THE MOST TRUSTED NAME IN TRAVEL: **FROMMER'S**

FROMMER'S EasyGuide to
RIVER CRUISING

By Fran Golden and Michelle Baran

P9-DME-669

Viking's Longship *Durnstein*.

CONTENTS

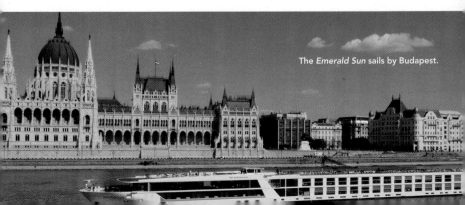

The *Emerald Sun* sails by Budapest.

A LOOK AT RIVER CRUISING

For thousands of years, the great rivers of the world—the Amazon and the Rhine, the Nile and the Danube, the Yangtze and the Volga—have been the "arteries" of civilization, the "highways" on which people traveled and transported products and goods. By taking a river cruise it is possible to witness many of the very same scenes, monuments and traditions—wonderfully unchanged in many instances—that our ancestors did. The same trips enable us to see the important modern cities—Cologne, Heidelberg and Moscow, Basel and Vienna, countless others—that commerce along rivers supports. Few travel opportunities are as informative, as exciting, and as fulfilling. Here are just a few of the sights and vessels you may experience.

An AmaWaterways ship visits Passau, a city that was once an ancient Roman colony, prized for its position at the confluence of three rivers.

Uniworld's *Maria Theresa* is as opulent as many of the castles and manor houses you'll visit when you cruise on the ship.

Dining on the Aquavit Terrace is a unique experience on Viking Longships.

Those who sail through the wine region of Bordeaux (p. 338) visit the wine capital's Place de la Bourse. It's often covered by an evocative fog, caused by a "water mirror"—a shallow, horizontal "fountain"—that was added to the royal square in 2006.

The weirdly shaped, stalagmite-like giant "Rocks of Belogradshik" are a highlight of many cruises along the Upper Danube.

The exquisite interior of St. Petersburg's Church of Our Savior on Spilled Blood.

Ah spas! Getting wet is part of the fun in Budapest (see p. 224) at the famed Szechenyi Thermal Baths.

Emerald Waterways' ships (see p. 177) are known for their streamlined design and indoor swimming pools (the *Emerald Sun* is pictured here).

Even the bar area aboard Uniworld's *Maria Theresa* is stately.

Wine tastings are paired with walks through the winding, medieval streets of Saint-Emilion on Bordeaux itineraries.

A canal in Amsterdam (see p. 235).

THE AMERICAS

The *American Queen* (see p. 158) is a classic paddle-wheeler.

Multonomah Falls is a "don't miss" shore excursion on Hood River cruises.

Old-fashioned music hall performances are a hallmark of the cruising experience aboard the *American Queen*.

Un-Cruise's S.S. *Legacy* (see p. 201).

Mississippi River cruises make many plantation visits, but we think Oak Alley Plantation is the most scenic.

Wine cruises of Oregon and Washington State are increasingly popular (pictured is a tasting at Dunham Cellars in the Walla Walla Wine Region).

Three-toed sloths are just one of the many critters visitors to the Amazon usually see.

Bird-watching on the Peruvian Amazon.

Kayaking the Amazon is one of the adventures offered by Aqua Expeditions.

Birders flock to Amazon cruises, and often double their "life lists", spotting such beauts as kingfishers (pictured), all sorts of macaws and other birds.

Native woods and decor are incorporated into the *Aqua Amazon*, a luxury vessel that takes visitors to some of the most remote spots in the Americas.

ASIA

The *Irrawaddy Explorer* employs locals as its servers in Myanmar and uses Burmese-style clothing for its uniforms.

As you float down the Irrawaddy River in Myanmar, you'll share the waters with fishermen trying for their daily catch.

Ballooning over the temples of Bagan at dawn is one of the most requested add-on excursions to cruises in Myanmar (p. 309).

Shwezigon Pagoda near Bagan was built in the 12th century and is thought to house a tooth and bone of the Buddha.

The *Mekong Navigator* (p. 186).

Angkor Wat in Cambodia is often "included" at the beginning or end of Mekong cruises (see p. 310).

Phnom Penh's Royal Palace, a wonder of Khmer architecture built in 1866, is visited on most Mekong cruises.

Ho Chi Minh City, the bustling start or end to a Mekong River cruise.

Yangtze River cruises often go through the locks of Three Gorges Dam (see p. 323). The dam is the largest power station on the planet.

On the banks of the Yangtze River, the Shibaozhai Pagoda is built up the side of a cliff.

Aboard the *Aqua Mekong* (p. 165), guests are served local delicacies like prawns with tumeric.

The traditional area of Chongqing, called Ciqikou (see p. 322), is a shopper's paradise. Yangtze cruises begin or end in Chongqing.

THE BEST OF RIVER CRUISING

River cruises are a hot vacation choice for good reason. You cruise calm waters to discover the interior of countries in Europe, the U.S., and elsewhere, often docking right in town (or in world-class cities).

Views from your ship might include castles and chateaux and hilltops covered in vineyards, or, on exotic itineraries, such sights as water buffalo, rice paddies, and houses built on stilts.

It's slow, casual travel on a comfortable ship, an easy way to see landmarks including UNESCO World Heritage Sites, and it's especially well suited to older travelers or busy boomers who like the idea of having most of their vacation experiences (including accommodations, meals, and excursions) well organized and well planned even before they leave home.

River cruises are not about rushing here and there. You visit key sights and explore the culture in places on and near a relatively small geographic stretch of river (though that stretch may take you through several countries). There's also time for languid afternoons on the sun deck, time to observe life along the river—kids swimming, fishermen, farmers tending their crops, passing cargo barges—while your ship cruises by at 5 mph (or even slower on the small barges in France).

The trips aren't cheap, and you may not have as much time for DIY exploration as you expect—you can't, as on, say, an inn-to-inn driving trip, love a place and decide at the spur of the moment to linger for a night (though you can extend your trip to do an itinerary of your choosing).

As you cruise, the scenery changes by the day and even the hour. You are fed decent food, there's a crew to offer attention and pampering, and you rest your head in a comfy bed.

Although accommodations on river ships once meant a choice between tight and cozy, today there are a lot of choices when it comes to ship accouterments. You can cruise on a sparkling contemporary ship or an over-the-top luxury vessel, or you can save bucks by choosing an older ship.

All the ships are intimate, most carrying fewer than 200 passengers and some under 100 passengers. River cruises are great for meeting people and are all about being social—you dine and tour as a group.

Since 1998, the industry has been growing in leaps and bounds (there's been double-digit growth for more than a decade), and it keeps growing. On popular waterways, such as the Rhine and the Danube, you will run into other river cruisers. Still, with most ships carrying relatively few passengers, river cruising is never going to be as mainstream a vacation choice as, say, ocean cruising.

Travelers ages 55 and up (most over 65) have embraced river cruising, and younger travelers are starting to take note. Efforts including a new relationship between Adventures by Disney and AmaWaterways may be the start of a new trend (in the Disney/AmaWaterways case, an attempt to appeal to the family market). Could Gen-Xers and millennials be next? Maybe. Adventure firm G Adventures, for one, has dipped a toe in the market, selling exotic river cruise itineraries (including on the Ganges, Peruvian Amazon, and Mekong rivers) and a barge option in Burgundy.

For the last several years, 20 or more ships have been introduced each year, the most recent bringing such amenities as glass walls that open at a push of a button, cushioned jogging tracks, indoor/outdoor pools, specialty dining, and wonderfully lit and scented massage rooms.

What Fran remembers most from her first river cruise in Germany more than 20 years ago is a very exuberant accordion player, lots of meat and potatoes, very tight accommodations, and that she was very much the youngster on board. It all felt very old fashioned yet brought her up close to the fantastic sights along the Danube. So she tried it again . . . and again . . . and again. In her opinion, with new amenities and new routes (including exotic itineraries), river cruises just keep getting better—though her enthusiasm may have to do in part with the fact that when she cruises now, she finds herself squarely in the majority demographic.

Michelle has sailed on dozens of river cruises and has been on every major river cruising waterway in the world. She is constantly impressed with the amount of innovation that is squeezed into the relatively limited size of the river cruise vessels (especially those in Europe). But in her opinion, what has always truly made river cruising great (it helps that the floating hotels keep getting nicer, don't get her wrong) is the sensation of floating down the river. There's really nothing quite like it.

We will warn you as you embark on your first river cruise or consider your second that river cruising can be somewhat addictive—do one, and you'll probably do another.

This is due partly to the fact that river cruise lines will tempt you with all sorts of offers and an expanding array of destinations, and partly because river cruising is so hassle-free and relaxing and really gets you away from the fast pace of everyday life (on some exotic itineraries, you will find you are pretty much cut off from the outside world completely, which can be a very good thing).

Fortunately, the diversity of rivers explored has grown in recent years to encompass several itinerary choices (of varying lengths) on legendary waterways, such as the Danube and the Rhine, the rivers of France, and also such far-off waterways as the Mekong in Cambodia and Vietnam and the Peruvian Amazon.

Closer to home, the Mississippi has seen a resurgence, and following the path of Lewis and Clark out west is in vogue. Although the Europe season is March to December, you can find river cruises in other parts of the world year-round.

Budgeting is easy, because river cruisers are all either mostly inclusive (you pay extra for cocktails and gratuities) or all-inclusive (you pay extra only if you want a fancier-than-fancy experience—or souvenirs).

All that said, river cruises are not for everybody. It's very much a packaged tour with shore excursions being part of what you pay for in your cruise fare. If you're not the type to travel on group tours, river cruises may not be for you.

The experience is also far different than what you might find on an ocean ship. Some travelers will love that river ships do not have a bunch of bars and lounges, casinos, show productions, or an all-day roster of activities, and that only a few lines welcome children; others may not.

As we said, speedy travel is never the goal. You will gain an understanding of the place you're visiting as well as an appreciation of why people have traveled rivers for millennia.

One of the best descriptions of river cruising we've ever heard comes from the unusual source of Joanna Lumley, the actress who played the wonderfully ditzy Patsy on the British comedy series *Absolutely Fabulous*; she is the godmother of the 190-passenger Viking River Cruises "longship" *Viking Odin* and was downright poetic when she accepted the honor, saying, "It's like the world is on a cloth and being dragged past you by captains sent from paradise."

THE best OF THE BEST

This book is designed to help you decide where to do your river cruise and with which line. Here we detail some of our favorite experiences.

o **The Best of the Mainstream River Ships:** The reference to historic Viking ships notwithstanding, **Viking River Cruises** with its cutting-edge, 190-passenger "longships" immerses guests in a wonderful contemporary Scandinavian environment. Light fills the two-deck atrium, you can dine with views whether indoors or out, there are cabins and suites with real balconies, and these ships even have "green" features, including solar panels (helping fuel the hybrid engines) and an onboard herb garden. They are both pretty and wicked smart.

o **The Best of the Budget River Ships:** Value-focused Australian line **Emerald Waterways** brings a surprising "cool" factor to river cruising with its 182-passenger "Star Ships." No, there's no *Star Trek* tie-in, but there is a bit more nightlife than you'll find on most river ships, thanks to fun-loving Australians on board—when the DJ spins Olivia Newton-John, the crowd goes wild. And we can't say enough about the wonderfulness of the infinity-style indoor pool (we do actually say more in "The Best for Amenities" entry, below).

o **The Best Ships for Luxury:** **Uniworld**'s SS *Maria Theresa* and SS *Catherine* are the beauty queens of the river cruise industry—spectacular floating palaces with over-the-top decor, including unabashed use of animal prints in the funky Leopard Bar, where there's also a small indoor pool. You'll find marble, lush upholstery, Murano chandeliers, baroque antiques—heck, even the window treatments are fab—and specially commissioned artwork everywhere. We'd be remiss if we didn't also mention **Scenic**'s latest crop of vessels, *Scenic Jasper, Opal,* and *Amber.* Upscale cruisers with a more modern aesthetic will greatly appreciate the sleek, clean lines on the Scenic ships, which have no shortage of high-quality hallmarks, from the all-marble lobbies to the mid-century modern furnishings. We're giving **Tauck** a shout-out too for the overall experience, focusing as much on wowing its guests off the ships (how do they find all those cool castles and chateaux for exclusive events?) as it is on spoiling them on board.

THE best FOR FAMILIES

o **AmaWaterways:** This line is testing the market for family cruises in a name-brand way, partnering with Adventures by Disney for select cruises on the Danube featuring kids' activities and Disney guides. The sailings are on the 170-passenger *AmaViola,* custom-built for the family market (including with several cabins that sleep three and some that connect).

o **Tauck:** Even more established in the family market is luxury line Tauck, which introduced multigenerational river cruising with its brand **Tauck Bridges** in 2008. Tauck will do 10 family-friendly departures on the Rhone, Rhine, and Danube rivers in 2016; 20 in 2017. Activities include kid-friendly adventures, such as a scavenger hunt in the Louvre in Paris, guided cycling in Austria, and interactive cooking demonstrations.

THE best FOR CUISINE

o **AmaWaterways:** The food on AmaWaterways ships puts emphasis on high-quality ingredients and is above standard river cruise fare—so much so the line has been recognized as a member of La Chaine des Roisseurs, the prestigious culinary organization. AmaWaterways was a pioneer in offering multiple dining options—including an excellent chef's table experience—and cruises themed on food and wine.

o **Uniworld:** Foodies will also be pleased with what they are served on Uniworld ships, especially if your tastes include such as extravagances as foie gras, fresh oysters and hard-to-find regional cheeses, expertly paired with wine. Uniworld does not hold back when it comes to bringing impressive delicacies and wine on board.

THE best FOR ONBOARD ACTIVITIES

o **Avalon Waterways:** Avalon Waterways does a particularly good job in historical and cultural immersion, with lectures by experts—for instance, a World War II historian comes on board cruises to Normandy. The line also has a large calendar of special-interest sailings with experts on board focusing on such topics as Jewish heritage, Impressionist art, European history, opera, jazz, wellness, and even craft beer.

THE best FOR AMENITIES

o **Emerald Waterways:** While ships that belonged to the company that was known as Haimark certainly improved the concept of onboard spas—moving massages literally out of the closet into more thought-out spaces—the pool on the Emerald Waterways "Star Ships" is our very favorite river ship amenity. Covered by a ceiling that can be open and closed for all-weather use and surrounded by cushy lounge chairs, it's the perfect spot to watch river views. The fact the space converts into a 25-seat cinema at night (with popcorn served) is an added bonus.

THE best FOR ENTERTAINMENT

o **Tauck:** Every line brings on visiting local acts, mostly singers, musicians, or folk dance troupes (in Myanmar, **Avalon Waterways** even hosts a family of renowned puppeteers). But we're giving the top accolades in this category to Tauck, because they include live shows and concerts on board *and* on shore.

o **American Queen Steamboat Company:** Deserving props, too, is American Queen Steamboat Company on the Mississippi, with its Dixie-land jazz and because it's the only river line we know of that occasionally has Elvis impersonators on board.

THE best FOR INCLUDED SHORE EXCURSIONS

o **Scenic:** Australian luxury line Scenic does your standard, escorted tour (where you listen to a guide through headphones) but goes a step further too, giving passengers the option of using a GPS gizmo called Scenic Tailormade. With these cellphone-size gadgets, you can head off on foot or bike and hear commentary that is automatically activated when you reach a point of interest. A screen on the device shows you the map of the route.

o **Tauck:** But we must also acknowledge Tauck, a tour company long before it was a river line, for delivering particularly well-planned and well-executed tours—often more than one a day.

o **AmaWaterways:** Avid bicyclists will applaud all of AmaWaterways' biking excursions, a program it is constantly growing and enhancing with more cycling outings; it has recently partnered with Backroads Tours, which specializes in bike-and-hike tours.

THE best FOR PRE- & POST-TOURS

o **Tauck & Avalon Waterways:** Both cruise lines are owned by established tour operators, and it shows. Tauck doesn't offer standard 2- and 3-day pre- and post-river cruise trip stays like some river cruise lines do, but the company does make it easy for you to combine your river cruise with a land tour or even a small ship ocean cruise (head from your Rhine cruise to the Baltic, for instance). Avalon Waterways is owned by **Globus,** with tour brands including Globus and **Cosmos** for organized tours and **Monograms** for independent travel, making it easy (and cost-effective) to do a pre- or post-cruise extension using the company's portfolio.

THE best ITINERARIES

Now that we've touted the attributes of the river cruise lines, here are our top picks of where to go on your river cruise.

o **The Danube (for Europe):** For first-timer river cruisers, we heartily recommend the Danube. You really can't go wrong with an Upper Danube cruise featuring the blockbuster cities of Vienna and Budapest—and Prague, if you do the optional add-on. The Upper Danube itinerary offers something for everyone, including castles, beer and wine, and opera. If you have the time, do the Upper Danube and the Lower Danube, from Germany to Romania, and explore highlights of Western and Eastern Europe, including Romania's Dracula haunts. We're also big fans of traveling in France, and for wine and food aficionados in particular, a cruise in Bordeaux or on the Rhone and Saone or both should be on your wish list.

o **The Mississippi (Stateside):** When it comes to the U.S., there are two main destinations for river ships: the Mississippi River in the middle of the country and the Columbia and Snake rivers in the Pacific Northwest. The two are as different as, well, Mark Twain and Lewis and Clark. Of the options, we've got to go with the Lower Mississippi, because you hit the fun-times city of New Orleans and in some cases also Memphis, the "Birthplace of Rock 'n' Roll." But no question, nature lovers will want to head west, where jaw-dropping gorges and waterfalls and other views are part of the scene (and there are good local wines in Washington State and Oregon, too).

o **The Mekong (for an Exotic Itinerary):** A cruise on the Mekong through Vietnam and Cambodia is thrilling and educational, an opportunity to observe the fascinating culture and explore the often-tumultuous history of a river that is an important lifeline to many. The ships are as comfortable as anything in Europe, and your itinerary includes time to explore bucket-list attractions, such as the mysterious ruins of Angkor Wat and the rapidly developing Ho Chi Minh City. But we're also keeping a close eye on India's Ganges as a potentially hot new exotic cruise destination.

WHY TAKE A RIVER CRUISE?

These days, a lot more people have become familiar with the concept of river cruising, and that's thanks in large part to Viking River Cruises having plastered our TV screens, and filled our mailboxes, with promos portraying a river cruise ship floating past picturesque European cities. But river cruising hasn't always been on travelers' radar. Compared to other vacation forms—ocean cruises, resort vacations, tours—river cruising (in its current form, as there was plenty rollin' down the river happening in the 1800s) has only more recently become a popular travel style, having only really started to take off, especially with the American market, in the early 2000s.

There are currently some half million Americans who hop the pond each year to take a river cruise in Europe, more than double the number who were river cruising in 2007 and more than seven times the number of North American river cruisers who sailed through Europe in 2001. And that number continues to grow. Consequently, more players and ships enter the river cruise game each year in an effort to capitalize on the novelty and buzz surrounding the river cruising industry. In other words, river cruising is having a moment.

The river cruising landscape of 2016 is vastly more sophisticated than its predecessor of even just 10 years prior. River cruising used to be a much simpler and more homogenous experience than it is now—picture relatively basic vessels with small, mostly balcony-less staterooms (we won't even discuss the bathrooms, though there's lore of toilets that were *inside* the shower), and a single, stark dining room that served up all three meals each day.

Fortunately for you, those days are long gone, and river cruising has evolved into a very upscale, very comfortable travel experience. If you're planning to take a river cruise in the coming months or years, you're benefitting from a very competitive marketplace of late that has upped the ante and vastly improved standards on the rivers.

Today, the norm is larger staterooms (often 200 sq. ft. and up), mostly with balconies, multiple dining venues on board, gourmet cuisine and well-curated wines, and onshore experiences that are getting ever more creative and engaging. So, congratulations, you've picked an excellent time to go on a river cruise.

IS RIVER CRUISING FOR YOU?

But even with all the improvements, river cruising is not for everyone. Here are some things to consider before booking your first river cruise (hopefully they'll help you get a sense of whether river cruising is truly for you).

Pros of River Cruising

IT'S A FLOATING HOTEL

Just like ocean cruising, river cruising benefits from the extreme convenience of only having to pack and unpack once, as you bring your floating hotel along with you. In other words, it's a downright leisurely way to get around, often to and through several countries.

RIVERS ARE WONDERFUL

There's something to be said for the soothing sensation of floating down the river. Whether you're gliding past castles on Germany's Rhine River, sailing by lavender fields on France's Seine River, drifting alongside fishing villages on Southeast Asia's Mekong River, or cruising past ancient Egyptian ruins on the Nile, being able to experience stunning landscapes from the vantage point of a comfortable, well-appointed river vessel could calm just about anyone's nerves.

THE FARE COVERS A LOT

Many people get sticker shock when they look into river cruising, as it's not a cheap travel product. But take into consideration that there are often very few extras or add-ons in river cruising compared to other travel styles. And in the case of some of the truly all-inclusive river cruise lines (such as Uniworld, Tauck, and Scenic), there are really virtually no extras beyond the brochure price, which means all your transfers, meals, excursions, and just about everything is taken care of along the way.

Cons of River Cruising

IT'S A PACKAGED TOUR

If you are a DIY type, you may have difficulty with the fact that much of your itinerary is preplanned.

YOU ARE TETHERED TO THE RIVERS

Rivers meander through some incredible geography and ports, but there are only so many rivers suitable for overnight passenger cruising, and being tied to the rivers means being relatively restricted in what you can see and do along the way. It also means that sometimes seeing certain points of interest requires a long bus ride.

SHIPS HAVE SPACE LIMITATIONS

Unlike today's massive ocean cruise ships, river cruise ships in Europe will never be larger than 38 feet wide by 443 feet long and four decks high due the constraints of the bridges and locks along Europe's inland waterways. Some rivers in the world don't have the same limitations, so you tend to see larger vessels on the Mississippi or on the Yangtze, for instance, but even on those wider rivers, you'll still never sail on a river cruise ship that can accommodate more than several hundred passengers. That means onboard amenities are limited too (no climbing walls or gargantuan water slides, folks). River cruise ships are not a destination unto themselves. They're meant to be the vehicle that takes you to and through the destinations.

A BRIEF HISTORY

Those who think that river cruising is some brand-new travel phenomenon suddenly taking the world by storm might be surprised to find out just how long this popular travel style has been around.

River cruising arguably had its first real heyday in the 19th century, when steamboats and paddle-wheelers became a popular mode of transportation for plying rivers from the Mississippi to the Irrawaddy. But this first incarnation of river cruising began to wane with the advent of rail networks. Slowly, river cruising became more of a novelty and less of a necessity.

As for river cruising's most recent renaissance, the springboard for which was European river cruising, it can be traced back to the 1990s, when some familiar names like Viking, Uniworld, and Grand Circle Travel, as well as the now-long-gone Peter Deilmann Cruises, began trying to sell the world on the idea of floating through Europe on a bargelike river cruise vessel.

By the early 2000s, river cruising was catching on like wildfire, stalled only briefly by a post-9/11 slowdown and the global economic recession of 2008 and 2009. Viking had purchased much of the inventory of a river cruise line called KD River Cruises that had gone under, which helped Viking quickly build up a fleet of a couple dozen vessels. Uniworld, which had been founded in 1976 by Serbian entrepreneur and river cruise pioneer Serba Ilich, was acquired in 2004 by a large travel conglomerate, the Travel Corporation, after which it began pivoting into the ultraluxury river cruise line it is today.

Seeing the growth that the river cruise market was experiencing during that first decade of the 21st century, several new players decided to get in on the river cruising action. Viking, Uniworld, and Grand Circle were joined by Avalon Waterways, AmaWaterways, Tauck, Scenic, and Emerald Waterways, among others. By 2010, six or seven players were solidly investing in this market, and that's when there started to be greater differentiation in the products, with each river cruise line realizing it needed to carve out a niche for itself if it was going to stand out from the pack.

Some, like Viking, Grand Circle, and CroisiEurope, went with the value-pricing model (Viking quickly became known for its attractive—if gimmicky—two-for-one deals). Others, including Tauck, Uniworld, Ama, and Scenic, went after the all- or mostly inclusive high-end market. Still others decided to offer upscale amenities at an affordable-luxury price point, such as Avalon and Emerald.

Today, there continues to be a surprising amount of innovation and investment in the river cruise market despite the seeming limitations of the size of the ships and of the rivers they sail. And regardless of gradually increasing concerns about whether the rivers in Europe are beginning to get a bit overcrowded, companies are continuing to build more, and new companies are still getting in on the game.

In 2015, Crystal Cruises became the first ocean cruise line to decide to build up its own river cruise fleet in Europe—its first ship launched in 2016, a purchased vessel the company is renovating, and four newly built river cruise "yachts," as Crystal is calling them, will launch in 2017.

Adventures by Disney, Disney's packaged tour operation, also decided to get in on the river cruising game by partnering with AmaWaterways on family-friendly river cruises, and Canadian company G Adventures is going to attempt to get millennial travelers into river cruising with some river cruise programs on the Amazon, Ganges, and Mekong rivers and in France's Burgundy region.

River cruising hasn't just been a smash hit in Europe. Mississippi River cruising experienced a complete rebirth in 2012 after being almost completely dormant for 4 years following the collapse in 2008 of what was then the main player in the U.S. river game, a company called Majestic America Line. A newly formed company, the American Queen Steamboat Company, purchased one of the former Majestic steamboats, the *American Queen;* fixed it up; and relaunched it in 2012, the same year that American Cruise Lines, another U.S. river and small ship ocean cruising outfit, christened a newly built paddle-wheeler, the *Queen of the Mississippi*—and it was off to the races.

Since then, American Queen Steamboat Company resuscitated another Majestic alum, the *American Empress* (formerly the *Empress of the North*), and launched it onto the Columbia and Snake rivers in the Pacific Northwest, and American Cruise Lines has built three more paddle-wheelers for the Mississippi and has plans for more new vessels throughout the U.S. In 2015, Viking said it too would begin building modern-style river cruise vessels for the Mississippi River that will launch 2017—we have yet to hear more on where those plans stand.

In addition to American Cruise Lines, other ocean lines with small ships have also gotten into the river cruise business, including Seattle-based UnCruise Adventures, with a ship on the Columbia and Snake rivers, and Lindblad Expeditions–National Geographic on the Amazon (using a ship chartered from Aqua Expeditions).

In Asia, river cruising along Vietnam and Cambodia's Mekong River and Myanmar's Irrawaddy River also kicked off at the turn of the 21st century. Scotsman Paul Strachan, founder of Singapore-based Pandaw River

Expeditions, was a real pioneer in the region, having first started taking people up and down the Irrawaddy River on a chartered vessel in Myanmar in 1995. By 2001, Pandaw had built its first company-owned vessel and started growing from there.

Several years later, river cruise lines that were experiencing a lot of success in Europe were looking for new destinations to offer their clients. AmaWaterways was among the first of the European-focused river cruise companies to look into the Mekong, and together with a Hanoi-based shipbuilder, AmaWaterways launched its first vessel on the Mekong in 2009. Since then, AmaWaterways has launched two newer ships and retired that first vessel, and numerous other river cruise lines have followed suit.

Every major river cruise line now has some inventory either on the Mekong or on the Irrawaddy or both, sailing generally much smaller ships than in Europe, but with large staterooms and suites and offering luxurious accommodations from which to explore these colorful and exotic destinations.

China's Yangtze River is a different story. Sailings along the Yangtze have been popular since long before the 2000s, but the Yangtze has struggled in the aftermath of the building of the Three Gorges Dam, which was completed in 2009 and vastly changed the makeup and landscape of the river and its banks. The 7,660-foot-long and 600-foot-high dam, the largest hydroelectric plant in world, caused hundreds of square miles of land along the river to be flooded, submerging entire cities and displacing 1.3 million people. Today one sees fewer of the quaint towns that used to dot the riverbank; and while there still are cliffs on shore, because the water has risen, they're no longer as soaring as they used to be (at least in looks).

In an effort to reignite the market, river cruise lines on the Yangtze, which is dominated by U.S.-based Victoria Cruises and Chinese company Century Cruises, invested heavily in their ships to bring five-star luxury to the Yangtze and court a new class of customers.

Not to be overlooked, the Peruvian Amazon is also an in-demand river cruise destination, especially for bird and nature lovers eager to get closer to the region's lush flora and fauna. Once a destination that only hosted a small handful of extremely basic river cruise vessels, the worldwide river cruise boom has resulted in some seriously fancy riverboats launching on the Peruvian Amazon.

The Nile River too is among the world's most impressive river routes, providing a scenic desert oasis-flanked highway through the heart of some of ancient Egypt's most significant relics, such as Luxor and the Valley of the Kings. In its heyday, and as recently as 2010, some 200 to 300 river cruise vessels were cruising up and down the Nile. But in the wake of the Arab Spring, many have been tied up and are now awaiting a time when Egypt's tourism industry will be reborn.

New rivers have come into play as well. In 2015, river cruise companies began building and offering river cruises on India's Ganges River between the well-known hubs of Kolkata and the fascinating holy city of Varanasi.

RIVER CRUISING VS. OCEAN CRUISING

Don't assume because you did an ocean cruise, even on a small ship, that you'll like a river cruise and vice versa. River cruises and ocean cruises are very different products. A river cruise is much more of a packaged tour with shore excursions and, often, some hotels (and even Wi-Fi and beer and wine with meals) included in the cruise fare. As we noted above, starting fares for river cruises are often higher than those of comparable premium-level ocean cruises. But with river cruises you get a lot more included in the price. Plus, there's the bonus with river cruises that you probably won't get seasick.

Here are some other key ways river cruises differ from ocean cruises.

It's All About the Group

Despite the fact water is involved, river cruising is much more akin to a bus tour than an ocean cruise. The experience is very much focused on the group and getting you and your fellow passengers to key sites both along the river and inland. It's all very carefully planned and structured. If you do the included tours (which you've paid for in your cruise fare), there isn't all that much free time in destinations on your own—an exception being in cities where you overnight. Frankly, the formulaic structure of river cruises may drive some DIY types crazy.

There's Nowhere to Hide

On a big ship with thousands of passengers, there is a sense of anonymity. Not so on river ships, which typically carry only 100 to 200 passengers (and sometimes even fewer). You'd better like your fellow passengers, as you'll be seeing a lot of them, including at open-seating meals—we don't recommend river cruises for those who *"vant to be alone."* If you're looking for a bunch of places to hang out on the ship, you're in for a shock. Ocean ships have multiple bars and discos and show lounges and restaurants and recreational areas, but most river ships have one main lounge and a dining room and maybe a library. There will be a sun deck where you can lounge outdoors. There may or may not be a Jacuzzi, a pool, or a spa.

Meal Times Are Regimented

Breakfast and lunch on river ships are typically buffets (sometimes with a short menu of dishes you can order). Dinner is from a menu, with waiter service. All are at set times with limited flexibility. On most ships, you aren't allowed to suddenly decide to show up for dinner at 8pm when it's scheduled for 7pm. Snacks may be available in the morning and afternoon near the 24-hour coffee setup, but even these are sparse—we've found ourselves on occasion begging the bartender in the lounge for chips or nuts to tide us over until the cocktail hour (which is usually accompanied by some nibbles). Think you'll just order room service? Forget about it. Room service is a rare offering on river ships.

Cabins Are Smaller

Most river ships today have comfortable cabins done up with hotel-style beds topped with fluffy duvets, but the cabins tend to be substantially smaller than on ocean ships in all categories. Plus there won't be as many categories—big ocean ships may have two dozen cabin configurations, but river ships may have six. Big spenders can book a suite on some ships, but it won't be apartment- or house-size as on ocean ships. Cabins that sleep more than two are rare on river ships, and so are connecting cabins for families. Accessible cabins modified for wheelchair access are extremely rare (river cruises are difficult for wheelchair users).

Entertainment Is Sedate

Don't expect much in the way of nighttime entertainment on river ships. Socializing with your fellow passengers over drinks, movie nights, and maybe a DJ or pianist playing danceable tunes at night (the DJ and pianist apt to be the same person) is about as exciting as it gets. There may be a performance one evening by a local dance or music troupe that you won't want to miss (in Germany, there may be an enthusiastic oompah band in lederhosen). During the day, you won't find a full roster of silly games and contests and activities as on big ships, but you may get a crew member talking local customs or language and/or a cooking demonstration.

There's a Schedule

Thinking of sleeping in? You can, but only if you're willing to miss the morning tour or on rare days when the ship is cruising in the morning. Most days you'll be up early; the schedule is filled with sightseeing, often involving getting on and off motorcoaches and a good deal of walking. You won't have relaxing multiple "sea days" as on ocean ships, though on some itineraries you can find 1 cruising day.

The Crowd Is Older

Most river cruise passengers are ages 60 and up—sometimes way up. The cruises are designed for a physically able older crowd; the tours conducted at a pace to suit this crowd; and the experience reflective of the fact that most people want to tour during the day and go to bed early to get ready for the next day's adventure. Younger folks on board—say ages 30 to 45— may find themselves referred to as "the kids." Still, we've met people under age 50 and even young honeymoon couples thrilled with the "packaged" aspect of the river cruise experience. Older teenagers who can socialize with adults will do fine on river cruises. But if you're thinking about a multigenerational trip, keep in mind there are no specific programs for kids except on a few family-friendly itineraries on select lines (such as Adventures by Disney sailings with AmaWaterways and Tauck's and Uniworld's family programs).

Small Crowd, Fewer Hassles

Because river ships are small, the service crew can get to know passengers and address their specific wants and needs. If you want to hang out with the officers, you can do that too, thanks to an open-bridge policy. On river ships, there is no hassle of long lines as on big ocean ships. When you arrive in a port, you'll often find yourself right in a town or city center (not some icky industrial port or touristy ocean cruise port), and you can walk right off the river ship into town. Boarding and disembarking a river ship is also more of a breeze than on ocean ships.

WHAT TO EXPECT

If you're familiar with ocean cruising and bus touring, river cruising is kind of a hybrid of the two.

Regardless of which river cruise line you have booked or plan on booking, you can expect a generally pretty comprehensive travel package. First and foremost, most river cruises begin with an included transfer from the airport, something you'll be absolutely grateful for, especially if you're abroad— there's nothing like being greeted by someone in a foreign airport who is there to take you (hopefully) swiftly to your accommodations.

The first day is usually for settling in either at the hotel, if you're doing a pre- or post-cruise included or added extension, or on the ship, if you're starting straight away with the cruise. There is often an optional tour or activity this day for guests who are up for it, but the first night is understandably generally pretty mellow. On board the ship, cabins may or may not be ready until midday or midafternoon, so be prepared to hang in the lounge groggily or walk around town until your stateroom is available.

Once you get into your cabin, you might be surprised by the relatively small amount of space compared to a hotel room. Even though river cruise lines are building increasingly larger staterooms, there is often little square footage beyond the bed and perhaps a small sitting area.

River cruise ships have gotten much better about providing more space for storing clothing, which helps alleviate space constrictions. And because you'll be on board for probably at least a week, you can unpack your clothes in the built-in wardrobes and drawers, and it helps to be able to store empty or nearly empty suitcases under the bed to clear some room as well. Bathrooms have gotten roomier too, including the standing showers, which were hard to even move around in before. All told, the dimensions can be a bit of an adjustment for a first-time river cruiser, but they are by no means a deal breaker, especially because the beds are generally extremely plush and comfortable, and all the in-room amenities are well designed.

Depending on the river route and itinerary, some river cruises can kick off with a bang, an intense 2 or 3 days of back-to-back sightseeing, whereas some might start off at a slower pace, perhaps with a relaxing sailing day within the first 2 days. Either way, the river cruise will likely proceed with a relatively balanced combination of very busy days, where you might be touring from morning until evening, and more leisurely sailing stretches that allow for some relaxation and recovery on board (although there are often lectures and demonstrations during sailings, it's not a bad idea to bring some books and/or an e-reader on board for down times).

There are usually at least 2 slightly more elegant evenings during the cruise, the welcome cocktail and dinner (traditionally hosted on the second evening), and the captain's and/or farewell dinner (traditionally hosted on the second-to-last evening). These are not black-tie events, but ladies have been known to break out their sparkly evening or flirty cocktail dresses, and men often wear a tie or a nice sport coat.

During the cruise, there could also be an evening outing, such as a concert or performance in town that also requires slightly more formal attire. Otherwise, the atmosphere on board and during the excursions is sophisticated casual.

Don't worry about knowing what is coming up each day. Every evening, there will be an orientation meeting before dinner to go over the next day's events, and a daily bulletin will be placed in your cabin each night with the following day's schedule.

There is generally a fair amount of walking during the daily tours, and for those who are more active, there might be an option for an active walking and/or biking excursion. Passengers with physical disabilities can opt for a slower-paced tour and/or discuss their best options with the cruise manager.

The tours are usually hosted by local guides, who may actually work different days for different lines, and the guide you receive is the luck of the draw. Some tour guides are leaps and bounds better than others and can truly make or break the excursion. If you get an average guide one day, or one who is clearly having an off day, you likely won't have the same one the next day as the river cruise vessel travels to a new destination (although sometimes guides do follow along, especially if the daily cruising distances aren't very far).

After the first few days of settling in, recovering from any jetlag you might have, exploring the ship, mingling with other passengers, and getting the overall sense of the daily rhythm on board, you'll find that most guests generally start finding their groove. By this point, you may have made some new friends whom you are dining with more frequently, you may have figured out which excursion groups you like best (for instance, the more active group or a gentle walkers' group), where your favorite hangout spots are on board, who your preferred server is in the dining room, and what you like to eat for breakfast, lunch, and dinner.

You're likely starting to feel more relaxed and are definitely personalizing the experience to your tastes and interests. Perhaps you're less inclined at this point to do every single activity and outing, because you just want to chill for a morning or afternoon. Maybe you're opting to skip out on a dinner in the dining room one night and instead do a light dinner in the casual dining venue and a movie in your cabin instead. Or maybe you're going all out and seeing

WHAT IS "rafting"?

If you ever get the feeling while you're on a European river cruise that somebody is watching you when you're docked in port, they just might be! Although the river cruise lines don't talk about it much, the practice of *rafting*, whereby several river cruise ships dock side-by-side, is relatively commonplace throughout Europe. Limited docking space and a growing number of river cruise ships often necessitate vessels' sharing a single landing.

For the most part this may not affect you much, if at all, but there are two annoying ways in which it could. For one, if you pull up alongside another vessel, you might suddenly find your once-private balcony has a view—into someone's stateroom a few feet away. If you know about it, that's fine. But rafting might happen overnight without your even realizing it, and when you go to open the curtains (hopefully while you are fully clothed), you could find someone else peering in. So, just be aware that this is a possibility and perhaps look outside your curtains before sweeping

them open and giving your neighbors a view they weren't expecting.

The other annoying thing about rafting is that if your vessel is docked farthest from shore, you will need to walk through or up and over the one or two vessels docked between you and the landing. It's not the most comfortable way to get on and off a ship, not to mention it can be awkward to walk through another vessel, and it can be particularly challenging for those with physical impediments when walking up and down additional steps is involved.

Unfortunately, the rafting phenomenon seemingly happens at random. You might experience a river cruise with no rafting at all and one where it seems like every day is a new rafting adventure, so there's no full-proof way to avoid it. Generally speaking, it happens more during the busy summer season when more vessels are docking in the same popular ports, so you have a better chance of avoiding it during the slower shoulder months in early spring and late fall.

But now that you know about it, you can at least be better prepared.

---

whether each night can top the last night's extravagances. Perhaps you're the one everyone is smiling at in the morning because you were cutting a rug in the lounge until the wee hours of the morning.

As the river cruise comes to a close, the sad reality that you're about to return to a world where no one will make you a customized omelet every morning and drive you around charming European villages every day is beginning to set in. You will either have a prearranged transfer to the airport or continue on to a pre- or post-cruise program or some other travel adventure you combined with the cruise.

Some passengers return home with a whole host of new Facebook friends, while others leave having had some quality time predominantly with their travel companion. Either way, given the high customer satisfaction ratings that river cruise lines tout and the market's seemingly unstoppable growth, chances are you had a pretty great time and are perhaps even already thinking about your next river cruise.

The Main Seven

If you're interested in taking a river cruise (and you likely are if you're reading this book), here's a breakdown of who the major players in Europe are (you can find out about all the river cruise lines, including those with river cruises beyond Europe, in chapters 7 and 8).

VIKING RIVER CRUISES

The river cruise company most travelers are familiar with is Viking River Cruises. With the most ships and the most marketing muscle, it's hard to avoid Viking when you're looking into a river cruise. Viking is known for aggressive promotions, and with its fleet of almost identical "longships" sailing through Europe, Viking passengers like the fact that they know what they're going to get when they sail with this company.

UNIWORLD BOUTIQUE RIVER CRUISE COLLECTION

A couple years ago, Uniworld declared itself a six-star luxury river cruise line in an effort to market itself in a class above the other river cruise lines. And in keeping with that six-star promise, the company has gone all out with its vessels, investing millions in lavish interiors filled with unique and original works of art. It also offers all-inclusive pricing that encompasses gratuities and unlimited beverages on board.

AMAWATERWAYS

Founded in 2002 by a trio of industry vets, AmaWaterways is that under-the-radar player that is gaining traction not with over-the-top ships or expensive advertising but by simply focusing on churning out high-class vessels and gourmet food and wine, all with an emphasis on high-satisfaction service. It's neither an uber-luxury player nor a bargain-basement one—its target market is the well-heeled, sophisticated river cruiser.

AVALON WATERWAYS

Like its well-oiled parent company, the Globus Family of Brands, Avalon Waterways is a no-fuss river cruise company that offers an extremely reliable river cruise experience at a slightly more manageable price point. This is a river cruise line going after the more relaxed passenger who wants well-executed excursions (which they're bound to be when your parent company is a major tour operator) and well-appointed staterooms, minus the pretention.

TAUCK

A river cruise line that was created by the 90-year-old tour company of the same name, Tauck is giving the high end of the river cruise market a run for its money. This truly all-inclusive river cruise company—gratuities and alcoholic beverages are included—may have a higher price tag than other lines, but Tauck doesn't cut any corners when it comes to onboard offerings or unique on-shore events.

GRAND CIRCLE TRAVEL

With an 11-ship fleet of older river cruise vessels, Grand Circle is focused on the four-star, retiree river cruise market. There's nothing fancy about these ships, and they are starting to show their age, especially compared to all the newer vessels launching of late, but it's hard to beat Grand Circle's prices. The company is a direct-to-consumer river cruise line, which means it doesn't work with travel agents. Instead, it targets older travelers through partnerships with AARP and through direct mailings.

SCENIC

In 2008, Australian company Scenic launched its first-ever river cruise program, which has since grown into a 14-vessel European river cruise fleet of sleek and modern ships. Scenic is also making a run at the high-end river cruise market with an all-inclusive model that is in line with Uniworld's and Tauck's. Scenic's trademark differentiator is its high-tech amenities, such as Scenic Tailormade, a GPS device that provides location-specific audio tours (pretty cool stuff).

ALL THE REST

In addition to the above river cruise lines, numerous other river cruise companies sail in Europe, many of which are foreign-owned. Although many of the below companies do not necessarily sell directly to the U.S. market, they may sell inventory to tour operators or travel agents stateside, so it's possible you might end up on one of their vessels if you book a river cruise—thus, it's good to know a bit about them.

One of the newer lines to have come onto the river cruise scene is **Emerald Waterways,** which was launched in 2014 by the same Australian parent company that owns Scenic. The idea was to introduce a sleek, four-star, mostly inclusive river cruise company to serve as a more affordable alternative—yet with newer ships. The five Emerald ships have some fun amenities, such as a pool that converts into a movie theater.

As far as European-owned companies, 40-year-old French river cruise company **CroisiEurope** began aggressively courting U.S. passengers with attractive pricing in 2013. It has 43 company-owned vessels (some older, some newer) and has been pursuing new rivers by designing vessels with paddlewheels and lower drafts that allow the vessels to sail in shallower waters (like the Loire and Elbe), and it has also been overhauling its ships' interiors to better compete with the big river cruise players. There is also **Luftner Cruises,** which is an Austrian company that sails the well-appointed Amadeus fleet of river cruise vessels. And German company **A-Rosa River Cruises** has a handful of river cruise ships of varying ages.

Vantage Deluxe World Travel is a Boston-based company with a fleet of five river cruise vessels—*River Venture, River Splendor, River Discovery, River Navigator,* and *River Voyager.*

Several companies are worth looking into if you're interested in barge cruising, which are sailings on much smaller 6-to-20-passenger barges that travel along the smaller canals and waterways of Europe. CroisiEurope has some canal barges in its fleet, but probably the main player in this market is British company **European Waterways,** which has a fleet of 17 canal cruisers. Luxury tour operator **Abercrombie & Kent** also offers canal barging as well as river cruises on Luftner's Amadeus fleet.

RIVER CRUISING SEASONS

The river cruising season in Europe generally gets rolling in late March and early April and runs until late November and early December, with the grand finale typically being the Christmas market and New Year's cruises that finish off the season. After that, river cruise vessels go into dry dock for the winter, during which they often get updated for the new spring season. The river cruising season is very similar in North America on the Mississippi and Columbia river systems.

In Asia, there are two seasons: the dry and wet seasons. The dry season is from November to April, and the wet season is from April through to November. Which is better? There's no definitive answer to that. It can get quite wet, and there can be flooding during the latter season, but in the dry season, it can be superhot, and there may be issues with low water. Typically, the high season for river cruising in Asia is January through March and October through December, but unlike in Europe, where there are a few months of the year when there are no sailings, river cruises in Asia run year-round.

River cruises run year-round on the Amazon River too, which experiences high water levels during the rainy season from December to May and lower waters during the dry season from May through December. There are advantages to both, as you'll read in chapter 10, "Exotic River Cruises."

On the Nile, the hot summer months are the slow season, and although sailings continue during the summer, they are lower in price and fewer are available due to the lower demand. November through March is typically a popular time to sail the Nile.

Danube vs. Rhine

(See more specifics on Europe itineraries in chapter 8.)

There are a number of other rivers and tributaries in Europe beyond the Danube and Rhine, but these two are the longest and most popular river routes in Western and Central Europe (the longest river on the continent is Russia's Volga River).

And they're popular for a reason. The Danube runs through some of the most iconic cities of Central Europe. It flows through Germany, Austria, Slovakia, Hungary, Croatia, Serbia, Romania, and Bulgaria, sailing right into the heart of Vienna, Budapest, and Belgrade along the way. There are few sights as spectacular as being docked along the river with a view of Budapest's jaw-dropping Parliament Building. And Vienna is a treasure-trove of music, art, and cafes. Indeed, the Danube is a great way to experience the grandeur of Western and Eastern Europe, and for this reason it is often the most popular first-timer's river cruise.

The Rhine is, quite simply, for castle lovers. It travels from the Swiss Alps to the North Sea in the Netherlands, passing through France and Germany along the way. The most-sought-after stretch is the Upper Middle Rhine Valley, a UNESCO World Heritage Site that runs for 40 miles between the German cities of Koblenz and Rudesheim and is dotted with ancient castles, historic towns, and vineyards. Other highlights include the fairy-tale-esque French city of Strasbourg and the canal-lined Amsterdam.

Other Places You Can Cruise in Europe

Beyond the iconic Danube and Rhine rivers, there are plenty of other river cruise destinations within Europe, most notably in France, home to three very different and distinct river cruising regions. There is the **Seine River,** which connects Paris to Normandy; the **Rhone and Saone rivers,** which sail into the heart of southern France's Burgundy and Provence regions; and the **Gironde and Garonne rivers** of the Bordeaux region. CroisiEurope also recently began offering sailings on France's chateaux-studded **Loire River.**

A little farther south, almost every major river cruise company offers cruises that wind between the sun-soaked, hillside vineyards of Portugal's **Douro River** Valley, a UNESCO World Heritage Site. Another unique river cruise destination—only offered by one river cruise line, Uniworld—is the **Po River** in Italy, which is more of a cruise tour, as there is little sailing, but the tidal river provides access to Venice and the scenic towns of northern Italy.

The shallow waters of Germany's **Elbe River** sometimes prove challenging, but that hasn't stopped Viking and CroisiEurope from offering river cruises between Prague and Berlin through the mountainous landscape of what is known as Saxon Switzerland. To read more on this, go to chapter 8.

Most river cruise companies already sail from Amsterdam to Maastricht in the Netherlands, weaving between Belgium and Holland along the two countries' vast network of canals and rivers, but Avalon Waterways recently created a new sailing that goes a bit farther south of Maastricht, along the **Meuse River** to the Belgian city of Namur.

Farther east, river cruises are available along Russia's **Volga River,** an itinerary that connects the country's blockbuster cities, Moscow and St. Petersburg, with unique churches and towns along the way. Viking is one of the only companies that also occasionally also offers Ukraine's **Dnieper River,** a river cruise bookended by stays in Kiev and Odessa.

Exotic Rivers

(See more on exotic rivers in chapter 10.)

For something very different from the European river cruising experience, there are ample exotic rivers throughout the world to cruise.

The **Peruvian Amazon** is a popular river cruise that is often tacked on to more comprehensive Peru itineraries that might include visits to Lima and Machu Picchu, for instance. This is an incredible river cruising destination, especially for the bird- and nature-loving set. Local outfits as well as some U.S. companies offer Amazon cruises on everything from more basic ships to some seriously decked out luxury vessels (Aqua Expeditions falls into the latter category).

In Asia, there are cruises on China's **Yangtze River,** which wind through scenic gorges and often include a visit to the controversial and impressive

Three Gorges Dam. Southeast Asia has been abuzz with development as river cruise companies build up vessels that are plying the **Mekong River** in Vietnam and Cambodia, anchored by bustling, motorbike-filled cities, the ancient ruins of Angkor Wat, and heart-warming floating villages along the way. As Myanmar has opened up more to the outside world and to tourism, so too has the vibrant country's **Irrawaddy River,** another exotic river hotspot.

More recently, India's **Ganges River** has been gaining traction as well, with several river cruise companies now offering luxury cruises along the fabled river, including Uniworld.

In Africa, the **Nile River** is the main game in town and offers the consummate river highway from which to visit some of Egypt's most important archaeological sites, from Luxor to the Valley of the Kings. Another river cruise destination of note is Botswana's **Chobe River,** where the luxury river safari company Zambezi Queen offers a comfortable vantage point for viewing the elephants, lions, buffalos, crocs, zebras, and other wildlife that come to swim and drink from the water.

U.S. River Cruising

(See more on U.S. rivers in chapter 9.)

For all the incredible river cruising experiences in far-flung destinations around the globe, there are some equally beautiful and interesting river cruises right here at home.

The two main river cruising regions in the U.S. are the **Mississippi River** and the **Columbia River** in the Pacific Northwest. Mississippi cruises run through the heartland of America between Minneapolis and New Orleans and can also be divided into shorter itineraries, such as Upper and Lower Mississippi cruises. There are also options to explore the region's **Ohio, Tennessee, and Cumberland rivers.**

The **Columbia and Snake rivers** are the scenic waterways that run near and along the Washington and Oregon border, traversing the breathtaking Columbia River Gorge.

QUIZ TIME: QUESTIONS TO ASK WHEN CHOOSING YOUR CRUISE

Before booking your river cruise, we suggest you ask yourself some questions about the type of experience you want and then read through our ship reviews and destination chapters to see which ships and destinations match your idea of a perfect river cruise vacation.

When looking through the attributes of the various ships, some determining factors will be no-brainers. For instance, if you're traveling with kids, you'll want one of the rare river ships and/or itineraries that cater to kids. If you're a foodie, you'll want to go with a line that puts a focus on food. If luxury is your thing, you'll want to make sure the line can meet your needs in terms of space, amenities, and onboard services.

Also ask yourself which shipboard features you can and can't live without. Do you mind if there's no pool, fitness center, or spa? Would you like the ship to have a fleet of bikes you can use? Or do you care more about having an educational or adventure experience? Do you want the ship to have an outdoor place where you can dine while catching the river views? Is value pricing your top consideration?

Here's a quick take on some of the pertinent questions and answers (you'll find more answers as you read the book).

HOW DO YOU GET A DEAL?

The best way to save is to check the offers about a year before you want to cruise. River cruises are a hot commodity, the ships are small, and the space is limited. The lines tend to put their best foot forward early on—even sweetening the pot with two-for-one deals, discounts on airfare, onboard spending credit, and such. They'd just as soon get you on their books early. If space is left 3 months before the sailings, there may be cheap, last-minute deals, but you can't count on it—especially in the height of the season, the ships sail full—so in waiting, you are basically taking a bet that someone else will cancel.

WHAT'S INCLUDED?

This varies by line, but the basic formula is your accommodations, food, wine, beer and soda with lunch and dinner (and sometimes mimosas at breakfast for those who want them), specialty coffees such as espresso, at least one shore excursion every day, and free Wi-Fi. Port charges and taxes are also included by some but not all. Airport transfers will be included if you book air through the cruise line and may also be available to those who don't. Gratuities for the crew, tour guides, and bus drivers are sometimes included but are often extra. There is also such a thing as all-inclusive river lines that include all the above plus have open bars.

HOW MUCH TIME IS SPENT ON THE SHIP & HOW MUCH IN PORT?

Fortunately the cruise lines offer very detailed itineraries on their websites so you can do some comparing, because the amount of time in port varies by line and itinerary. The ships cruise the same rivers but don't necessarily stop at the same places. Most days, though, you will visit a town or city (or even disembark on a river bank) to see major sights along the river and inland (although rarely more than a 2-hour motorcoach ride from the river). Some days you may visit two places. You may spend an overnight docked in a city, such as Vienna, so that you can partake in the nightlife. Some itineraries may include a relaxing day shipboard without a stop so you can check out the scenery—such as in the Rhine's midsection with its dozens of castles and the famous cliff known as Loreli. Rarely do river ships do 2 nonstop cruising days in a row.

WHAT ENTERTAINMENT DOES THE SHIP HAVE?

Again, this varies by line, but pretty standard (except on small ships on exotic routes) is some sort of live music at night so those who want to can dance, and at least one visit by a local troupe, either musicians or dancers. Some lines, such as Emerald Waterways, also do a crew show. In addition, there might be an occasional (perhaps connected to the destination) movie night, but mostly movies are available on demand through in-room entertainment systems.

ARE THERE SHIPBOARD ACTIVITIES?

Yes, but not at all the frenetic lineup you'll find on ocean ships. When they aren't out exploring on included shore excursions, most river cruise ship passengers are content to sit with a good book (indoors or out on the sun deck), play a game of Scrabble, or socialize over drinks or coffee. Organized activities may include some lectures, a local language class, a discussion of local customs by members of the crew, and/or a cooking demonstration by the chef. Depending on your ship, you may also be able to indulge in spa treatments or get your hair and nails done. You may also find a tempting selection of movies on your in-cabin TV.

IS THE CRUISE FORMAL OR CASUAL?

Even on fancy lines, river cruises are casual, although people may dress in "smart casual" at night. Men need bring a jacket only if they want to (some will wear one to the captain's party). Rarely does anyone wear a tie. In the evenings, women dress anywhere from smart casual to slightly more formal. There are no black-tie evenings.

WHAT ARE THE OTHER PASSENGERS LIKE?

Most on board will be retirees, most will be ages 55 and up, and most will be fit enough to do walking tours. They tend to be a friendly group that likes to socialize, although not usually late into the wee hours (most people are in bed by 11pm so they'll be fresh for the next day's tours).

I AM TRAVELING ALONE. WILL I FIT IN? DOES IT COST MORE?

Solo travelers occasionally get a break but often will find themselves paying the full fare for two (or 100 percent more than they would if they were sharing a room). Look for deals, though. With more solo travelers interested in river cruises, more lines are offering breaks on the single supplement fee. Some ships have tiny cabins, designed and priced for one, and Grand Circle Line also offers a same-sex roommate-matching service for singles (so you can share a cabin and pay the shared room rate). We give more information on solo travel in chapter 3.

No worries about fitting in. As we said, river cruisers are social. Don't be surprised if you find yourself "adopted" by several couples, or if you meet other travelers going it alone on their trips.

IS SHIPBOARD LIFE HEAVILY SCHEDULED?

Yes and no. Meal times are scheduled, and you are expected to be on time (see "What Are Meals Like?" below). There is always a nightly cocktail hour when the cruise director briefs you on what's happening the next day, and you won't want to miss this. But otherwise, when you are not off on a shore excursion or exploring on your own on shore, you are free to do what you like on the ship, including nothing.

WHAT ARE THE CABINS LIKE?

We give detailed descriptions in chapter 3. But in general, expect them to be smaller than in hotels and even smaller than what you may have experienced on ocean ships. You will have a private bathroom, most likely with a standing shower (bathtubs are a river ship rarity). And even in the most value-priced cabins, you will have some sort of view, either through a half window (you might have to stand on your bed to see out) or full window. Fancier cabins have French balconies (windows or doors that open) or full balconies that you can actually step out on. Typical amenities include bath products, a safe, a hairdryer, and a TV (usually a flatscreen). You may or may not get a bathrobe or slippers (on Viking, you need to request them). Some lines provide an in-cabin minifridge.

WHAT ARE MEALS LIKE?

Meals are open seating. Tables for two are rare, so you should plan on sharing a table. Breakfast and lunch are typically buffet-style, while dinner is a sit-down, four- or five-course affair with waiter service. You are expected to dine within certain hours—say, 7 to 9am for the breakfast buffet—ditto for the lunch buffet, and at a set time, often 7pm, for dinner. Some ships have the option of alternative dining at dinner (such as Viking, with its Aquavit Terrace) for which you may or may not need a reservation and which may or may not have a set start time. House beer, wine, and sodas are typically served at lunch and dinner. You may be able to upgrade to fancier wine for a fee. In general, the food is Continental, with the addition of some local dishes reflecting the destination you are cruising through. The chef may have daily suggestions.

DOES THE SHIP HAVE A CHILDREN'S PROGRAM?

Many do not. As we said, the cruises are geared toward an older crowd. Some lines don't even let kids under age 12 on board. However, a new albeit small phenomenon is select cruises geared toward multigenerational families, with shipboard activities and itineraries that keep kids' interests in mind. Lines offering family-friendly cruises include AmaWaterways (with Adventures by Disney), Tauck, and Uniworld.

WILL I GET SEASICK?

It's unlikely. If you have a problem with motion sickness, you're more likely to feel movement on the motorcoaches during excursions than on the river ship (snag a set of seats in the front of the bus, if that helps). Pack an over-the-counter product, such as Dramamine or Bonine, or try homeopathic methods, such as ginger pills or Sea-Band Wristbands (based on acupressure). You aren't going to feel enough movement on river ships to justify anything stronger.

IS THERE SMOKING ON RIVER SHIPS?

Smokers should expect to be left out in the cold, literally. Don't expect to smoke indoors on the ship at all. You may be able to light up in a specially designated section on the sun deck. There also may be smoking restrictions when it comes to shore excursions; you won't be able to smoke on

I Have a Disability. Will I Have Trouble Taking a River Cruise?

River cruises are in general difficult for those who have walking limitations. That said, if you don't mind missing some tours that require walking and more challenging steps and climbs, you can catch some wonderful views from the ship. You need to be honest about what you can and can't do and what accommodations you require. Walkers may be allowed, but scooters are usually banned (there's no room to store or maneuver them). You will want to have a collapsible wheelchair. Newer river ships in Europe have elevators, but they are unlikely to reach the sun deck and may not even reach the value cabins on the lower deck—meaning both will be accessible only by stairs. At many stops, you will disembark the ship via a gangway, which may or may not be a ramp and may require you to walk through other ships (see the "Rafting" box, p. 16). From the gangway, you may face stairs, sometimes many stairs, and on more exotic itineraries, there may not even be stairs—you may have to climb a steep riverbank, with the crew there to lend a hand. Wheelchair-accessible cabins are a rarity on ships in Europe, although Scenic is among the lines that have some.

The towns in Europe themselves may also be hard to negotiate (think lots of cobblestones). Keep in mind that river ships have small crews who may not always be able to assist you. You will want to travel with a companion who can assist you on the voyage and excursions and in the event of an emergency.

In the U.S., ships tend to be more accessible (although not ADA-compliant), but even then, elevators may not reach all decks; you will likely encounter raised door thresholds and narrow passageways; and you may find yourself precluded from some excursions due to gangways.

motorcoaches and may be restricted on where you can smoke off the coach (some of the attractions you'll visit will have their own rules).

WHAT IF I AM CELEBRATING A SPECIAL OCCASION?

If your river cruise is for a birthday, anniversary, family reunion, or other special event, let the cruise line know in advance. The crew will help you celebrate—a birthday, for instance, might bring a cake topped by a sparkler and a chorus of singing celebrants.

SHOULD I HONEYMOON ON A RIVER SHIP?

River cruises work for honeymooners in that they are an easy, one-stop shopping form of travel and visit several countries and romantic places, which in Europe include historic cities with cobblestone streets and castles; and in Southeast Asia, more exotic treks. You can book a suite and have a big bed, a balcony, and room to spread out, and maybe even a bathtub. But you should keep in mind there won't be a lot of time to be together just the two of you—except if you go off on your own on shore or hang out in your cabin. You may have to share a table with others at dinner (tables for two are rare), there won't be much nightlife, and you will be traveling with mostly older couples. On the other hand, it's easy to extend your celebration with pre- and post-cruise hotel stays in amazing cities, such as Paris, Prague, and Budapest. We've met honeymooners both younger and older who have been perfectly happy celebrating on a river cruise.

BOOKING YOUR RIVER CRUISE

3

Okay, you've thought about what type of river cruise vacation experience you might like. You've decided when and for how long you'd like to travel. You know what sort of itinerary interests you. And after reading through our ship reviews in the following chapters, and narrowing your focus down to a couple of river cruise lines that appeal to you, you'll be ready to get down to brass tacks and make your booking. Here's what you need to know.

BOOKING A CRUISE: THE SHORT EXPLANATION

Every river cruise line has a brochure, often many different brochures, full of beautiful glossy photos of beautiful glossy people enjoying fabulous vacations. They're colorful! They're gorgeous! They're enticing!

They're confusing!

They'll include rate charts with published prices that may be nothing more than the pie-in-the-sky wishes of cruise execs. Or those same rates may be crossed out in the brochure so that offers of 2-FOR-1 pricing and such can be included. Did we mention cruise brochures can be confusing?

Basics first: We strongly suggest you consider **booking your river cruise at least a year in advance** to take advantage of the best offers. And even though new ships are proliferating, a lot of prime season sailings sell out a year in advance. Does that mean if you're looking for a river cruise in March or April for that year that you're already out of luck? Not necessarily. There may be pockets of openings, especially in the slower fall season. But it does mean if you want first dibs on popular routes and popular cabins and popular dates, you may be better off looking further ahead.

So how do you book your river cruise? A lot of people book through **travel agents.** When you're spending $6,000 or more for two on your vacation, it certainly makes sense to have a guiding hand. But you may be wondering: Hasn't the traditional travel agent gone the way of typewriters and eight-track tapes and been replaced by the **Internet?** Not exactly. Travel agents are alive and kicking, although the Internet has indeed staked its claim alongside—which is why most traditional travel agencies have their own websites on which you can source initial information.

So which is the better way to book a cruise these days—by calling an agent or via the Internet? Good question. The answer can be both. If you're computer savvy, have a good handle on all the elements that go into a river cruise, and have narrowed down the choices to a few cruise lines that appeal to you, websites are a great place to gather information and do price and itinerary comparisons. On the other hand, you'll barely get a stitch of personalized service searching for and booking a cruise online. If you need help, for instance, getting a refund, arranging special meals or other onboard matters, or deciding on a cabin category, you're on your own. In addition, agents may have access to cruise discounts that the river cruise lines don't publicize on their websites. Some agents also get exclusive add-ons or upgrades with specific lines, so ask about that as well.

However you arrange to buy your river cruise, what you basically have in hand at the end is a contract for transportation, lodging, dining, entertainment, tours, housekeeping, and assorted other miscellaneous services that will be provided to you over the course of your vacation. That's a lot of services, involving a lot of people. It's complex, and like any complex thing, it pays (and saves) to study up. That's why it's important that you read the rest of this chapter.

BOOKING THROUGH A TRAVEL AGENT

The majority of passengers book at least their first river cruise through agents. Most of the river cruise lines are happy with this system and commission agents to do the work. In some cases, if you try to call a cruise line to book your own passage, you may be advised by the line to contact an agent in your area. The cruise line may even offer you a choice of names from its list of preferred agencies, and there are often links to preferred agencies on some of the lines' websites.

Patrick Clark, managing director of Avalon Waterways, estimates at least 80 percent of river cruise bookings are made through agents. Grand Circle is an anomaly, working only directly with consumers and not with travel agents at all. Viking River Cruises, which is aggressive with its direct marketing (after you make initial contact), may do a higher number of direct bookings. But even Viking encourages first-timers to use travel agents.

And why not? Good agents can give you expert advice, save you time, and (best of all) will usually work for you for free or a nominal fee—**the bulk of their fees are paid by the cruise lines.** (Many agents charge a consultation fee—say, $25—which is refunded if you eventually give them the booking.) In addition to advising you about the different ships, an agent can help you make decisions about the type of cabin you will need, any special airfare offerings from the cruise lines, pre- and post-cruise offerings, and travel insurance. All of these can have a big impact on your cruise experience. We've heard complaints from people who booked a cabin with a half window at the waterline and had to stand on their bed to see any view. Had they asked an experienced agent, they might have been advised that the cabin was cheap because it didn't have a full river view.

It's important to realize that **not all agents represent all cruise lines.** To be experts on what they sell, and to maximize the commissions the lines pay them (they're often paid more based on volume of sales), some agents may limit their offerings to one or more preferred lines. If you have your sights set on a particular line or have narrowed down your preferences to a couple of lines, you'll have to find an agent who handles your choices. As we mentioned above, you can call the lines themselves to get the name of an agent near you. It's also a good idea to ask the agent you are working with whether he or she has actually been on a river cruise with the line you're looking at so you can determine whether you are receiving firsthand advice.

It's rare to find a deal not offered by travel agents. The cruise lines tend to communicate deals and offers to their top agents first, before they offer them to the general public, and some of these deals will never appear in your local newspaper, on bargain travel websites, or even on the websites of the cruise lines themselves. When the river lines themselves *do* post specials on their websites, the same deals are usually also available through travel agents. The lines don't want to upset their travel-agent partners and generally try not to compete against them. In fact, travel agents are frequently in contact with the river lines and are continually alerted by the lines about the latest and best deals and special offers.

Depending on the agency you choose, you may run across other incentives for booking through an agent. Some agencies buy blocks of space on a ship in advance and offer it to their clients at a group price available only through that agency. These are called **group rates,** although "group" in this case means savings, not that you have to hang out with the other people booking through the agency. In addition, some agencies are willing to **negotiate,** especially if you've found a better deal somewhere else. It never hurts to ask. Finally, some agencies are willing to give back to the client a portion of their commissions from the cruise line to close a sale. This percentage may be monetary, or it might take the form of a perk, such as a free bottle of champagne or a limo ride to the ship (hardly reasons to book in and of themselves, but nice perks nevertheless).

Finding a Great Agent

If you don't know a good travel agent already, try to find one through your friends, preferably someone who has done a river cruise before. For the most personal service, look for an agent in your area, and for the most knowledge-able service, look for an agent who has river cruising experience. It's perfectly okay to ask an agent questions about his or her personal knowledge of the product, such as whether he or she has ever done a river cruise with one of the lines you're considering.

WATCH OUT FOR scams

It can be difficult to know whether the travel agency you're dealing with to make your river cruise booking is or isn't reliable, legitimate, or, for that matter, stable. The travel business tends to attract more than its share of scam operators trying to lure consumers with incredible come-ons.

o **Unsolicited contact is the hallmark of many scams.** Whenever you get a solicitation to buy travel by phone or e-mail from someone you have not contacted, consider it a scam. Legitimate travel agents do not cold-call. If you get an unsolicited pitch, call your state consumer-protection agency or the local office of the Better Business Bureau, or you can check with the cruise line to see whether it has heard of the agency in question. Be wary of working with any company, be it on the phone or Internet, that won't give you its street address.

o **Get a referral.** A recommendation from a trusted friend or colleague is one of the best ways to hook up with a reputable agent.

o **Use the river cruise lines' agent lists.** Some cruise-line websites include agency locator lists, naming agencies around the country with which they do business. These are by no means comprehensive lists of all good or bad agencies, but an agent's presence on these lists is usually another good sign of experience.

o **Beware of snap recommendations.** If an agent suggests a cruise line without first asking you a single question about your tastes, beware. Because agents work on commissions from the lines, some may try to shanghai you into cruising with a company

that pays them the highest rates, even though that line may not be right for you.

o **Always use a credit card to pay for your cruise.** A credit card gives you more protection in the event the agency or cruise line fails. (Trust us! It happens occasionally.)

o **Check where the first payment went.** When your credit card statement arrives, make sure the payment was made to the cruise line, not to the travel agency. If you find that payment was actually made to the agency, it's a big red flag that something's wrong. If you insist on paying by check, you'll be making it out to the agency, so it may be wise to ask whether the agency has default protection. Many do.

o **Always follow the cruise line's payment schedule.** Never agree to a different schedule the travel agency comes up with. The lines' terms are always clearly printed in their brochures and usually require an initial deposit of $250 to $500 (depending on the line) with the balance due no later than 90 days before departure. If you're booking 3 months or fewer before departure, the full payment will be required at the time of booking.

o **Keep on top of your booking.** If you ever fail to receive a document or ticket on the date it's been promised, inquire about it immediately. If you're told that your cruise reservation was canceled because of overbooking and that you must pay extra for a confirmed and rescheduled sailing, demand a full refund and/or contact your credit card company to stop payment.

a full-service agency. If you are calling a full-service travel agency, ask for the **cruise desk** or for someone with **river cruise experience.** A good and easy rule of thumb to maximize your chances of finding an agent who has cruise experience and who won't rip you off is to book with an agency that's a member of the **Cruise Lines International Association (CLIA;** ℡ **754/224-2200;** www.cruising.org), the main industry association. Members are cruise specialists with expertise in a variety of ocean lines; look for ones who also list river cruise experience. Membership in the **American Society of Travel Agents (ASTA;** ℡ **800/275-2782;** www.astanet.com) ensures that the agency is monitored for ethical practices, although it does not designate cruise experience. You can tap into the websites of these organizations to find reliable agents in your area.

There are also numerous large national and global agencies with vast networks of travel agents. Some of the larger travel agencies include Carlson Wagonlit Travel, AAA, Travel Leaders Group, Frosch, Valerie Wilson Travel, and Avoya, to name just a few. Agency networks, known as consortia, can also be incredibly helpful in helping you track down a river cruise specialist. Some of the largest and most well-known consortia are Virtuoso, Signature Travel Network, Ensemble Travel Group, and Vacation.com.

BOOKING ON THE INTERNET

For those who know exactly what they want (we don't recommend online shopping for first-time cruisers), you can book river cruises on the Internet. Sites that sell river cruises include top online travel agencies (Travelocity.com, Expedia.com, Orbitz.com) and agencies that specialize in cruises (icruise. com, Cruise.com, Cruise411.com).

There are also some good sites on the Internet that specialize in providing cruise information, including on river cruises. The best site dedicated to cruising in general (rather than linked with one line) is **Cruisecritic.com** (now owned by Expedia.com). This website includes reviews by professional writers, ratings and reviews by cruise passengers, useful tips, frequent chat opportunities, and message boards. For updated cruise news, no one does it better than Gene Sloan at his **USA Today Cruise Log Blog** (www.cruises.usatoday. com), where you'll also find a very active discussion forum. **Shermans Cruise.com** is a newer site with concise information about cruise companies and itineraries. In addition, nearly all the cruise lines have their own sites, which are chock-full of information—some even give virtual tours of specific ships. You'll find the website addresses for the various cruise companies in our cruise line reviews in chapter 5.

CRUISE COSTS

In chapter 5, we include the brochure rates for every ship reviewed, but, as noted above, these prices may actually be higher than any passenger will pay. Prices fluctuate based on any special deals the cruise lines are running. The volume of travelers interested in cruising in a particular river region may influence prices. If a ship does not achieve certain predetermined passenger volume goals, the river line might begin slashing rates to goose the market. The prices we've noted are for the following three basic types of accommodations: standard (which will have a window but often at the waterline), balcony (which includes cabins with French balconies), and suite. Remember that cruise ships generally have several different categories of cabins within each of these three basic divisions, all priced differently. That's why we give a range. See "Choosing Your Cabin," p. 36, for more information on cabin types.

The price you pay for your cabin represents the bulk of your cruise vacation cost, but there are other costs to consider. Whether you're working with an agent or booking online, be sure that you really understand what's included in the fare you're being quoted. Are you getting a price that includes the cruise fare, port charges, taxes, fees, and insurance, or are you getting a cruise-only fare? Are airfare and airport transfers included, or do you have to book them separately (either as an add-on to the cruise fare or on your own)? One agent might break down the charges in a price quote, while another might bundle them all together. Make sure you're comparing apples with apples when making price comparisons. Read the fine print!

It's important when figuring out what your cruise will cost to remember which extras are not included in your cruise fare. The items discussed in the section below are not included in most cruise prices and will add to the cost of your trip.

Shore Excursions

Unlike ocean cruises, river cruise lines include excursions in the cruise fare. These can be anything from city tours lasting a few hours to full-day tours that take you a considerable distance from the river to a key attraction, with lunch included (usually at a local hotel or restaurant, but occasionally at the homes of locals). In some locations there may be optional shore excursions priced from about $60 to $150, or more for, say, a flightseeing opportunity, depending on your cruising destination. On Europe cruises, these may include such luxuries as a wine tasting at a famous vineyard or a tour of a truffle farm with lunch. In chapter 8, we recommend specific excursions based on each river.

Gratuities

Some lines—including Scenic, Tauck, and Uniworld—include gratuities in the cruise fare, but others do not. You'll want to add tips for the ship's crew to your budget calculations. Tips are supposed to be "discretionary," but they are very much expected. Because some people find the whole tipping process very confusing, your cruise line will recommend an amount, which you can adjust up or down. Viking River Cruises in Europe, for instance, spells out tips for the program director, onboard staff, local city guides, and coach drivers that total about $19 (based on the exchange rate at press time) per guest, per day, or $259 per couple for a 1-week cruise. But amounts differ by destination—Russia tends to be higher—and by cruise line (you can find this information in advance at the cruise line website).

The tips can be paid in cash (in euros or other local currency or U.S. dollars) or put on your credit card at the end of your cruise. You may have the option of prepaying gratuities in advance of your trip. The amount you give is a lump sum that is divvied up between the crew. If a particular crew member has given you special service, such as the bartender, you are free to also tip him or her separately.

You may also be asked to tip tour guides and bus drivers separately (although some lines will include these in the cruise fare, so check first), in which case a standard tip is $3 to $5 per person for the guide and $1 for the bus driver. An automatic tip may be added to spa services. If not, you can add a tip to the bill.

Booze & Soda

Most river ships include soft drinks, specialty coffee (espressos and lattes), and beer or house wine with meals as part of the cruise fare. Some lines including Tauck, Uniworld, and Scenic are all-inclusive, with all drinks included in the cruise fare (although they may still charge extra if you want, say, a fancy cognac). But on most ships, there is an extra charge for all cocktails and liquor, although typically very reasonably priced from $6. In a river cruise oddity, during cocktail hour, if you want a glass of wine you have to pay (save for the welcome or farewell cocktail party), although if you wait until dinner, you don't. In addition to the house pour of the day, there may be the option of finer wine selections at dinner, ranging from about $30 per bottle to upward of $300.

Port Charges, Local Taxes & Fees

Every ship has to pay docking fees at each port. It also has to pay some local taxes per passenger in some places. These fees are passed on to customers. Port charges, taxes, and other fees are sometimes included in your cruise fare, with Viking River Cruises and Uniworld among lines that include them. If they are not included, these charges can add on average between $160 and $170 per person. Make sure you know whether these fees are included in the cruise fare when comparing rates.

MONEY-SAVING STRATEGIES
Early-Bird & Last-Minute Discounts

As we said earlier, the best way to save on a river cruise and have a good choice of available cabins is to book well in advance, preferably more than a year before your departure date, which is when most of the deals come out. Itineraries are typically announced 1 year to 15 months in advance. River ships have limited space on board, and despite the fact there are many more ships on the river now than there were even 6 years ago, they tend to book up early. That doesn't mean there aren't periods where you are likely to find discounts, however. A popular time for discounting is fall, when enough inventory has sold for the following year that river cruise lines know which itineraries and departures they need to push a little harder to fill. Another wave of discounts will often crop up after the New Year, a time when many people start realizing they haven't yet made plans for the summer. Prices may get reduced closer to the sailing if cabins don't sell. But before they do that, the lines offer incentives—such as free or discounted air and two-for-one pricing—to get you to book in advance. Because the ships are small and fill up quickly, you can't count on there being much last-minute availability—especially if you have a precise cruise date you're interested in. Planning your river cruise vacation in advance and taking advantage of early booking discounts is still the best way to go, in our opinion.

Shoulder-Season Discounts

In Europe, you can also save by booking a cruise in the shoulder months of **March and April** or **October through December** when cruise pricing is usually lower than during the more popular summer months. Airfares are lower in these months as well. June, July, and August are peak season. May and September bring the advantages of typically decent weather (not too hot in Europe). And although the shoulder seasons may not always come with perfect weather, remember that the traditional high-season summer months bring massive crowds, especially in popular European cities. A coat and umbrella in exchange for a bit of sightseeing exclusivity isn't necessarily the worst trade-off.

Solo-Traveler Discounts

Most river ship accommodations are for two passengers, either in twin beds or beds combined to make a queen-size bed. Single supplements range from 50 to 100 percent. In other words, travel alone and pay through your teeth. The good news is that river cruise lines are increasingly recognizing the growing popularity of solo travel and the importance of catering to the passenger traveling alone, and these supplements are being waived or reduced in greater frequency than in the past, which means solo travelers can get a deal. Tauck, at press time, was waiving the single supplement in Category 1, its least-expensive cabins, on all Europe river cruises—solo cruisers paid the same amount one person sharing a cabin was charged; it also was offering a $1,000 discount for solo travelers in some fancier categories. AmaWaterways, Uniworld, Avalon Waterways, Scenic, and Emerald Waterways have all been known to roll out waived or reduced single supplements, too. Keep an eye out for other offers, which are not necessarily year-round. Some ships also offer the option of a small cabin with a twin bed or sofa bed designed and priced for one.

Past-Passenger Deals

River cruise lines, like ocean cruise lines, reward repeat passengers for their loyalty—they'd love for you to do all your vacations with them from now on and will offer you discounts as enticement. Viking River Cruises, for instance, has a repeat passenger program called Viking Explorer Society. You are automatically enrolled after your first cruise, and if you book within a year, you receive $200 in travel credit (book within 2 years and receive $100 in travel credit). Viking also has incentives for those who make referrals to family and friends—refer 13 friends and receive a free cruise (each person referred also gets a $100 discount). AmaWaterways' Privilege Rewards Program gives you $100 off plus an invitation to a repeat-guest reception on your second cruise (and the more you cruise, the more the perks increase). With Avalon Waterways, those who travel on any brand of parent company Globus becomes a Journeys Club Member and receives a 5 percent repeat-passenger discount. Uniworld's River Heritage Club for repeat cruisers brings special offers and such perks as $150 per person off 7- to 12-day cruises ($250 off on longer sailings).

Group Discounts

One of the best ways to get a cruise deal is to book as a group, so you may want to gather family together for a reunion or convince your friends or colleagues they need a vacation, too. A "group," as defined by the river cruise lines, is generally **at least 8 to 10 people** (depending on the line) in four or five cabins. Your group will receive a discount and may receive additional perks. In some cases, the 11th passenger in a group may be free—and the group members can split the savings.

Some travel agencies buy big blocks of space on a ship in advance and offer it to their clients at a group price available only through that agency. These are called group rates, although, as we mentioned earlier in the chapter, "group" in this case means savings, not that you have to hang out with (or even know) the other people booking through the agency.

Other Deals

Lines tend to offer cut rates for their sailings on their older vessels, as many passengers are often eager to get onto the newest and latest models. The thing is that even though the ships have aged several years, due to aggressive annual renovating and updating programs, they might not feel a day older than some of their newer counterparts, so it's definitely worth it to look into some of these time-tested vessels. (Read our reviews later in this book to see which boats these are.)

Also, every river cruise destination goes through highs and lows. Sometimes that's just because of random trends in popularity (for the past couple of years, river cruisers couldn't get enough of the French waterways), and sometimes it could be based on turmoil or negative PR in the region (the Nile River has struggled in the aftermath of the Arab Spring, and Russia's Volga River has been distressed ever since the Crimea crisis). To stimulate demand on less popular rivers, the lines will roll out deals, often pretty incredible ones. Of course, if you aren't comfortable going, you should never do so. But if it's safe to go, this can be a great way to experience a wonderful river cruising region at an affordable price—indeed, if it really is too dangerous, most river cruise companies will halt operations to the region altogether and will only go back when they feel it is safe. Look at the State Department website (www.state. gov/travel) and talk to your agent about his or her thoughts on when and where to go to get a deal—an agent should be tuned in to all the latest travel warnings, and some agents who have been to the region in question will be better able to tell you whether it's a good idea to take advantage of the attractive prices and go.

SIX AIRFARES & PRE-/POST-CRUISE HOTEL DEALS

Air Add-Ons

Your cruise package may or may not include international air. Especially during promotional periods, the lines may have free air offers. For instance, in December 2015, Viking River Cruises was offering airfare discounts and, in some cases, free air on November and December 2016 Grand Europe and Romantic Danube sailings.

You are always free to book your vacation as cruise-only or land-and-cruise-only and do your air separately. What it comes down to is convenience. The cruise line will likely offer coach and upgraded business-class airfares, if not on a direct flight, then on a route with an easy connection. More than half of river cruise passengers book air with the cruise line. Why? The fares are decent, if not the cheapest, and it's one-stop shopping. Booking air with the cruise line also allows the line to keep track of you. If your plane is late, for instance, the line may actually hold the ship, although not always. When you book air travel with your cruise line, the lines include **transfers** from the airport to the ship, saving you the hassle of getting a cab. (If you do cruise-only and book your air travel on your own, you may still be able to get transfers separately—ask your agent about this.) *Tip:* Be aware that once the air ticket is issued, you usually aren't allowed to make changes.

All that said, is it possible to book cheaper air on your own (or via your travel agent)? Yes, likely, especially if you get one of the lesser-known discount carriers, such as WOW or Norwegian, or fly via, say, Dublin on Aer Lingus, and then catch an intra-European flight. If you have frequent-flier miles, go ahead and use them for a free flight. If you are particular about which carrier you fly or which route, or if you have an airline you always fly and stand a chance at an upgrade, go for it, because you are more or less at the mercy of the cruise line in terms of carrier and route if you take its air deals. *Tip:* If you're booking your own air and your travel schedule is flexible, it's often easier to get the carrier and the flight time you prefer if you choose a cruise that leaves on a Wednesday or Thursday—or other times considered nonpeak by the airlines.

On the plus side, if airfare is part of the cruise package but you choose to book your air transportation, you will be refunded the air portion of the fare.

Intra-Vacation Air

Another area of possible expenditure that needs to be included in your planning is air within the country or countries you are visiting. Your ship may not dock in the same city you arrive in after your international flights. In Europe, transfers to your port of disembarkation are typically by bus, but in more exotic destinations, you may have to fly to meet your ship on a plane chartered by the cruise company. There is a charge for these flights, which may be required (transport on your own won't be an option) and that may or may not be included in your cruise fare, so read the fine print. Intra-vacation flights can add several hundred dollars per person to your cruise vacation costs.

Pre- & Post-Cruise Hotel Deals

Even if you don't take a cruise tour, you may want to consider spending a day or two in your port of embarkation or debarkation either before or after your cruise. (See details on exploring the port cities in chapters 5 and 6.) An advantage to coming in a day or two early is that you don't have to worry if your flight is running late.

Just as with airfare, you need to decide whether you want to buy your hotel stay from the cruise line or make arrangements on your own. The river lines negotiate **special deals with fancy hotels** at port cities (often four-star). They may have decent rates at that hotel, but what you are really paying for, as with airfare, is convenience. You are likely to find much better rates at other hotels on your own, as long as you don't mind the getting-there-on-your-own part.

When evaluating a cruise line's hotel package, make sure you review it carefully to see what's included. See whether the line provides a transfer from the airport to the hotel and from the hotel to the cruise ship (or vice versa); make sure that the line offers a hotel that you will be happy with in terms of type of property and location; and ask whether any escorted tours, car-rental deals, or meals are included. You'll also want to compare the price of booking on your own. (Keep in mind that cruise lines usually list rates for hotels on a per-person basis, whereas hotels post their rates on a per-room basis.)

CHOOSING YOUR CABIN

Once you've looked at the ship descriptions in chapter 5, talked over the options with your travel agent, looked at the cruise line's website and any virtual tours online, and selected an itinerary and ship, you'll have to choose a cabin. You can go with a basic cabin with a view just above the waterline or opt for a two-room suite with balcony. Most cabins have twin beds that are convertible to queen-size (you can request which configuration you want), plus a private bathroom with a shower and sometimes a bathtub (although this is a rarity). Some cabins have solo cabins with fixed sofa beds. Most cabins sleep two. Suites that sleep more than two and connecting cabins are new phenomena on select ships.

Most cabins, but not all, have flatscreen televisions. Some also have extra amenities, such as safes, minifridges, bathrobes (either provided or available on request), and hair dryers. Most cabins have individual thermostats so that you can control air-conditioning and heat. A bathtub is considered a luxury on river ships and will usually be found only in more expensive cabins. You can expect your bathroom to be equipped with amenities including shampoo and conditioner and liquid soap (maybe even fancy products, such as L'Occitane). If you prefer bar soap, check in advance, as we've run into situations on exotic routes where it's not provided.

Some cabin choice considerations:

1. Look at the deck plan of the ship on the line's website or in the line's brochure, note the location of the ship's lounge and other loud public areas, and try not to book a cabin that's too close or underneath.
2. Also take note of the location of the engines—they can be loud and can vibrate intensely when they are starting up as well as when the ship is moving, which can be a rude awakening when you're trying to catch some Zs.
3. Cabins that adjoin elevator shafts or staircases might be noisy (although proximity makes it easier to get around the ship).
4. If you are looking for a suite with two separate rooms, make sure that's what you're getting. "Suite" is a term used to denote a larger cabin (not necessarily with two rooms).
5. Want a balcony that you can step out on? Make sure that is mentioned. A "French balcony" just means you have a large window that opens.
6. If you are mobility-impaired, carefully consider location and the size of the cabin (you may want more room to maneuver). The prime areas where you will spend time will be the dining room and main lounge, which on newer ships in Europe should be accessible by elevator. Other decks may only be accessible by stairs.

Cabin Types

What kind of cabin is right for you? Price will likely be a big factor here, but so should the vacation style you prefer. The typical river ship has several types of cabins, which are illustrated by floor plans in the cruise line's brochure. The cabins are usually described by **price** (highest to lowest), **category** (suite, deluxe, standard, and other types), and **furniture configuration** ("with sitting area"). Fancier cabins may come with **verandas** (also referred to as **balconies**) that give you a private outdoor space to enjoy river views, or **French balconies,** which mean large windows or glass doors that open. An advantage of both is that you can experience fresh air and the sounds of the river—although for safety and bug-control reasons, it is generally recommended that you keep doors closed at night. Balcony sizes vary, so if you're looking to do more than stand on your balcony, make sure the space is big enough to accommodate deck chairs, a table, or whatever else you require. Also keep in mind that these verandas are not completely isolated—your neighbors may be able to see you, and vice versa.

Noise can be a factor that may influence your cabin choice. See the list of cabin choice considerations, above, for more on that topic. Note that the loudest areas of a ship vary depending on how well insulated the different areas are, so if noise will be a problem for you, ask what the quietest part of the ship is when you are booking your cabin. We would say that, generally, midship on a higher deck will be the quietest area (unless, of course, you're near the lounge). Occasionally, though, guests in upper cabins can hear people walking on the jogging track on the sun deck above.

If you plan to spend a lot of quiet time in your cabin, you should probably consider booking the biggest room you can afford, and you should also consider taking a cabin with a picture window or, better still, a private veranda. If, conversely, you plan to be off on shore excursions or on deck checking out the river views and using your cabin only to change clothes and collapse at the end of the day, you might be happy with a smaller (and cheaper) cabin. Usually, cabins on the higher decks are more expensive, even if they are the same size as cabins on lower decks. **Luxury suites** are usually on upper decks, with lots of space to stretch out, but not necessarily a separate room—the term "suite" is used loosely (to mean "bigger" space). The suite will be elaborately decorated on Uniworld. On some lines, including Uniworld and Scenic, those in top digs also get butler service. Otherwise, expect nice contemporary decor, room to stretch out, and special services—including room service—not available with other cabins.

You may want to keep in mind that, just as with real estate, it's sometimes better to take a smaller cabin in a nicer ship than a bigger cabin on an older, simpler ship.

Cabin Sizes

The size of a cabin is described in terms of square feet. This number may not mean a lot unless you want to mark it out on your floor at home. But to give you an idea: 90- to 120-square-feet and under is low end and cramped, 170-square-feet is midrange (and the minimum for people with claustrophobia), and 250-square-feet and up is suite size.

YOUR DINING OPTIONS

On river ships, all meals are open seating, meaning you can sit with whomever you want. Meal times are set—say breakfast from 7 to 9am, lunch from 12:30 to 1:30pm, and dinner at 7pm. Unlike on ocean ships, there isn't much flexibility on dinner time. You are requested to get to your meal as close to the set time as possible—show up at 8pm, and you'll get stares from the crew.

Specialty Dining

Some lines have alternative dining options, such as nighttime meals at Viking River Cruises' Aquavit Terrace or AmaWaterways' chef's table restaurant at the aft of its newer ships, which require advance reservations—check with your onboard concierge for specifics. In most cases on river ships, these alternative eateries do not have an extra charge.

Table Size

Tables for one or two are rare on river ships, so you should plan on dining with others. What happens organically is you find people you like during the sailing and pair up. We generally start out trying to snag a table of six or eight, which provides enough variety so that you don't get bored and also allows you to steer clear of any individual you don't particularly care for. If you are traveling as a family or other group, notify the waitstaff, and they may be able to save you a spot.

Special Menu Requests

The cruise line should be informed at the time you make reservations about any special dietary requirements you have. Some lines provide kosher menus, and all have vegetarian, vegan, low-fat, low-salt, and sugar-free options. It's also important to notify the ship in advance and once on board of any allergies. If you have included meals on shore, make sure to reiterate your allergies to your tour guide, who can translate your needs to the restaurant.

DEPOSITS & CANCELLATION POLICIES

You'll be asked by your travel agent to make a **nonrefundable deposit,** typically a fixed amount between $250 and $500. You'll then receive a receipt in the mail from the cruise line. You'll typically be asked to pay the remaining fare usually no later than 3 months before your departure date. Note that special offers may have different payment terms.

The cruise lines have varying policies regarding **cancellations,** and it's important to look at the fine print in the line's brochure to make sure you understand it. Most lines allow you to cancel for a refund of 35 percent of your fare 89 to 60 days before your cruise and 50 percent 59 to 30 days before. If you cancel within 30 days, you will pay 80 percent of your cruise fare up to no refund at all, depending on the line.

TRAVEL INSURANCE

Hey, stuff happens. Given today's unpredictable geopolitical situation, economic woes, and extreme weather conditions, you just never know what might occur. A cruise could be canceled, for example, because of mechanical breakdowns, low water levels on the river, the cruise line's going out of business, or an act of war. For all these reasons—worries about travel, worries about river cruise lines canceling, sudden illness or other emergencies, missed flights that cause you to miss the ship, or even if you just change your mind—you may want to think about purchasing **travel insurance.**

When you pay for your river cruise, your travel agent or the cruise line will likely give you a pitch to buy insurance to cover your vacation. The agent gets commissioned, and travel insurance is a profit area for cruise lines. A big selling point will likely be that you're making an investment in your vacation and will want to protect that investment should you need to cancel.

You can dismiss travel insurance for your cruise as a waste of money, and for some people that's true. But there are circumstances where people will want to be insured, including if you or a close relative has a medical condition that could flare up, if you're cruising in a potentially bad weather season or caught in a geopolitical crisis, or if you're not covered internationally for medical insurance (especially vital if you're covered primarily by Medicare, which won't cover you in international destinations).

The most common travel insurance policies sold by agents and cruise lines bundle coverage for trip cancellation and interruption, baggage protection, medical expenses, and emergency evacuation. There might also be a set amount of death and dismemberment insurance. But you may not need all that. Your homeowner's policy, health insurance, and credit cards may already cover you in some areas—meaning the cruise line's bundled plan may provide coverage you already have.

And the reality is you can often find less-expensive policies through third-party insurers. Travel insurance policies will typically cost you from 4 to 10 percent of your total trip cost—so you lay out $200 to $500, based on a $5,000 river cruise vacation. If you go with the cruise line policy, you are opting for the cruise line's set pricing structure, which may be on the high side. Go with a third party, and you can pick and choose what you believe you really need. (See below for advice on how to book your insurance directly.)

No matter what you choose, it's absolutely crucial to read the fine print, because terms vary from policy to policy and even line to line. Be aware that cruise line polices tend not to apply to preexisting medical conditions, for instance. The cruise line policies also won't cover you for any air tickets you purchase on your own (not through the cruise line). On the plus side, if you buy from the cruise line, you can pay for your insurance at the same time that you pony up for your cruise fare.

Trip cancellation and disruption insurance requires extra scrutiny. Look at what timeline may apply—does the insurance kick in after 12 hours, 24 hours, 48 hours, or another amount of time? You'll also want to look at whether a cruise line's policy will give you cash back or whether the reimbursement is in the form of credit for a future cruise.

Cancel for any reason insurance is the most expensive type and has some drawbacks—including that you can't usually cancel last minute. Another misnomer is that emergency evacuation means you'll be airlifted wherever you say. It doesn't. It means you are covered for treatment at the nearest hospital that can handle your medical issue.

Reputable third-party insurers include **Allianz** (© 800/284-8300; www.accessamerica.com), **Travel Guard International** (© 800/826-4919; www.travelgaurd.com), and **Travel Insured International** (© 800/243-3174; www.travelinsured.com). Two useful websites, **Squaremouth** (© 800/240-0369; www.squaremouth.com) and **InsureMyTrip** (insuremytrip.com), let you easily compare various third-party insurance options. For evacuation coverage in the event of a major medical emergency, **MedJet Assist** (© 800/527-7478; www.medjetassist.com) has both short-term and annual policies (and will get you to a hospital of your choice). Be aware that travel insurance

Onboard Medical Care

River ships rarely have a doctor on board except in China and Russia, in which case they charge a fee for their services. On other routes, a member of the crew may be trained to deal with emergencies. But generally, because you are in such close proximity to land, if you run into a medical issue, you will be referred to a doctor on shore, at your expense.

does not cover changes in your itinerary, which are at the discretion of the cruise line.

Lost-luggage insurance doesn't make much sense for most travelers, so if you have the option to skip that one, do. On domestic flights, checked baggage is covered up to $2,800 per ticketed passenger. On international flights (including U.S. portions of international trips), baggage is limited to about $1,500 per checked bag. If you plan to check items more valuable than the standard liability, see whether your valuables are covered by your homeowner's policy, get baggage insurance as part of your comprehensive travel insurance package (contact one of the travel insurance providers listed above), or buy Travel Guard's BagTrak product. Be sure to take any valuables or irreplaceable items with you in your carry-on luggage, as many valuables (including books, money, and electronics) aren't covered by airline policies.

If your luggage is lost, immediately file a lost-luggage claim at the airport, detailing the luggage contents. For most airlines, you must report delayed, damaged, or lost baggage within 4 hours of arrival. The airlines are required to deliver luggage, once found, directly to your house or destination free of charge.

[FastFACTS] RIVER CRUISING

Business Hours Not every place you visit will operate on a 9-to-5 basis. Check in advance on opening hours. In Europe, some shops close for extended lunch periods in the afternoon. And there are still a lot of cities and towns in Europe where many shops and restaurants are closed on Sundays. Check on local holidays too, as they are (obviously) different than U.S. holidays and businesses will often be closed then.

Calling Home You may be able to purchase a global plan for your cellphone so that you can make calls, send texts, and check e-mails during your trip.

Check with your provider before your trip about rates. Another option is to purchase a SIM card for your phone locally once you get to your destination. If you're thinking of using Skype to call home, be aware that while most river cruise lines do offer Wi-Fi, the connection isn't always good enough for video calls (it tends to be best when docked in port).

Cash, Banks & ATMs Banks and automated teller machines (ATMs) will be available in most cities and some towns on your route. A fee may be charged to withdraw cash and for money exchange. Make

sure to notify your bank that you will be traveling internationally.

Credit Cards Notify your credit card companies about which countries you'll be visiting so they know that it is you using the card and they don't deny any charges. Be aware that not all credit cards work everywhere—we've run into situations where only Visa or MasterCard is accepted and others where none of our credit cards worked at all, such as in Romania.

Inoculations Whenever you travel, you should make sure your vaccines, such as for tetanus or the flu, are up to date. If you are traveling

41

to an exotic destination, such as Southeast Asia, China, Egypt, or the Amazon, additional shots and preventative medications may be advised. A great source for this information is the Traveler's Health website operated by the **CDC** (Centers for Disease Control and Prevention; wwwnc.cdc.gov/travel).

Local Customs It's a good idea to study up before your trip, especially if you're visiting an exotic destination. In Asia, for instance, it's customary to present money using both hands. Your cruise line will likely provide advice, and you can also find information at world etiquette websites, such as **ediplomat.com.**

Lost or Stolen Credit Cards Be sure to tell all of your credit card companies the minute you discover your wallet has been lost or stolen, and file a report at the nearest police precinct. Your credit card company or insurer may require a police report number or record of the loss. Most credit card companies have an emergency toll-free number to call if your card is lost or stolen; they may be able to wire you a cash advance immediately or deliver an emergency credit card in a day or two.

News If your ship has in-cabin TVs (most now do), you will likely have access to news and information networks, such as CNN, Fox,

the BBC, CNBC, and ESPN International. Be aware, though, that signals may be sporadic, and there may be times when you can't see anything but fuzz or a frozen screen.

Seasickness Seasickness isn't a problem for most on river cruise ships, as there is much less swaying (if any) than on the open seas, but those particularly susceptible to motion sickness may feel the motion of river ships. And you also have buses to worry about (sitting in the front may be your best bet). We suggest if you are prone to seasickness or motion sickness that you pack over-the-counter medication, such as Dramamine, Bonine, or Marezine. Some people swear by ginger capsules, and there's a lollipop product called Queasy Pops (and a hard candy called Queasy Drops) that some people swear helps with seasickness (find them at pharmacies, natural food stores, and online at Amazon.com). You might alternatively want to use acupressure wristbands, known as Sea-Bands.

Tipping Guidelines for Restaurants/Taxis
One way Americans sometimes appear culturally ignorant is by overtipping. Tips in countries outside the U.S. tend to be less than 10 percent, and in some places no tips are expected at all. In tourist restaurants, service charges may be automatically added, so check your

bill first before leaving extra. Porters will gladly accept a dollar or a euro, but again, it may not be expected.

Traveler's Checks
While you may be able to use this secure method in Western Europe and the U.S., it's hard to find vendors (other than your ship) who will accept them in such places as Asia and Eastern Europe.

Voltage Carefully read up on voltage in the countries you'll be visiting and on your ship. Most laptops and cellphones and other smart devices are now dual-voltage, but if you're in doubt, use a converter. We've had more than one device fried by plugging into 220V (as opposed to 110V). Your river ship will likely have 110V and/or 220V outlets for standard (U.S.) two-prong plugs and outlets as well as outlets for European three-prong plugs, but you will likely stay at some hotels where you will need multiprong travel plugs or converters. Note that the ship outlets will not likely be grounded.

Water Water is not potable in all river cruise destinations, so when you are on shore, you may be advised to go with bottled water. Your ship will also provide bottled water in your stateroom and will let you know whether the water on board is drinkable (it typically is in Europe, not so in Asia).

THE CRUISE EXPERIENCE

N ow that you've made most of the hard decisions—choosing and booking your river cruise vacation—the rest of your planning should be relatively easy. From this point on, the cruise lines take over much of the work, particularly if you've booked a package that includes hotels and air travel.

With river cruises it is particularly important to read the pre-trip information sent to you by your chosen cruise line. The river lines do a good job in addressing commonly asked questions—in addition to printed materials sent to your home you can find details on the line's website. Because the lines know their customers to be inquisitive sorts, they may also recommend additional reading material, both fiction and non-fiction that we highly recommend you check out.

4

PACKING FOR YOUR CRUISE

Our main advice here is to pack light. Use the old pile-a-bunch-of-stuff-on-a-bed method before deciding what you really need—the principle at play being "If in doubt, leave it out."

On your ship you will have a closet and some drawers in your cabin, but you won't find the amount of storage you have at home, or even in a standard hotel room. A good thing about cruises in general is once you're on the ship you can unpack and hide your suitcases under the bed for the rest of the cruise (if there is not enough space under the bed ask the ship personnel if they can store your suitcases elsewhere). But when you add hotel stays to the mix, you really don't want to find yourself constantly rummaging through your suitcase for that important item that always somehow gets lost on the bottom, under your carefully folded stacks of clothes.

Wherever you go, plan on the weather being unpredictable. We've frozen in the middle of summer in Germany and felt overheated in the "cooler" fall in Asia. Going with layers of wrinkle-resistant, easy-care clothes you can layer on or peel off is your best bet.

River cruises are all casual or "smart-casual" day and night, so there's no reason to pack overly formal attire. There will be some passengers who dress up a little at night (a man or two may put on a jacket, women may don casual dresses), but others will stay in pretty much the same outfit all day, maybe putting on a different top or heels at night. An exception is if there's a Captain's Party or Farewell Dinner, where people are more likely to dress up a tad (but definitely not black tie). Shorts may or may not be allowed in the dining room at night (check with the line). How informal or fancy you get is up to you—we like to go with nice tops and jeans or pants and occasionally will put on a skirt or dress just because it makes us feel special. It is a good idea to have a nice outfit if you plan to eat at finer restaurants (some may require men to wear a jacket) or to attend special events such as an opera performance in Vienna.

In most places, a rain jacket and sweater or sweatshirt that can go underneath will serve you well in chilly temperatures, though if you are cruising October to December in Europe or the U.S. you will want to also have a warmer jacket, a hat, a scarf and gloves. An umbrella is a must-have on river cruises, but before you take up space with one, check and see if your line provides them (many do). If your ship has a pool or hot tub, or you plan to visit pools and spas on land, pack a swimsuit.

Our big packing issue always involves shoes. You will do a lot of walking, comfortable walking shoes or sneakers are essential. In Asia, you will want to have shoes that easily slip off since you will be visiting Buddhist temples that require everyone entering to be barefoot (some people bring disposable socks for use when these are allowed). We usually also bring a pair of fancier flats or sandals and black patent heels, which are great for dressing up jeans.

You've probably heard it before, but sticking with one basic color and doing mix and match is the way to go. If you're focusing on black, you might want to add in some red or blue just to shake things up a bit.

Essentials

What you choose to pack obviously involves a lot of personal choice, but here's a checklist of items that everyone should bring along:

- A waterproof jacket or lightweight raincoat (big enough to fit a sweater or sweatshirt underneath
- A sweater or sweatshirt
- An umbrella
- A wrap or light sweater (for air-conditioning on the ship, in buses and in restaurants)
- Two to four pairs of pants or jeans
- A choice of tops ranging from t-shirts to dress shirts
- One or two pairs of walking shoes or sneakers (which you can wear on uneven surfaces such as cobblestones)
- Plenty of socks and underwear (so you can avoid the cost of laundry and also because socks take forever to dry in humid temps)
- Sunscreen (SPF 15 or higher)
- Bug spray (rivers can get buggy everywhere)
- Sunglasses and a sun hat

- Binoculars (unless provided by the river line)
- A camera, preferably with zoom or telephoto lens (plus extra flashcards or film and batteries)
- Smart-casual nighttime attire
- Travel-size toiletries and medications (with the meds in your carry-on)
- Grooming items such as an electric shaver, curling or straightening iron (the major river lines provide hairdryers)

Additional Stuff to Pack

We also have our own lists, as frequent cruisers, of what we bring on trips. Some of these items we keep in little travel bags in our closets so we can grab them whenever we hit the road. We share these just to give you an idea of other things you might think about.

- A Kindle (or other e-reader) pre-loaded with a selection of books
- A power strip (so we can plug in all our devices at once)
- A converter and/or plug adapter (with a choice of prongs)
- A spare pair of contacts or glasses
- Gallon-size sealable plastic bags which we use to protect cameras in the rain, for damp bathing suits and to protect hot sauces, honey, jams and other products we like to buy as souvenirs
- Big safety pins (so we can close curtains tightly)
- A couple of clothes pins, because we always have something to wash
- Hand sanitizer and packages of Kleenex (because you can't always count on what's in washrooms)
- Bonine or another motion sickness medication, more for the buses than for the river ships
- A battery operated sound machine or sound machine app on a cellphone (the white noise helps light sleepers)
- A small backpack or tote to use on day trips
- A battery-operated fan for hot weather (we haven't used them, but friends swear by them)
- If you don't have a cellphone with an alarm, we'd also suggest a travel alarm clock
- A first-aid kit (working on the principle if you bring one you probably won't have to use it)

Baggage

Another incentive not to overdo the packing is that airlines and river cruise lines have established luggage limits and may charge extra if you exceed them (see your specific airline and river line for their rules). Note that international flights usually have larger allowances than domestic flights or flights within Europe, so if you're traveling on a non-connecting flight, what may have passed muster on the intercontinental flight may incur a fee on other legs of your journey. Typically porterage for one large suitcase per person is included in your cruise fare (there may be limits on how large and heavy that bag can be). You can also bring a carry-on bag in which you should place all your important stuff including medications, your passport and all your other trip documents. There may be a limit in the size of carry-on you can bring on buses during your cruise, so having an additional small backpack or daypack to bring stuff for excursions is a good idea.

Laundry Services & Dry Cleaning

An easy way to cut down on what you pack is to plan on doing some laundry en-route. You ship will have laundry service available for an additional fee and may have a clothesline in the shower you can use if you prefer to wash stuff in your sink. Travel irons are banned from ships as a fire hazard, though there may be an iron you can use in the laundry room. You are allowed to bring a portable travel steamer. Pressing service will also be available for a fee. Dry cleaning services will not be available, except at hotels.

4 BUDGETING & BILLS

There are few forms of travel that are as inclusive as river cruises. You've already paid for the lion's share of your vacation when you step onboard the ship. Still, you should budget for some temptations on your trip, such as meals at local restaurants, exploration on your own and souvenirs. We like to do a little advance research online prior to our trip to determine what those temptations might be, what we might want to buy or otherwise sample—be it lacquer ware in Myanmar, a special lunch in France or a public bath experience and massage in Budapest.

For shipboard expenses such as bar bills, either when you board or at some point in your river cruise you will be asked to present a major credit card or pay for onboard expenses, which again, will likely be minimal. You can often also opt to pay gratuities with your credit card and if that's the case, there will be a separate form to fill out to specify how much you would like the cruise ship to charge your account. The ship may preauthorize your account (with your credit card company) for a set amount, say $200 per person, an amount that is refunded if you don't spend it. At the end of the cruise, you will have the option of paying your bill with cash (U.S. dollars, euros or other local currency), traveler's checks or in some cases a personal check—all this will be spelled out in your pre-trip materials.

In lieu of paying cash each time, any extra excursions you do, souvenirs you buy onboard, laundry services, bar drinks, massages or other extras will be automatically added to your shipboard bill. The last night of your cruise you will receive the final bill. If there are any discrepancies you can address that with the front desk staff.

Drinks Packages

Your cruise fare will cover bottled water, tea and coffee (including in most cases espresso and cappuccinos) and soft drinks, and on most lines house wine and beer with meals. Some ships are more all-inclusive, covering most

THE COST OF STUFF ON BOARD

Beer*	$3–$4
Mixed Drink	$4–$8.50
Wine*	$5–$8
Soda*	$3
Laundry	$2–$7 per item
Massage	$40–$70
Logo souvenirs	$3–$50

* Prices are for drinks in the lounge; soda, wine, and beer are typically complimentary at lunch and dinner.

or all alcohol (there may be a charge for top-shelf drinks so make sure to check). But if you're not on an open-bar ship and like to indulge in cocktails or are a wine aficionado who may not be satisfied with house pours, you may want to consider purchasing a drinks package. Pricing is based on the number of nights you cruise—Viking's Silver Spirits Premium Beverage Package, for instance, is priced at $210 per person for a 7-day cruise. Whether or not this is a value depends on how much you plan to drink. We suggest before buying you take a look at the bar menu, which you should be able to find online at the cruise line's website, and do the math to determine if you'll save buying a package (note that drinks such as Bourbon on the rocks tend to be what we'd call "short" pours).

Have Some Cash on Hand

In all destinations, you should have some local cash on hand for when you stop in port, to pay for cabs, make small purchases, buy soda and snacks, tip tour guides, and so on. Having $1 bills (or the equivalent in local currency) is especially helpful for these purposes. Credit cards will be accepted in most shops and restaurants, but not at markets (where you can also find the best bargains).

Your ship may have money exchange, but your best bet will be to find an ATM when you first land in a destination (a fee may be involved but it's usually less than you'd pay at a tourist exchange center). Don't take more than you need though, especially if you are visiting several countries with different currencies during your trip.

It's recommended that you not leave large amounts of cash in your room, unless in your safe. If there is no safe, you can leave cash and other valuables at the purser's desk for safekeeping. You should also store your plane ticket, passport (unless collected by the purser) and other ID papers in the safe.

SMOKING

Smoking will typically be allowed only on a designated area of the sun deck. There is no smoking on motorcoaches, and many historical sites will also have smoking restrictions.

water levels—A CAUTIONARY TALE

Ever read or watch the news and see disconcerting images of rivers that have breached and flooded their surroundings, or heard of riverboats that have been grounded due to low water levels? Well, if you're gearing up to take a river cruise, these are issues you should at least be aware of as high and low water levels do impact rivers—and even, occasionally, the routes of ships that glide along them.

Rivers are susceptible to unpredictable and often uncontrollable levels of water, and this is a hurdle for the river cruise industry. If the water gets too high or too low it can disrupt a cruise or prohibit river ships from operating altogether. In Europe, for instance, river cruise ships often have to pass under low bridges. If water gets too high, that section of the river becomes impassable. Conversely, if the water is too low, ships risk running aground.

HOW WORRIED SHOULD YOU BE?

While water levels are a concern, only a very small fraction of river cruises are impacted by high or low water levels each year. The vast majority of river cruises operate as normal every sailing season.

That being said, hardly a year goes by when there isn't some kind of water level issue, however minor, on the world's rivers.

The first question people often ask is when and where they should book a river cruise in order to have the highest chance of avoiding the issue. Well, folks, we regret to inform you that when Mother Nature is in charge, there is no magic formula here. Sometimes you can

have the very same river be flooded one year and dried up the next, even around the same time of the year.

Not surprisingly, hot and dry months tend to lead to potentially lower waters and the rainy seasons may result in higher waters or flooding. But with weather patterns being increasingly erratic around the world, even these simplistic guidelines are all but null and void (in 2013, Central Europe saw some record flooding in early summer, and 2 years later Europe entered a drought period around the same time that impacted rivers throughout the continent).

WHICH RIVERS ARE MOST AFFECTED?

There are, however, some rivers that are more susceptible to high and low water issues. The **Elbe River** is a notoriously low-water river and thus as soon as there are drought conditions, including lower-than-average rainfall and hotter temperatures, the Elbe is usually impacted. When there are high water issues or flooding in Europe, it's not uncommon for the **Danube or Rhine rivers** to be involved. But when massive flooding occurred in Central Europe in 2013, it was the Elbe, a notoriously low-level river, and the Danube that were most effected. So it just goes to show, you really never can tell.

CONTINGENCY PLANS

When there are disruptions, each river cruise line comes up with different contingency plans. Your cruise won't necessarily be canceled. One common work-around is what is called a **ship swap.** Two vessels will sail as close as

SAFETY & SECURITY

On the first day of your cruise you will be asked to attend a safety briefing with the Captain and crew, which will include a demonstration of how to use a lifejacket. It's important to pay close attention. Fire is a particular concern they can to a point that cannot be bypassed, such as a bridge they can't sail below or a low-water area, and then passengers will pack up their belongings and be moved to the vessel on the other side of the problematic area for the remainder of the cruise.

In instances like this, river cruise lines with larger fleets, such as Viking, have a big advantage in that they have more inventory to play with and Viking's ships can, in essence, help each other out. On the flipside, larger fleets also mean more ships facing disruptions, which can be a logistical nightmare. While it's not any-one's first choice, not least the river cruise line's, to put passengers through a ship swap, the thinking is that at least the cruise can continue onward.

Another fix is to essentially convert the remainder of the cruise into a **quasi-bus tour.** Since river cruise ships often don't sail huge distances each day, sometimes river cruise lines can simply bus passengers to some of the destinations they can't reach. Sure enough, each day those destinations might get further and further from where the ship is stuck moored, but the thinking is that at least passengers will still get to see the cities and sights they came to Europe to see. A river line may also put passengers up in a hotel or an extra night or two at either end of the cruise to help facilitate further sightseeing from perhaps a better vantage point.

No solution is perfect or ideal, but river cruise lines will generally do everything in their power not to cancel the cruise. And often times they throw in so many added perks and upgraded experiences during a disrupted river cruise that some passengers leave almost thankful for the disruption (other passengers will leave grumbling, and will make their opinions known on social media, where you can find plenty of weigh-ins about water level issues).

SO WHAT SHOULD YOU DO?

Our advice is to go ahead and book your river cruise for whenever you would like to book your river cruise. More important than the time of year and the river you are sailing is how the river cruise line will respond if there is a disruption or worst-case scenario, if the cruise is canceled. While most lines are accommodating in the event of a high or low water level disruption, some are more so than others.

You should get in touch with the river cruise line and ask what their policy is with regards to changes or cancelations due to water level issues. For instance, AmaWaterways has a policy whereby it credits passengers for each day their cruise experiences a disruption (AmaWaterways is also one of the river cruise lines with fewer disruptions because the company really tries to navigate around risky rivers), credits passengers can then put towards a future cruise.

When a sailing needs to be canceled, most river cruise lines will try to accommodate you on another ship or route, refund you the entire price of the river cruise and/or give you a pretty generous future cruise credit. However, any change or cancelation fees associated with your airfare may be on you (or your travel insurance company, depending on what type of policy you purchased).

on all cruise ships, which is why they are required to have fire safety equipment onboard (ships built after 1990 have sprinkler systems in Europe).

The tragic sinking of the ship on the Yangtze in 2015 notwithstanding, in most cases, river ships are not in particularly deep water, with there being more likelihood they would get stuck in a shallow patch than capsize. Those built after 2007 in Europe have two propulsion systems (in case one fails). Newer ships are also built with several watertight compartments—so should not sink even if one is flooded. Should a ship get stuck, another ship would likely come alongside to remove passengers. River ships do not have safety boats as their larger cruise ship peers.

When it comes to security, you probably won't notice much. There will be security personnel, but cruise lines are reluctant to give too many details for obvious reasons. Every time you leave your ship you will be given a boarding card with your room number that you will present when you return onboard— this allows ship personnel to keep track of who is on shore and who is onboard. We've never been asked to show an ID when re-boarding a river ship. The river lines will say this is because the ships are small enough that the crew can remember faces.

Ships also dock not only in cities or towns but also on some routes in pretty remote places. You'd think you'd spot security personnel patrolling the perimeter all night, right? If they do they do it really invisibly because we've rarely seen security personnel, with the exception of armed guards in the Amazon and Egypt.

On this note, if you have a cabin with windows or a door that opens we suggest you keep it closed both at night and any time you're not in your cabin.

YOUR VERY IMPORTANT DOCUMENTS

About 3 weeks to a month before your departure you will receive in the mail your **river cruise documents.** If you want your documents earlier a fee may be involved. Included will be a Passenger Ticket Contract, which you should at least skim before your trip. It's basically your contract for travel, and outlines the cruise line's obligations and yours—for instance, you are responsible for notifying the cruise line if you have a medical condition that may require attention during your trip. You will also have received your **air tickets** (or e-tickets that you can download online). If you haven't alerted the airline of your frequent flier number now is the time to do it (though keep in mind you don't get points with some negotiated fares). While you're at it you can obtain or change seat assignments. It's important to look at your air tickets to make sure your name is spelled out correctly (the TSA requires this) and that you have the correct flight times—with plenty of time to make any connections and to get to the ship well before departure.

There will also be a pamphlet with all sorts of other specifics about your cruise including details on **transfers from the airport** and your specific cabin number (make sure it's the category and location you requested). You'll find details of your hotel reservations and also about any optional tours you can purchase once on the ship (or sometimes in advance). Again, it's a good idea to review all this information. For instance, if you don't see a voucher for a transfer from the airport but were sure it was included or wanted to add one, you'd best square this away *before* you arrive at the destination, tired and groggy and transfer-less.

You will also find boarding forms you are asked to fill out listing any allergies and your emergency contact information. All this information you can deliver once on the ship, but it's best to fill out the forms ahead of time.

All of the above may come in a neat folder or more elaborate backpack. It's a good idea to keep it all in one place. Make sure to carry all these documents in you carry-on rather than in your checked luggage, since you may have difficulty traveling without them. There may also be luggage tags included, which help the crew identify your bags.

It's a good idea to leave a copy if your itinerary, including flight and hotel information, with a friend or relative should any emergency arise. While you're making copies, get a photocopy of your passport (useful in the odd event you lose the actual booklet).

Passports, Visas & Necessary Identification

For river cruises outside the U.S. you will be required to have a passport, both for air travel and for check-in at hotels and on your ship. If you are doing a cruise on the Mississippi or its tributaries or on the Columbia & Snake rivers a valid driver's license or other government-issued photo ID will suffice. If you are not a U.S. citizen but live in the United States you will have to carry your alien registration card and passport. Foreign-born travelers who do not reside in the U.S. will be required to show a valid visa to enter the U.S.

For more information about passports and to find a regional passport office, consult the Department of State website (http://travel.state.gov) or call the National Passport Information Center's automated service at ℂ 877/487-2778. *Note:* In many countries you are **required to have at least 6 months remaining on your passport.** If your passport is about to expire you should have it renewed.

Some river cruise destinations such as Russia, China, Egypt, India and the countries in Southeast Asia also require U.S. travelers to have a valid visa. River cruise lines or your travel agent can recommend third party companies that for a fee (a stiff one at that) can help with processing. A cheaper way to

Embassy Websites Where You Can Apply for Visas on Your Own

CAMBODIA: www.embassyofcambodia.org/visa.html
CHINA: www.china-embassy.org/eng/visas/
MYANMAR: http://evisa.moip.gov.mm
INDIA: https://indianvisaonline.gov.in
EGYPT: www.egyptembassy.net
RUSSIA: www.russianembassy.org
UKRAINE: http://mfa.gov.ua/en
VIETNAM: http://vietnamembassy-usa.org

go is to contact the appropriate embassy and download applications online (see websites above), and pay the embassy's processing fee.

Applying for a visa takes time, so you should start the process as soon as you book your cruise (although in some cases such as Myanmar, you may be required to apply closer-in to your trip). Your application may require an "invitation letter," which you can obtain by contacting your cruise line. In some cases, such as Vietnam, you may need to apply for a double- rather than a single-entry visa, based on the cruise program. You will be required to submit passport-size photos, which you can have taken at your local CVS pharmacy or other retail outlets. If this all sounds confusing, it can be, which is why some choose to spring for a visa specialist to help.

GETTING TO THE SHIP & CHECKING IN

Before you leave for the airport, attach to each of your bags one of the luggage tags provided by the cruise line (in your documents kit). Make sure to correctly fill out the information requested such as your name, departure date and cabin number. Put a luggage tag on your carry-on as well because helpful crew may insist on carrying your carry-on when you get to the ship.

Airport Arrival

If you booked your travel and transfers through the cruise line, when you arrive at your destination you should see a **cruise-line representative** either in the baggage area or in the arrivals hall. He or she will be carrying a sign with either your name or the name of the cruise line. If for some reason you don't see such a person, give a call to the number that will be listed in your travel documents. All details about what to do on arrival will be listed in your travel documents.

The cruise-line representative will ask you to identify your luggage, which will then be whisked away, taken to either your hotel (if you have a pre-cruise stay) or directly to the ship (your luggage may not go in the same motorcoach you're in). You may or may not be asked to identify your luggage once again before it's delivered to your room or cabin. Since river ships are small, missing bags are rarely a problem—it's not like crew are handling thousands of bags as on the big ships. Still, if you are at all concerned, ask the crew when your bags will arrive.

On the question of identifying your luggage, don't simply rely on appearance. One Samsonite looks just like another, even though yours may have a distinctive red ribbon on the handle. Check the ID tags as well.

If you booked air on your own, claim your luggage as you normally would when flying. You're on your own to get to the ship or your hotel. Don't forget to stop at an airport money exchange or ATM to get local currency (don't assume a cab or public transport will accept credit cards). It's important to note carefully what time you are expected at the ship. *Note:* Some docking locations can be a little obscure as they're often not a traditional address that

what to do IF YOUR FLIGHT IS CANCELED OR DELAYED

First of all, if your plan was to head right to the ship (and you weren't planning to spend a pre-cruise day at a hotel) tell the airline personnel at the airport you are a cruise passenger. They may be able to get you on a different flight. Second, either call the cruise line or ask the airline folks to make the call to advise them of your delay. There should be an emergency travel number included in your cruise documents, with someone answering 24 hours a day. Before you panic, keep in mind you may not be the only passenger delayed, and the line may be able to hold the ship until your arrival.

Unlike with ocean ships, which may be at sea, if you do miss the boat it's fairly easy, in many cases, to get you to the next day's destination (though you may end up spending your first night in a hotel and if you booked air on your own you may get stuck paying). River ships move slowly and don't cover great distances. Nor do they spend time on a bunch or hard-to-reach islands.

a cab is used to getting from most passengers (this is becoming a bit less of a problem as river cruising becomes more popular and taxis become more familiar with the ports, but it's still not uncommon to end up driving around a bit in search of a particular docking location). It's not a bad idea to make sure you have a printout or a GPS-mapped location of the ship's location to show the driver to help him/her find the vessel.

At the Pier

Once at the pier you will be directed onboard, often offered a welcome drink, handed your key at the front desk (or pierside) and then shown to your cabin—if it's ready. Often staterooms won't be ready until later in the afternoon. So be prepared to wait a bit. A light lunch will usually be served onboard and the public areas will be available to lounge around in, or you can head into town for some fresh air.

It's not typically necessary to do a formal check-in (the purser will get your credit card information later), though you may be asked to turn over your passport based on local regulations

Again, because you are on a small ship check-in tends to be much more hassle-free than on big ships with thousands of passengers arriving at the same time. There is unlikely to be much of a line, if any.

Your first get together on river ships is typically a welcome reception, where you will meet the officers and crew.

KEEPING IN TOUCH

Your cell phone may be your best bet for phone calls home. Make sure you've squared away your international coverage before you leave! We've heard horror stories of travelers going over their data or minute usage while abroad and racking up heart-stopping bills. Most U.S.-based **mobile providers have**

A LOVE (or hate) OF LOCKS

It's late afternoon and you're just hanging out in your stateroom, maybe catching up on some e-mails or watching a classic 1990s flick as you take a load off after a busy morning of sightseeing. And suddenly, the entire stateroom goes dark. Really dark. You're obviously sinking. This is it, your Titanic moment. Be brave.

Or, you're just going through a lock, what many people consider an engineering marvel that allows river cruise ships to bypass the many dams along the rivers, especially in Europe (you would think those dams would better help regulate the high and low water levels we discuss in "Water Levels—A Cautionary Tale").

WHAT IS A LOCK?

Okay, so what is the lock we tell of? The best way we can think of to describe it is to picture a really big rectangular bathtub. Your river cruise vessel will sail into one side of the bathtub, and the tub will either be filled with water to raise the ship up to the level of higher water on the other side of the dam, or water will be released to bring the ship down to lower water level on the other side of the dam.

In other words, a lock is a mechanism that allows river cruise ships to be lifted or lowered.

When the ship is in the bottom of the lock, the lock's walls are generally very close to the sides of the vessels—it's a fun exercise in navigational

precision—which is why you get the blackout effect described above. The standard 39-foot width of the majority of locks in Europe is also why most river cruise vessels are limited to a width of 38 feet, so as to have that 6 inches on either side to clear the lock. So as you can see, it's a tight squeeze!

Once you get used to it, it will be less of a shock than the first time you experience it (and you won't go lunging for your life vest). You will maybe even be converted into one of the many lock lovers on the rivers that look so forward to watching the mechanism at work that they will head up to the sun deck or onto their balconies to get a better view of the process.

If it's a particularly impressive lock, the cruise manager will often let passengers know, in case they want to come out on deck to watch.

Sometimes entering a lock can be a bit bumpy as river cruise ships tap the sides of the lock slightly, edging their way in. This might be among the few times during a river cruise that someone with motion sickness could experience a short spell. The bumpiness tends to be very fleeting.

TYPES OF LOCKS

Locks range from relatively small in height to pretty massive and technologically advanced.

various international packages (the more data you want, the more you pay), but even with those you need to make sure that all the countries you are visiting are covered equally. In some more remote countries that are not as well connected, you can usually buy a local **SIM card** for a nominal fee that you can pop into your smartphone to use while you're there. But again, check in on your usage because once you're out of data or time, you're stuck until you find another store that sells SIM cards.

If there is a **phone in your stateroom,** costs for calls will be pricey. Your cruise line will provide you in advance of your trip a shipboard phone number you can leave with friends and relatives in case an emergency arises at home.

The standard lock is called a **pound lock** and is what you will mostly see on Europe's rivers. It has gates that open and close at both ends to allow ships to sail in and out before or after water is raised or released.

The higher or larger in volume the lock, the more impressive it tends to be. Along the Rhine-Main-Danube Canal there are more than a dozen locks, among which a couple have a lifting height of up to some 80 feet—that's 80 feet a large river cruise vessel has to either be lifted and lowered by the mechanics.

In canal barging, you will often see much smaller locks and some that are hand-operated by the barge crew, which is just as interesting to watch (though you can also imagine it gets tiresome for them, being regularly interrupted by these hand-operated locks).

On the Canal de la Marne au Rhin in northeastern France an inclined plane, or boatlift, transports boats in a tank up and down a 146-feet high and 422-feet wide incline. It's a sight to behold.

A defining feature of the Three Gorges Dam on China's Yangtze River is a five-step ship lock that carries vessels 370 feet up or down through the graduated locks. It takes about 2 hours and 40 minutes to pass through the lock system. There is also a 370-foot-high shiplift that can carry 3,000-ton vessels in about 30 minutes. You have to see it to believe it.

MORE OR LESS LOCKS

While for some people locks are a real treat, for others they can quickly become a bit of a drag. For better or for worse, they can slow things down a bit, depending on the river traffic. So whether you want to flock to the locks or avoid them, here are some rivers that are more "lock-y" than others.

The **Danube** (19 locks), **Main** (34 locks), **Seine** (34 locks) and the **Rhine-Main-Danube Canal** (16 locks) are among the rivers and waterways with the most locks. You go through the two locks of the Iron Gate on Lower Danube cruises. Most of the other river cruising rivers in Europe have at least a handful of locks. Often times you'll stop noticing whether you're going through a lock, or you will go through at night while you're fast asleep. In other words, the locks can kind of become white noise once you get used to them, so it's really not worth planning your river cruise around them.

There are dozens of locks along the Mississippi, all of which are north of St. Louis.

And then there are the free-flowing rivers of the world—the Amazon, Nile, Ganges and Mekong—where locks are a total non-issue. So if for some reason you're very lock averse, looks like an exotic river cruise is the one for you.

Your in-cabin TV will be programmed with news channels such as CNN, Fox and the BBC. Some ships also print out a few copies of daily news from a wire service that you can borrow from the reception desk or find in the library. On shore, those who want to keep up on the news in English should be able to find copies of the International Herald Tribune at newsstands.

Internet

Nearly every river ship has **complimentary Wi-Fi.** Expect access to be slow and even non-existent, at times. Bandwidth will be minimal. Wi-Fi tends to be better when the vessel is docked in port as opposed to when sailing. The best way to get access to send photos or e-mails with attachments is to wait until everyone else goes to sleep at night, heads to a meal or off the ship for an excursion, or try in the wee hours of the morning.

Don't plan on sending or streaming any videos—there is unlikely to be capacity for that. Skype-ing with family or friends will probably be more frustrating than gratifying—although you shouldn't rule it out altogether. The river cruise lines are constantly improving connectivity and there can be brief, wondrous, random moments of Internet connectivity greatness. If you don't bring your own laptop or iPad, your ship may have some computers for guest use and iPads you can borrow (but check in advance).

> ### Insider Tip
>
> AmaWaterways has a cool service whereby the line will send off as many of its provided postcards (and they aren't all terrible marketing images) as guests would like, free of charge.

Another option, if you bring your own device, is to use the Wi-Fi in cafes in towns and cities you visit. Buy a coffee or beer and ask for the access code. It's also an opportunity to mingle with locals.

Sending Mail & Postcards

The purser's desk on your ship will be able to mail any letters and postcards and will have or be able to get local stamps—a slight fee may be charged for this service.

CURRENCY EXCHANGE

Your ship may be able to offer currency exchange on a limited basis, but you should plan on exchanging larger amounts at banks. ATMs are a handier and often cheap way to get cash, and can be found in major cities and airports and also in some towns. Exchange bureaus tend to have lousy exchange rates and numerous fees, so we suggest avoiding those when you can.

DAY-BY-DAY DETAILS

Each day you will find in your cabin the **daily program** noting times for meals, departures for tours and the daily briefing, plus any special programming such as lectures or nighttime entertainment. You'll want to read all this so you don't miss anything. Every evening during cocktail hour the cruise director will also do a briefing on what's coming up the next day. It's important that at least one person in your stateroom attend the briefing—since it's during the cocktail hour it's also one of the fun events of the day, a chance to recap what you've seen and get excited about what's coming next.

> ### Religious Services
>
> While the ship will not have clergy onboard, the reception desk should be able to direct you to churches or temples in the towns and cities you will be visiting.

Listening Devices for Tours

In your cabin you will find a listening device and headphones that you will want to take with you every day on tour. This will allow you to hear what the guides are saying, and to adjust the volume to what works for you. If you wear hearing aids, you may want to bring the case each day (you won't need the aids with the headphones). The listening devices will come with a string you can wear around your neck or you can put the device in a pocket. Some come with a stand and should be recharged nightly. Others run on batteries—if your batteries run low, alert your tour guide or reception staff and they will replace them. If you forget your device don't be stoic about it, tell the guide. They'll probably be equipped with a spare.

Arriving in Ports

Days without a stop are rare on river ships. When you arrive at a destination the ship may have to be cleared by local officials and a ramp will be set. It's usually a pretty quick process. From there, the cruise director will give everyone a heads-up of about 15 minutes until when tours are departing. When you near the destination, it's a good idea to start getting ready. If you're heading off on your own you can just walk off the ship as soon as you hear the all clear, or later.

It's a much easier process than on ocean ships except for this big caveat: Sometimes there is no there, there. Don't expect to always walk off the ship onto a shiny pier or even a pier at all. In some cases you may have to disembark through other river ships (see "What Is 'Rafting'?" in chapter 2). In others you may have to climb a riverbank (especially in remote areas of Southeast Asia, though not usually in Europe where the river cruising infrastructure is much more developed), with the crew there to help. The ship may bring you right into the center of a city or town, or the ship may be tied up in a more remote location within walking distance of nothing in particular—a motorcoach or other transport (small boats, mules, ox carts—yes, we said ox carts) waiting to get those on tour to the arranged destination.

You are in no way required to do every tour or get off at every port. It's perfectly okay to take a break and hang out on the ship, which may actually be moving onto another destination up or down the river after the tours depart (the passengers on tour will rejoin the ship at the other destination).

Essentials: Don't Leave the Ship Without Them

You will be given a boarding pass to bring with you, which you'll return when you get back to the ship. You'll want to remember to bring your provided listening device, and will be offered a bottle of water as you disembark (it's smart to stay hydrated). Don't forget too to bring a little cash and/or a credit card in case you want a soda or coffee or snack or run into tempting souvenirs along the way. You'll also want to remember any other items that you find essential, such as your camera, hand sanitizer, Kleenex, a sweater or shawl (for the air conditioning on the motorcoach, or changes in outdoor temperature), and so forth. It's best to keep all this in a backpack or tote you carry onshore (for safety reasons you may be better off leaving your fancy pocketbook or purse on the ship).

Watch the Clock

It's hugely important if you leave the ship to explore on your own that you note the ship's departure time. It should be posted, but if you're unclear ask. You should also ask the reception staff to write down the exact address where the ship is tied up and to give you an emergency number to call if you get lost.

You're generally required to be back at least a half hour before the ship is scheduled to disembark. If tours run late the ship will wait. Not so for those who wander off on their own. If you are on your own and run into a situation where you know you won't get back to the ship on time, call the number provided. The ship may be able to wait, but if not you will likely have to pay to get to the next port on your own.

DEBARKATION & HEADING HOME

A nice thing about river ships as opposed to many ocean ships is you are not forced off the ship at the crack of dawn if you have a flight departing later in the day or plans to stay over in the port city. You can linger over breakfast and maybe even lunch. You will, however, be asked to vacate your cabin at a set time in the morning so that the crew can get it ready for the next passengers.

Settling Your Shipboard Account

The last evening of your cruise you will be asked to settle your account, which you can do with cash or the credit card you provided. Feel free to question anything with the purser that doesn't look quite right. You're best off doing this early to avoid lines at the purser's desk. You can also ask for a preliminary bill a day or two earlier if you want.

Luggage Procedures

If you want assistance with getting your bags off the ship you will be asked to put your larger suitcases, with provided tags, into the corridor early on disembarkation day. The cruise director will give directions at the last evening briefing.

Reclaiming VAT

If you purchased any pricy souvenirs in Europe you may be able to collect a refund on the Value Added Tax (VAT). To qualify for a refund you have to spend above a set amount, ranging from about $40 to $300 (the amount varies by country) at one time. You will need to fill out a special form at time of purchase and to show your passport. You will then need to bring a copy of this form and receipts to a special counter at the airport, where you'll get the form stamped, before you depart Europe.

Allow time to stand in the VAT refund line. Complicating matters is that you aren't supposed to use or wear the items in advance, and may be required to show them at the airport in order to collect the refund. You may be able to get the refund in cash (in a currency of your choice) right at the airport for a small fee and by standing in a second line, or mail in the form to have it applied to your credit card.

It's not an infallible system, and you should be aware the refund might not be as much as you expect. The price you paid includes the tax and then a percentage of tax comes out based on the original price and not what you paid. It's complicated. Still, getting at least something back may be worth the effort.

Customs & Immigration

When you fly out of a country you will be required to show your passport to immigration officers and may have to fill out a customs and/or immigration form. When you return to the U.S. you will also clear U.S. Customs and Border Protection (CBP) and will be required to show your passport and a completed customs declaration form (the forms will be handed out on the plane).

There are restrictions on what you can bring back to the U.S., including in regards to fresh food products, and on how much you can spend aboard without paying a duty (tax). Find details at the CBP website, www.cbp.gov/travel.

THE MAIN RIVER CRUISE LINES

S even dominant players got into the river cruise game early on in Europe and together carry the bulk of North American river cruise passengers along Europe's inland waterways and beyond.

Some of these lines, such as Grand Circle, Viking and Uniworld, have been doing this since the 1980s and 1990s, while the remainder entered the market in the early 2000s, when river cruising started to boom. These cruise lines represent some of the most extensive and comprehensive river cruise fleets in the business. They are in this chapter because they've either built a shocking number of new ships in the last few years (Viking, we're looking at you), because they are very popular despite *not* having built many new ships recently (Grand Circle comes to mind), or because they have been consistently expanding their fleets, introducing innovative new concepts on and off-board, and have established large and loyal followings among an increasingly avid river cruising public.

Their European fleet sizes vary widely, from Tauck's nine vessels to Viking's 60, with the bulk landing somewhere in the middle with between 14 and 16 ships (not including the ship charters and leases most of them have elsewhere in the world). But what these vessels represent is the diverse tastes, interests and price levels river cruise passengers are looking for, from a much more expensive and more upscale river cruising experience (Uniworld, Tauck, AmaWaterways and Scenic fit into this category) to something more mainstream (Viking and Avalon), to a river cruise experience that is completely pared down and basic (like Grand Circle).

There are river cruise lines that have been around for decades that are not in this chapter, such as French river cruise company Croisi-Europe, which has some 30 vessels in its fleet and is celebrating its 40th anniversary in 2016. But CroisiEurope only recently began courting U.S. passengers and still only represents a small fraction of the market. And Pandaw River Expeditions, which has been carving a hardcore niche for itself along the scenic waterways of Southeast Asia where it will have 15 company-owned vessels in 2016. You will find these and many other river cruise lines in the following chapter.

But here, we really wanted to focus on the seven most well-known, the seven most popular and the seven river cruise lines that will likely come up the most in your river cruising conversations.

5

We kick off with the big dog, Viking River Cruises, and list the other main lines in backwards alphabetical order from there, because sometimes it's good to switch things up a little.

THE COMPONENTS OF OUR CRUISE-LINE REVIEWS

Each cruise line's review begins with a quick word about the line in general and a short summation of the kind of cruise experience you can expect to have aboard that line. The text that follows fleshes out the review, providing all the details you need to get a feel for what kind of vacation the cruise line will provide.

The individual ship reviews following the general cruise-line description then get into the nitty-gritty, giving you details on the ships' accommodations, facilities, amenities, comfort levels, and upkeep.

We've listed each ship's vital statistics, such as number of decks, year built, number of cabins, number of crew—to help you compare. *Note:* When several vessels are members of a class—built with the same or very similar design— we've grouped the ships together into one review.

Stars
THE RATINGS

To make things easier on everyone, we've developed a simple ratings system that covers those things that vary from line to line—quality and size of the cabins and public spaces, decor, number and quality of dining options, gyms/ spas (if any) and whether the line is a good choice for children or not. We've also rated enrichment, an important aspect for many river cruisers. We've given each line an overall **star rating** based on the combined total of our poor-to-outstanding ratings, translated into a 1-to-5 scale:

1	=	Poor	4	=	Excellent
2	=	Fair	5	=	Outstanding
3	=	Good			

In instances when the category doesn't apply to a particular ship—for instance no kids allowed—we've simply noted "not applicable" (N/A) and absented the category from the total combined score, as these unavailable amenities will be considered a deficiency only in certain circumstances (for instance, if you plan to travel with kids).

Now for a bit of philosophy: The cruise biz today offers a profusion of experiences so different that comparing all ships by the same set of criteria would be like comparing a Paris apartment to an A-frame in Aspen. That's why, to rate the ships, we've used a sliding scale, rating ships on a curve that compares them only with others in their category. Once you've determined what kind of experience is right for you, you can look for the best ships in that category based on your particular needs.

Itineraries

Each cruise-line review includes a chart showing itineraries. We did this by river line rather than ship because river ships tend to move around—the same ship may do several different itineraries in a year and several ships may do the same itinerary. All itineraries are subject to change. Consult the cruise-line websites or your travel agent for exact sailing dates.

For your convenience, we've listed some of the **pre- and post-cruise** options you can book with your cruise line, though these vary greatly by route, so you'll want to see what's available for the particular itinerary you choose by checking with the cruise line or your travel agent.

Also, we did not include holiday cruises. Most river cruise lines offer what are often called **"Christmas market" cruises**—many of Europe's towns and cities are decked out with the popular Christmas markets in December, stalls upon stalls often set up in the main town square that sell everything from souvenirs and home-made gifts to sweets and mulled wine. The Christmas market cruises generally sail several of the identical itineraries offered the rest of the year, but at a slightly lower price due the chilly temperatures. They were, and remain, a smart way to extend the season a bit before the ships go into winter dry dock. The cruise lines will usually decorate their vessels and have other festive activities and entertainment both on and off the ships. Some cruise lines also offer New Year's Eve cruises. Some past river cruisers think these are just the most charming cruises, even if you have to bundle up a bit, and for other people, the thought of cruising through Europe in the frigid cold is a terrible idea—so to each his/her own.

Prices: Don't Get Sticker Shock

We've listed starting brochure prices for cabins, and starting prices for cabins with balconies (including French balconies). If the starting price is for "cabins/balconies" that means it's an all-balcony ship, as many of them are in Southeast Asia, for instance. If there is no starting price for balconies, that means there are no balcony cabins. Suites will be higher priced than the starting prices we have listed. We stress that all the prices listed reflect the line's **brochure rates,** so depending on how early you book and any special deals the lines are offering, you may get a rate substantially below what we've listed. Rates are all per person, per cruise, based on two people sharing a cabin (rates for a solo passenger in a cabin will usually be higher).

VIKING RIVER CRUISES

www.vikingrivercruises.com. ☎ 877/668-4546.

Pros

- **Extremely well-oiled operation.** You can expect a high quality experience on any of Viking's ships.
- **Innovation.** The Viking "Longships" with their snub-noses, outdoor dining, "green" features (including solar panels), and cabins with balconies did no less than change the course of river cruising—for the better.

Cons

- **No pool, spa, or fitness facilities.** The line will make recommendations for facilities you can visit along the way but doesn't believe in using space for that sort of stuff on board.

- **Not kid-friendly.** Kids under 16 are discouraged (under 12 not allowed).

THE LINE IN A NUTSHELL   For many people Viking River Cruises *is* river cruising. It's the Big Kahuna of the industry with more than 60 ships and it's the line you've seen in those exquisite ads on TV. Affordable, destination-focused cruising on comfortable ships is Viking's calling card.

Frommer's Ratings (Scale of 1–5)

Cabin comfort & amenities	5	Public spaces	5
Decor	5	Dining	4
Fitness, spa and pool	2	Service	4
Family-friendly	2	Enrichment	4

THE EXPERIENCE   In many ways, Viking created "Modern River Cruising." Founded in 1997 by cruise industry veteran Torstein Hagen, Viking started with cruises in Russia and has had a meteoric rise to become the king of the river cruising world with more than 60 ships. The company in 2016 represents about 50 percent of the worldwide river cruise market.

The model for the river product (adopted by the ocean product as well) is value-priced, mostly inclusive cruises, with wine and beer at mealtimes, Wi-Fi, airport transfers, port charges and, most importantly, daily shore excursions included in your cruise fare. The cruises are geared towards adults age 55-plus who really want to see and experience the destinations they are sailing through.

The line's "Longships," first introduced in 2012, brought with them a whole new era of river cruising. The size of river ships is limited by the need to go under short bridges and by the width of locks, but these wonderfully contemporary ships were cleverly designed with a snub-nose rather than a traditional pointy bow. This change allowed the line to add a partially windowed, open-air outdoor dining area—what Viking calls the Aquavit Terrace. Founder Hagen, with the help of the ship architects Yran & Storbraaten (who also created interiors for ocean ships including the Disney Dream and luxury line Seabourn's Odyssey-class ships), also cleverly had the idea to move the hallways to one side so the ships could offer true two-room suites, plus cabins with real, step-out balconies as on ocean ships, without going over the river width restrictions. The de-centralized hallway also allowed for a greater number of cabin configurations and categories. "Green" advances included hybrid diesel-electric engines partially fueled by solar panels.

Viking's smart sponsorship of PBS's *Masterpiece Theater* with the hit British drama *Downton Abbey* has been credited with not only popularizing Viking but making the very idea of taking a river cruise mainstream.

The line's ships offer all the comforts of a decent hotel—the "Longships" may remind some of W Hotels with their streamlined, contemporary decor and upscale accouterments. You sleep in a cabin with a comfortable bed and can pay extra for perks such as a French balcony or a real veranda or even a two-room suite. You hang out in cushy spaces including the main lounge. All cruises come with three meals a day, with wine and beer included at lunch and dinner (you can also request complimentary mimosas at breakfast). Daily tours are included, premium tours available for an extra fee—such as a BMW Factory experience in Munich or an evening Fado concert in Lisbon.

That said, Hagen does things his way or the highway, and if you don't like his style, well too bad. On his ships you won't find many bathtubs (he prefers showers). You won't find pools or fitness rooms or spas on most of the ships because Hagen believes those are underused, wasted spaces. But you will find salmon available every day (he's Norwegian!). He also loves oatmeal and Viking ships always offer hearty, delicious oatmeal with all the fixings as part of the breakfast buffet.

A lot of people agree with Hagan's tastes. Viking is the dominant cruise line in Europe and also offers cruises in Russia, China, in Southeast Asia (the Mekong and Irrawaddy) and in Egypt. The line is gearing to introduce cruises on the Mississippi in 2018; and started offering ocean-going cruises in 2015.

Perhaps most surprising, is Viking has managed to maintain a consistent level of quality as it has grown. Itineraries are well planned and very much focused on making sure you see the key sights en route. The idea is that you explore a region without being nickel-and-dimed.

THE FLEET   The fleet is the largest in the industry with more than 60 ships and counting. Viking has been phasing out older ships to make way for the new, though a few classic ships remain. On the company's cutting-edge, 190-passenger "Longships," dozens introduced beginning in 2012, you can watch the scenery from the veranda of your cabin or two-room suite, or while dining al fresco. There are also smaller ships with similar features as the "Longships" specifically designed for rivers that can't handle the larger ships, including the Elbe and Douro. The 188-passenger *Viking Legend* launched in 2009, and the 188-passenger *Viking Prestige* (2011), preceded the "Longship" building boom, and introduced some of the features found on the newer ships, including eco-friendly hybrid engines. In Russia, the line has totally rehabbed three older ships (all built in East Germany, when there was an East Germany) to keep them up to modern standards. The company's largest ship, *Viking Emerald* (operated under charter), carries 256 passengers and is more resort-like than the line's other ships—there's a big presidential suite and even a pool and spa. Likewise, the line provides a slightly fancier ambience with the two ships it charters in Egypt, the **MS *Omar El Khayam*** and **MS *Mayfair.*** On the Mekong in Southeast Asia, Viking charters small river ships hand-crafted locally in teak. For the Mississippi ships, the line was looking to build at an American shipyard, though details weren't available at press time.

PASSENGER PROFILE   Viking gears its entire product to age 55-plus. Many on board will be *way* plus, though still active enough to do the included tours. Nearly all on board will be English-speakers and most Americans. The dress code is casual at all times (though some dress up slightly at night) and the folks on board like it that way. Expect mature, social fellow passengers who are interested in history and culture and travel.

DINING OPTIONS   Meals are served in the main dining room, and on newer ships there is alternative dining in the Aquavit Terrace, which is an *al fresco* extension of the main lounge. Breakfast and lunch are buffet style. Dinner is a multicourse menu that includes a choice of local specialties and continental dishes. Improved menus have added a more modern slant, so you might have potato ravioli with sabayon sauce and a sautéed black cod, tuna sashimi and carved roast veal. Always available are New York-cut steak and salmon. A light buffet is available at breakfast and lunch (the latter will be at the Aquavit Terrace on the "Longships," or on other ships in the lounge) Offered once on each sailing on the Sun Deck, don't miss the buffet of local snacks (the line calls the spread "A Taste Of...") featuring such treats as pretzels and sweet mustard leberwurst and Kölsch (beer) in Germany or grilled local sausages, vegetable skewers with feta, *cevapcici* (minced meat kabob), baklava and local beer in the Balkans. House wine and beer are included with dinner, and you can order complimentary mimosas if you want at breakfast. Cocktails and premium wine are extra (added to your tab each time you order). Viking also has the option of Beverage Packages that include cocktails and wine for those who prefer an all-inclusive drinks experience (priced at $210 per person for a 7-day cruise).

ACTIVITIES   Lectures and multimedia presentations on local history and culture are part of every cruise. So, on Bordeaux itineraries there might be a presentation on local wine; in Holland, an included lecture could tell tales of the Dutch Masters artists; and on many sailings, the cruise director teaches words and phrases in the local language. The newer ships have a walking/jogging track and a putting green on the Sun Deck. There are no bikes on board and most of the ships do not have fitness facilities, spas or pools.

CHILDREN'S PROGRAM   There are none. Viking does not encourage kids on board (under 12 are banned, and under 16 discouraged). There are no connecting cabins. That said, well-behaved teenagers who can converse with adults might actually enjoy the experience.

ENTERTAINMENT   Local entertainers, singers and dance groups, come on board at select ports—such as a Hungarian folk dancing troupe on the Danube or a Fado singer in Portugal. A piano player entertains in the lounge at night, doing classical music or pop melodies, including during cocktail hour. Depending on the ship, a combo may play for dancing. The lounge may also double as a movie theater, the films chosen for their local connection.

SERVICE   The hardworking crew focuses on efficiency, but the atmosphere is friendly and few passengers have any complaints. In fact, the line is so sure your needs will be attended to they offer a service guarantee—if a problem is not corrected within 24 hours you can leave the ship and get a refund. Gratuities are not included in your cruise fare, but are collected at the end of the cruise (you can pay in cash or by credit card,) in one lump sum, which is then divided among the crew. Recommendations vary by itinerary, but in Europe

VIKING ITINERARIES

9-day Upper Danube ("Bavaria to Budapest"), Nuremburg to Budapest, $3,022, balconies from $4,322, May–Oct

11-day Danube ("Imperial Cities of Europe") with 8-day cruise, Berlin to Budapest, $3,806, balconies from $4,606, Mar–Oct

17-day Yangtze ("Undiscovered China") with 5-day cruise, Shanghai to Beijing, cabins/balconies from $5,616, Mar–Oct

11-day Yangtze ("Imperial Jewels of China") with 5-day cruise, cabins/balconies from $3,117, Feb–Oct

14-day Mekong ("Magnificent Mekong"), with 7-day cruise, Hanoi to Ho Chi Minh City, cabins from $3,699, no balconies, Jan–Apr and July–Oct

14-day Irrawaddy ("Myanmar Explorer") with 7-day cruise, round-trip from Bangkok, cabins from $5,799, no balconies, Jan–Apr and Aug–Oct

15-day Yangtze ("Roof of the World") with 5-day cruise, Beijing to Shanghai, cabins/balconies from $5,010, Apr–Oct

11-day Upper Danube ("Castles & Legends) with 7-day cruise, Munich to Budapest, $4,406, balconies from $4,606, Mar–Oct

11-day Saone and Rhone ("Paris, Burgundy & Provence), with 7-day cruise, Paris to Avignon, $3,906, balconies from $4,606, Mar–Oct

14-day Saone and Rhone ("France's Finest"), Paris to Avignon, $5,111, balconies from $5,311, Mar–Oct

7-day Saone and Rhone ("Lyon & Provence"), Lyon to Avignon, $2,556, balconies from $3,256, Mar–Oct

15-day Elbe ("Poland, Prague & the Elegant Elbe") with 7-day cruise, Berlin to Warsaw, $5,199, balconies from $5,899, Mar–Oct

9-day Elbe ("Elegant Elbe") with 7-day cruise, Berlin to Prague, $3,299, balconies from $3,499, Mar–Oct

9-day Rhine ("Switzerland to the North Sea"), Basel to Amsterdam, $3,172, balconies from $4,072, Apr–Oct

9-day Moselle and Rhine ("Rhine Rhapsody") with 7-day cruise, Paris to Basel, $2,956, balconies from $3,656, Mar–Apr

18-day Rhine, Main and Danube ("Grand European Tour & Belgium") with 14-day cruise, Ghent (Belgium) to Nuremburg, $5,712, balconies from $6,812, May–Oct

the recommended total adds up to about $15.25 per person, per day ($2.18 for the program director and the rest for the waitstaff, bar team, room stewards and other service crew).

TOURS   Daily excursions (at least one in every port) for the most part consist of half-day introductory tours designed to show you the highlights of the destination. On all the tours local guides lead the way and motorcoaches are often used to transport passengers from the ship to the city or landmark they will be visiting on their excursion. All passengers are provided with a Quiet-Vox amplifier and headset so you can hear what the guide is saying even from quite a distance. In addition to the introductory tour you can purchase a more

Viking River Cruises

THE MAIN RIVER CRUISE LINES

14-day Rhine and Danube ("Grand European Tour"), Amsterdam to Budapest, $4,462, balcony cabins from $5,462, Mar–Oct

7-day Rhine ("Rhine Getaway"), Amsterdam to Basel, $2,656, balcony cabins from $3,356, Mar–Oct

10-day Lower Danube ("Passage to Eastern Europe") with 7-day cruise, Budapest to Bucharest, $3,056, balconies from $3,756, Mar–Oct

7-day Upper Danube ("Danube Waltz"), Passau (Germany) to Budapest, $2,456, balconies from $3,156, Apr–Oct

11-day Rhine ("Rhineland Discovery"), with 10-day cruise, Bruges (Belgium) to Basel, $3,906, balcony cabins from $4,606, Mar–Oct

7-day Upper Danube ("Romantic Danube"), Budapest to Nuremburg, $2,556, balcony from $3,356, Mar–Oct

9-day Belgian and Dutch Canals ("Tulips & Windmills"), round-trip from Amsterdam, $3,272, balconies from $422, Mar–May

11-day Rhine, Main and Danube ("Cities of Light") with 7-day cruise, Paris to Prague, $3,156, balconies from $4,456, Mar–Oct

22-day Rhine, Main and Danube ("European Sojourn"), Amsterdam to Bucharest, $6,317, balconies from $8,117, Mar–Oct

9-day Douro ("Portugal's River of Gold) with 7-day cruise, Lisbon to Porto, $3,290, balconies from $3,756, Mar–Oct

7-day Dordogne and Garonne ("Chateaux, Rivers & Wine), round-trip from Bordeaux, $2,456, balconies from $3,256, Mar–Oct

7-day Seine ("Paris & the Heart of Normandy"), round-trip from Paris, $2,556, balconies from $3,256, Mar–Oct

12-day Volga ("Waterways of the Tsars"), St. Petersburg to Moscow, $5,296, balconies from $6,396, May–Oct

11-day Nile and Lake Nassar ("Pathways of the Pharaohs") with 7-day cruise*, round-trip from Cairo, cabins/balconies from $4,198, Jan–Apr and Sept–Oct
*4 days on the Nile and 3 days on Lake Nassar

Note on this chart: Itineraries may also be available in the reverse direction. The first price is the lowest available price for all cabin categories, and the second price is the lowest balcony price, including French balcony cabins.

detailed tour or spend some time exploring a destination on your own. Some people love having the free time but others may feel lost without a scheduled outing, so it's important to know how important having guided excursions are to you (and budget accordingly). Culturally enriching "Local Life" excursions include, on some itineraries, visits to private homes or local markets. The line's "Working World" excursions take you to place such as a porcelain factory in Meissen (where you'll see how the product is made and have opportunity to buy if you want) and wineries in France. Viking's beefed up half- and full-day "Privileged Access" tours (for an extra charge) take you to such places as a truffle farm with lunch in France, or on private visits to museums, with prices ranging anywhere from $39 to $299.

PRE- & POST-CRUISE STAYS   In addition to any hotel nights including in your cruise fare, pre- and post-cruise extensions are available on all itineraries. Hotels are "superior first class" but those who want can also upgrade to Premier Hotels, such as the Budapest Four Seasons or Prague Four Seasons. A Viking representative will be on site at hotels to answer any questions you might have, and to help in areas such as where to make dinner reservations (only breakfasts are included in the packages). You also get one city familiarization tour, with transfers from the ship included.

Prices for the tour extensions vary by time of year and itinerary. On a Grand European Tour from Amsterdam to Budapest, guests can extend their 15-day cruise with a pre-cruise extension in Amsterdam, with 2 nights at the Mövenpick Hotel Amsterdam City Centre, priced from $549; and then do a post-cruise extension so you can explore Prague, the 3-night package including a stay at the Hilton Prague Hotel (or similar property), priced from $749 to $799. Tours in more exotic destinations may have more meals and tours included. Do a 3-night post-cruise extension in Bangkok on a Southeast Asia cruise, from $899.

Viking Longships

The Verdict

Forget the old and stodgy. These ships, named for Norse gods and heroes, bring a whole new take on river cruises.

Specifications

Passengers	190	Total cabins/balcony cabins	95/70
Passenger decks	3	Crew	50
Year entered service:			
Viking Aegir, Viking Bragi, Viking Embla, Viking Freya, Viking Idun, Viking Njord, Viking Odin	2012	Viking Atla, Viking Forseti, Viking Jarl, Viking Lif, Viking Magni, Viking Rinda, Viking Skadi, Viking Tor, Viking Var	2013
Viking Alsvin, Viking Baldur, Viking Bestla, Viking Buri, Viking Delling, Viking Eistla, Viking Gullveig, Viking Heimdl, Viking Hermod, Viking Hlin, Viking Idi, Viking Ingvi, Viking Kvasir	2014	Viking Eir, Viking Gefjon, Viking Kara, Viking Lofn, Viking Mani, Viking Mimir, Viking Modi, Viking Skirnir, Viking Ve, Viking Vidar, Viking Vili	2015
Viking Alruna, Viking Egil, Viking Kadlin, Viking Rolf, Viking Tialfi, Viking Vilhjalm	2016		

THE SHIPS IN GENERAL   Viking has had particular success with these contemporary 190-passenger "Longships," with their innovative design and contemporary environs, and for good reason. On some river ships, accommodations get pretty cozy, but these stylish ships break the mold. They are stunning, floating, Scandinavian-inspired boutique hotels (think W Hotel) with refreshingly airy public spaces, the option of large cabins and suites with balconies and even al fresco alternative dining. Less visible are the ship's cutting edge "green" advances, including hybrid diesel-electric engines that are partially fueled by solar panels on the Sun Deck.

CABINS   Viking wanted to move beyond just French balconies, which have become a standard feature on many river ships, and with these ships they did. Thirty-nine 205-square-foot cabins and nine suites have real step-out verandas, albeit mostly small ones, with room for two chairs and a small table. The two 445-square-foot Explorer Suites come with separate living and French-balconied bedroom area and a large wraparound veranda (with space to entertain). Veranda Suites are 270-square-feet with a small living room with veranda and separate bedroom with French balcony. Another 22 cabins (tight at 135 sq. ft.) have French balconies; while 25 value-priced cabins (150-square-feet) are at the waterline of the Main deck and serve up views via portholes. Everyone gets such niceties as hotel-like queen-size beds (that can also be configured as twins), fluffy European duvets and bathrooms with rounded sinks, glass showers and heated floors. Modern Norse art is part of the decor of what is a very comfortable sleeping environment. All cabins are equipped with a mini-fridge and safe, as well as a handheld hairdryer and a large Sony HD flatscreen TV (a cool feature is the TVs also list ship information including names of every member of the crew). If you want a bathrobe and slippers, you can request them (they are not automatically provided).

PUBLIC AREAS   As you step on board, light fills the subtly colored two-story atrium with its stunning grand staircase and many windows. The sense of space and airiness continues in the lounge, which serves up views through floor-to-ceiling windows and has a bar on one end and on the other end the Aquavit Terrace, a casual, open-air cafe with windbreaks to cut the breeze. Plush chairs and stools around the bar make the lounge a prime place to hang out. There's a dance floor too, and some nights the room is transformed into a movie theater with a big screen coming out of the ceiling. Everyone gathers in the lounge for nightly cocktail hour during which the program for the next day is reviewed by the Program Director.

There's a library/internet corner on the upper level of the atrium, which is also a nice place to sit and people watch—grab a coffee or latte from the 24-hour, serve yourself machine in the corner.

Up on top of the ship is a large Sun Deck with cushioned loungers and chairs in the sun and shaded under canopies, and the best views of the river. There's also a shuffleboard court and golf putting greens and the very pleasant feature of an organic herb garden.

DINING OPTIONS   The food and beverage program isn't necessarily where Viking shines, especially in comparison to lines like Uniworld and AmaWaterways that go all out. The food will be tasty and reliable, but nothing worth bragging about or snapping shots of for social media. In the windowed, open-seating main dining room, cuisine is international but includes local tastes. Breakfast and lunch are buffet-style (though you can also choose menu options) and dinner is a multicourse affair. The nine tables of the Aquavit Terrace in the ship's snub-nosed bow are the place to be at lunchtime on a sunny day. At night, if you wish, you can skip the multicourse meal in the main dining room and head to the cafe for a burger or Caesar salad, among other options. One day up on the Sun Deck there might be a local "street food" snack in between meals such as pretzels and beer as you cruise past views of the German countryside. Don't miss it. At all meals you can get complimentary soft drinks, wine and beer. Cocktails are available for purchase. Wines more premium than the house wines are available for an extra charge. If you want to bring your own wine on board—say, pick up a bottle at a winery in Bordeaux—there is no corkage fee.

> **Trivia Fact**
>
> In 2013, Viking set a Guinness World Record when it christened 10 new Viking "Longships" in a single day. The line then proceeded to break its own record when it christened 14 in 1 day the following year.

POOL, FITNESS, SPA, BIKES
The ships do not have a spa or fitness center, nor pool or hot tub, but Viking has agreements with luxury hotels in several of the cities the ship visits, allowing passengers to use the hotels' health facilities. There is a walking/jogging track and a putting green on the Sun Deck.

Viking Hemming, Viking Osfrid & Viking Torgil

The Verdict
These contemporary ships are similar to the "Longships" but smaller in length to fit Portugal's Douro River. They also have the added benefit of a pool on top.

Specifications

Passengers	106	Total cabins/balcony cabins	53/37
Passenger decks	3	Crew	36
Year entered service:			
Viking Hemming, Viking Torgil	2014	Viking Osfrid	2016

THE SHIPS IN GENERAL   The streamlined decor on these ships, custom-built for the Douro River, embraces Portuguese elements including colorful tiles. But they share a lot of the same attributes as the "Longships."

CABINS   All staterooms on the Middle and Upper decks have a full veranda or French balcony. The 302-square-foot Veranda Suites are two full rooms with a veranda off the living room and a French balcony on the bedroom, and 40-inch TVs in both rooms. In addition to the suites, the staterooms that have balconies are the Veranda staterooms at 185-square-feet each, and the French Balcony staterooms at 150-square-feet each. The Standard Staterooms on the lower deck are 155-square-feet each and just feature a window—no balcony.

PUBLIC AREAS   A spacious, modern lounge with floor-to-ceiling windows serves up views from comfortable club chairs and is the gathering spot for drinks, socializing, lectures (including about port wine) and entertainment. The open-air Aquavit Terrace is at the bow end. The Sun Deck has shaded loungers and an organic herb garden. There's also a library area and boutique. There is an elevator between the passenger decks.

DINING OPTIONS   The open seating, river-view restaurant in the middle of the ship serves a buffet breakfast and lunch and a sit-down five-course dinner. Ingredients from the organic herb garden add spice to contemporary and regional Portuguese dishes.

POOL, FITNESS, SPA, BIKES   There's a small pool as well as a golf putting green on the Sun Deck.

Viking Astrild & Viking Beyla
The Verdict

These modern ships are smaller versions of the "Longships," designed specifically for the height restrictions and shallow water of Germany's Elbe River.

Specifications

Passengers	98	Total cabins/balcony cabins	49/21
Passenger decks	2	Crew	28
Year entered service	2015		

THE SHIPS IN GENERAL   Like the larger "Longships" these ships have a partially glassed-in Aquavit Terrace with indoor and outdoor seating in their expanded snub-nosed bow, lots of windows for views and some staterooms with real, step-out balconies. "Green" features include hybrid diesel-electric engines for a cleaner and quieter ride, solar panels and an organic herb garden on the Sun Deck. There is no elevator.

CABINS   All staterooms on the Upper Deck have either full or step-out verandas, and all staterooms have some sort of river view. The 250-square-foot Veranda Suites are two separate rooms with a veranda off the living room and French balcony in the bedroom. Veranda staterooms are 180-square-feet, standards 140-square-feet, and French balcony staterooms are a tight 122-square-feet. Big flatscreen TVs feature a variety of channels including CNN and movies on demand.

PUBLIC AREAS   The Lounge is the main gathering spot and has floor-to-ceiling windows and club chairs and a fancy bar setup. The Sun Deck has a shaded sitting area and views of both the river and organic herb garden. There's also a library corner and a boutique.

DINING OPTIONS   The open seating, river-view dining room in the middle of the ship serves a buffet breakfast and lunch and a sit-down five-course dinner. You can also dine al-fresco at the Aquavit Terrace. An onboard organic herb garden brings extra flavor to the contemporary and regional cuisine that's served.

POOL, FITNESS, SPA, BIKES   The only fitness offering is a golf putting green on the Sun Deck. Passengers can also walk or jog on the top deck. For fun, there's also a Giant Chess Set. Those wanting more can arrange use of spa, gym and pool facilities on land via the concierge.

Viking Legend & Viking Prestige

The Verdict

These Europe river ships blazed the trail for the "Longships" introducing features including the Aquavit Terrace, an outdoor casual dining spot, and hybrid diesel-electric engines for a cleaner, quieter ride.

Specifications

Passengers	188	Total cabins/balcony cabins	99/74
Passenger decks	3	Crew	40
Year entered service			
Viking Legend	2009	Viking Prestige	2011

THE SHIPS IN GENERAL These eco-friendly ships are sleek and done up in contemporary Scandinavian decor. They are very much a precursor for what was to come on the "Longships," revolutionary for their time but without some of the bells and whistles of their successors. The bold new concept first introduced on *Viking Prestige* was the Aquavit Terrace in the bow, a casual space with open glass walls and indoor and outdoor seating.

CABINS The majority of staterooms have a French balcony and Veranda Suites have two. Standard cabins are 170-square-feet and the ships also have five small cabins with single foam beds (not regular, larger hotel-like mattresses as in the other cabins) that crew members can transform into sofas upon request and are designed and priced for solo travelers. Two, two-room suites on the Upper Deck are 337-square-feet. All staterooms have flatscreen TVs, hair dryers, and individual climate control among amenities.

PUBLIC AREAS A large lounge with a bar in the corner and floor-to-ceiling windows is the prime hangout spot. The Atrium is a large, airy space with a grand staircase to an upper lobby sitting area. The ship also has a nice big library aft. The Sun Deck has seating including under shaded canopies.

DINING OPTIONS The main dining room serves up scenery through panoramic windows, a breakfast and lunch buffet and a sit-down dinner. Despite this being an older vessel, you can expect food to be of a similar quality as on other Viking ships. You can also enjoy a light buffet at the Aquavit Terrace on *Viking Prestige* (but not *Viking Legend*).

POOL, FITNESS, SPA, BIKES There are no gym facilities, but Viking can help make arrangements at luxury hotels en route.

Viking Fontane & Viking Schumann

The Verdict

These older sister ships don't have the hip factor nor space of the line's newer ships. But they still provide comfortable environs for seeing Europe's rivers.

Specifications

Passengers	112	Total cabins/balcony cabins	56/8
Passenger decks	2	Crew	32
Year entered service	1991		

THE MAIN RIVER CRUISE LINES

THE SHIPS IN GENERAL   There two classic Viking ships were built to navigate the Elbe, with customized hulls and engines. A complete refurbishment in 2010 (*Schumann*) and 2011 (*Fontane*) resulted in streamlined Scandinavian interiors.

CABINS   All staterooms have river views and amenities including 42" flatscreen TVs. The top accommodations are the eight 200-square-foot French Balcony cabins, with floor-to-ceiling sliding glass doors and beds that can be configured as a queen. Standard A-category cabins (a tight 135 sq. ft.) come with a large picture window that opens and fixed twin-size beds. Standard categories B, C, and D have a window that doesn't open and twin beds.

PUBLIC AREAS   The updated decor and intimate atmosphere are appealing, though you won't find as much space to spread out as on the larger "Longships." The main Lounge has floor-to-ceiling windows and serves as the ships socializing, educational and entertainment hub. There's a small library near the bar. The Sun Deck has both sunny and shaded sitting areas. There's also a small boutique. There are no elevators, making these ships difficult for those who can't handle stairs.

DINING OPTIONS   In the windowed dining room, there's a breakfast buffet, a soup and sandwich bar (as well as served entrees) at lunch and a five-course dinner includes a choice of several entrees and regional specialties.

POOL, FITNESS, SPA, BIKES   As with the other older Viking ships, there is no gym or pool but the line will provide a list of fitness facilities you can use (for a fee) en route.

Viking Emerald
The Verdict

The *Viking Emerald* is a big river ship, so much so that it feels a bit like an oceangoing vessel. But big brings advantages including a variety of public spaces and room to stretch out.

Specifications

Passengers	256	Total cabins/balcony cabins	125/125
Passenger decks	5	Crew	138
Year entered service	2011		

THE SHIP IN GENERAL   Viking charters this ship from Century Cruises, and it's the largest river ship operated by Viking and has more of an oceangoing ship feel, with its elegant five-story atrium, public areas that get their design cues from Vegas casinos, and larger staterooms with plenty of windows. It's the line's sole ship on the Yangtze, and while most of the line's ships draw a mostly older adult audience, this one also attracts a number of families and younger couples.

CABINS   All staterooms are generously sized—standards are 250-square-feet—and have a veranda, accessible through sliding glass doors. Amenities include flatscreen TVs, European linens, and duvets and L'Occitane beauty products. This ship's two-room Explorer's Suites are the largest in river cruising—at 603-square-feet, with private, wrap-around verandas and big bathrooms with shower and tub. There are also smaller suites and junior suites.

PUBLIC AREAS The classy Observation Lounge & Bar, where lectures are held and movies screened, has floor-to-ceiling windows and comfortable seating. Above, and connected by a staircase, is the river-view Emerald Lounge & Bar on the Sun Deck. Other public rooms include a reading room. The Sun Deck has shaded sitting areas. The ship has two glass elevators. A shop sells Chinese souvenirs and the ship also has its own tailor shop where you can order custom-made garments.

DINING OPTIONS There's open seating dining and panoramic views in the restaurant. The ship's state-of-the-art Western kitchen offers Asian and European cuisines (hotel and catering services are overseen by Viking's Swiss management team).

POOL, FITNESS, SPA, BIKES Bigger ship, more amenities. There is a spa and hair salon as well as gym and sauna. Tai chi classes are offered.

Viking Mekong
The Verdict

You will be cruising the exotic Mekong through Cambodia and Vietnam, but you'll have all the creature comforts of home on this handcrafted ship.

Specifications

Passengers	56	Total cabins/balcony cabins	28
Passenger decks	2 1/2	Crew	25
Year entered service	2014		

THE SHIP IN GENERAL Done up in French Colonial style with teak, mahogany and brass decor, this ship provides an intimate environment for exploring the Mekong. The two main decks have wraparound promenades. There are no elevators.

CABINS The comfortable, 168-square-foot cabins are all impressively mahogany-paneled and include such accouterments as hairdryers, air conditioning and walk-in showers, plus sliding French doors opening onto a shared terrace with seating.

PUBLIC AREAS The air-conditioned restaurant is the main indoor spot, with activities including entertainment also taking place on the Sun Deck, where you'll find the bar. There's also an enclosed lecture room (where movies are shown) and salon on the on the Sun Deck, as well as a small library area and little shop selling local souvenirs.

DINING OPTIONS The open-seating restaurant has tables for six and river views. Breakfast and lunch are buffets while dinner is a multicourse, waiter-service meal featuring regional dishes.

POOL, FITNESS, SPA, BIKES There's a small spa for massages, and Tai Chi is offered early morning on deck. No fitness room.

Viking Akun, Viking Ingvar & Viking Truvor

The Verdict

These older Volga ships were given a major facelift—everything was ripped out and new carpets, walls, window coverings, Scandinavian furniture, hotel-style beds, you name it, were introduced.

Specifications

Passengers	204	Total cabins/balcony cabins	104/71
Passenger decks	4	Crew	105
Year entered service			
Viking Akun	1990	Viking Truvor	1984
Viking Ingvar	1988		

THE SHIPS IN GENERAL   Acquired by Viking these older Volga river ships were extensively refurbished in 2013/2014, including the addition of veranda staterooms and decor inspired by the Viking "Longships." An elevator connects the public decks.

CABINS   The ships have both veranda and deluxe staterooms, done up with the standard Viking accouterments including flatscreen TVs and a nice, contemporary decor. Two 400-square-foot suites have panoramic windows leading to substantial veranda, bathtubs and separate shower. Two junior suites (335 sq. ft.) and 67 veranda staterooms (225–230 sq. ft.) also have outdoor sitting areas. Deluxe staterooms have picture windows and range from 140 to 160-square-feet.

PUBLIC AREAS   There are two bars, The Panorama Lounge, where lectures and entertainment takes place, and the Sky Bar, with indoor and outdoor seating on the Sun Deck. The library has comfortable seating and room to play cards and board games and a good-sized shop where you can buy a decent array of Russian souvenirs on the Main Deck.

DINING OPTIONS   The windowed main dining room is opening seating with tables for 6, 8 and 10 guests. Breakfast and lunch are buffet style while dinner is a five-course affair (typically at 7pm) with a good choice of international dishes and regional specialties (up for trying some *bliny,* Russian pancakes, or *zakuski,* assortments of cold cuts, cured fish, pickles, caviar and darker rye-style bread?).

POOL, FITNESS, SPA, BIKES   There is no gym, pool, or spa, but Viking can arrange access to facilities at luxury hotels en route.

MS Omar El Khayam

The Verdict

Niceties on this ship—which has been adequately updated—include a large pool on the Sun Deck and staterooms that all have their own balcony and bathtub.

Specifications

Passengers	160	Total cabins/balcony cabins	80/80
Passenger decks	5	Crew	88
Year entered service	2008		

THE SHIP IN GENERAL   Named for a Persian philosopher, mathematician and astronomer, the MS *Omar El Khayam,* chartered by Viking, carries 160 passengers in spacious suites and staterooms and is Viking's only ship on Egypt's Lake Nasser.

CABINS   All staterooms and suites have a veranda and everyone also gets a bathtub. The top four suites are located on the Middle and Main decks and are 388-square-feet with verandas. The other staterooms are a generous 258-square-feet. These are clean and upscale accommodations with nice furniture and subtle but tasteful decor.

PUBLIC AREAS   Passengers on the MS *Omar El Khayam* relax in three cushy lounges on the Upper, Observation (with bar) and Lower decks. Off the Upper Deck lounge is a card room and billiards room. The ship also has a small library and boutique. An elevator connects the public areas.

DINING OPTIONS   Meals are open seating in an attractive restaurant with panoramic views. Breakfast and lunch feature buffets—at lunch including a soup and sandwich bar. During dinner service, five-course menus feature Egyptian specialties such as grilled meats and dips like the eggplant spread *baba ghanoush* and the popular Middle Eastern sesame spread *tahini.*

POOL, FITNESS, SPA, BIKES   Amenities on the MS *Omar El Khayam* are more extensive than on most Viking cruisers, including a pool and Jacuzzi on the Sun Deck, where there are also cushy loungers, both in the sun and shade. The ship also has a small gym, sauna and steam room and an indoor Jacuzzi. Massage services are available.

MS Mayfair
The Verdict
This fancy, hotel-like ship takes cruisers down the Nile in high style.

Specifications

Passengers	148	Total cabins/balcony cabins	74/2
Passenger decks	4	Crew	70
Year entered service	2010		

THE SHIP IN GENERAL   This 150-passenger ship, chartered by Viking, is surprisingly elegant, with an extravagant two-deck lobby done up in marble and with chandeliers and a winding grand staircase leading to the second level.

CABINS   All staterooms have French balconies or verandas, bathtubs and classy, Art Deco-inspired decor. Standard staterooms are a generous 277-square-feet, and 10 in categories A and B have verandas. The top two suites have bedroom and living room areas (separated by a partial divider) and verandas, and are 377-square-feet.

PUBLIC AREAS Passengers schmooze, imbibe, attend lectures and enjoy local music in a cushy, windowed lounge. There is also a Lounge Terrace for outdoor coffee and drinks; a library; and a small boutique.

DINING OPTIONS The restaurant brings views and features regional dishes. Breakfast and lunch are buffet spreads while dinner is a five-course, sit-down affair.

POOL, FITNESS, SPA, BIKES On the top Sun Deck, passengers lounge like Cleopatra around the pool and two Jacuzzis—on daybeds positioned in the sun and under shade-providing canopies. The ship also has a spa, with massage services available.

UNIWORLD

www.uniworld.com. ℰ 800/257-2407.

Pros

o **High design.** You cannot talk about Uniworld without talking about the interior design of this company's river cruise ships. We have three words for you: Over. The. Top. Think extensive marble details, lush upholstery, and tons of commissioned artwork, which have made the vessels something of a destination unto themselves.

o **Gourmand's delight.** Uniworld's vessels are not just a feast for the eyes, they are a feast for the taste buds too. The company does not hold back when it comes to bringing impressive delicacies and wine on board.

Cons

o **Price.** Uniworld's fancy-schmancy six-star, all-inclusive offering comes at a price. These river cruises are not cheap.

o **Impractical inventory.** These decked-out riverboats are often weighed down by all the divine details inside and that means that Uniworld vessels can sometimes be at a disadvantage when river water levels are low, a situation that favors lighter boats with lower drafts.

THE LINE IN A NUTSHELL Uniworld has grabbed a hold of the highest end of the river cruise market and has firmly planted itself there. When it comes to opulent interiors, paired with fine dining and wine, Uniworld is in a class of its own.

Frommer's Ratings (Scale of 1–5)

Cabin comfort & amenities	4	Public spaces	4
Decor	5	Dining	5
Fitness, spa and pool	5	Service	5
Family-friendly	5	Enrichment	4

THE EXPERIENCE Beyond its ritzy river cruise ships, Uniworld has a secret weapon similar to Avalon Waterways'—it too is owned by a major travel conglomerate, The Travel Corporation, a company that owns well-established tour brands such as Trafalgar, Insight Vacations, Brendan Vacations, and the hotel company the Red Carnation Hotel Collection. What that means is that Uniworld isn't just a fleet of fancy ships. It is backed by some serious tour operating experience and decades of travel expertise.

That kind of tour operating pedigree means that Uniworld has the ability to create land programs in line with the level of expectation set by the onboard experience, whether that means finding exclusive chateaux for wine tastings in Bordeaux or taking its passengers truffle hunting in the south of France.

Back on board, you will find that, despite a certain old-world elegance that the ships evoke, Uniworld in fact has some very modern ideas about the kinds of offerings today's contemporary river cruiser might want. For instance, the company is getting much more into health and wellness. So it offers yoga and exercise classes and TRX training equipment in the more traditional fitness room. Bikes are also available to cruisers.

And passengers may find they could use that extra workout as Uniworld cuisine makes it hard to resist temptation (there are healthy options too, but who wants to eat healthy when there are mounds of pastries at breakfast, a heaping cheese station at lunch and multicourse dinners?).

Uniworld is making strides in terms of sustainability, too, having developed an Environmental Sustainability for River Cruising guide in 2013, a set of best practices for how river cruise lines can reduce their environmental impact. Since then, Uniworld (and other river cruise lines are making strides as well) has cut back on energy consumption by "plugging in" to shore-side electricity supplies when docked. And Uniworld also gives its guests two refillable aluminum bottles at the start of the cruise, then provides them with large glass containers of water in their staterooms for refilling the bottles.

THE FLEET　The Uniworld fleet is a testament to the fact that age actually does not matter when it comes to river cruise vessels—not if you're willing to invest big bucks to completely reinvent old hardware. Uniworld has been around since the 1980s when the company founder, Serbian entrepreneur Serba Ilich began bringing Americans through Europe on riverboats. Uniworld still has some more mature ships in its fleet, its oldest dating back to 1993 (it has two others that were built in the late 90s and a whole batch of ships from the early 2000s). But if you step on any Uniworld ship today, you would never see the evidence of the passage of time. Uniworld has done such a stellar job revamping its older ships that they truly are as striking as their newer counterparts. In a way the company has done with its ships what its sister company Red Carnation Hotel Collection has done with some of its hotel properties—completely updated vintage exteriors with refreshed and reinvigorated interiors. The only giveaway, as you'll see when you read about the individual ships below, is some of the dated layouts that give way to smaller staterooms and fewer balconies on the older ships.

Regardless of whether you're boarding one of its newest or older vessels, stepping on board a Uniworld vessel is similar in feel to when you walk through the doors of some of the more exquisite hotels in the world. It has a bit of that fantasy feel. It isn't for everyone. Some people might say the vessels are too gaudy or perhaps stuffy feeling, but anyone with a flair for the fancy will probably revel in it all.

Just as one example of just how far Uniworld goes with its ships, the company invested more than $1 million in the purchasing and commissioning of the extensive collection of art pieces on board just one of its ships—the 159-passenger S.S. Catherine, which sails on the Rhone and Saone rivers in France's Burgundy and Provence regions. Other extravagant details include the intricate mosaic-tiled indoor swimming on Uniworld's newer Super Ship class of vessels, the safari-themed Leopard Lounge at the aft of several of its ships and the 10-foot blue Strauss Baccarat chandelier with sapphires, which once hung in the former Tavern on the Green in New York's Central Park and now hangs in the lobby of the S.S. *Antoinette.*

More so than in any other river cruising fleet, the vessels in the Uniworld fleet each truly do have their own personality. While there is an identifiable look and feel to a Uniworld ship, rooted in elaborate window dressings, antique-style furniture and ornate decor, each individual ship has been uniquely designed with its own color palette (or rather color palettes as they can change dramatically from one room to the next), distinctive artwork and details.

Last year, Uniworld launched its newest Super Ship class vessel, the 150-passenger S.S. *Maria Theresa,* bringing the company's European fleet size to 14 ships. Of those, Uniworld owns 12, and has long-term lease agreements on the *Queen Isabel* in Portugal and on the *River Victoria* in Russia.

In January of 2016, Uniworld also began its first-ever sailings on India's Ganges River with the launch of the all-suite, luxury river cruise vessel, the 56-passenger *Ganges Voyager II.*

The company also has sailings on the 58-passenger *River Orchid* on the Mekong River, offers Yangtze River cruises on the Century Legend and Century Paragon ships, and has a beautiful all-suite vessel on Egypt's Nile River, the 82-passenger *River Tosca.*

PASSENGER PROFILE   Like many river cruise lines, Uniworld's mainstay are baby boomers, but in recent years Uniworld has been attracting a wider variety of guests, including a greater number of younger passengers. Along those lines, Uniworld has been building up its wellness program, which as of 2016 includes higher paced "Go Active" excursions, complimentary yoga classes and TRX training, bicycles on board and Nordic walking sticks that guests can use. Uniworld also offers family-friendly departures, which helps bring down the age range of passengers.

DINING OPTIONS   Just like it doesn't skimp on artwork and interiors, Uniworld doesn't cut corners when it comes to its culinary program.

14-day Danube, Main and Rhine ("European Jewels"), Budapest to Amsterdam, from $7,099, balconies from $8,769, Apr–Nov

9-day Rhine ("Tulips & Windmills"), Amsterdam to Antwerp (Belgium), from $3,599, balconies from $4,724, Mar–Apr

7-day Rhone and Saone ("Burgundy & Provence"), Avignon to Lyon, from $3,299, balconies from $4,394, Mar–Nov

14-day Seine, Saone and Rhone ("Grand France"), Paris to Avignon, from $7,499, balconies from $9,794, Mar–Oct

21-day Seine, Garonne, Saone and Dordogne ("Ultimate France"), Paris to Avignon, from $10,999, balconies from $15,094, Mar–Oct

7-day Rhine ("Castles along the Rhine"), Basel to Amsterdam, from $2,999, balconies from $3,974, Mar–Nov

7-day Danube ("Enchanting Danube"), Budapest to Passau (Germany), from 2,899, balconies from $3,794, Apr–Nov

12-day Rhine and Moselle ("Legendary Rhine & Moselle"), Amsterdam to Basel, from $5,399, balconies from $7,294, May–Nov

9-day Rhine ("Tulips & Windmills"), Amsterdam to Antwerp (Belgium), from $3,349, balconies from $4,844, Mar–Apr

7-day Dordogne and Garonne ("Bordeaux, Vineyards & Chateaux"), round-trip from Bordeaux, from $2,999, balconies from $4,364, Mar–Nov

9-day Po ("Gems of Northern Italy"), with 7-day cruise, Milan to Venice, from $3,999, balconies from $5,544, Apr–Nov

14-day Po ("Splendors of Italy"), with 7-day cruise, Milan to Rome, from $6,999, balconies from $8,244, Apr–Nov

11-day Danube ("Highlights of Eastern Europe & Istanbul"), with 9-day cruise, Budapest to Istanbul, from $4,999, balconies from $6,594, May–Sept

25-day Danube, Rhine and Main ("Ultimate European Journey"), with 23-day cruise, Amsterdam to Istanbul, from $11,798, balconies from $15,693, May–Sept

9-day Danube and Main ("Delightful Danube & Prague"), Budapest to Prague, from $3,299, balconies from $4,794, May–Nov

20-day Danube ("Portraits of Eastern Europe"), with 14-day cruise, Prague to Istanbul, from $8,898, balconies from $11,888, Apr–Oct

Passengers can expect meals that incorporate local delicacies like impressive selection of smoked salmon at the breakfast buffet, foie gras in France, hard-to-find regional cheeses throughout Europe (seriously, their cheese displays are massive) and very specialized wine pairings. This high quality, locally sourced gourmet dining experience alleviates some of the potential frustration that eating most of your meals on the ship during a river cruise can cause. Uniworld makes it feel like you are experiencing a high-end local restaurant, rather than just generic cuisine that could be from anywhere in Europe.

Uniworld hasn't embraced the multiple dining venue trend and appears to be more focused on simply wowing in the main restaurant.

14-day Danube ("Grand European Discovery"), Basel to Vienna, from $5,899, balconies from $7,824, May–Oct

7-day Dutch and Belgian Canals ("Holland & Belgium at Tulip Time"), Brussels to Amsterdam, from $3,099, balconies from $4,124, Mar–Apr

9-day Danube ("Rhine Discovery & Prague"), with 7-day cruise, Prague to Basel, from $3,699, balconies from $4,724, May–Nov

7-day Seine ("Paris & Normandy"), round-trip from Paris, from $3,349, balconies from $4,424, Mar–Oct

12-day Douro ("Jewels of Spain, Portugal & the Douro River"), with 7-day cruise, Lisbon to Madrid, from $5,599, balconies from $6,624, Apr–Oct

10-day Douro ("Portugal, Spain & the Douro River Valley"), with 7-day cruise, Lisbon to Porto, from $3,849, balconies from $4,874, Mar–Nov

12-day Volga ("Imperial Waterways of Russia"), Moscow to St. Petersburg, from $5,149, balconies from $6,944, May–June

12-day Ganges ("India's Golden Triangle & the Sacred Ganges") with 7-day cruise, New Delhi to Kolkata, cabins/balconies from $7,599, Jan–Dec

10-day Yangtze ("Highlights of China & the Yangtze"), with 3-day cruise, Beijing to Shanghai, cabins/balconies from $4,249, Mar–Oct

11-day Yangtze ("Treasures of China & the Yangtze"), with 4-day cruise, Shanghai to Beijing, cabins/balconies from $4,449, Mar–Oct

13-day Yangtze ("China, Tibet & the Yangtze"), with 4-day cruise, Beijing to Hong Kong, cabins/balconies from $6,599, Mar–Oct

17-day Yangtze ("Grand China & the Yangtze"), with 4-day cruise, Shanghai to Beijing, cabins/balconies from $4,449, Mar–Oct

14-day Mekong ("Timeless Wonders of Vietnam, Cambodia & The Mekong"), with 7-day cruise, Ho Chi Minh City to Hanoi, from $5,649, Jan–Dec

11-day Nile ("Splendors of Egypt & the Nile"), with 7-day cruise, round-trip from Cairo, cabins/balconies from $5,649, Jan–May

Note on this chart: Itineraries may also be available in the reverse direction. The first price is the lowest available price for all cabin categories, and the second price is the lowest balcony price, including French balcony cabins.

It's also important to note that as part of Uniworld's all-inclusive pricing, unlimited beverages are available throughout the cruise including some premium spirits such as Grey Goose, Crown Royal, and Glenfiddich.

ACTIVITIES Uniworld's discerning clientele expects lofty and engaging lectures relevant to the history, culture or current events of the region, and deeper insights into the local culinary traditions and wines of the regions through tastings and cooking demonstrations and thus that's what Uniworld strives to provide.

CHILDREN'S PROGRAM   Uniworld does not encourage children on its regular sailings, but it doesn't prohibit them either. The company doesn't recommend the experience for young children, especially those under 4, stating that they "are simply not yet old enough to enjoy river cruising." Children under 18 must be accompanied by an adult 21 or older at all times, and there are no kid-friendly arrangements or activities for them.

All that said, for those who would like to bring the little ones on a river cruise, Uniworld has a long-standing family river cruise program that dates back to 2007. Currently, Uniworld has 13 family-friendly departures on nine different itineraries throughout Europe, including on the Rhine, Danube, Seine and Po rivers, with departure dates focused around the summer months and holiday season. To make these itineraries kid-friendly, Uniworld injects them with more active excursions such as biking and kayaking, more arts and crafts, opportunities to visit various amusement parks or a gladiator school (that's a thing? … apparently in Rome it is…), hands-on food activities, and anything spooky (ghost walks), creepy (such as the Medieval Crime and Justice Museum in Rothenburg, Germany) or just plain weird that "kids" will get a kick out of. Just the kids. Because it's not like us adults want anything to do with that stuff. Okay, let's be honest, the kids' stuff is often way cooler and more fun than the adult stuff. There, we said it.

ENTERTAINMENT   As the number of river cruise ships on Europe's rivers increases exponentially, it's getting harder for each line to try to offer something a bit different. You go to Vienna and everyone offers a classical music concert. When you sail through Portugal, the inevitable Fado singer will come on board. And while there's absolutely nothing wrong with these performances, Uniworld tries to shake things up a bit, whenever it can (it offers plenty of the typical entertainment, too). So, maybe instead of the Viennese opera singer in the main lounge one night, they might have an American-born, Europe-residing jazz family in the Leopard Lounge at the aft of the vessel instead. Also, they really go all out to find something particularly special for their New Year's cruises.

SERVICE   There's a certain expectation in the luxury cruising category and Uniworld certainly makes every effort to ensure that extremely well-trained staff are on-hand to meet and hopefully exceed customers' expectation. It could be something small like crew remembering passengers' names and preferences, to something more involved like helping passengers make special onshore arrangements and celebrate special occasions—Uniworld is tuned in to these details and appears to be aware that without them it really doesn't matter how glamorous the ships are.

Furthermore, Uniworld stepped it up a notch last year by offering in-suite butler service for guests staying in the suites on four of its vessels—the River Beatrice, S.S. *Antoinette,* S.S. *Catherine,* and S.S. *Maria Theresa.* The service includes packing and unpacking assistance, in-room breakfast if desired, a daily fruit and cookie plate, and evening snack, a bottle of wine upon arrival, shoe shine and free laundry service. These guests are also invited to a special dinner in the Bar du Leopard.

Uniworld includes gratuities in its pricing.

TOURS   As mentioned previously, Uniworld is part of a larger tour operator powerhouse, The Travel Corporation, and thus has the connections and clout to create reliable and sophisticated daily half- and full-day excursions. Most excursions are included, but there might be a very exclusive tour here or there that passengers have to sign up and pay extra for. Recently, Uniworld has been placing a greater emphasis on more "local" experiences, such as insider tours of various cities, or what it calls village visits, which give passenger a more intimate look at how people in the communities along the rivers live.

PRE- & POST-CRUISE STAYS   Uniworld's river cruise extension options generally consist of 3- and 4-day packages that passengers can add on in front of or behind their river cruise and that include deluxe hotel accommodations, daily breakfast, gratuities, a city tour, a local expert and all transfers.

Super Ships—S.S. Maria Theresa, S.S. Catherine & S.S. Antoinette

The Verdict

Uniworld certainly didn't hold back with its newest class of vessels, which it calls its Super Ship class (hence the S.S. at the start of the names). From the almost reckless investment in stunning amounts of original artwork to the mosaic-tiled indoor pools, these ships provide as much eye candy as the rivers they sail.

Specifications

Passengers			
S.S. *Maria Theresa*	150	S.S. *Antoinette*	154
S.S. *Catherine*	159		
Total cabins/balcony cabins			
S.S. *Maria Theresa*	75/65	S.S. *Antoinette*	77/62
S.S. *Catherine*	80/67		
Passenger decks	3	Crew	57
Year entered service			
S.S. *Maria Theresa*	2015	S.S. *Catherine*, S.S. *Antoinette*,	2014

THE SHIPS IN GENERAL   After several years of not launching any new ships, Uniworld restarted its shipbuilding process with a bang. Beginning with the S.S. *Antoinette* in 2014, the strategy appeared to be to draw inspiration from the opulence of the palaces and castles to which these ships sail. You can see elements of Versailles in the many mirrored walls of the S.S. *Catherine,* and Uniworld said it took inspiration from the Baroque period during which Maria Theresa, the Archduchess of Austria, ruled the Habsburg dynasty (1740 to 1780) for its vessel of the same name—the S.S. *Maria Theresa*. In terms of onboard amenities, there are similarities between the three vessels (they all have one main restaurant and lounge, for instance), as well as several differences—two of the three vessels have a small cinema (S.S. *Maria Theresa* and S.S. *Antoinette*), and two of the three feature the popular Bar du Leopard with its adjoining pool area (S.S. *Maria Theresa* and S.S. *Catherine*), while the S.S. *Antoinette* instead has a larger pool area with a juice bar.

The differences not just in the layout of the ships, but in the look and feel of them, is very refreshing in a river cruising industry where it has become commonplace to churn out like vessels year after year after year. You can expect that individuality to extend into the suites and staterooms, which are all done up with different motifs, prints and upholstery. For some people, the layered patterns and designs that have become a Uniworld trademark can seem a bit dizzying or, quite frankly, just too much. You have really got to be into this look as it suits a very specific taste. For those that are, though, they are in for a treat. The *Maria Theresa* sails the Rhine and Danube rivers, the *Catherine* sails the Rhone and Saone and the *Antoinette* sails the Rhine.

CABINS   On each of these vessels, the cabin breakdown is a bit different. On the S.S. *Maria Theresa,* there are seven categories of cabins ranging from the lower deck Category 4 and 5 cabins that are 162-square-feet each and do not have balconies (just porthole windows), to the 410-square-foot Royal Suite with its separate salon (it feels like it should be called that on these ships) and a full-sized bathtub. The majority of the staterooms are the Category 1 and 2 staterooms (194-square-feet) on the second and third deck that feature Uniworld's drop-down balcony concept, transforming the floor-to-ceiling window into a French balcony with the push of a window-lowering button. There are also 10 individually decorated suites that are 305-square-feet each.

On the S.S. *Catherine* there is one 120-square-foot single cabin on the lower deck with a sleeping sofa (a great, if cozy, option for solo travelers as there is no extra charge) alongside the 12 lower deck cabins that are 162-square-feet. All the cabins down here are balcony-less—just sealed-shut windows to peer out of. The majority of staterooms are Category 1, 2 and 3 cabins on the second and third deck that measure 194-square-feet each and feature those drop-down French balconies. And for those who want to go big or go home, there are five suites at 305-square-feet each and the Royal Suite at 401-square-feet and with that coveted full bathtub.

Lastly, on the S.S. *Antoinette,* there are the 163-square-foot cabins on the lower deck (no balconies); the 196-square-foot cabins with French balconies on the second and third deck; the 294-square-foot suites on the third deck (there are eight of these guys); and the 391-square-foot Royal Suite, with its separate sitting area and bathtub.

Now, cabin sizes aside, all of these staterooms have some common amenities including marble bathrooms outfitted with towel warmers and L'Occitane bath products; Savoir Beds (a fancy British mattress company—read: a good night's sleep); hair dryer, safe, individual thermostat, flatscreen TV with info-tainment system and satellite channels, and bottled water.

Cabin sizes and amenities aside, all of the staterooms on these vessels have a certain regal rococo-ness to them. Every aspect of the decor is defined by multiple layers of details, from the plethora of patterns (wallpapers, uphol-stery and bedding are all fair game when it comes to motifs) to numerous textures and treatments—for instance, window dressings aren't just simple curtains, they're curtains with trim, and fridge, and tassels. You get the idea.

PUBLIC AREAS   The S.S. *Maria Theresa* and the S.S. *Catherine* are most similar in terms of their common areas as they both have the popular Bar du Leopard at the aft of the vessel, adjacent to an indoor pool with safari-themed mosaic tile-work. The pool area walls are sheer glass so if you want to take a quiet swim at night, don't count on it, you'll have the bar crowd peering in. On the S.S. *Maria Theresa,* there is also the Serenity River Spa, the Lipizzan Cinema, a small screening room, a fitness room, and a 24-hour coffee station all located on the lower deck. There is one main dining room and the larger bar and lounge area with an outdoor terrace. The S.S. *Catherine* also features a 24-hour coffee station and fitness room on the lower deck, where there is also a small boutique. The Serenity River Spa is located one deck up at the aft of the vessel. Here too you have one main dining room and one larger bar and lounge area, which includes an outdoor terrace.

The S.S. *Antoinette* does not have the Bar du Leopard, and instead has a larger pool area at the aft of the second deck, where the Serenity River Spa is also located. There's a small indoor cinema and coffee station on the lower deck, and a main restaurant, bar and lounge. All of these public areas are done up with opulent decor and furniture. The color schemes will be unique from one room the next and there will be old-world influences alongside more modern touches.

DINING OPTIONS   Unlike other cruise lines that have moved towards offering multiple dining venues, on these vessels there is one main destination for your daily bread (and it's a lot more than just bread, trust us): the Baroque Restaurant on the *Maria Theresa,* the Cezanne Restaurant on the *Catherine* and the Restaurant de Versailles on the *Antoinette.* In all three restaurants, tables accommodate groups of two, four and six. The breakfast and lunch buf-fets are elaborate displays of choice (heaps of fruits for breakfast, and salad choices for lunch, alongside heartier omelet and chef station entrees), and for the dinners, all we can say is, bring your stretchy pants.

POOL, FITNESS, SPA, BIKES   On all three vessels there are indoor pools, though let's be clear, you aren't going to be doing some serious laps on these things—a few strokes will get you across to the other side. In addition is the River Serenity Spa room, offering massages and full-body treatments involving oils and exfoliation, and a fitness room. There are also bikes and Nordic walking sticks available for passengers to use.

River Beatrice

The Verdict

Not as flamboyant as the Super Ships, Uniworld hadn't hit its stride with the interior designs on the River Beatrice, but it is still a swanky ship to be sure.

Specifications

Passengers	156	Total cabins/balcony cabins	78/67
Passenger decks	3	Crew	53
Year entered service	2009		

THE SHIP IN GENERAL The River Beatrice is a slightly less inspired ship than some of Uniworld's more eccentric vessels but it still has many of the Uniworld marks of distinction, such as elaborate patterned wallpaper and upholstery, and artwork strewn throughout. This Danube vessel may actually be a good choice for customers who love Uniworld's service, food and amenities but think the Super Ships are just a bit too over the top (and remember it's all relative, since a "toned down" Uniworld vessel is still a lot more ornate than most other river cruise ships).

CABINS There are five categories of cabins on the River Beatrice, starting with the lower deck, Category 4 and 5 cabins, which are each 150-square-feet and have windows but no balconies. Category 1-3 cabins on the second and third decks are not any larger at 150-square-feet each, but these do feature a French balcony. Partially making up for all those small cabins is the fact that there are a fair amount of suites—there are 14 of the 225-square-foot Suites and one Owner's Suite at 300-square-feet, featuring a rain shower and a tub and a secluded toilet and bidet area. The staterooms all have marble bathrooms and L'Occitane products (no towel heating racks though), those comfy Savoir beds, heat and cooling controls, safes, hair dryers, flatscreen TV with movies and TV, and bathrobes and slippers.

PUBLIC AREAS As you enter the ship, the reception is located in a bright and open lobby with marble floors and white accents (there is a strong white color scheme throughout the Beatrice), including the lobby's main statement piece, a large white chandelier. Behind the reception is the main dining room. One deck up is the main bar and lounge and the 24-hour coffee station (these come in very handy morning, noon and night). At the aft of the third deck is a library and lounge area, which offers a quiet alternative to the main lounge. There is also a Sun Deck, as well as a spa and fitness room all the way down on the lower deck.

DINING OPTIONS Hungry? Head to the main restaurant where meals will be served at set times with open seating. Tables sit four and six and there are some longer communal tables where passengers can separate into smaller groups or join together as one slightly larger group. Breakfast and lunch are self-service buffet meals, with both hot and cold offerings, and dinner is a served meal ordered off the nightly (changing) menu.

POOL, FITNESS, SPA, BIKES   There's a fitness room with cardio equipment, a spa treatment room, and bikes and Nordic walking sticks on board. There is no pool.

River Royale, River Countess, River Duchess, River Empress & River Princess

The Verdict

This group of Uniworld vessels really showcases such a fun and wide variety of design styles—it's entertaining to just flip through all the photos of these ships and see how the spaces were imagined quite differently, the way you might voyeuristically flip through a home decor magazine, except that if you want to, you can actually make these vessels your home for a week or so.

Specifications

Passengers	130		
Total cabins/balcony cabins			
River Royale	65/27	River Countess, River Duchess, River Empress, River Princess	65/22
Passenger decks	3	Crew	41
Year entered service			
River Royale	2006	River Empress	2002
River Countess, River Duchess	2003	River Princess	2001

THE SHIPS IN GENERAL   A testament to Uniworld's aggressive capital refurbishment plan, these vessels have been updated so well that they could compete with any of the newer vessels on the rivers. The only drawback to their age is that they were constructed prior to the balcony-building fervor that took off around 2010. Thus, these vessels only offer French balconies on the upper passenger deck and have no balconies on either the second or lower deck. If not having a balcony isn't a deal breaker (and there are still plenty of balcony cabins on that upper deck), then this is an absolutely fabulous group of ships. Fewer balcony cabins aside, you can expect a lot of the same amenities as on all Uniworld vessels, such as those lovely marble stateroom bathrooms. Because of the way these vessels were designed, they also have some of the nicer fitness rooms on the rivers (more on that below). Everyone has their favorites among the eclectic Uniworld ships, but we particularly love the funky black and white lobby, bar and lounge of the *River Princess* and the eclectic portraits in the lobby of the *River Empress*.

CABINS   The cabin situation on these five vessels is pretty straight forward. All of the staterooms are 151-square-feet each, including those with balconies on the upper deck, larger windows on the second deck and smaller porthole windows on the lower deck. There is one suite on the *River Royale* and four suites on the remaining four vessels that are all 214-square-feet each. The staterooms and suites all have their individual design character (some are lighter and brighter with a clean two-color palette accented by a delicate throw here and some heavy drapes there, and others are all about the bold wallpaper, and contrasting patterns that really pop), and are outfitted with all the usual—marble bathrooms, L'Occitane bath products, and flatscreen TVs with movies and satellite channels.

PUBLIC AREAS   These ships were designed differently than most river cruise vessels that you see today. On contemporary European river cruise ships, the main restaurant and the bar and lounge area sit one on top of the other (the bar and lounge is typically on the reception deck and the restaurant is one deck below) occupying the bow portion of the ship. But back in the day, it wasn't uncommon for the restaurant to be at the aft of the vessel, which is exactly where it is on all of these ships except the *River Royale,* which has its restaurant upfront. Part of the reason the restaurant was shifted away from the aft on newer models was to get it away from the occasional rattle of the engines. On the other four vessels, all the major public spaces are on the third deck, with just the boutique, fitness center, spa and a 24-hour coffee station one deck below. These ships also have a partially shaded Sky Lounge located on the Sun Deck, and the *River Royale* also has a hot tub on the Sun Deck.

DINING OPTIONS   All meals are served in the one main restaurant on these ships, where passengers will go for buffet breakfast and lunch and Uniworld's more elegant sit-down dinners.

POOL, FITNESS, SPA, BIKES   There's a whirlpool on the *River Royale,* and a spa and fitness centers on all five vessels, as well as bikes on board. On newer vessels, fitness centers are often shoved into the basement, so to speak (they're often on the darker, more claustrophobic lower deck). But on these ships, the fitness centers actually occupy prime real estate on the second deck where they have nice views and a solid roster of cardio equipment. On the *River Royale* the fitness center is on the third deck, facing the aft of the ship, an ideal place to sweat it out to passing river views.

River Queen
The Verdict

A very unique vessel with a sort of Dutch houseboat inspired exterior and funky Art Deco and mid-century modern furniture and vibe within—and it has a real fireplace in the lounge too.

Specifications

Passengers	128	Total cabins/balcony cabins	64/20
Passenger decks	3	Crew	41
Year entered service	1999		

THE SHIP IN GENERAL   The *River Queen* has a certain charm and uniqueness that usually only vintage vessels have. The ship has a very identifiable exterior with brown-beige and navy blue accents, a stark contrast to the mostly white facades of most contemporary river cruise ships. Again, this is one of the older vessels that was built before balconies were a priority so only the third deck staterooms have them. The interiors are defined by a bold blue and white color scheme, accented by porcelain pieces made of the same colors. But the most distinctive feature inside is a working fireplace in the lounge. How is that even allowed? We're not sure and we love it.

CABINS All of the staterooms on the *River Queen* measure 151-square-feet, save for the four Suites, which are 215-square-feet each. Only the third deck cabins have French balconies and the remaining cabins have either larger windows, on the second deck, or smaller ones on the lower deck. Despite the smaller size of the cabins, Uniworld still managed to cram plenty of design details into the staterooms, such as nail button trimmed headboards, embellished wallpaper, and accent chairs and lamps galore, which are both colorful and varied. They feature marble bathrooms, plush bedding and towels.

PUBLIC AREAS The restaurant, bar and lounge are all located on the third deck, which is also home to the reception area, an Internet corner, a 24-hour coffee and tea station and the Captain's Lounge and Library (a good place to relax with a coffee station cappuccino). There is a fitness center and Serenity River Spa treatment room on the second deck, and a guest laundry room on the lower deck. The Sun Deck is outfitted with lounge chairs and shaded seating.

DINING OPTIONS Buffet breakfast and lunch and a multiple-course dinner are all served in an open seating format in the main restaurant.

POOL, FITNESS, SPA, BIKES This ship boasts a fitness room with cardio equipment and a spa treatment room. There are also bikes on board. The *River Queen* does not have a pool.

River Baroness & River Ambassador
The Verdict
These smaller sister ships, dating back to the 90s, make up for in look and style what they lack in size.

Specifications

Passengers	116	Total cabins/balcony cabins	58/30
Passenger decks	2	Crew	43
Year entered service			
River Baroness	1997	*River Ambassador*	1993

THE SHIP IN GENERAL The further back we go in terms of when Uniworld ships were built, the more we see just how much serious investments in overhauling interiors can serve to make the vessels' age irrelevant. Beautifully updated staterooms and public spaces aside, art lovers will revel in all the art lining the hallways and common areas in these two vessels.

CABINS There's no two ways about it, these cabins are tight. All of the staterooms on these two vessels are a cozy 128-square-feet each and the four Suites are 256-square-feet each. My how times—and cabin sizes—have changed. They still have marble bathrooms and Savoir beds and all of the Uniworld design flare, but trying to get around the bed at the same time as your travel companion may require some negotiation.

PUBLIC AREAS   River cruise lines kept it simple 20 years ago—a main restaurant, a bar and lounge, a reception, a library, a fitness room and a Sun Deck. But all the fun design details—the art gallery-esque hallways, the eclectic furniture, and the multicolored rooms—keep things fresh.

DINING OPTIONS   All meals, including the buffet breakfast and lunch, and the nightly full-service dinner, are served in the main restaurant on the lower deck (which is actually not as dark as you would think a lower deck restaurant might be—thanks to plenty of windows and light and bright dining room accents).

POOL, FITNESS, SPA, BIKES   There's a fitness center—nothing huge, just a couple cardio machines and a window to watch the passing scenery through—and bikes on board available for passengers to use. There is no pool or spa on these two ships.

Queen Isabel

The Verdict

This Douro River vessel brings some of Uniworld's flare, but with a more modern twist, to Portugal.

Specifications

Passengers	118	Total cabins/balcony cabins	59/44
Passenger decks	3	Crew	33
Year entered service	2013		

THE SHIP IN GENERAL   The vast majority of vessels on Portugal's Douro River are built by the local shipbuilding magnate, Porto-based DouroAzul. DouroAzul retains ownership of the vessels and charters them out to different river cruise lines. Fortunately for Uniworld, AmaWaterways and Viking (a few of the lines that work with DouroAzul), the company's founder and CEO, Mario Ferreira, couldn't be a more charming fellow and is perfectly willing to build the ships according to each individual river cruise company's specifications and overall design aesthetic. In the case of Uniworld, that meant bringing some of that classic Uniworld glamour to the Douro, but perhaps with a slightly different interpretation. So, there are marble bathrooms but not the gleaming white and grey marble that Uniworld incorporates into its other vessels—instead it's beige and emerald-green marble on the *Queen Isabel*. There is also a strong emphasis on the outdoor areas on this vessel, such as the pool on the Sun Deck, which is on the larger side for river cruise ship pools, is lined with more lounge chairs and has wait service, giving it a much more resort experience feel.

CABINS   On the lower deck are 161-square-foot cabins with porthole windows. Cabins on the second deck are the same size, but with French balconies. And on the upper deck there are 18 junior suites at 215-square-feet each and two suites at 323-square-feet each. All the upper deck suites and junior suites feature full step-out balconies with a small table and chairs. The staterooms have the some of the standard Uniworld amenities, such as L'Occitane bath products and comfy slippers and robes. The suites and junior suites also have iPod speakers, a Nespresso coffee and tea unit come with daily fresh fruit service. You'll still see some of those classic Uniworld accents, like floral-patterned carpets, ornate wallpaper and plush headboards, but in more delicate and muted tones of brown, beige and light blue.

PUBLIC AREAS The public areas include the Sun Deck (the heart of a lot of the action during the warmer months), which has a decent-sized wading pool as well as lounge chairs for sun bathing and shaded seating for those who would prefer to avoid the rays. On the upper deck, there is the reception area, and the bar and lounge, which also has an outdoor lounge area where drinks are served. One deck down is a 24-hour coffee and tea station and the restaurant, which has both indoor and some outdoor seating. A fitness center and the Serenity River Spa are located on the lower deck. All the public areas have a certain pizzazz but not the same level of pizzazz as other Uniworld ships.

DINING OPTIONS A breakfast and lunch buffet, with hot and cold items, is served in the restaurant as is a sit-down dinner. And don't forget to try the port wine after dinner. Just as on Uniworld-owned vessels, food and wine on the *Queen Isabel* are of a high quality, with an emphasis on local products, such as Portuguese wines, cheeses, fish (especially cod) and seafood.

POOL, FITNESS, SPA, BIKES There's a gym, spa and a pool, as well as bike on board.

River Victoria
The Verdict
Uniworld did what it could to transform what would otherwise be a pretty stark, unimaginative Russian vessel into a very Uniworld-esque river cruise ship and the results are impressive.

Specifications

Passengers	202	Total cabins/balcony cabins	101/72
Passenger decks	4	Crew	110
Year entered service	1982		

THE SHIP IN GENERAL In May 2011, Uniworld re-launched this older Russian riverboat after the design team from its sister company Red Carnation Hotels went in, stripped it down and worked its magic. The cabin sizes were increased, an elevator was added and all the public areas were given the Uniworld touch—bold-patterned carpets, faux-vintage furniture, floral arrangements and art accents. The fact that Uniworld is no stranger to major refurbs shows in how well it was able to transform the spaces to make them feel, well, not of a Communist-era aesthetic, ultimately making the *River Victoria* a lovely vehicle for visiting the people and sights along the fascinating Volga.

CABINS On the two lower decks, passengers can squeeze into the 135-square-foot and 161-square-foot cabins, or they can opt for a bit more space on the third and fourth decks, home to 210-square-foot balcony cabins,

269-square-foot Deluxe Suites, 334-square-foot Junior Suites and 409-square-foot Presidential Suites. Don't expect marble bathrooms, but there will still be nice bedding and towels and pleasing design details. Staterooms also have flatscreen TVs with movies and satellite channels, hair dryers, safes, thermostats, bottled water, and those coveted L'Occitane products.

PUBLIC AREAS   The lounge is actually located on part of the Sun Deck (kind of cool and different—why not? The views are always best from high up). There is a bar one deck below and the main restaurant one deck below that. The reception, a library, boutique, coffee and tea station and Internet corner are located on the second deck. And there is a fitness center and spa on the lower deck—it may feel a bit claustrophobic down here in the basement but for those who want to get in some cardio or a massage in, they do the trick.

DINING OPTIONS   As with all Uniworld cruises, every meal is provided in the restaurant. Breakfast and lunch are served up as choose-your-own buffet offerings and dinner is a sit-down service. Don't expect the same high quality of food and service as on the Uniworld vessels in the rest of Europe.

POOL, FITNESS, SPA, BIKES   There's a gym and a River Serenity Spa with massage and body treatments.

River Tosca

The Verdict

Uniworld is the only major river cruise line that has its own vessel in Egypt, the advantage for Uniworld being that it has total control of the ship's style, features and in training its crew.

Specifications

Passengers	82	Total cabins/balcony cabins	41/41
Passenger decks	3	Crew	60
Year entered service	2009		

THE SHIP IN GENERAL   A true gem on the Nile, the *River Tosca* is among the most luxurious vessels plying Egypt's iconic river. From the all-balcony cabins to the public spaces outfitted with rich wood and marble finishings that combine Middle Eastern details with Western creature comforts, the *Tosca* creates a very welcoming environment to come back to after long, hot days visiting ancient temples. The pool area, with its covered cabanas, has a particularly resort-y vibe that makes it a great place for some post-temple-touring relaxation.

CABINS   There are three categories of suites on the *River Tosca* and all of them feature a French balcony, custom-made beds, a hair dryer, safe, individual thermostat, iPod docking station, flatscreen TV with satellite channels, and bathrooms with a bathtub and shower.

PUBLIC AREAS   The Sun Deck, with its swimming pool area and covered cabanas, is a great place for relaxing to Nile River views, but if it's too hot up here in the shade, passengers can chill in the main lounge on the second deck.

There is also a massage room, gym, library and boutique. The restaurant is located on the lower deck.

DINING OPTIONS   Passengers will head down to the lower deck restaurant for all their meals. Breakfast and lunch are offered as a buffet and include Egyptian standards such as the popular bean spread known as *foul* as well as plenty of Western cuisine. Dinner is served and is a bit more formal with menus that detail the options for the three courses (apps, entrees and desserts). There are also some fun, themed dinner events such as the *galabeyya* party where both men and women are encouraged to wear the traditional longer dress-like clothing donned by Egyptians.

POOL, FITNESS, SPA, BIKES   There's a decent dipping pool on the Sun Deck, as well as a gym and spa on board.

River Orchid
The Verdict

For the *River Orchid* Uniworld partnered with Pandaw River Expeditions, which built this ship for Uniworld to charter on the Mekong River. The result is classic Pandaw construction with some Uniworld touches.

Specifications

Passengers	58	Total cabins/balcony cabins	29/0
Passenger decks	2	Crew	28
Year entered service	2013		

THE SHIP IN GENERAL   This classic Mekong vessel has all the makings of a Pandaw ship—the wrap-around common promenade, the strong reliance on wood details and construction—but with subtle Uniworld touches like fancy window dressings, and delicate floral arrangements throughout.

CABINS   Staterooms are all 170-square-feet (save for the two slightly larger suites) with high quality beds, individually controlled air-conditioning, bottled water, bathrooms with standing showers, robes and slippers, and a hair dryer. The staterooms aren't anywhere near as ornate as Uniworld's European river ships, and might be considered a bit of a downgrade by some (despite every effort by Uniworld to enhance with textured throws, cushions, window treatments and headboards).

PUBLIC AREAS   The Sun Deck has a much-used covered bar area. On board are also a reception area, a restaurant, a lecture and movie room and a massage room.

DINING OPTIONS   Meals are served in the restaurant where passengers will find Southeast Asian specialties along with international standards. Breakfast and lunch are served as a buffet and dinner is a seated meal with menus and options to choose from.

POOL, FITNESS, SPA, BIKES   There's a spa room on the lower deck for various massage treatments.

TAUCK

www.tauck.com. ✆ 800/788-7885.

Pros

o **Lofted lower decks.** For its newest class of vessels, Tauck created lofted lower-deck staterooms with high ceilings and a raised seating area that are a welcome departure from their smaller, darker, porthole-windowed predecessors.

o **Unique on-shore outings.** Tauck usually hosts at least one or two unique outings shore-side during each cruise, so passengers might find themselves having a candlelit dinner in an ancient chateaux or being treated to a surprise musical performance in a museum.

o **Great service.** Taking a river cruise with Tauck is not necessarily going to be easy on the wallet, but you can expect that every single detail will be arranged to a tee.

Cons

o **Pricey.** If you like the idea of having that very exclusive Tauck experience, be prepared to shell out for it.

o **Small fleet.** As of 2016, Tauck's fleet consisted of nine vessels, which means the company only sails on the most traditional river routes in Europe (Danube, Rhine, Rhone and Seine), and space is limited.

THE LINE IN A NUTSHELL The Tauck model seems to be, "Yes, we're expensive, but we'll make it worth it." In other words, if you're willing to pay to play, Tauck will absolutely deliver on a luxury river cruise experience.

Frommer's Ratings (Scale of 1–5)

Cabin comfort & amenities	5	Public spaces	4
Decor	4	Dining	5
Fitness, spa and pool	4	Service	5
Family-friendly	5	Enrichment	5

THE EXPERIENCE Tauck is truly a full-service river cruise and land operator at the highest end of the river cruising spectrum (where it shares company with Uniworld and Scenic). Nothing is skimped on, from the food and wine to the tours and included extras. This is the river cruise experience for those who don't want to worry about a thing. A Tauck river cruise would also make for a great special occasion trip, like an anniversary or family reunion, because of the high level of service.

Tauck's secret weapon? Well, it certainly doesn't hurt that the company has 90 years of experience in

> ### Trivia Fact
>
> Tauck likes to surprise its guests with *lagniappes*. The word is taken from the French spoken in Louisiana and it means something given as a little bonus or extra. The company tries to incorporate at least one lagniappe into all of its tours and river cruises. So don't be surprised (or do) when some little souvenir or token of appreciation shows up randomly.

guided tours. And it shows in how meticulously it executes on the daily land excursions. Tauck's operations team must search far and wide, scouring the European countryside for the awesome venues it contracts with for on-shore events, from candle-lit wine caves to ancient castles and mansions.

If you're more of a do-it-yourself traveler, there may be a bit too much hand holding in the Tauck experience for you. But if you like the idea of disconnecting and relaxing, only needing to know where to be, at what time and in what attire, safe in the knowledge that whatever awaits will not disappoint, Tauck is certainly an option to look into.

THE FLEET   When Tauck got into the river cruise game a decade ago, right out of the gates the company knew it wanted to put an emphasis on quality not quantity, a concept that began with its Jewel Class of vessels, which were built to carry fewer passengers per square foot than competing lines, in order to allow for larger stateroom space and more hands-on service.

Tauck vessels are all decorated in a modern and tastefully elegant style. Think subtle and soothing hues of browns and tans, accented by delicate details, reminiscent of a slightly toned down Ritz-Carlton.

The company has two classes of river cruise vessels. The Treasure, Swiss Emerald, Swiss Jewel, Swiss Sapphire and the Esprit make up Tauck's **Jewel class,** each measuring 361 feet in length and carrying up to 118 passengers. And in 2014, Tauck introduced its **Inspiration class** of ships, vessels that measure 443 feet in length and carry up to 130 passengers. They include the Inspire and Savor, which in 2016 were joined by the Grace and Joy. While they are 23 percent longer than the Jewel class of vessels, they only accommodate 10 percent more passengers, with Tauck having opted to instead use the additional space for more suites and for the innovative lofted lower deck cabins the company conjured up.

PASSENGER PROFILE   Tauck's river cruise customers tend to be culturally curious, English-speaking travelers. They are primarily from North America, but there are also some Brits and Aussies that come on board. They are generally in the 50-to-70 age range, are active, and enjoy socializing with others. They definitely like the fact that Tauck curates their travel for them.

DINING OPTIONS   Tauck's riverboats have one main dining room and a more casual alternative dining venue at the aft of its vessels. But Tauck is also committed to getting its passengers off the ships for one or two meals during each sailing. And when it does, the venue tends to be something more unique than a typical tourist-trap restaurant. Tauck will often find settings, such as a historic mansion or castle, in which to host these surprise seatings. Of note, Tauck's prices include most alcoholic and nonalcoholic beverages on board, save for premium and top-shelf alcohol. Whether on or off the ship, you can expect the quality of food to compete with the other high-end river cruise lines and is often among the several "wow" factors of the cruise. Here too, Tauck does not skimp and your taste buds will not be disappointed (your waistline, now that's a different story).

ACTIVITIES   Tauck is very much about getting its passengers off the ship to experience more of the destinations it sails to and through. Which means there often isn't much time spent on board. When there is, a relevant presentation might be given about the language, culture or cuisine of the region.

CHILDREN'S PROGRAM   Tauck introduced family-friendly river cruises under its family brand, Tauck Bridges, in 2008. Currently, Tauck offers three family itineraries on the Rhone, Rhine and Danube rivers. The company has seen so much demand for these river cruises that it will be doubling the number of family-friendly departures it offers to 20 in 2017, up from 10 in 2016. In order to better accommodate families on board, the suites on Tauck's riverboats have pull-out sofas that allow for three or four people to stay in one stateroom. Activities on the family river cruises include kid-friendly adventures such as a scavenger hunt in the Louvre in Paris, guided cycling in Austria, and interactive cooking demonstrations. The company does not recommend its Tauck Bridges program for children ages 3 and younger.

ENTERTAINMENT   Again, Tauck is all about providing that balance of on- and off-ship experiences, and that goes for entertainment as well. Like other river cruise lines, Tauck will bring local talent onto the vessels for various live performance on board, but also treats its guests to concerts and live shows onshore.

SERVICE   A high-end product means high-touch service. Not only does Tauck celebrate customer's special events such as birthdays and wedding anniversaries (as do most river cruise lines—in fact, sometimes it's comical how many birthday and anniversary celebrations there will be on a single sailing, regardless of the river cruise line), but the company will often throw in additional gifts, such as local souvenirs, for guests to bring home with them. The company is very tuned in to both the little and big things that make travelers feel special, and that's a level of service it takes a truly experienced company to provide. Gratuities are included in Tauck's prices. Tauck also has a Tauck Director and three Tauck Cruise Directors—as opposed to just one cruise director, which is standard on other river cruise lines—on board all its river departures to assist passengers at all times. A Tauck Director is what Tauck calls its tour directors. On its river cruise ships, this person serves as an additional point of contact and resource and will be with the groups both on and off the ship (whereas cruise directors usually stay on). They add another level of customer service and of simply helping everything to go smoothly.

TOURS   Remember, Tauck is one of those river cruise lines that was a tour operator long before it was a river cruise line, so you can not only expect that there will be at least one or two tours offered each day, but that they will be well executed ones. Because of its long-standing tour operating business, Tauck also has an extensive rolodex of local tour guides that it works with throughout Europe who are vetted by and contracted directly with Tauck, so you can expect the local guides for the daily tours to be of a really good quality (they will have excellent English skills, loads of experience and insights),

TAUCK ITINERARIES

9-day Rhone ("French Waterways"), with 7-day cruise, round-trip from Lyon, $4,490, balconies from $4,890, Apr–Oct

9-day Rhone ("A Taste of France"), with 7-day cruise, Paris to Lyon, $5,590, balconies from $5,990, May–Oct

13-day Rhone and Saone ("French Escapade: Monte-Carlo to Paris"), with 9-day cruise, Monte Carlo to Paris, $5,990, balconies from $6,390, Apr–Oct

9-day Seine ("Rendezvous on the Seine"), with 7-day cruise, round-trip from Paris, $4,290, balconies from $4,690, Apr–Oct

13-day Seine ("Cruising the Seine, plus Versailles, Paris & London"), with 9-day cruise, round-trip from Paris, $6,490, balconies from $6,890, Apr–Oct

22-day Seine, Rhone and Saone ("Belle Epoch: London to Monte-Carlo"), with 18-day cruise, London to Monte Carlo, $11,990, balconies from $12,790, Apr–Sept

12-day Rhine and Moselle ("The Rhine and Moselle"), with 11-day cruise, Amsterdam to Basel, $4,890, balconies from $5,440, Apr–Oct

9-day Rhine ("The Rhine, Swiss Alps & Amsterdam"), with 7-day cruise, Amsterdam to Basel, $4,690, balconies from $5,090, Apr–Oct

7-day Rhine ("The Romantic Rhine: Amsterdam to Basel"), Amsterdam to Basel, $3,590, balconies from $3,990, Apr–Oct

11-day Danube ("The Blue Danube"), with 7-day cruise, Regensburg (Germany) to Budapest, $4,490, balconies from $4,890, Apr–Oct

11-day Danube ("Musical Magic Along the Blue Danube"), with 7-day cruise, Budapest to Regensburg (Germany), $5,690, balconies from $6,090, June–Oct

11-day Danube ("Danube Reflections"), Vienna to Regensburg (Germany), with 7-day cruise, $4,690, balconies from $5,090, May–Sept

14-day Rhine, Main and Danube ("Amsterdam to Budapest by Riverboat"), Amsterdam to Budapest, $5,690, balconies from $6,340, Apr–Oct

7-day Belgian and Dutch Canals ("Belgium & Holland in Spring"), Brussels to Amsterdam, $2,890, balconies from $3,345, Apr

11-day Danube ("Budapest to the Black Sea"), with 7-day cruise, Budapest to Cernavoda (Romania), $4,890, balconies from $5,290, May–Aug

23-day Rhine, Main and Danube ("Grand European Cruise"), with 22-day cruise, Amsterdam to Cernavoda (Romania), $10,090, balconies from $11,140, May–Aug

7-day Danube ("Blue Danube: Family Riverboat Adventure"), Budapest to Regensburg (Germany), $3,690, balconies from $4,090, July

9-day Rhone ("Bon Voyage! France Family River Cruise"), with 7-day cruise, Paris to Lyon, $4,690, balconies from $5,090, June–July

7-day Rhine ("Castles on the Rhine: Family Riverboat Adventure"), Basel to Amsterdam, $3,790, balconies from $4,190, June–July

---

Note on this chart: Itineraries may also be available in the reverse direction. The first price is the lowest available price for all cabin categories, and the second price is the lowest balcony price, including French balcony cabins.

as opposed to the catch-as-catch-can guides that some of the other river cruise lines rely on. Daily excursions usually consist of either one half-day tour, two half-day tours before and after lunch, or a full-day excursion. So you can expect a mix of being on the move as well as some time to relax on board during morning or afternoon sailings. Either way, Tauck will always have something in store for its passengers—and it likely won't just be the same stereotypical landmark all river cruise lines will stop at on a given route. Tauck is very good at pushing the touring envelope and adding unique and unexpected sights and experiences to its itineraries.

PRE- & POST-CRUISE STAYS While Tauck doesn't offer standard 2- and 3-day pre- and post-river cruise trip stays like some river cruise lines do, the company does have a massive roster of land tours and small-ship cruises (Tauck also offers sailings on the Le Boreal yacht ships on the Mediterranean and Baltic seas for instance) that customers can combine with their European river cruise. Also, look through the itineraries carefully because many of them already include a pre- or post-cruise stay, such as in Paris or in Monte Carlo on France sailings.

Jewel Class

The Verdict

This first generation of Tauck vessels has ample roomy suites and staterooms and the same level of style and service as their next-gen successors.

Specifications

Passengers	118	Total cabins/balcony cabins	59/50
Passenger decks	3	Crew	40
Year entered service			
Swiss Emerald	2006	Treasures	2011
Swiss Sapphire	2008	Esprit	2015
Swiss Jewel	2009		

THE SHIPS IN GENERAL Tauck's Jewel class of vessels paved the way for Tauck's model of hosting fewer passengers on board, having larger state-rooms and more suites, and putting an emphasis on service. Don't be turned off by the fact that most of them are a bit older than the newer Inspiration class ships. They are adequately updated each year (and are about to get a *major* overhaul) and for those who like the idea of being on one of the more intimate ships on the rivers—these vessels have only 118 passengers when many if not most other river cruise vessels host around 140 passengers or more—then the Jewel ships are where it's at. Added bonus: By 2018, the Jewel class of vessels will be totally reconfigured, with Tauck currently investing to replace the 30 cabins on the second passenger deck (Ruby Deck) that measure 150-square-feet each with 20 cabins measuring 225-square-feet each, which will result in the number of passengers being reduced to 98.

CABINS Currently, the Jewel-class ships have 14 Suites that are 300-square-feet each (with a pull-out sofa that allows for up to four-guest capacity), and the remaining staterooms range from between 150- and 183-square-feet. But as you have read above, that is about to change. All of the staterooms are outside facing and 85 percent (those on the two upper stateroom decks) have French balconies with sliding glass doors.

PUBLIC AREAS The public spaces include a main dining room with panoramic windows, a casual dining venue at the aft of the vessel, a bar and lounge, and a sun deck with a Jacuzzi, putting green and additional seating and lounge chairs. There is also an elevator that operates between the second and third deck (no access to the first or Sun Deck), and a small boutique.

DINING OPTIONS Three meals a day are served in the main dining room (except for when there is an on-shore meal offered) on the second deck, where passengers can go for tempting buffet breakfasts and lunches, as well as sophisticated, wait-service, multicourse dinners. When looking for a lighter, more casual option, there is a less formal venue at the aft of the vessels. That venue too will see some upgrades. Over the next 2 years, the ships' second dining venue, now called The Bistro, will receive its own dedicated kitchen and chef, an expanded menu and will be renamed Arthur's, a tribute to company founder Arthur Tauck Sr.

Breaking News

As Tauck converts all its Jewel class ships to have larger staterooms and a proper second dining venue, which will happen in two waves—one for the 2017 season, and the second for 2018, it is doing away with its distinction between the two classes of vessels. Once those transformations are complete, Tauck will instead refer to its ships collectively as the **Tauck Destination Fleet.**

POOL, FITNESS, SPA, BIKES Tauck's Jewel-class ships feature a Jacuzzi, fitness room, putting green, and bikes on board. Massage services are also available.

Inspiration Class
The Verdict

The newest generation of Tauck vessels are an amped up version of their Jewel-class predecessors, with more suites and hard-to-resist lofted lower deck staterooms (with higher ceilings and a raised seating area).

Specifications

Passengers	130	Total cabins/balcony cabins	67/53
Passenger decks	3	Crew	43
Year entered service			
Savor, Inspire	2014	Grace, Joy	2016

THE SHIPS IN GENERAL Tauck exclusively charters its river cruise ships from a Swiss company Scylla, and for the inspiration class of ships, the two companies put their minds together to try to resolve a dilemma in the river cruise industry. Most ships sell from the top down, meaning the most expensive, largest suites and staterooms sell first. The smaller, lower-deck cabins, with just porthole windows (aka no balconies) are a tougher sell. Thus, they came up with the lofted lower-deck concept, lower deck staterooms that by borrowing square footage from the deck above are able to feature high ceilings, two-deck-high windows (that crack open) and a raised seating area. Most lower decks cabins don't have any seating area, let alone a seating area with a decent view, so with this move, Tauck completely transformed the lower deck experience, bringing in more light, more space and unique high ceilings to the once cramped and dark quarters of the cabins down below. And to compliment those, Tauck added some solo-passenger cabins on the lower deck as well. While they were at it with enhancements, they also added a spa, massage room and hair salon, and an elevator that goes all the way down to the lowest deck (features that don't exist on the Jewel class vessels).

CABINS   On the top deck of the Inspiration vessels there are 22 Suites that are 300-square-feet each (with a pull-out sofa that allows for an up to four-guest capacity). The eight, lofted lower-deck staterooms, along with two other categories of staterooms are 225-square-feet each. We can't recommend the lofted lower deck cabins enough though. They seriously are a super fun change of pace, especially for lower-deck cabins. The high ceilings and soaring windows alone make them stand apart from anything else on the rivers. Granted the beds end up being in the "lower" portion of the loft, with the seating area in the "raised" part of the loft, which can make the bedroom area feel a bit dark and removed from the window and the scenery, so for many people the second and third deck cabins will still be the preferred choice. But for once it's not a total bummer to be on the lower deck. And the remaining cabins are either 150- or 190-square-feet each.

PUBLIC AREAS   The public spaces include the classy and understated main dining room (think white tablecloths, crystal chandeliers and cushioned seating in muted tones) as well as an alternative, casual-dining venue named Arthur's (after the company's founder) at the aft of the vessel. There is also the bar and lounge, which has a sort of country club lounge feel, both upscale and causal all at once. The sun deck is home to a Jacuzzi and putting green. And on the lower deck, there is a fitness room, two spa and massage treatment rooms and a hair salon. The elevator operates between the first and third deck (no access to the Sun Deck), and there is also a small boutique on board.

DINING OPTIONS   Onboard meals are served either in the main dining room or at Arthur's for lighter fare. You can expect buffet breakfasts and lunches that offer Western standards like omelets and salads alongside local specialties. Dinner is a single-seating, wait-service meal with multiple courses and choices.

POOL, FITNESS, SPA, BIKES   Tauck's Inspiration-class ships feature a Jacuzzi, fitness room, putting green, and bikes on board. The fitness room isn't huge but has about four cardio machines (generally two treadmills and two exercise bikes), weights, yoga mats and an exercise ball. If you want to sweat off those hard-to-resist dinners, there is no excuse not to. There are spa and massage treatment rooms as well as a hair salon.

THE MAIN RIVER CRUISE LINES

SCENIC

www.scenicusa.com. ℂ 855/517-1200.

Pros

o **High tech.** Scenic has really pushed the envelope in terms of river cruise-enhancing technologies. They hand out custom-made GPS devices to passengers for wireless touring and have a very high tech in-room entertainment system, too.

o **All-inclusive.** With Scenic's all-inclusive pricing model, you really don't need to spend much beyond the cruise price and airfare. Rates include all meals, complimentary drinks all day, all shore excursions, complimentary e-bikes, all gratuities, and all transfers to and from the ship.

Cons

o **Stiff competition.** Scenic is going after a luxury space in river cruising where companies like Uniworld and Tauck already have a very strong foothold and reputation.

THE LINE IN A NUTSHELL   Despite arriving a smidge late to the river cruising party, Scenic is rapidly making a name for itself as a strong player at the high end of the market, with its all-inclusive pricing (meaning gratuities and alcoholic beverages, too), sleek ship interiors and high-tech enhancements.

Frommer's Ratings (Scale of 1–5)

Cabin comfort & amenities	5	Public spaces	4
Decor	5	Dining	5
Fitness, spa and pool	4	Service	5
Family-friendly	3	Enrichment	4

THE EXPERIENCE   One of Scenic's strongest selling points is to what lengths it has gone to ensure that there are plenty of options for dining, sightseeing and engaging both on board and off the vessels.

For one, since Scenic began operating river cruises in 2008, the company has had six dining options available to passengers on it vessels (more on that in the dining section below). Scenic also has a Free Choice excursion program, which means that in addition to the blockbuster sightseeing tours it offers in each major port call, there are usually one or two additional excursions on offer that might be a bit off the beaten path or might have a unique theme, such as the Szechenyi Thermal Bath in Budapest or shopping with a chef in central Vienna's open-air food market, Naschmarkt.

And as competition heats up on the rivers, Scenic is continuing to add service options, including butler service, which covers early-morning coffee and tea, shoeshine service and help with making on-shore arrangements such as private transportation or obtaining theater tickets (the butler thing is a bit gimmicky, but it definitely makes some passengers feel a little more special).

Then there is also the high-tech component to Scenic cruises, starting with the high-tech GPS devices that the company provides passengers in lieu of the wireless tour guide systems most other river cruise companies use. The Scenic version, which the company calls Scenic Tailormade, is a touch-screen device slightly larger and thicker than an average smartphone. From the device, passengers can access the traditional wireless tour guiding systems (which allows passengers to listen to their local guides via a wireless microphone and headset system), but they can also access a selection of self-guided city tours with information about various points of interest at each port call. And Scenic Tailormade also features a river guide, which includes a follow-along map of the river cruise and commentary about sights along the river—this last feature allows Scenic to bypass providing that commentary over the loud speaker on its ships, which can disturb passengers trying to rest, read or do other activities. Frankly, reaction to the devices can go two ways: Guests either love them or they get frustrated with them—ship staff definitely have to be prepared for the requisite handful of passengers who find the devices difficult to use.

Another technology-based feature is the entertainment system in the staterooms. In addition to the movies on demand, satellite TV and Internet access that most of river cruise lines' in-room systems have, Scenic's version has an Internet tracker that shows how strong the Wi-Fi signal is along the river (Wi-Fi signal strength can vary quite drastically along the rivers and can range from quite good in port to nonexistent during sailings—but it's getting better and more consistent each year thanks to investments and enhancements by river cruise lines like Scenic), plus fact sheets about each port call and the option for passengers to check their invoices.

THE FLEET   Scenic's vessels have a very sleek and modern look and feel to them, even more so than most other river cruise ships. The branding is very clean (the Scenic logo is black with a gold or white trim) as are the interiors, which are grounded in polished tones of black, white and grey. You can expect lots of marble details, glass and subtle and sophisticated lighting. Scenic ships remind us of the Loews hotel brand, chic and upscale without being even remotely fussy or too colorful.

In addition to having multiple dining venues, many of Scenic's newer vessels have a pool on the Sun Deck, fitness centers and spas. Scenic also carries electric-assist bicycles (also known as e-bikes, electric-assist bicycles provide the option to turn on an electric-powered motor that can help propel the bicycles up hills, for instance, or provide greater speed to the bicycles) on some of its ships to give increasingly popular cycling outings a little more oomph.

Another tech-driven amenity in Scenic's staterooms are the drop-down balcony windows. Similar to the systems in place on Uniworld vessels, Scenic has installed windows in the balcony suites and staterooms that can be lowered with the touch of a button to create a balcony. The result is an indoor/outdoor seating area that can be used in good weather and in bad.

Scenic has a 14-vessel fleet in Europe, including its two newest vessels, the 169-passenger *Scenic Amber* on the Rhine, Main and Danube, and the 96-passenger *Scenic Azure* on Portugal's Douro River. Scenic also launched two sister ships on the Mekong in 2016, the 68-passenger *Scenic Spirit* and *Scenic Zen,* as well as the 44-passenger *Scenic Aura* on Myanmar's Irrawaddy. Scenic is one of the only river cruise lines besides Viking currently offering sailings on Russia's Volga river on the 112-passenger *Scenic Tsar.*

PASSENGER PROFILE Scenic's bread-and-butter is the 55-plus crowd. Passengers tend to be well-traveled, well-educated, and financially well-off. They typically have already done some upscale ocean cruising prior to river cruising. This is a social bunch. They like to get to know the other passengers on board as well as the local citizens in the countries they are sailing in.

DINING OPTIONS As mentioned above, Scenic vessels all offer six dining options, so there is no shortage of variety. On each ship, there is Crystal Dining, the main dining room; either a Portobellos, an Italian-themed, or L'Amour, a French-themed specialty dining restaurant; Table La Rive, an invitation-only, six-course, wine-pairing dinner experience offered exclusively to passengers in the upper-deck Suites and second-deck Junior Suites; River Café, a casual cafe open from 6am to 6pm, offering a range of light meals (think mini sandwiches and small pre-prepared salads), snacks and beverages that guests can grab at their whim; Sun Deck Barbeque, a traditional barbeque (from burgers to seafood) served on the Sun Deck at least once per week, weather permitting; and 24/7 in-room dining. The variety makes for a more fun and dynamic onboard dining experience, and the food churned out at each venue is first-rate. It doesn't have the uber-gourmet feel of Uniworld dining, but is rather more contemporary-chic style dining, with each venue putting its own little twist on things (the River Café, for instance, is where to go for light and fresh tapas-style bites, whereas the Table La Rive is where the chef gets more experimental with a unique nightly tasting menu, including fun dishes like a lemongrass crème brûlée appetizer). Dining on board is more casual and social, less fussy and forced. And while you'll likely see plenty of European woven throughout the menus, Scenic doesn't shy away from incorporating other international influences such as Asian cuisine and spices, into its meals.

ACTIVITIES Don't expect anything hokey or forced in terms of onboard activities. For one, Scenic provides its guests with tools for keeping engaged on their own while cruising, including the Scenic Tailormade GPS device it hands out to all its passengers, which in addition to serving as a listening device during guided shore excursions has commentary available for sights along the rivers so that passengers can relax and follow along on their headsets—kind of like an audio tour at a museum. When and where it makes sense to do so, Scenic will also bring a relevant lecturer on board or offer an interactive demonstration such as a wine or food tasting.

SCENIC ITINERARIES

14-day Rhine, Main and Danube ("Jewels of Europe"), Amsterdam to Budapest, $4,595, balconies from $6,390, Mar–Oct

20-day Rhine, Main and Danube ("Jewels of Europe with Paris & Prague"), with 14-day cruise, Paris to Prague, $7,710, balconies from $9,505, Mar–Oct

7-day Upper Danube ("Gems of the Danube"), Nuremburg (Germany) to Budapest, $3,150, balconies from $4,045, May–Oct

7-day Upper Danube ("Iconic Danube") Munich/Passau (Germany) to Budapest, from $2,795, balconies from $3,690, April

14-day Rhine and Moselle ("Romantic Rhine & Moselle"), Basel to Amsterdam, from $4,795, balconies from $6,590, Mar–Oct

18-day Rhine and Moselle ("Romantic Rhine & Moselle with Switzerland"), with 14-day cruise, Amsterdam to Zurich, $8,065, balconies from $9,860, Apr–Sept

7-day Rhine ("Rhine Highlights"), Basel to Amsterdam, $2,995, balconies from $3,890, Apr–Oct

11-day Rhine ("Rhine Highlights with Switzerland"), with 7-day cruise, Zurich to Amsterdam, $5,265, balconies from $6,160, May–Sept

8-day Dutch and Belgian Canals ("Dutch Sights & Belgian Delights"), round-trip from Amsterdam, from $2,435, balconies from $3,330, Apr–May

22-day Rhine, Main and Danube ("North Sea to the Black Sea"), Amsterdam to Bucharest, from $9,410, balconies from $12,100, Apr–June

29-day Rhine, Main and Danube ("North Sea to the Black Sea with Gallipoli"), with 21-day cruise, Amsterdam to Istanbul, $12,495, balconies from $15,185, Apr–June

10-day Lower Danube ("Black Sea Explorer"), with 7-day cruise, Budapest to Bucharest, from $3,940, balconies from $4,835, Apr–June

17-day Lower Danube ("Black Sea Explorer with Gallipoli"), with 7-day cruise, Budapest to Istanbul, $7,025, balconies from $7,920, Apr–June

15-day Danube ("Danube Delta Discovery"), Vienna to Bucharest, from $5,850, balconies from $7,645, Apr

13-day Rhone and Saone ("Spectacular South of France"), Paris to Nice, from $6,425, balconies from $7,870, Apr–Oct

18-day Rhone and Saone ("Spectacular South of France with Barcelona"), with 12-day cruise, Paris to Barcelona, $10,270, balconies from $11,715, Apr–Sept

8-day Rhone and Saone ("Enchanting Rhone"), Paris to Marseille, from $3,535, balconies from $4,445, Apr–Sept

CHILDREN'S PROGRAM   Scenic does not encourage children under the age of 12 on board its vessels and does not offer any specific programs geared towards kids.

ENTERTAINMENT   In addition to the nightly music in the lounge, Scenic will bring additional musical and dance groups on board during the cruise to showcase the local culture. That could be a boisterous oompah band in Germany or folk dancers in Hungary. Scenic also offers onshore entertainment in

13-day Rhone and Saone ("Enchanting Rhone with Paris and Monte Carlo"), with 7-day cruise, Paris to Monte Carlo, $7,365, balconies from $8,275, May–Sept

10-day Seine ("Gems of the Seine"), round-trip from Paris, $5,180, balconies from $6,490, Apr–Oct

22-day Seine, Rhone and Saone ("Gems of the Seine & South of France"), Paris to Nice, from $11,510, balconies from $14,265, July, Sept

11-day Gironne and Garonde ("Breathtaking Bordeaux"), Bordeaux to Bordeaux, from $5,250, balconies from $6,560, Apr–Oct

20-day Seine, Dordogne and Garonne ("Gems of the Seine & Breathtaking Bordeaux"), Paris to Bordeaux, from $10,285, balconies from $12,905, Apr–Sept

10-day Douro ("Unforgettable Douro"), round-trip from Porto, from $4,945, balconies from $6,540, Oct

16-day Douro ("Unforgettable Douro with Lisbon & Madrid"), with 10-day cruise, Lisbon to Madrid, $7,565, balconies from $9,160, May–Sept

14-day Volga ("Jewels of Russia"), St. Petersburg to Moscow, from $6,395, balconies from $8,190, June–July

7-day Mekong ("Luxury Mekong River Cruise"), Siem Reap to Ho Chi Minh, cabins/balconies from $2,195, year-round

11-day Mekong ("Essence of Vietnam"), Hanoi to Ho Chi Minh, cabins/balconies from $4,795, year-round

16-day Mekong ("Gems of South East Asia"), with 7-day cruise, Bangkok to Ho Chi Minh, cabins/balconies from $7,835, year-round

17-day Mekong ("Journey along the Mekong"), with 7-day cruise, Ho Chi Minh to Luang Prabang, cabins/balconies from $8,275, year-round

26-day Mekong ("Grand Indochina and Luxury Mekong River Cruise"), Hanoi to Luang Prabang, cabins/balconies from $11,170, year-round

10-day Irrawaddy ("Luxury Irrawaddy"), Yangon to Mandalay, cabins/balconies from $4,845, Oct–Dec

13-day Irrawaddy ("Mystical Irrawaddy"), Yangon to Mandalay, cabins/balconies from $7,195, Oct–Dec

17-day Irrawaddy ("Mystical Myanmar"), Yangon to Yangon, cabins/balconies from $9,200, Oct–Apr

Note on this chart: Itineraries may also be available in the reverse direction. The first price is the lowest available price for all cabin categories, and the second price is the lowest balcony price, including French balcony cabins.

cities where that is popular or where it is available. For instance, in Vienna, passengers may take in a classical music concert in a beautiful Viennese palace. Vienna is, after all, the City of Music.

SERVICE   With its new butler service (which is included for all guests), Scenic has kicked its service standard up a notch to white-glove level. But don't expect the butler to be at your beck and call 24/7. The butlers have other duties on board the vessel, so they are there to help fulfill some personal requests such as laundry service, but for everything else you will still need to get assistance from the very helpful reception staff. All tips and gratuities are included in Scenic's pricing.

TOURS   Thanks to Scenic's Free Choice excursion program, passengers can choose between more traditional overview tours, as well as more quirky, off-the-beaten path excursions, all of which are enhanced by the high-tech headsets Scenic gives each of its guests. Not only do they serve as a wireless touring device, which allows tour guides to speak into a microphone as tour-goers listen in, but there is also a self-guided touring option that provides information about popular landmarks in the various cities and towns on the itinerary. So if you're not into touring with the pack, you can go off and do your own thing but still access intriguing history and trivia about the destination.

PRE- & POST-CRUISE STAYS   As an off-shoot of a massive tour operator Scenic, not surprisingly, has plenty of pre- and post-cruise extension options. Unlike some other river cruise lines that price the extensions out separately, Scenic will often bundle the extension together with the cruise. So, for instance, Scenic's 11-day "Unforgettable Douro," a cruise along Portugal's Douro River from Porto and back, is priced from $5,320. With a 3-day Lisbon pre-cruise extension, it's priced from $5,890, and with both a pre-cruise Lisbon stay and a post-cruise extension in Madrid, the entire 17-day package is priced from $7,565. Similarly, its 8-day "Gems of the Danube" itinerary from Budapest to Nuremberg is priced from $3,400, or from $3,985 if you opt for the 3-day Prague extensions. Pre- and post-cruise options typically include accommodation, breakfast and at least one included sightseeing tour.

Scenic Jasper, Scenic Opal, Scenic Amber

The Verdict

These latest Scenic vessels are about as sleek as it gets. From the all-marble lobby, to the modern art and furniture, you'll feel like you're staying in a high-class boutique hotel.

Specifications

Passengers	169	Total cabins/balcony cabins	85/72
Passenger decks	3	Crew	53
Year entered service			
Scenic Amber	2016	Scenic Jasper, Scenic Opal	2015

THE SHIPS IN GENERAL   Scenic's newest vessels find that great balance of being luxurious without being overstated. It's luxury without flaunting it. At first glance, the clean lines and details simply make the ships look pristine. But upon closer inspection, you start to notice that there are actually some pretty pricey finishings all around, whether it's a lobby with floor-to-ceiling marble or mid-century modern dining chairs.

CABINS   All of the suites and staterooms on the upper two passenger decks feature what Scenic calls its "Sun Lounges," drop-down windows that allow passengers to convert an indoor balcony area into an open-air balcony, essentially a fancy quasi-French balcony, but it totally works. And Scenic has actually built a proper little balcony area into the rooms with faux hardwood floors that make them seem like a real, separate balcony (they have chairs and a little table and are separated from the rest of the room by a sheer curtain). Cabins also feature Apple TV monitors that are linked to a MiniMac computer, offering Wi-Fi access, individual temperature control, plush bedding, walk-in showers, L'Occitane products and a glass-front minibar fridge that is replenished daily. Staterooms include the 160-square-foot cabins on the lower deck with porthole windows, and Balcony Suites that are 205- or 225-square-feet each, and 240-square-foot Junior Suites. There is also a 360-square-foot Royal Balcony Suites with a separate seating area and a full-size bathtub, and 475-square-foot Royal One-Bedroom Suite (aka Panorama Suites) with a separate living area and full-sized bathtub as well.

PUBLIC AREAS   In addition to the main restaurant, these three vessels also have a Panorama Lounge and Bar, which houses the casual dining venue the River Café. In front of the lounge, at the bow of the vessels, is the Panorama Deck, an outdoor seating area with glass panes to shield from the wind. On the Sun Deck there are lounge chairs with umbrellas and canvas coverings, a walking track, and an over-sized chessboard. This is where the occasional barbeque lunch is served, as well. There is also a fitness room and wellness area, and the lobby and reception area, adjacent to which is the small gift shop. An elevator travels between the second and third deck.

DINING OPTIONS   The main meal service takes place in the Crystal Dining room, where buffet breakfast and lunch are served with a la carte items available for order, as well as full-service, sit-down dinners. A fun alternative is to head to Portobellos or L'Amour (each ship has one or the other) for a five-course Italian of French meal at the aft of the ship (with some great views). If you're lucky to have booked a suite or junior suite, you'll be invited to have a dinner at Table La Rive, an Executive Chef's table. It seats just 10 people (essentially a long table in the front of the main restaurant slightly sectioned off by a large floor-to-ceiling wine refrigerator), and offers a six-course degustation menu with paired wines. The communal table dining style of this experience also makes it a fun way to meet and mingle with other passengers. There's also the casual River Café in the lounge, open from 6am to 6pm for light snacks and meals, or the occasional Sun Deck barbeque. And if you're really feeling like "staying in" for a meal, there is round-the-clock room service, which is not an amenity offered by most river cruise ships.

POOL, FITNESS, SPA, BIKES   A small but adequate pool occupies the Sun Deck; there's also a fitness room with cardio and weight equipment; a spa, which offers up facials (ranging from 39€ for 30 minutes to 99€ for 90 minutes), massages (39 to 79€) and manicures (36€); and a hairdresser's room for cuts and styling. Scenic also carries electric-assist bikes, or e-bikes (see p. 102) on board for passengers to use along the route.

Scenic Crystal, Scenic Jewel, Scenic Jade, Scenic Gem

The Verdict

The predecessors to the *Scenic Jasper, Opal,* and *Amber,* these ships are still sleek, just not *as* sleek.

Specifications

Passengers			
Scenic Crystal, Scenic Jewel, Scenic Jade	169	*Scenic Gem*	128
Total cabins/balcony cabins			
Scenic Crystal, Scenic Jewel, Scenic Jade	85/72	*Scenic Gem*	64/57
Passenger decks	3		
Crew			
Scenic Crystal, Scenic Jewel, Scenic Jade	53	*Scenic Gem*	44
Year entered service			
Scenic Crystal	2012	*Scenic Jade and Scenic Gem*	2014
Scenic Jewel	2013		

THE SHIPS IN GENERAL   In terms of the staterooms, there are a lot of similarities between these and the suites and staterooms on Scenic's newest vessels. The accommodations have a really clean and contemporary feel, accented by luxury amenities like marble countertops and chic window treatments. The public areas are super light and open and modern. Scenic put a big emphasis on having large, floor-to-ceiling windows on these ships, which completely opens them up and showcases the passing scenery.

CABINS   These ships offer five categories of cabins: the Standard Suite (calling these lower-deck cabins a "suite" is just wrong—that word gets thrown around way too much in river cruising), which is 160-square-feet and has just a window, no balcony; the Private Balcony Suite, which is 205-square-feet; the Private Balcony Deluxe Suite, which is 225-square-feet; the Junior Balcony Suite, which is 250-square-feet; the Royal Balcony Suite, which is 315-square-feet (and has a separate seating and full-size bathtub); and the Royal Panorama Suite, which is 325-square-feet with a separate seating area and full-size tub as well. As is standard on Scenic ships, there's the Apple TV monitor with Internet and Wi-Fi, in-room movies, and stocked minibars. (On the *Scenic Gem,* all the cabin sizes are the same except for the two larger suite categories, which on the *Gem* are the 305-sq.-ft. Royal Balcony Suite and the 455-sq.-ft. Royal One-Bedroom Suite.)

PUBLIC AREAS   Starting from the top, there's the Sun Deck with the Riverview Terrace, an al fresco eating and sitting area, a walking track and various lounge chairs both exposed and shaded. One deck down is the Diamond Deck, where the lounge and bar are located, along with the River Café, the specialty dining restaurant and the outdoor lounge area at the bow of the ship. This is also home to the reception area and gift shop. An elevator travels between this deck and the one below it, which is the Sapphire Deck. The

Sapphire Deck is where Crystal Dining and Table La Rive are housed. And the lowest deck, Jewel Deck is where you'll find the fitness and wellness rooms.

DINING OPTIONS   As on all Scenic ships, you'll find the same six dining options—Crystal Dining (the main restaurant), Portabellos/L'Amour (specialty Italian or French), River Café (casual), Table La Rive (fancy and exclusive), Sun Deck barbeque (grilled lunch) and room service. While the venues may look and feel slightly different (they may have felt very modern a few years ago but they've already been shown up by the newer Star Ships), the concepts and the execution of the food are the same as on the Scenic Star Ships.

POOL, FITNESS, SPA, BIKES   There's a fitness room with cardio and weight equipment and a spa treatment room, and these vessels carry electric-assist bikes on board. Alas, these boats don't have pools.

Scenic Sapphire, Scenic Emerald, Scenic Diamond, Scenic Ruby, Scenic Pearl
The Verdict
Older vessels often get a bad rap, but before you rule any of these out simply due to age, you should know that Scenic invested nearly $10 million to completely gut renovate them in 2013.

Specifications

Passengers	167	Total cabins/balcony cabins	84/70
Passenger decks	3	Crew	53
Year entered service			
Scenic Sapphire, Scenic Emerald, Scenic Diamond	2008	*Scenic Pearl*	2011
Scenic Ruby	2009		

THE SHIPS IN GENERAL   These five vessels are where it all began for Scenic, when in 2007 the company laid down $100 million to start building its first river cruise ships and get in on the hot river action. The foundations were there and many of the amenities that were put in place remain today, including balcony suites, a spa and the main fine dining restaurant. But with the extensive gut renovations in 2013, the vessels were outfitted with the Scenic Sun Lounges, those fun drop-down windows that transform into a balcony, the casual River Cafe eatery and Table La Rive. And just about everything inside was stripped down and redone, including wallpaper, adding marble desks in the staterooms, marble to the bar area, updating furniture and carpeting, all of it. Around this time, Scenic also implemented an upgraded Wi-Fi system fleet-wide that uses both satellite and universal mobile technology to help amp up onboard Internet speed. It was a valiant and costly effort and the result is that these five ships don't show their age (as much).

CABINS   Staterooms range from the 160-square-foot lower deck cabins to the largest 315-square-foot upper deck suites. All staterooms (aka suites) on the second and third deck feature the Sun Lounges. You can expect the stocked minibar, the in-room entertainment system with movies, satellite TV and Internet/Wi-Fi, and L'Occitane products.

PUBLIC AREAS   The Sun Deck has a walking track and lounge areas. There is also a bar and lounge, the casual River Café, the specialty dining restaurant, and outdoor lounge area at the bow of the ship, a reception area and gift shop, the main dining room, and fitness and wellness rooms. An elevator travels between the second and third deck.

DINING OPTIONS   As on all Scenic ships, you'll find the same six dining options—Crystal Dining (the main restaurant), Portabellos/L'Amour (specialty Italian or French), River Café (casual), Table La Rive (fancy and exclusive), Sun Deck barbeque (grilled lunch) and room service. The venues are all done in Scenic's more contemporary style, but definitely don't reach the level of sophistication (in appearance) as the newer vessels' dining areas. However, you can expect food quality and variety to be on par with the rest of the fleet.

POOL, FITNESS, SPA, BIKES   There's a fitness room with cardio and weight equipment and a spa treatment room, and these vessels carry electric-assist bikes on board. There is no pool.

Scenic Azure
The Verdict

Launched on Portugal's Douro River in 2016, the *Scenic Azure* is a smaller but equally sexy version of the company's newest river cruise ships in Europe.

Specifications

Passengers	96	Total cabins/balcony cabins	48/42
Passenger decks	3	Crew	36
Year entered service	2016		

THE SHIP IN GENERAL   Ships on the Douro are smaller than ships on other rivers in Europe due to the constraints of the locks and bridges in Portugal. Thus with 96 passengers on board, the *Scenic Azure* will feel a bit more intimate than its counterparts in the rest of Europe. Despite the smaller size of the vessel, Scenic is still including many of its trademark amenities such as multiple dining venues and room service. The nice thing (or terrible thing if you're heat averse) about Portugal is that the summers get really balmy, which means the ample outdoor spaces on the *Scenic Azure,* such as the pool on the Sun Deck and the Riverview Terrace at the bow of the vessel, really come in handy because you will want to sit outside—it's too pleasant not to.

CABINS   Despite being a smaller vessel, the cabins are all actually slightly larger than on other Scenic vessels in Europe so you can spread out a bit more in your digs. There are four cabin categories on the *Scenic Azure:* the 172-square-foot Standard Suite, lower deck cabins with windows but no balcony; the 215-square-foot Private Balcony Suite, with a balcony; the 247-square-foot Junior Suite, with balcony; and the 420-square-foot Royal One-Bedroom Suite, with a living area, a balcony and a bathtub in the bathroom.

PUBLIC AREAS The *Scenic Azure* features a sun deck with a decent-sized pool area (as mentioned above, the pool comes in handy during Portugal's hot summers) and ample lounge chairs. One deck down is the bar and lounge area as well as some of the alternative dining venues. The reception and gift shop are here as well. Below that is the main dining room, and the spa and fitness rooms. There are no public spaces on the lowest passenger deck, just cabins. There is an elevator that travels between the three passenger decks.

DINING OPTIONS For the majority of your meals, the Crystal Dining on the second deck (Sapphire Deck) is the place to be. Here there will be a full-blown breakfast and lunch buffet and a nice sit-down dinner with table service. La Table River, Scenic's more exclusive 10-person dinner experience for guests staying in the second and third deck suites, is located towards the front of the restaurant. An Italian-themed specialty restaurant Portobellos is located at the back of the lounge. The lounge is also where diners can opt for some casual grab-and-go fare from the River Café, which they can either eat inside or take outside to the Riverview Terrace.

POOL, FITNESS, SPA, BIKES As we noted, there's a pool on the sun deck, plus a fitness room and spa room and electric-assist bikes on board.

Scenic Tsar

The Verdict

Like all ships on Russia's Volga River, the *Scenic Tsar* was rebuilt on an existing older hull, but the refurbishments were so extensive Scenic was allowed to register it as a newly launched ship in 2012. The vessel does look pretty sweet inside.

Specifications

Passengers	112	Total cabins/balcony cabins	56/52
Passenger decks	3	Crew	71
Year entered service	2012		

THE SHIP IN GENERAL As we mentioned in our write-up about Russia's Volga River, it is almost impossible to build ships from the ground up in Russia due to various strict regulations, so river cruise lines are forced to work with older hulls—which is why you will notice that Volga vessels just do not have the same look or feel as their counterparts in the rest of Europe. While they don't necessarily carry more passengers they tend to be a bit taller and wider, as the Volga is a very wide river and is not constrained by the smaller locks and lower bridges of rivers such as the Danube and Rhine. Despite working with "used merchandise" (aka an older hull), Scenic still managed to make the *Scenic Tsar* feel relatively modern by incorporating very geometric furniture and decor, tasteful pops of brown, red and beige and shiny white walls throughout (even the bar is one big slab of white).

CABINS There are numerous cabin categories, ranging from 161-square-foot cabins on the lower, to the 215-square-foot balcony cabins on the second deck; to the 300-square-foot Royal Suites; and 334-square-foot Royal

Panorama Suites on the third deck. Ninety-three percent of the cabins have private balconies. There are also en suite bathrooms (outfitted with clean white tiles and modern sinks), satellite TV, an in-room safe and mini-bar. As for decor, the cabins have patterned carpeting, duvets and curtains, plush headboards and quiet floral artwork, all of which is toned down and kept looking clean by those shiny white surfaces that weave throughout the vessel.

PUBLIC AREAS At the aft are a Sun Deck with lounge chairs and some chairs and tables, the outdoor Neva Lounge and, the Crystal Dining room, also at the aft, the main Panorama Bar and Lounge, a beauty salon and spa. An elevator connects the first three decks. Complimentary Wi-Fi is available throughout the ship.

DINING OPTIONS Don't expect seven dining options here. All meals are served in the Crystal Dining restaurant, including the breakfast and lunch buffet (which also include a la carte items) and served dinners. Meals are during set times and are open seating.

POOL, FITNESS, SPA, BIKES Alas, there's only a spa and hair salon on this boat, making it a less-than-ideal pick for fitness addicts.

Scenic Spirit
The Verdict

This Mekong yacht-style vessel is attempting to bring Scenic sleekness beyond Europe.

Specifications

Passengers	68	Total cabins/balcony cabins	34/34
Passenger decks	3	Crew	50
Year entered service	2016		

THE SHIP IN GENERAL Scenic's contribution to the constant one-upmanship on the Mekong River, the *Scenic Spirit,* boasts some seriously spacious suites (the smallest—*smallest*—is 344 sq. ft. and the largest is more than 800 sq. ft.), and some nifty amenities like a steam room and an open-air cinema on the Sun Deck. And in a part of the world where most vessels only have one dining room, Scenic sought to at least have one more option, its more casual dining venue the River Café.

CABINS Okay, this is one vessel on which we think it's fair that Scenic refers to all its cabin categories as suites. When the lowest category is the 344-square-foot Deluxe Suite with a separate living area, that's legit. There's also the 430-square-foot Grand Deluxe Suite with a walk-in closet and extra roomy bathroom, and the pièce de resistance, the 861-square-foot Royal Panorama Suite, "the largest suite on the Mekong" according to Scenic and we can't think of one larger. There are two on board and both have a separate dining and lounge area, and a bathroom with a separate shower and bathtub.

PUBLIC AREAS The public areas include the reception area and gift shop, the main dining room, a small library, both and outdoor and an indoor lounge, the River Café (located inside the indoor lounge, aka the Spirit Lounge), a decked out pool and bar area, and an open-air cinema on the Sun Deck.

DINING OPTIONS   All meals including buffet breakfast and lunch and full-service dinner are served in the main Crystal Dining restaurant on the second deck (Jewel Deck). But if you're looking for a light bite, head one deck up to the River Café in the Spirit Lounge.

POOL, FITNESS, SPA, BIKES   There's a gym, steam room, beauty salon and spa room. There's also a pool and bar on the fourth deck. No bikes on board.

Scenic Aura
The Verdict
In 2016, Scenic is also taking its first stab at the booming Irrawaddy market—if the renderings translate into reality, this will be one gorgeous cruise ship.

Specifications

Passengers	44	Total cabins/balcony cabins	22/22
Passenger decks	3	Crew	35
Year entered service	2016		

THE SHIP IN GENERAL   It was still just renderings when this book went to press, but if the renderings hold up, this Irrawaddy cruiser will give the other luxe ships on the river something to ogle at.

CABINS   Suites—and as with all Scenic boats all rooms are called suites—range from 258- to 753-square-feet and all have balconies and a separate seating area ranging from relatively small to pretty sizeable.

PUBLIC AREAS   The public areas include the reception area and gift shop, the main Crystal Dining restaurant, a library, an Outdoor Lounge, an indoor Aura Lounge, the River Café, an outdoor pool and bar, and an open-air cinema on the Sun Deck.

DINING OPTIONS   The Crystal Dining restaurant on the second deck (Jewel Deck) will serve breakfast and lunch (buffet-style), and a sit-down dinner, and the River Café will have light bite alternatives.

POOL, FITNESS, SPA, BIKES   The boat carries a gym, spa and a pool. No bikes are on board.

GRAND CIRCLE LINE
www.gct.com. ✆ 800/221-2610.

Pros
o **Enrichment.** Prior to the cruise guests can expect to receive a lot of detailed information regarding destinations. Onboard guests can expect daily enrichment lectures from local experts in history along with various local cuisine cooking demonstrations and even the occasional folk dancing troupe.

- **Solo-traveler friendly.** GCL has a large supply of small cabins designed and priced for one; it also provides a roommate matching service for those sailings where solo cabins aren't available (solos bunk with another passenger of the same gender and pay the double passenger rate without a singles supplement). Best of all: It offers reduced-rate single-supplements for those who want their own larger room.

Cons

- **Limited dining options.** Don't expect any specialty dining options. Every ship has one dining room with strict feeding times. Additionally, the food, while varied, can be quite basic and uninspired.
- **Beds are twins.** Most cabins have fixed twin beds that cannot be combined. This could be problematic for some romantic couples.

THE LINE IN A NUTSHELL   Grand Circle Cruise Line caters mainly to budget-conscious American retirees who are culture aficionados and prefer substance over style.

THE EXPERIENCE   The line is part of Grand Circle Travel, a tour company which was founded by a retired school teacher and was once associated with the American Association of Retired Persons (AARP). The line does not work with travel agents, relying instead on direct marketing and sales to consumers (get on their list and you will be barraged with all sorts of tempting marketing brochures for river cruises and other tours).

The company prides itself on being tailored to American tastes and expectations, making sure guests feel at home throughout their voyage—Grand Circle only sells cruises to Americans; there may be an occasional Canadian on board, but they must have a U.S address in order to process the cruise fare. They make the onboard experience totally geared towards American comforts from the menu choices (steak anyone?) to entertainment options. Grand Circle's dozen ships are older than a lot of their competition, but they have been refurbished in a basic comfortable style and are meticulously maintained.

Grand Circle places great emphasis on immersive travel as a form of enrichment. The line takes great pride in not "sugar coating" destinations by embracing cultural differences and controversial topics. Included tours go beyond the norm. On signature excursions, for instance, you visit local families in their homes or stop by a school to meet with local kids.

Personalization is another thing that sets Grand Circle apart. To enhance the onboard and destination experience guests are divided into color-coded groups of no more than 45 persons and assigned to an onboard, English-speaking Program Director. These affable directors are chosen for their knowledge of history, geography, politics and local culture. So they act as tours guides, but they also are true hosts, there to make sure no guest gets lost in the crowd: In addition to answering all questions about the destination, and thus taking care of the intellectual needs of the participants, he or she is the go-to person for everything from special diets to extra care for passengers with physical limitations. The relationships starts a week before departure when an e-mail is sent

GRAND CIRCLE ITINERARIES

14-day Rhine and Danube ("Great Rivers of Europe"), Amsterdam to Vienna, from $3,095, balconies from $3,495, Mar–Nov

14-day Rhine and Moselle ("Romance of the Rhine and Mosel") Antwerp to Basel, from $2,895, balconies from $3,195, Mar–Nov

12-day Lower Danube ("Eastern Europe to the Black Sea"), Budapest to Bucharest, from $2,495, balconies from $3,095, Mar–Nov

12-day Elbe ("Essence of the Elbe: Berlin to Prague"), with 7-day cruise, Berlin to Prague, from $2,095, balconies from $2,295, Mar–Nov

11-day Upper Danube ("Old World Prague & the Blue Danube") with 8-day cruise, Prague to Budapest, from $2,595, balconies from $3,195, Mar–Nov

11-day Upper Danube ("Old World Prague & the Blue Danube: President's River Cruise"), with 9-day cruise, Prague to Budapest $3745, balconies from $4395, Mar–Nov

11-day Rhone and Saone ("Cruising Burgundy & Provence to the Cote d'Azur"), with 8-day cruise, Paris to Nice, from $2,795, balconies from $3,495, Mar–Nov

11-day Seine ("The Seine: Paris to Normandy"), with 10-day cruise, Paris to Honfleur, from $2,695, balconies from $3,295, Mar–Nov

10-day Dutch and Belgian Canals ("Holland & Belgium in Springtime"), Antwerp to Amsterdam, from $2,295, balconies from $2,695, Mar–Apr

Note on this chart: Itineraries may also be available in the reverse direction. The first price is the lowest available price for all cabin categories, and the second price is the lowest balcony price, including French balcony cabins.

to each guest from their Program Director, discussing the itinerary along with important reminders and offering to answer any questions.

THE FLEET   Grand Circle owns and operates 12 river ships (though one in Russia was parked for 2016), as well as several ocean-going vessels. The fleet is older, but well maintained. Decor is best described as dated but comfortable with dark woods, colors and heavy rich fabrics—think 1990's Marriott hotel.

In your stateroom, you'll get a hairdryer and toiletries and all the ships have flatscreen TVs with news, enrichment, and movie programming. Not all the ships have elevators (the ones that don't are a difficult choice for those passengers who have a hard time with stairs).

PASSENGER PROFILE   Fellow guests are often well-traveled retired teachers and professors, as well as doctors, engineers and such, most with a knack for conversation, and nearly everyone 55 and up. Expect the same crowd that might be attracted to Road Scholar, but are looking for more of a bargain. Many have traveled with Grand Circle before—the company has a loyal and somewhat fanatical customer base. Passengers are exclusively American which limits the onboard opportunities for cultural interplay.

DINING OPTIONS   Everyone eats in the main dining room at the same time daily. Snack options are sparse—though there may be cookies sometimes at the coffee station. Breakfast and lunch are a combination of a decent buffet spread and made-to-order entrees. Regional specialties are available and for those who get homesick you can always order a burger and fries. Dinner is a full-service, sit-down affair. The food is solidly tasty, but is more basic comfort-food than anything cutting edge. Select wine, beer, and soft drinks are complementary during lunch and dinner, but cost extra out of the dining room. There is a coffee, cappuccino, and tea machine available 24-hours. Special requests are an area where the line seems to struggle, particularly when it comes to vegans (entrees arrive late and can be tasteless). There is no room service.

ACTIVITIES   Enrichment lectures are the big activity every day, with local experts brought on board, including war veterans on Danube routes. When guests aren't busy touring there are opportunities for card games, trivia, and exercise on the limited exercise equipment available or, weather permitting, a few laps around the Sun Deck. There's also a whirlpool and sauna on board some of line's vessels. On most voyages a masseuse may be available.

CHILDREN'S PROGRAM   Grand Circle does not allow children on board.

ENTERTAINMENT   The emphasis is on enrichment lectures and demonstrations from local experts brought on board. Most guests turn in early, but there is evening musical entertainment provided by a solo keyboard singer/musician. The musical stylings are akin to Bill Murray's character from Saturday Night Live, "Nick The Lounge Singer."

SERVICE   Onboard crew is very friendly and service is very efficient. Due to the smaller size of the vessels (some have fewer than 100 passengers on board) it's common to be addressed by name from all crew ranks. Gratuities are collected at the end of the cruise, with the recommended amount $10 to $12 per passenger, per day, which gets split among the crew (you can pay in cash or by credit card). In addition, it's recommended you tip the Program Direct $4 to $6 per person, per day in cash (dollars or euros). Your cruise fare includes tips for the local guides and tour drivers.

TOURS   Daily tours are included in the fare; however, there are also optional special tours available for a fee. All passengers are provided with a personal headset so you can hear what the guide is saying even from quite a distance. Thanks to the company's tour operation and long-standing relationships with many cities, all guests will be able to partake in the line's signature excursions—a "home visit" with a local family and a school visit. These visits are often the highlight, offering an enlightening experience that enhances the understanding of different cultures.

PRE- & POST-CRUISE STAYS   An extensive array of pre- and post-cruise optional tours are available on all itineraries.

Frommer's Ratings (Scale of 1–5)

Cabin comfort & amenities	3	Public spaces	3
Decor	3	Dining	3
Fitness, spa and pool	2	Service	4
Family-friendly	N/A	Enrichment	5

MS Chardonnay & MS Provence
The Verdict

The smallest vessels in the Grand Circle fleet have the highest customer ratings, according to the line. We're including them here as ships, because that's what the line calls them, but they are really a barge-ship hybrid. (a barge without the fancy stuff you expect on barges). See chapter 7 for more on barge cruises.

Specifications

Passengers	46	Total cabins/balcony cabins	27/8
Passenger decks	2	Crew	14
Year entered service			
Chardonnay	1999	Provence	2000

THE SHIPS IN GENERAL   These 40-passenger, barge-like ships were specifically designed for the smaller rivers of France. While not sister ships, both provide a very cozy onboard ambiance—by the end of the trip, you'll definitely know everyone on board and who you do (and don't) want to sit with at dinner. The onboard Program Director will serve as your guide.

CABINS   Cabins are larger than on the other GCL ships, 190- to 200-square-feet, and come with a nice desk. Some have armchairs and sofas too. Beds are stationary twins (you can't combine them). The bathroom is very small with a curtained shower. But on the plus side everyone gets view. Eight balcony cabins have step-out spaces large enough for two chairs; lower level cabins have a porthole. All power outlets are 220v, so be sure to bring adapters.

PUBLIC AREAS   There's a casual French flavor to the decor. The ships have a Sun Deck equipped with wooden loungers and tables with wicker chairs, but otherwise there's a small windowed lounge, bar, games area and reception area, and that's it. The *Chardonnay* was refurbished in 2015 and the *Provence* in 2012. Complimentary Wi-Fi internet access is available in public areas and cabins. Neither ship has an elevator.

DINING OPTIONS   Everyone dines together three meals a day, dinner service typically at 7pm. You will find some French regional specialties on the menu, alongside GCT's usual comfort food.

POOL, FITNESS, SPA, BIKES   There are Jacuzzis on the Sun Decks, but that's it for fitness or pampering services.

MS River Allegro
The Verdict

This smaller, older ship, was extensively refurbished in 2011 and feels like a larger version of a quaint canal barge.

Specifications

Passengers	90	Total cabins/balcony cabins	48/0
Passenger decks	2	Crew	29
Year entered service	1991		

THE SHIP IN GENERAL Expect comfort, just not anything fancy in terms of accommodations or public spaces. This is old-style river cruising.

CABINS All cabins are only 120-square-feet (tight!) with a window that does not open and stationary twin beds that convert to sofas during the day. Expect your bathroom to be very small, with small curtained shower (though plenty of storage space for your toiletries).

PUBLIC AREAS Grand Circle reduced the number of passengers carried when it renovated this ship, knowing onboard space was at a premium. It helped a bit. Hangout spots include the Sun Deck, a lounge with bar (expanded in the redo and right off the dining room), a library corner and a reception area. Complimentary Wi-Fi internet access is available in public areas and cabins. The ship does not have an elevator.

DINING OPTIONS Everyone eats together at a set time. Breakfast and lunch consist of an American-style buffet and salad bar with additional menu options. Lunch always starts off with a regional-based soup followed by several set entrees and dessert options. Dinner is a multicourse serviced event with numerous dining options with one option being locally inspired.

POOL, FITNESS, SPA, BIKES There is a massage room, where guests can get Swedish, deep tissue, lymphatic drainage or a personalized combination massage.

MS River Chanson

The Verdict

This small ship brings to Bordeaux a 1930's vibe with nautical touches including teak decor.

Specifications

Passengers	90	Total cabins/balcony cabins	44/0
Passenger decks	2	Crew	24
Year entered service	2001		

THE SHIP IN GENERAL Acquired by Grand Circle in 2014 from luxury tour operator Abercrombie & Kent, and launched in 2015, after a complete refurbishment, the 90-passenger MS *River Chanson*'s smaller size offers a relaxing experience cruising France's waterways. The vessel's 1930s comes from the heavy use of teak decor and nautical brass details throughout the public areas.

CABINS The Main Deck cabins are 150-square-feet with large picture windows and one queen-size bed. Lower Deck cabins are 120-square-feet and have two porthole windows and stationary twin beds. Bathrooms are small but offer plenty of shelves and under sink storage for toiletries. All cabin electrical outlets are 220v so all 110v appliances will need plug adapters. Cabin interiors are more subdued with wooden walls painted in lighter colors that are adorned with traditional artwork.

PUBLIC AREAS Comfortable facilities include a bar and lounge, library, and a teak-covered Sun Deck. Complimentary Wi-Fi Internet access is available in public areas and cabins. There is no elevator.

DINING OPTIONS Breakfast and lunch are a combination of buffet and set menu items, the majority of which will be regionally influenced. Dinner is a multicourse extravaganza with popular French options of onion soup, beef bourguignon, crepes Suzette, and cheese course at the end of dinner.

POOL, FITNESS, SPA, BIKES Sorry: There's nothing for fitness buffs on the ship, but there is a massage room where guests can get Swedish, deep tissue, lymphatic drainage or combination massage to one's preferences.

MS Bizet

The Verdict

The 120-passenger MS *Bizet* brings easy, breezy GCL-style cruising to the Seine. But like the other ships in the fleet, it's pretty plain

Specifications

Passengers	120	Total cabins/balcony cabins	60/28
Passenger decks	2	Crew	33
Year entered service	2002		

THE SHIP IN GENERAL Despite an update in 2012, the 120-passenger MS *Bizet* offers an old-fashioned (think kitschy, dated furniture) yet intimate environment to explore from Paris to Normandy. Resident Program Directors enhance the enrichment of this historic area.

CABINS All cabins have views and are 160-square-feet with twin beds that convert into sofas (but can't be combined). Those on the Soprano Deck have sliding glass doors that open to balcony space (big enough for two chairs, but tight); lower deck cabins have two large picture windows that cannot be opened. All cabin electrical outlets are 220v, and bathrooms are compact.

PUBLIC AREAS The lounge and bar and reception area are outfitted with furniture and decor that is newer (so it's clean and fresh) and yet still feels older (in terms of look and style). There's also a library corner and library corner and a gathering spot called the Pub. The prime spot to catch views on a fair weather day is the Sun Deck. Complimentary Wi-Fi Internet access is only in select public areas and cabins. The ship does have an elevator (though it does not reach the Sun Deck).

DINING OPTIONS In the upper deck dining room everyone dines together in the open-seating dining room. There is an attempt at French cuisine with crepes, bouillabaisse, foie gras, and cheeses.

POOL, FITNESS, SPA, BIKES There are none.

MS River Concerto, MS River Harmony, MS River Melody & MS River Rhapsody

The Verdict

The names are purposefully musical for these comfortable and versatile, 140-passenger sister ships, the first ships built specifically for Grand Circle. The size works well on various European waterways.

Specifications

Passengers	140	Total cabins/balcony cabins	70/15
Passenger decks	3	Crew	34
Year entered service	1999/2000		

THE SHIP IN GENERAL Launched in 1999 and 2000, sister ships MS *River Concerto,* MS *River Harmony,* MS *River Melody,* and MS *River Rhapsody* host 140 passengers in comfortable style—despite the dated details, the vessels are still elegant and charming (in fact some of the dated decor adds to that charm; you won't find funky twin cabins that convert into a seating area that looks like the dining car tables on a train anymore).

CABINS All are 160-square-feet with two twin beds that convert into sofas, and views. The Serenade Deck balcony cabins have large sliding glass doors to a small balcony space, with two chairs; lower deck cabins have two large picture windows that cannot be opened. The bathrooms are very small but with lots of cabinet storage. There is a hairdryer in each cabin, but all 110v American appliances will require plug adapters since all cabin electrical outlets are 220v.

PUBLIC AREAS Ship amenities include a bar and lounge, pub area, library, Sun Deck and reception area. All the ships were refurbished in 2011 and 2012, so you can expect fresher carpeting and finishings. Complimentary Wi-Fi access is available throughout the vessels. The ships have an elevator but it doesn't reach the least expensive cabins on the lower deck nor the Sun Deck.

DINING OPTIONS In the open seating, windowed dining room menus are regionally inspired. For example, Rhine River itineraries offer more German fare like sausages and sauerkraut. Danube voyages may offer goulash-type entrees and a proper Viennese strudel.

POOL, FITNESS, SPA, BIKES On board these ships you can get a massage, hangout in the sauna or whirlpool and workout in the small fitness room.

MS River Adagio & MS River Aria

The Verdict

The newest and largest river ships in the Grand Circle fleet, this pair was still built before river cruising took a decidedly contemporary turn in interiors, but you'll still be comfortable as you explore the Upper and Lower Danube.

Specifications

Passengers	164	Total cabins/balcony cabins	82/20
Passenger decks	3	Crew	38
Year entered service			
River Adagio	2001	River Aria	2003

THE SHIP IN GENERAL Launched in 2001 and 2003, sister ships MS *River Adagio* and MS *River Aria* while hardly modern, do offer such resort-like facilities as a whirlpool and sauna.

CABINS All cabins are 160-square-feet with some sort of view and two twin-size beds that that fold up into couches during the day (making the space at least look and feel a tad bigger). Cabins on Serenade Deck have large sliding glass doors that lead to a small balcony, equipped with two chairs; lower decks have either one large, two medium, or two small windows that cannot be opened. The bathrooms are tiny, with a curtained off shower.

PUBLIC AREAS Ship amenities include a windowed lounge furnished like grandma's living room, but with a bar. There's also a small library off reception and a Sun Deck where you can watch the word go by from sling-back style cloth loungers. There's Wi-Fi in some public areas and cabins. The ships have an elevator.

DINING OPTIONS There are a lot of choices on the buffets. At dinner in the windowed dining room you'll sit with other passengers—tables are for six and up. Look for regional specialties such as chicken paprikash and goulash as you cruise the Danube. Cruising the Rhine, you'll find spätzle and schnitzel, which you can wash down with delightful pilsner beer.

POOL, FITNESS, SPA, BIKES The ships are equipped with massage room, fitness center, whirlpool and sauna.

AVALON WATERWAYS

www.avalonwaterways.com. ℂ 877/797-8791.

Pros

o **Resources.** Avalon Waterways hugely benefits from the fact that it is owned by a large travel company, the Globus Family of Brands, which translates into great value for Avalon passengers. Also, should any itinerary changes or complications arise, a global operations team is on-hand to create a quick fix.

o **Views.** Avalon's trademark floor-to-ceiling panoramic sliding glass doors in the staterooms on its 10 Suite Ship class of vessels offer sweeping views of the passing scenery, further enhanced by the fact that stateroom beds on Avalon ships face outwards towards said sweeping views.

Cons

o **Lacking character.** While competitors have created stronger identities (Uniworld is flashy, Viking is Scandinavian-modern), Avalon ships are lacking more defining characteristics making it hard to distinguish between the Avalon ships themselves as well as what makes Avalon different or better than others.

THE LINE IN A NUTSHELL There's something very straight forward and no-fuss about Avalon. If you like clean, contemporary design, well-executed itineraries and solid cuisine, Avalon Waterways is probably a good choice for you. Avalon offers upscale amenities like marble bathrooms and L'Occitane bath products, minus the pretension.

Frommer's Ratings (Scale of 1–5)

Cabin comfort & amenities	5	Public spaces	4
Decor	4	Dining	4
Fitness, spa and pool	5	Service	5
Family-friendly	2	Enrichment	5

THE EXPERIENCE   Being owned by the tour operator company Globus, Avalon has solid tour operating skills backing it. You can expect well-executed excursions and VIP access to popular venues where Globus has long-held connections (don't be surprised if you skip the line at tourist hot-spots like the Eiffel Tower in Paris or at the Rijksmusuem in Amsterdam).

Avalon is also big on flexibility. In 2012, the company introduced the Avalon Choice program, the idea being to offer passengers the ability to personalize their cruise a bit more, for instance with more dining options (such as additional venues and room service), bedding options (such as choice of pillows and bed configurations), and sightseeing options (more on those below). With MyAvalon, the company's online service center, passengers can pre-select included excursions, choose and pre-pay for optional excursions, set bed configuration preferences (joined or separated), and select special celebration packages.

Avalon is definitely making a run at that middle-of-the-road segment of the river cruise market, travelers who don't want or can't afford the more luxury lines but who also like the idea of sailing on sparkling new ships with some of the latest amenities. If that sounds like you, read on.

THE FLEET   Avalon river cruise ships can be summed up in three words: clean, contemporary and consistent. There's nothing overly flashy about them and there's nothing low-budget about them, either. In 2011, Avalon introduced its now hallmark Suite Ships class off vessels, ships with staterooms that feature a floor-to-ceiling and wall-to-wall sliding glass door that transforms the entire stateroom into an open-air balcony. The 200-square-foot staterooms (hardly true suites, but this is where the aggressive marketing comes into play) also have a comfortable sitting area and even more comfortable bedding (we love their quality sleep-inducing bedding). They also have some souped-up amenities like marble bathrooms. And generally speaking, like many of its competitors, Avalon has been improving upon its river cruise ships each year, adding more dining venues and onboard options, plus little things like stocked minibars in all its cabins. In river cruising, you'll come to find out, it really is all about the little things—given that the ships just really aren't all that big.

In 2016, with two new Suite Ship class of vessels launched, Avalon's European fleet size grows to 16 vessels, 12 of which are Suite Ships. Avalon also has exclusive charters on vessels on the Mekong in Vietnam and Cambodia and on Myanmar's Irrawaddy. The company also offers river cruise through partnerships on China's Yangtze River (the 398-passenger Century Legend and Century Paragon, which both launched in 2013); on the Peruvian Amazon (the freshly built 44-passenger Amazon Discovery); and on Egypt's Nile River (the 114-passenger Sonesta St. George).

PASSENGER PROFILE   Avalon passengers span a wider age range than you might think based on stereotypes about river cruising attracting only a much older clientele. According to the company, 22 percent of passenger are 69-plus; 24 percent are ages 59 to 68; 21 percent are in the 50 to 58 range; 20 percent are ages 34 to 49; and 13 percent are between 19 and 33. The average age is mid-60s. Many hail from the ocean cruising world, with 84 percent having cruised in the past.

DINING OPTIONS   In the main dining room, Avalon passengers will find open-seating breakfasts and lunches served in elegant buffet-style. Dinners are four-course affairs served by the wait staff—the meal has one start time each evening but is open seating. Weather permitting, sometimes an al fresco lunch will be served on the Sun Deck. On the Suite Ships an alternative dining venue, the Panorama Bistro, was added at the aft of the vessels for light breakfast, lunch and dinner options for those who want a quiet respite from the main restaurant.

Avalon includes complimentary sparkling wine with breakfast, and beer and wine during dinner, though passengers can also buy fancier bottles of their choosing. In addition to the daily captain's menu of dinner selections, which often include regional dishes with an emphasis on local meat and fish specialties, there are always a standard selection of healthy and comfort meal options such as vegetarian, salmon and steak dishes. There are also always healthy options at the breakfast and lunch buffet with fruit smoothies available at breakfast and an expansive salad buffet at lunch. You can always expect a made-to-order-eggs chef's station during breakfast, as well as popular sweet breakfast options such as French toast or pancakes. There are plenty of cereals, pastries, yogurt and often oatmeal or cream of wheat, as well. At lunch, the chef's station is often a carving table, but can also be a made-to-order pasta station or will be serving up some other daily special. There are always hot and cold dishes available in the buffet, including both local flavors and dishes for those who are feeling a bit homesick.

ACTIVITIES   During sailings, Avalon embraces the cultural immersion aspect of travel with lectures by experts in various relevant fields—for instance, a World War II historian comes on board during the company's Paris-to-Normandy sailing on the Seine River to give an in-depth talk about the D-Day landings passengers will visit on the itinerary. There are also food and wine tastings to give guests the opportunity to try regional cheeses, charcuterie and wine varietals you've never heard of—especially the German ones! There is also the occasional arts, craftwork, or cooking demonstration, with the latter always ending up being a highlight (and something you can try to replicate back home to impress friends and family).

CHILDREN'S PROGRAM   Avalon does not allow children younger than 8 years of age on board and doesn't have any special programs or activities geared specifically towards kids.

ENTERTAINMENT   Entertainment will come in the form of the nightly live piano or keyboard player who takes up residence in the lounge, and usually gets going after dinner. Occasionally he or she will be joined by a singer or there will be a more elaborate performance put on by local entertainers, such as a dance troupe. Later in the evening, a DJ might take over to get the

14-day Rhine, Main and Danube ("Magnificent Europe"), Amsterdam to Budapest, $4,799, balconies from $6,897, Mar–Oct

15-day Rhine and Rhone ("Rhine & Rhone Revealed"), with 7-day cruise, Amsterdam to Cote d'Azur, $5,658, balconies from $7,756, Apr–Oct

8-day Dutch and Belgian Canals ("Enchanting Belgium"), with 7-day cruise Amsterdam to Namur (Belgium), $2,699, balconies from $3,348, Apr

23-day Rhine, Main and Danube ("North Sea-Black Sea Cruise"), with 22-day cruise, Amsterdam to Bucharest, $8,679, balconies from $11,976, May–Aug, Oct

9-day Rhine and Moselle ("Canals, Vineyards & Paris"), with 7-day cruise, Amsterdam to Paris, $3,539, balconies from $4,188, May–Nov

12-day Rhine and Moselle ("The Rhine & Moselle"), Amsterdam to Basel, $4,299, balconies from $7,554, Sept–Oct

12-day Rhine, Main and Danube ("European Splendor"), Amsterdam to Vienna, $4,449, balconies from $6,247, May, July–Oct

7-day Dutch and Belgian Canals ("Essential Holland & Belgium"), Amsterdam to Vilvoorde (Belgium), $2,559, balconies from $3,698, Apr–Sept

7-day Rhine ("Romantic Rhine"), Amsterdam to Basel, $2,199, balconies from $3,298, Apr-Dec

12-day Upper Danube ("Blue Danube Discovery"), with 7-day cruise Budapest to Prague, $3,289, balconies from $4,338, Apr–Nov

9-day Lower Danube ("Balkan Discovery"), with 6-day cruise, Budapest to Bucharest, $3,409, balconies from $4,308, Apr, June-July, Sept–Oct

11-day Upper Danube ("Danube Dreams"), with 7-day cruise, Budapest to Prague, $3,319, balconies from $4,368, Mar–May

16-day Moselle, Rhine, Main, and Danube ("Jewels of Central Europe"), with 14-day cruise, Budapest to Paris, $6,419, balconies from $8,067, May–Oct

7-day Upper Danube ("A Taste of the Danube"), Budapest to Melk (Austria), Apr, Oct–Nov $1,839, balconies from $2,117

10-day Rhone and Saone ("Burgundy & Provence"), with 7-day cruise, Paris to Cote d'Azur, $3,549, balconies from $4,248, Mar–Nov

7-day Dutch Canals ("Tulips of Northern Holland"), round-trip from Amsterdam, $2,549, balconies from $2,718, Apr–May

15-day Rhone, Saone and Seine ("Grand France"), Cote d'Azur to Paris, $5,209, balconies from $7,157, Mar–Nov

dance floor moving, and the dance floor can get pretty hopping, depending on the passengers. In general, the entertainment can be hit or miss.

SERVICE   There is rarely slack service on river cruises and Avalon is no exception. The Avalon crews find that delicate balance of being helpful but not overly so. It's a very good experience for those that like the idea of a crew that works their magic behind the scenes. Gratuities for the crew and cruise manager are not included in Avalon's prices, and according to the company are considered to be "discretionary."

10-day Upper Danube ("The Legendary Danube"), with 7-day cruise, Prague to Budapest, $2,859, balconies from $3,908, Apr–Dec

17-day Danube ("Grand Danube Cruise"), with 13-day cruise, Prague to Bucharest, $5,889, balconies from $7,837, Apr, June–Oct

11-day Upper Danube and Main ("Central European Experience'"), with 7-day cruise, Nuremberg to Remich (Luxembourg), $3,829, balconies from $4,878, May–Oct

13-day Danube ("Blue Danube to the Black Sea"), with 10-day cruise, Bucharest to Vienna, $4,839, balconies from $6,338, Apr–May, July, Sept–Oct

9-day Upper Danube ("Danube Dreams"), with 7-day cruise, Prague to Budapest, $2,739, balconies from $3,838, Mar–May

7-day Seine ("Paris to Normandy's Landing Beaches"), round-trip from Paris, $2,449, balconies from $3,148, Mar–Nov

8-day Upper Danube ("Danube Symphony"), with 5-day cruise, Munich to Vienna, $2,989, balconies from $3,774, Apr–May, Aug–Sept

12-day Main and Rhine ("Highlights of Germany"), with 9-day cruise, Munich to Basel, $4,589, balconies from $5,573, May–June, Aug–Sept

16-day Moselle, Rhine, Main, and Danube ("Jewels of Central Europe"), with 14-day cruise, Paris to Budapest, $6,139, balconies from $7,437, May–Oct

11-day Rhine ("The Upper Rhine to the City of Music"), Zurich to Vienna, $4,249, balconies from $5,319, May–Sept

12-day Mekong ("Fascinating Vietnam, Cambodia & the Mekong River"), with 7-day cruise, Siem Reap to Ho Chi Minh City, cabins/balconies from $4,068, Feb–Apr, June–Dec

13-day Irrawaddy ("Golden Myanmar & the Alluring Irrawaddy"), with 10-day cruise, from Yangon to Yangon, cabins/balconies from $5,849, Feb–Apr, Sept–Dec

8-day Nile ("Highlights of Egypt"), with 4-day cruise, cabins/balconies from $2,667, Feb–Dec

11-day Yangtze ("Magical China & The Yangtze River), with 3-day cruise, Beijing to Shanghai, cabins/balconies from $3,499, Apr–Oct

18-day Yangtze ("Cultural China & Tibet with Yangtze River Cruise and Hong Kong"), with 4-day cruise, cabins/balconies from $4,939, May–Oct

Note on this chart: Itineraries may also be available in the reverse direction. The first price is the lowest available price for all cabin categories, and the second price is the lowest balcony price, including French balcony cabins.

TOURS Avalon is all about options and that includes its daily excursions. There are always included sightseeing options, and these are available at several different paces. In some ports there will also be special-interest excursions offered. And in some destinations there will be optional premium excursions for an additional cost. Passengers can see and pre-select their excursions through the MyAvalon program, an online registration option that allows passenger to pre-order their tours, whether they're included or not. The company offers "Essential Sightseeing" guided tours, which hit the blockbuster sites; "Leisurely

Sightseeing" guided tours, for those that want to go at a gentler pace; and "Independent" exploration options for those who want to explore on their own. In some European ports, Avalon will offer off-the-beaten-path tours like a Jewish Heritage Walk in Cologne, or a tour of the WWII Rally Grounds in Nuremberg. Avalon is also big on health and wellness (there are always healthy food options in the dining venues, and all their ships have a fitness room), and along those lines the company has partnered with bicycle tour operators in Amsterdam; Bernkastel, Germany; Cochem, Germany; Durnstein, Austria; and Breisach, Germany, to offer optional, guided biking excursions in those destinations.

PRE- & POST-CRUISE STAYS   With sister brands that offer both tours (Globus and Cosmos) and semi-independent travel options (Monograms), it's possible to create a large variety of pre- and post-cruise extensions—anything from a few extra hotel nights before or after the river cruise to adding on a whole tour or sightseeing package. There are plenty pre-packaged pre- and post-cruise extensions that Avalon includes in many of its river cruises, or you can check with your travel agent or an Avalon representative to build out some unique options for you. But if you can think of it, the Globus Family of Brands can probably put something together.

5 | Avalon Suite Ships
The Verdict

In 2011, Avalon launched the *Avalon Panorama*, the first of what would become its Suite Ships class of vessels. With the *Avalon Panorama*, the company introduced a new concept: suite-like staterooms that feature a floor-to-ceiling and wall-to-wall sliding glass door that transforms the stateroom into an open-air balcony.

Specifications

Passengers			
Avalon Panorama, Avalon Vista, Avalon Expression, Avalon Impression, Avalon Illumination, Avalon Passion	166	Avalon Visionary, Avalon Artistry II, Avalon Poetry II, Avalon Tapestry II, Avalon Tranquility II, Avalon Imagery II	128
Total cabins/balcony cabins			
Avalon Expression, Avalon Impression, Avalon Illumination, Avalon Passion	83/67	Avalon Visionary, Avalon Artistry II, Avalon Poetry II, Avalon Tapestry II, Avalon Tranquility II, Avalon Imagery II	64/52
Avalon Panorama, Avalon Vista	84/66		
Passenger decks	3		
Crew			
Avalon Panorama, Avalon Vista, Avalon Expression, Avalon Impression, Avalon Illumination, Avalon Passion	47	Avalon Visionary, Avalon Artistry II, Avalon Poetry II, Avalon Tapestry II, Avalon Tranquility II, Avalon Imagery II	37
Year entered service			
Avalon Panorama	2011	Avalon Poetry II, Avalon Impression, Avalon Illumination	2014
Avalon Vista, Avalon Visionary	2012	Avalon Tapestry II, Avalon Tranquility II	2015
Avalon Artistry II, Avalon Expression	2013	Avalon Passion, Avalon Imagery II	2016

THE SHIPS IN GENERAL   There is something to be said for straightforward, understated style and that is what the Avalon Suite Ships have (though we do take some issue with the overuse/abuse of the word "suite" on river cruise vessels). The look and feel of the vessels are reminiscent of Radisson Hotels, a reliable brand that is clean, modern, comfortable and efficient. The staterooms feature the trademark panoramic sliding glass doors that define this entire class of vessels. With the added space that was gained by creating an advanced French balcony system (rather than a square foot-sucking step-out balcony), a comfortable sitting area was incorporated into all the staterooms on the upper two passenger decks. The design was so simple and successful, that Avalon has stuck with it ever since. The staterooms also have beds that face outward towards those large windows and passing views, something you won't find on very many other river cruise lines, which generally position their beds facing one of the walls. And the dining areas and public spaces are equally as streamlined as the staterooms.

CABINS   There are three categories of staterooms on the Avalon Suite Ships: Deluxe Staterooms, generally 172-square-foot staterooms on the lower deck of the ship which have just porthole windows; Panorama Suites, 200-square-foot staterooms that occupy the majority of the second and third decks, featuring the hallmark panoramic sliding-glass door/balcony, and a sofa and small sitting area; and Royal Suites, 300-square-foot suites on the upper passenger deck with a separate living area, a bathroom with a double sink and the wall-to-wall sliding glass balcony doors. All of the staterooms have a stocked minibar, a flatscreen satellite TV with movie channels, and L'Occitane bath products.

PUBLIC AREAS   The variety of public spaces is a huge plus on the Avalon Suite Ships, which feature multiple dining venues, as well as several different areas in which to socialize and relax. In addition to the main dining room, there is the Panorama Bistro adjacent to the lounge area, where light meals are served, the Club Lounge at the aft of the vessel with a 24/7 coffee station, and the Sky Bistro on the Sun Deck where an occasional grilled lunch al fresco is prepared. The Panorama Bar and Lounge are the heart of the social scene on these vessels, but passengers can also hang out in the outdoor Observation Lounge. There is also an open and airy reception area, an Internet Corner with computers for guests to get online (although there is also Wi-Fi throughout the ships), a whirlpool on the Sun Deck, a hair salon and a fitness room.

DINING OPTIONS   As on most river cruise vessels, the heart of the food and beverage service on the Avalon Suite Ships is in the main dining room, where breakfast and lunch are served as a buffet (with chef stations for egg orders and daily lunch specials), and where dinner is served restaurant style, complete with menu options, four courses and full wait service. Complimentary sparkling wine is available at breakfast, soft drinks at lunch and beer and wine with dinner. More casual, lighter meals are served in the Panorama Bistro and in the Club Lounge. Occasionally, an al fresco lunch will be served at the Sky Bistro on the Sun Deck. For an added fee, room service is available for a continental breakfast. There are low fat and vegetarian options always on the menu, in addition to standing steak and fish entrees each night.

POOL, FITNESS, SPA, BIKES There is a whirlpool on the sundeck and a fitness room with several cardio machines. There is no spa, but there is a hair salon. There are no bikes on board but Avalon does host biking excursions in some ports.

Avalon Scenery, Avalon Creativity, Avalon Affinity, Avalon Luminary & Avalon Felicity

The Verdict

The predecessor to Avalon's Suite Ship class of vessels, the main difference between these ships and their Suite Ship counterparts is that Avalon hadn't yet implemented its clever panoramic suites concept yet, which means staterooms on these vessels are a bit smaller and less open and bright (though plenty comfortable and functional nevertheless).

Specifications

Passengers			
Avalon Scenery, Avalon Affinity, Avalon Luminary, Avalon Felicity	138	Avalon Creativity	140
Total cabins/balcony cabins			
Avalon Scenery, Avalon Affinity, Avalon Luminary, Avalon Felicity	69/58	Avalon Creativity	70/59
Passenger decks	3	Crew	39
Year entered service			
Avalon Scenery	2008	Avalon Luminary, Avalon Felicity	2010
Avalon Creativity, Avalon Affinity	2009		

THE SHIPS IN GENERAL Before the Avalon Suite Ships came along, Avalon had already begun to establish its contemporary aesthetic with this group of vessels. And while the cabins are not as open and airy as their Suite Ship counterparts, Avalon was already brightening things up in the rest of the ship by, for instance, introducing a skylight into the main lobby area to give it an atrium feel. With this flock of ships, Avalon also started incorporating new and alternative dining options, like its al fresco dining option on the Sun Deck, where grilled lunches are served when the weather is cooperating. It's hard to compete with the newer, nicer models of anything, but all told there is absolutely nothing inadequate about this group of ships, which have been reliably updated on a regular basis to keep up with their younger siblings.

CABINS There are three categories of staterooms on these vessels: the 172-square-foot Deluxe Staterooms that occupy the lower deck of the ship and have just porthole windows (the same as on the Suite Ships); the 172-square-foot Deluxe Staterooms that take up the majority of the second and third decks and feature a French balcony; and the 258-square-foot Suites (there are two of these each on the *Avalon Scenery* and *Avalon Creativity* and four each on the *Avalon Affinity, Luminary* and *Felicity*), which have a French balcony and an additional seating area. All of the staterooms have a stocked minibar, a flatscreen satellite TV with movie channels, and those L'Occitane bath products. Don't expect a plethora of patterns or colors—staterooms tend to have a few details that make them a bit cozier (a colored throw here, a subtle piece of art there), but otherwise provide simple, clean accommodations to rest in (think pared down Ikea-style cabinets, nightstands and closets).

PUBLIC AREAS   This class of vessels feature one main dining room, a bar and lounge with an adjacent observation lounge, a reception area with an Internet corner, a club lounge at the aft of the vessel, a fitness room, a hair salon, and a Sun Deck with a whirlpool, lounge chairs, a shaded awning and the Sky Bistro, an al fresco dining venue. The design of these ships isn't as open and airy as on the Suite Ships (for instance the reception area is not as light-filled as the lobbies on the Suite Ships), but they still have the trademark clean, contemporary lines and design features that Avalon has integrated into all its vessels with a few really subtle details, like a funky chandelier here or some textured wall coverings there.

DINING OPTIONS   Most of the eating action takes place in the main dining room, where breakfast and lunch are served buffet style and dinner is served as a sit-down affair with menu options and wait service for a four-course meal. You can expect the same reliable quality of food as on any other Avalon vessel. Complimentary sparkling wine is available at breakfast, soft drinks at lunch and beer and wine with dinner. An occasional lunch will be served outside at the Sky Bistro on the Sun Deck, weather permitting—this outdoor grill and seating area is definitely a great way to switch things up. It sits up to 40 people (passengers will have to make reservations when the sailings are full), and a casual lunch such as grilled sausages, steak, corn on the cob, baked potatoes and a salad bar will be served in the shaded, patio-style seating area. For dessert, they often offer up ice cream sundaes in keeping with the fun-in-the-sun outdoor theme. Wine, beer, iced tea, soft drinks and water are also available with this meal. And for an additional fee, passengers can opt for continental breakfast room service. There are generally low-fat and vegetarian options always on the menu, in addition to standing steak and fish entrees available each night.

POOL, FITNESS, SPA, BIKES   A whirlpool is the centerpiece of the Sun Deck; also on the boat is a fitness room with several cardio machines. There is no spa, but there is a hair salon. There are no bikes on board but Avalon does host biking excursions in some ports.

Avalon Siem Reap & Avalon Myanmar
The Verdict

With these two vessels, the idea was to bring the concept of Avalon's Suite Ship class of vessels to Southeast Asia. So, guests can expect many of the same amenities and services they would receive on an Avalon ship in Europe, including those sliding glass panoramic doors in the staterooms.

Specifications

Passengers	36	Total cabins/balcony cabins	18/18
Passenger decks	2	Crew	24
Year entered service			
Avalon Siem	2014	Avalon Myanmar	2015

THE SHIPS IN GENERAL In the past, Avalon had chartered vessels in this part of the world, but with these two ships, the company worked directly with the ship builders to create a style more in line with what Avalon offers in Europe. The resulting vessels are much smaller (as are most of the river cruise ships on the Mekong and Irrawaddy rivers) versions of the Avalon Suite Ships, with some Southeast Asian touches and styling. In some ways, these vessels are a bit more ornate than their European counterparts, and feature more colorful design elements, such as floral carpeting and upholstery, intricate woodwork ceilings and furniture (the dining rooms have some really intricate wood-carved pieces), and locally inspired art and craftwork on the walls. Along the lines of that ornateness, the crew provides slippers which passengers wear around the ship (or they can bring your own), to keep the wood floors clean (you leave your shoes to be cleaned every time you come back from an excursion).

CABINS All 18 staterooms on board both vessels are 245-square-feet and feature Avalon's characteristic wall-to-wall sliding glass doors that transform the entire room into an open-air balcony (with an insect screen to protect from mosquitoes when open). There is also individually controlled air-conditioning and heating, an in-room safe, a mini-bar stocked with complimentary local beer, soft drinks and bottled water, a small seating area and a flatscreen TV (depending on the signal you may be able to watch CNN or other news stations). The beds are outfitted with Avalon's premium mattresses and bedding. Passengers also have their choice of bed configuration—two twins or one king. The bathrooms are sizeable.

PUBLIC AREAS The public areas consist of a dining room with a buffet in the center and cooking station where chefs prepare daily special dishes. There is a windowed lounge with a bar and a forward-facing outdoor lounge with cushy lounge chairs. There's also a second open-air lounging area facing aft on the top deck, in addition to a reception area, a small gym and spa treatment rooms with traditional Southeast Asian therapies.

DINING OPTIONS On these smaller vessels, all meals are served in the sole dining room on board. At every meal the chef offers a choice of regional or western cuisine, so you can sample Southeast Asian dishes or go with an option such as pasta. Complimentary soft drinks, beer and wine are served with lunch and dinner, and complimentary spirits are also offered during dinner. There is also a welcome reception with open bar and cocktail hours during which hors d'oeuvres will be passed around along with a cocktail of the day.

POOL, FITNESS, SPA, BIKES There is a spa treatment room and a small gym, but no pool or bikes.

AMAWATERWAYS

www.amawaterways.com. ℂ 800/626-0126.

Pros

o **Food and wine.** AmaWaterways has several dining venues on each of its vessels with an emphasis on high-quality ingredients and unique recipes. The company also brings an impressive selection of wines on board and has a large portfolio of wine-themed cruises.

o **Least itinerary disruptions.** AmaWaterways' president and co-owner Rudi Schreiner is one of the forefathers of modern river cruising. Schreiner's insider knowledge of inland waterways and his careful deployment of vessels means that AmaWaterways usually experiences the least (or no) disruptions on its river sailings when water levels are acting up.

o **Customer service.** With a strong emphasis on providing top-notch customer service, AmaWaterways often makes decisions that are not necessarily in its best financial interest (think generous refunds when things go wrong) to ensure that customers go home with a positive impression.

Cons

o **Playing it safe.** Because AmaWaterways doesn't like to take risks on emerging and less predictable rivers (such as the notoriously shallow Elbe River in Germany), it generally sails on more run-of-the-mill rivers.

THE LINE IN A NUTSHELL It may not be cheap (few river cruises are), but if you want the lowest risk of having any itinerary disruptions and some of the best customer service on the rivers, you'll get your money's worth if you book this more under-the-radar gem of a river cruise line.

THE EXPERIENCE Founded in 2002 by Rudi Schreiner (the river cruise pioneer), Kristin Karst (the customer service guru) and the late Jimmy Murphy (a tour company veteran), AmaWaterways was originally called Amadeus Waterways. Following some confusion with a former partner company, German river cruise line Luftner Cruises, which operates ships that have Amadeus in their name (such as Amadeus Rhapsody, Amadeus Symphony—you get the point), the company decided to go with AmaWaterways instead.

In recent years, as competition has heated up in the river cruise industry, the various river cruise lines have attempted to shift into better defined segments of the market and AmaWaterways landed squarely in the high-end category (with perhaps only Uniworld or Tauck being a step above) with its mostly inclusive style of river cruising. AmaWaterways includes all meals on board, at least one excursion in each port, and beer and wine with lunch and dinner.

AmaWaterways is one of the river cruise lines that is trying to find that balance between taking very good care of its passengers with well-executed excursions and outings while also giving them the free time to explore on their own. Thus, if you want a fully inclusive river cruising experience, AmaWaterways may not be the river cruise line for you—they aren't about hand-holding the same way a company like Tauck for instance is. But if you like the idea of very well-appointed staterooms and tastefully done restaurants, lounges and a swim-up pool bar on board with the option to do your own thing with your partner, friends or family, AmaWaterways is probably a better fit.

The company does a great job catering to special groups too, which can be anything from a full-ship charter, or just a larger group traveling together, so if you're looking for a line to host a meeting, special event or reunion, this is a forte of theirs. They also have bikes and biking excursions available to guests (AmaWaterways recently partnered up with active bike-and-hike outfit Backroads, which will be hosting several cycling-centric Danube river cruises in 2016) an attractive option for fitness-focused travelers. And the company is pushing fervently into the family market by, for instance, having partnered with Adventures by Disney (more on that below).

For those to whom it's critically important to be connected, AmaWaterways invests a lot of money into its onboard free Wi-Fi to ensure the best connection possible—it's still a bit spotty in between ports but it seems to be getting more reliable each year.

THE FLEET AmaWaterways builds vessels that are both unique but that are also distinctly AmaWaterways. Each river cruise ship has its own individual color palette (think neutrals and metallic combined with pops of color) and/or theme (perhaps a subtle floral or nautical theme) and the public spaces are laid out slightly different—but all have a modern, European styling. Since its first ship launched a decade ago, the company has been tweaking and evolving its fleet with additional enhancements with every new or new generation of ships. For instance, in 2010, AmaWaterways introduced a small pool with a swim-up bar on the sundeck, and recently added two private dining spaces for larger parties on its newest vessels, as well. As of 2016, AmaWaterways will have 16 vessels sailing throughout Europe, the two newest of which, the *AmaViola* and *AmaStella,* launched in spring 2016. For those interested in more exotic river adventures, the company also sails two ships in Vietnam and Cambodia on the colorful Mekong River, the *AmaDara* and *AmaLotus,* as well as one ship on Myanmar's (aka Burma's) Irrawaddy River, the *AmaPura.* Want to take an AmaWaterways river cruise in southern Africa? Sure, why not— AmaWaterways also charters the 28-passenger boutique safari riverboat *Zambezi Queen* on the Zambezi River in Botswana.

PASSENGER PROFILE With a focus on wine and themed cruises, AmaWaterways caters to oenophiles and enthusiasts of all kinds (craft beer connoisseurs, art aficionados and history buffs are all likely to find a specialty AmaWaterways cruise that suits their fancy). In its own words, AmaWaterways' passengers are often seasoned travelers who are both affluent and well-educated. With a strong biking program, there tends to be a more active contingency on board and the average age range is 50 years old and up.

DINING OPTIONS AmaWaterways was among the pioneers of creating multiple dining experiences on board its river cruise vessels, including one of its venues that is now a signature, AmaWaterways' reservation-only Chef's Table dinner venue at the aft of the vessel, now available on the *AmaCerto,*

AmaReina, AmaSonata, AmaPrima, AmaVerde, and *AmaBella.* These five-course dinners are served in an intimate restaurant at the aft of the vessel, with a view into the glass-encased kitchen where the chef and his/her team are hard at work. There will often be chef's welcome, a small teaser bite of something savory. Appetizers are delicious and light dishes, such as smoked salmon or tuna tartare. These are followed by a soup course and then a choice of two entrees, say a heartier tenderloin or rack of lamb, and either an innovative vegetarian option or a lighter poultry dish such as roasted duck. Dessert will often be a plate with three or four small dessert bites beautifully splayed across it, and of course there is always the cheese cart, from which guests can choose a selection for a custom-made cheese plate. There are also suggested wine pairings for the Chef's Table dinner, generally one white and one red. AmaWaterways also recently began introducing some interesting nonalcoholic sparkling wines as an alternative option with rhubarb and celery essence, among others. Dining at the Chef's Table restaurant is available to all passengers on board—they need to make sure to reserve a table as it's a smaller venue.

Weather permitting, there is also an alfresco grilling venue for casual lunches on the Sun Deck on the *AmaVista, AmaSerena, AmaSonata, Ama-Reina, AmaPrima, AmaCerto,* and *AmaVida.* This is a popular spot for serving up grilled sausages and sauerkraut, with a mug of beer to wash it down.

The *AmaVista, AmaSerena, AmaSonata, AmaReina, AmaPrima,* and *Ama-Certo* also feature charming private dining wine rooms adjacent to the main dining room for larger groups of about 10 that would like to sit together.

What kind of food should you expect from the main restaurant? There will be a decked-out breakfast and lunch buffet featuring an assortment of American standards—anything from eggs benedict and waffles for breakfast, to grilled ham and cheese sandwiches and familiar pasta dishes for lunch—alongside regional fare, with the European soups being particularly delicious.

The multicourse dinner in the main restaurant is accented by impressive details such as fresh, in-house-baked bread at dinner with multiple butters and spreads to choose from (always a good start). Also, there always seems to be subtle Asian influences in the cuisine on board AmaWaterways ships (something the company perhaps picked up from its investments in Southeast Asia?), whether it's Vietnamese *pho* noodle soup being served at lunch, or Asian flavors infused in the dinner entrees. It's a nice counterbalance to the European dishes.

Lighter fare is also available in the lounge during meal times, for those who would prefer a small soup or salad and a bit of solitude.

Insider Tip

If you're sailing on one of the ships that has the Chef's Table restaurant, make sure to book a dinner there as it's a fun and palette-delighting experience, complete with an open kitchen and a more intimate atmosphere than the main dining room.

AMAWATERWAYS ITINERARIES

7-day Dutch and Belgian Canals ("Tulip Time Cruise"), round-trip from Amsterdam, $2,499, balconies from $3,398, Mar–May

12-day Dordogne and Garonne ("Taste of Bordeaux") with 7-day cruise, round-trip from Bordeaux, 4,399, balconies from $5,298, Mar–Nov

9-day Seine ("Paris & Normandy") with 7-day cruise, round-trip from Paris, $3,499, balconies from $4,398, Mar–Nov

13-day Rhone & Saone ("Provence & Spain") with 7-day cruise, Paris to Barcelona, $4,699, balconies from $5,598, Mar–Nov

10-day Upper Danube ("Romantic Danube"), with 7-day cruise, Prague to Budapest, $3,479, balconies from $4,378, Mar–Dec

10-day Upper Danube ("Melodies of the Danube") with 7-day cruise, Budapest to Munich/Prague, $3,499, balconies from $4,398, Mar–Dec

10-day Upper Danube ("The Legendary Danube") with 7-day cruise, Prague to Budapest, $3,379, balconies from $4,278 Mar, May–Nov

12-day Upper Danube ("Blue Danube Discovery") with 7-day cruise, Budapest to Prague, $3,779, balconies from $4,678, Mar, May–Oct

13-day Lower Danube ("Gems of Southeast Europe"), with 7-day cruise, Vienna/Budapest to Istanbul, $4,699, balconies from $5,598 Apr, June–Aug, Oct

11-day Rhine ("The Enchanting Rhine"), with 7-day cruise, Amsterdam to Zurich, $3,759, balconies from $4,658, Mar–Dec

12-day Main and Moselle ("Europe's Rivers & Castles"), with 7-day cruise, Luxembourg to Prague, $4,719, balconies from $5,618, May–Oct

14-day Rhine, Main, Upper Danube ("Magnificent Europe"), Amsterdam to Budapest, $6,399, balconies from $8,197, Apr–June, Aug–Sept

ACTIVITIES While the emphasis on AmaWaterways cruises is more often on giving passengers options for things to see and do off the ship, during the occasional longer daytime sailings, there will be informative lectures and/or demonstrations on board that highlight the theme or region of the cruise. For instance, there might be a wine lecture and tasting during a Douro River sailing, or an art history discussion on the Rhone and Saone rivers. AmaWaterways also offers a fair amount of themed sailings such as wine-themed, beer-themed or art-themed cruises, during which there will be enhanced lectures by an expert or experts and/or tastings relevant to the theme.

CHILDREN'S PROGRAM While AmaWaterways allows children as young as 4 years old on board, the company does not recommend its cruises for children under the age of 8. All guests under the age of 18 are required to share a cabin with an adult. Children between the ages of 4 and 10 may share a cabin with two adults provided the child is able to share the bed with the

21-day Danube ("Grand Danube Cruise") with 14-day cruise, Vilshofen (Germany) to Istanbul, $7,878, balconies from $9,676, Apr, June–Oct

10-day Douro ("Enticing Douro"), with 7-day cruise, Lisbon to Porto, $3,849, balconies from $5,048, Apr–Nov

13-day Douro ("Port Wine & Flamenco") with 7-day cruise, Lisbon to Madrid, $4,519, balconies from $5,718, Apr–May, July–Oct

19-day Moselle, Main and Danube ("Ultimate River Cruise") with 14-day cruise, Paris to Budapest, $7,898, balconies from $9,696, May–Oct

9-day Main and Rhine ("Treasures of the Main & Rhine") with 7-day cruise, Prague to Amsterdam, $3,319, balconies from $4,218, Dec

15-day Mekong ("Vietnam, Cambodia & The Riches of the Mekong"), with 9-day cruise, Hanoi to Ho Chi Minh City, cabins/balconies from $4,498, Jan–Apr, Aug–Dec

9-day Chobe ("Discover Africa") with 4-day cruise, Cape Town to Johannesburg, cabins/balconies from $8,499, Apr–Nov

12-day Chobe ("Rivers & Rails of Africa") with 4-day cruise, Cape Town to Johannesburg, cabins/balconies from $12,695, Apr–May, July–Oct

14-day Chobe ("Star of South Africa") with 4-day cruise, Cape Town to Johannesburg, cabins/balconies from $11,695, Apr–Nov

16-day Chobe ("Golden Trails of East Africa"), with 4-day cruise, Johannesburg to Arusha (Tanzania), cabins/balconies from $13,495, Apr–Nov

13-day Irrawaddy ("Golden Treasures of Myanmar") with 10-day cruise, round-trip from Yangon, cabins/balconies from $5,339, Jan, Mar–Apr, Sept–Nov

15-day Irrawaddy ("Hidden Wonders of Myanmar") with 14-day cruise, round-trip from Yangon, cabins/balconies from $6,279, Jan–Feb, Apr, Aug–Dec

Note on this chart: Itineraries may also be available in the reverse direction. The first price is the lowest available price for all cabin categories, and the second price is the lowest balcony price, including French balcony cabins.

adults (no additional bed will be provided). On the company's Africa program, there is a minimum age limit of 12 years old.

ENTERTAINMENT   When it comes to entertainment on board, AmaWaterways does a fair amount of vetting and scouting of local talent. There is nightly live music in the lounge on AmaWaterways' ships and usually at least one or two additional special acts (think a French songstress or a Spanish flamenco troupe) brought on board during the cruise.

SERVICE   AmaWaterways realized early on that service was key to surviving and thriving in a competitive river cruise marketplace and has thus placed a lot of attention on hiring, training and retaining its crew members. The river cruise operator has done particularly well in recruiting charismatic and charming cruise directors—they have some of the best in the biz. The crew tend to be very hands-on and accommodating to passengers' personal requests.

disney BRINGS FAMILIES TO THE RIVERS

Traditionally known to be more popular with the baby boomer set, river cruising is gradually evolving into a more family-friendly product, and AmaWaterways made a huge step in that direction when it inked a deal last year with Adventures by Disney, Disney's tour brand, to have it charter several family-friendly departures. Disney now offers seven Danube River sailings on AmaWaterways' 170-passenger *AmaViola*, which was custom-built to cater to families. Family-friendly features include six sets of connecting staterooms as well as 12 staterooms that can accommodate three people, with an armchair that converts into a single sleeper, and four suites that can accommodate four people with a pullout sofa bed.

Adventures by Disney sailings will feature movies, karaoke, relay games, chess lessons on an oversize board, video games and themed nights for children and teens as well as wine tastings, fine dining, music, dancing and an onboard fitness center geared to adults. There will also be a biking option in every port, and eight Adventures by Disney guides will be on each sailing in addition to the existing AmaWaterways crew.

The Adventures by Disney sailings are priced slightly higher than a regular AmaWaterways departure but have more inclusions, including all gratuities, additional excursions and port charges. Adventures by Disney recommends the cruises for children ages 8 and older, and the minimum age allowed on board is 4 years old.

Gratuities for the cruise director and ship crew are not included in the cruise price, and AmaWaterways recommends about 15 euros per day for gratuities, as well as a couple euros each for daily tour guides.

TOURS As is pretty standard in river cruising, AmaWaterways gives its guests several options on included shore excursions, which usually consist of a guided tour in each port call. That can mean a morning visit in one town in the morning, a short sailing during lunch and then another afternoon visit. Or if a vessel is docked in a larger city, AmaWaterways might provide a half-day city tour in the morning and free time in the afternoon in the city. Passengers are divided into smaller groups to be able to visit the cities and towns along Europe's rivers in a more intimate atmosphere. There is a "gentle walkers" option for those that would like to visit at a more leisurely pace; an "active walkers" option for those who want to cover more ground; and a "late starter" group for passengers who would like to sleep in a bit.

Where the company excels is in its bike program, which it implemented before it was commonplace to do so and has developed into a comprehensive self-bike or bike touring option that has become very popular given how pleasant it is to cycle along the rivers of Europe or through many of the continent's bike-friendly cities.

PRE- & POST-CRUISE STAYS AmaWaterways does offer an extensive pre- and post-cruise program with offerings attached to most of its river cruises. Pre- and post-cruise stays can either be in a destination not included in the river cruise, in another city in the country where you are starting or ending your cruise, or in another country altogether. Or, passengers can opt to simply extend their time in ports of embarkation or disembarkation. The company typically offers 2 or 3 additional nights in a hotel and one or two included tours in destinations including Prague, Istanbul, Barcelona and Paris. A 2-night extension in Paris is priced at $560 per person, a 2-night stay in Budapest goes for $500, and a 3-night extension in Siem Reap with daily breakfast and included tours is $799.

Frommer's Ratings (Scale of 1–5)

Cabin comfort & amenities	4	Public spaces	5
Decor	4	Dining	5
Fitness, spa and pool	5	Service	5
Family-friendly	4	Enrichment	5

AmaViola

The Verdict

The *AmaViola* was designed by AmaWaterways with input from Adventures by Disney to be better suited to the family travel market, which means that in addition to the standard AmaWaterways features, the *AmaViola* also has connecting staterooms (a new concept for AmaWaterways), as well as suites that can accommodate up to three and four passengers.

Specifications

Passengers	170	Total cabins/balcony cabins	82/70
Passenger decks	3	Crew	50
Year entered service	2016		

THE SHIPS IN GENERAL While it may be designed to better accommodate families traveling with kids, adults will appreciate the sophisticated decor and details on board the *AmaViola* such as the Chef's Table restaurant and plush bedding. There are activities on board that the entire family can engage in, such as the in-room infotainment and on-demand internet, TV and movie system that all the AmaWaterways vessels benefit from, as well as more family-friendly experiences that will be available specifically on the *AmaViola*—family karaoke and group movie nights, for instance. Indeed, the *AmaViola* is designed to satisfy all its passengers, no matter their age.

CABINS With an emphasis on accommodating larger groups that may be traveling together, the *AmaViola* has a large percentage of cabins that are more than 200-square-feet each, with the total range being lower deck cabins that are 160-square-feet each to upper deck Suites that are 350-square-feet each. There are six sets of adjoining cabins that can accommodate families of up to five; four suites with convertible sofa beds that can accommodate families of up to four; and 12 staterooms that can accommodate up to three family members each. The majority of cabins feature a twin balcony (a French balcony adjacent to a step-out balcony) or a French balcony, and all the staterooms have a safe, flatscreen television, and a desk. All lower deck cabins only have porthole windows and no balconies.

PUBLIC AREAS   Like the ships before it, the *AmaViola* has multiple dining venues, including the main restaurant, the Chef's Table restaurant at the aft of the ship, and the option for al fresco dining on the Sun Deck. The boat has a heated pool and walking track on the Sun Deck, a panoramic lounge and bar, a gift shop, fitness room, massage room and hair salon. An elevator connects the main entrance deck (the second deck, it also houses the reception area) and third deck.

DINING OPTIONS   Passengers can either head to the main restaurant for a buffet breakfast or lunch, or for a multiple-course served dinner, or they can make a reservation at the Chef's Table restaurant for a unique dinner experience. Light meals are also served in the lounge and observation deck area and occasionally a grilled lunch is served outside on the Sun Deck, weather permitting. All meals are open seating. Wine, beer and soft drinks are included with lunch and dinner.

POOL, FITNESS, SPA, BIKES   A hair and massage salon, as well as a fitness room are located on the lowest deck. The Sun Deck is outfitted with a walking track and a heated pool. There are also bikes available both for passengers to use on their own or for use during organized, optional biking excursions. During the Disney sailings there will be at least one biking excursion offered daily.

AmaVista, AmaSerena, AmaSonata, AmaReina, AmaPrima, AmaCerto, AmaVerde & AmaBella

The Verdict

This newest generation of AmaWaterways vessels definitely benefits from years of experience and customer feedback that culminated in additional amenities such as a swim-up pool bar on the Sun Deck and private dining rooms.

Specifications

Passengers			
AmaVista, AmaSerena, AmaSonata, AmaReina, AmaPrima, AmaCerto	164	AmaVerde, AmaBella	161
Total cabins/balcony cabins			
AmaVista, AmaSerena, AmaSonata, AmaReina, AmaPrima, AmaCerto	82/65	AmaVerde, AmaBella	81/62
Passenger decks	3	Crew	49
Year entered service			
AmaSerena, AmaVista	2015	AmaCerto	2012
AmaSonata, AmaReina	2014	AmaVerde	2011
AmaPrima	2013	AmaBella	2010

THE SHIPS IN GENERAL These are not just AmaWaterways' newest vessels, they are also among the company's longest with a bow-to-stern length of 443 feet (which means more space for suites and cool public areas). Most of the suites and staterooms on board feature AmaWaterways' twin balcony concept: one full step-out balcony adjacent to a French balcony for a combination of indoor and outdoor balcony seating. The public areas offer a pleasant variety of dining, relaxing and entertainment opportunities, making these river cruise ships the crème de la crop of the AmaWaterways fleet.

CABINS There are seven categories of cabins, ranging from the 160-square-foot lower deck staterooms to 235-square-foot balcony cabins to 300-square-foot suites. The staterooms feature a sitting area, en suite bathrooms with standing showers, a wardrobe for hanging clothes, a hair dryer, safe and an in-room infotainment system with a flatscreen monitor that offers Internet access, on-demand TV shows, movies, and music.

PUBLIC AREAS One of the central social hubs of the ships is the main lounge, located on the third deck, which houses the bar, a piano and dance floor, as well as a round-the-clock, complimentary coffee and tea station. There is also a library area with a charming faux fireplace adjacent to the lounge. This deck (aka the Violin Deck) is home to the Chef's Table restaurant, fitness room, hair and massage salon, all of which are located at the aft of the ships. Behind the reception area on this deck, sits the small gift shop. One deck below, on the Cello Deck, is another important hub, the main dining room. An elevator travels between the second and third decks.

DINING OPTIONS There are several dining venues on board. The main dining room features a combination of booths and round tables that are configured for four, six, or eight diners. Larger parties can also arrange for private dining in one of the two wine rooms located at the entrance to the dining room. For a more intimate dining experience, the Chef's Table restaurant at the aft of the vessels offers a gourmet, reservation-only dinner service. Alternatively, light meals are served in the lounge and observation deck area and occasionally a grilled lunch is served on the Sun Deck, weather permitting. Breakfast and lunch are served buffet style and dinner is a multiple-course meal with several menu options to choose from. All meals are open seating. Wine, beer and soft drinks are included with lunch and dinner.

POOL, FITNESS, SPA, BIKES On the second deck are a hair and massage salon, as well as a fitness room. The Sun Deck is outfitted with a walking track and a heated pool with swim-up bar (essentially a dipping pool with built-in seats that you can bring your bar drink to). There are also bikes available on board both for passengers to use on their own or for use during organized, optional biking excursions.

AmaCello, AmaLegro, AmaDagio, AmaLyra, AmaDolce & AmaDante

The Verdict

These ships may not have all the bells and whistles as their newer counterparts, but they are still just as classy and their constant updating means you'll feel just as pampered on one of these as on any of the newer class of AmaWaterways ships.

Specifications

Passengers			
AmaLyra, AmaDolce, AmaDante	146	AmaLegro, AmaDagio	150
AmaCello	148		
Total cabins/balcony cabins	74/62	Crew	44
Passenger decks	3		
Year entered service			
AmaLyra, AmaDolce	2009	AmaLegro	2007
AmaDante, AmaCello	2008	AmaDagio	2006

THE SHIPS IN GENERAL These 360-foot vessels are perfect examples of the simple elegance that defines the AmaWaterways fleet—they remind us of European boutique hotels, where modern design and workmanship meet both classic and statement art pieces and florals. No, these slightly smaller ships don't have such amenities as the swim-up pool bar or twin balconies that AmaWaterways added on its newer ships. But for many passengers, French balconies are more than enough, and the time on land is more precious than time in a pool. The majority of staterooms are also a bit smaller than on the newer ships, so divas be warned.

CABINS Most of the staterooms on these vessels are 170-square-feet each, and all of the cabins on the upper two levels have French balconies. There are also four, 255-square-foot Suites on the upper deck (also with French balconies), and two of the staterooms on the *AmaCello, AmaLyra, AmaDolce,* and *AmaDante* are 140-square-foot cabins designed for solo travelers (they have French balconies too and being for solos means no single supplement—score for single travelers). All lower deck cabins only have porthole windows and no balconies

PUBLIC AREAS On board these sister vessels, there's a bar and lounge, main dining room, Chef's Table restaurant, fitness room, hair and massage salon. On the Sun Deck, there's a whirlpool and walking track. An elevator connects the second and third deck. Each ship has a unique color palette (the *AmaLyra* for instance is based in warm hues of brown, red, turquoise and white, while the *AmaDagio* has more muted brown and beige details), and artwork touches all its own, ranging from more dramatic pieces to classic European paintings. So even though the layouts are almost identical, you feel subtle identity differences on each.

DINING OPTIONS The main dining room serves American standards alongside local specialties. Breakfast and lunch are large buffet spreads and dinners are multicourse waitered meals—passengers pick their preferred appetizers, entrees and desserts. Alternatively, the Chef's Table restaurant at the aft of the vessels is a reservation-only specialty restaurant, featuring an open kitchen and dinner served in a more intimate setting. There is complimentary and unlimited wine, beer and soft drinks with lunch and dinner, sparkling wine served at breakfast, and free bottled water, specialty coffees and teas for passengers.

POOL, FITNESS, SPA, BIKES   On board are a small fitness room, hair and massage salon and a whirlpool; bikes available for passengers as well.

AmaVida
The Verdict

Ships that sail Portugal's Douro River are required to be a bit smaller than ships that sail Europe's other rivers, so think of the *AmaVida* as a pocket-size version of a regular AmaWaterways ship.

Specifications

Passengers	106	Total cabins/balcony cabins	53/38
Passenger decks	3	Crew	30
Year entered service	2013		

THE SHIPS IN GENERAL   The *AmaVida* has a distinctly sleek and modern interior design, accented by stylish wood finishings. Due to its smaller size (the *AmaVida* only measures 260 feet in length, compared to the 360- to 443-foot vessels that ply the main rivers of Europe), the *AmaVida* doesn't have as many staterooms or the same public spaces as its larger equivalents. There is no Chef's Table restaurant on board, but in addition to a main restaurant that churns out quality meals, there is also a casual outdoor venue for meals served al fresco in an intimate space at the bow of the ship, something to take advantage of with the warmer temps in Portugal. The relatively sizeable pool on the sundeck is also a great place to cool off during those hot Portuguese summers.

CABINS   There are three cabin sizes: the 161-square-foot lower deck cabins; the 215-square-foot balcony cabins on the second and third deck; and the two, 323-square-foot Suites on the third deck. All of the staterooms have an in-room safe, hair dryer, closet space, wireless telephone, terry cloth bathrobes, complimentary bottled water replenished daily and individually controlled air-conditioning.

AmaWaterways

Insider Tip

The actress Sharon Stone is the godmother of the *AmaVida* and christened the vessel when it launched in 2013. She stayed in what is now known as the "Sharon Stone Suite," which is Room 319, if you want to have stayed-in-the-same-stateroom-as-a-celebrity bragging rights.

PUBLIC AREAS   There is one main restaurant, a bar and lounge area, a gift shop off to one side of the reception area, a fitness room, spa and pool. An elevator travels between all three stateroom decks.

DINING OPTIONS   The main dining room is outfitted with cushioned bench seating (with backs) and oval tables. There are tables for two, four and eight passengers and meals are open seating, with breakfast and lunch served buffet style and dinner served by the wait staff as a three-course meal. There is also an al fresco dining area adjacent to the restaurant, where passengers can reserve seats for a three-course dinner that is different than the main restaurant menu in a more casual setting. Local wines are included with lunch and dinner.

POOL, FITNESS, SPA, BIKES   There is a small but adequate heated pool on the Sun Deck and a fitness room and spa on the lower deck. There are no bikes on board but bike touring outfits offer cycling excursions.

AmaDara & AmaLotus

The Verdict

These Mekong River cruisers are built and designed in a slightly different style than their European counterparts (vessels on the Mekong are generally taller and shorter than in Europe), but AmaWaterways made sure to incorporate all the creature comforts one would expect from a luxury river cruise line, including air-conditioned interiors, plenty of balconies and top-notch food and service.

Specifications

Passengers	124	Crew	50
Total cabins/balcony cabins			
AmaDara	62/62	AmaLotus	62/56
Passenger decks			
AmaDara	3	AmaLotus	4
Year entered service			
AmaDara	2015	AmaLotus	2011

THE SHIPS IN GENERAL   It's very East-meets-West on the *AmaDara* and *AmaLotus,* with style and design touches that give a decided nod to the aesthetics of Vietnam and Cambodia (you'll find silk prints on the cushions in the lounge and on the throws on the bed, and local floral artwork on the walls, among other shout-outs to the destinations), but an onboard experience that is mostly in line with the standards of river cruising passengers have come to expect in Europe—think high-touch service, comfortable air-conditioned staterooms and public spaces, and food that evokes both Western and Southeast Asian favorites. The overall experience is a bit more adventurous with many of the daily excursions taking place on motorboats for instance, not to mention the exotic nature of the destinations overall. With the *AmaDara* and *AmaLotus,* AmaWaterways has created extremely agreeable accommodations from which to see and experience life along the Mekong River.

CABINS   The smallest of the spacious cabins are 226-square-feet each. On the *AmaLotus* there are 10 Suites measuring 290-square-feet and two sprawling, Luxury Suites at 624-square-feet each. On the *AmaDara* there are 12 Suites that measure 334-square-feet each, and two Luxury Suites at 452-square-feet each. All of the staterooms on the *AmaDara* feature AmaWaterways' twin balconies, and all but the lower deck staterooms on the *AmaLotus* do as well (the lower deck staterooms on the *AmaLotus* have porthole windows).

PUBLIC AREAS   Both vessels have a main dining room, called the Mekong Restaurant, and the *AmaDara* has an alternative dining venue, the Tarantula Grill, with an outdoor terrace. Both have a spa, swimming pool and lounges. The *AmaDara* also has a fitness room and hair salon.

DINING OPTIONS   In the Mekong Restaurant, passengers will find Western specialties sitting side-by-side with Southeast Asian fare. Breakfast and lunch are served buffet style, often with a specialty grilling station where dishes are made to order. We highly recommend trying the Vietnamese *pho* soup for breakfast. It's a light beef or chicken broth soup with noodles, choice of meat added (shrimp, beef, chicken or pork) and garnished with lime, tons of fresh herbs and whatever chili sauce you want to add. It is quite a soothing way to wake up. Dinners are served in an open seating environment with a nightly menu of options to choose from, also with an East-meets-West vibe (think a Cambodian fish dish alongside a baked chicken entrée). In the Tarantula Grill on the *AmaDara,* passengers will be able to sit indoors or in a shaded terrace and will be offered local options cooked by local chefs. Complimentary wine is served with lunch, and complimentary house spirits, local beer, soft drinks and bottled water are available all day, free of charge.

POOL, FITNESS, SPA, BIKES   There is a pool and spa (they give some serious, knot-untangling massages) on both vessels, and a fitness room on the *AmaDara.* No bikes on either of the Mekong vessels.

AmaPura

The Verdict

Similar in look and feel to AmaWaterways' Mekong vessels, the *AmaPura* marries Burmese design with luxury accommodations and amenities.

Specifications

Passengers	56	Total cabins/balcony cabins	28/28
Passenger decks	2	Crew	30
Year entered service	2014		

THE SHIPS IN GENERAL   The *AmaPura* provides a comfortable and fashionable floating hotel from which to explore Myanmar's Irrawaddy River. This small vessel has few, but very tastefully appointed, public spaces (where European antique-style furniture are detailed with patterned, silk pillows), and offers an air-conditioned refuge in which to rest in between excursions.

CABINS   All 28 staterooms have either a French or full balcony or both. The majority of cabins are 285- to 290-square-feet and there are two larger, 420-square-foot staterooms. Most have a small seating area, and all have a desk, in-room infotainment system, wardrobe and en suite bathroom. The

420-square-foot cabins feature a full bathtub. The modern stylings of the staterooms are made to feel more welcoming by artwork depicting Burmese scenery.

PUBLIC AREAS   On board the *AmaPura,* there is a main lounge and bar, a pool, sundeck, a main restaurant and a spa on the lower deck.

DINING OPTIONS   All meals are served in the main dining room, where passengers can choose from an array of both Western and Asian dishes at the buffet breakfast and lunch. Dinners are a three-course affair with menus changing nightly.

POOL, FITNESS, SPA, BIKES   There is a small pool and spa on board. No bikes or fitness room.

OTHER RIVER CRUISE LINES

A s we stated in the previous chapter, there are a lot of river cruise companies out there (more than you probably ever realized or imagined!). In this chapter we are going to introduce the other major players.

Many of these companies are specialized in a specific region of river cruising, such as U.S. rivers (American Cruise Lines and American Queen Steamboat Company, for instance) or Southeast Asia rivers (such as Pandaw River Expeditions). Some of them are also predominantly "wholesale" river cruise lines, meaning they own and operate the ships but most of their inventory is actually leased or chartered out to river cruise lines or travel companies you're more familiar with—Chinese company Century Cruises is a perfect example of this as it sells its ships through Uniworld and Avalon, among others.

If you go online to search for river cruises, and you find a company that is not listed in one of these two chapters, chances are it either doesn't cater to American travelers (we aren't the only ones who are crazy about river cruising), is very, very small, or, most probably, is a river cruise reseller, companies that contract with river cruise lines for a certain amount of inventory and then resell that inventory (see box on p. 146 for more on those companies).

The companies we focused on here are bona fide river cruise lines that build and operate their own river cruise fleets. Because they operate in different parts of the world, their products vary drastically both because the standards and the shipbuilding styles are so unique in different regions of the world, but also because the rivers themselves have distinctive characteristics. Many rivers outside of Europe are much more vast, allowing for taller or wider ships. This chapter is, in fact, where river cruising starts to get really dynamic and we get to see how different the riverboats, pricing, and overall river cruising experience can be throughout the world.

THE COMPONENTS OF OUR CRUISE-LINE REVIEWS

Just as in the last chapter, each cruise line's review begins with a quick word about the line in general and a short summation of the kind of cruise experience you can expect to have aboard that line.

The text that follows fleshes out the review, providing all the details you need to get a feel for what kind of vacation the cruise line will provide.

The individual ship reviews following the general cruise-line description then get into the nitty-gritty, giving you details on the ships' accommodations, facilities, amenities, comfort levels, and upkeep.

We've listed some of each ship's vital statistics, such as number of decks, year built, number of cabins, number of crew—to help you compare. *Note:* When several vessels are members of a class—built with the same or similar design, with usually only minor variations in decor and attractions—we've grouped the ships together into one review.

Stars
THE RATINGS

To make things easier on everyone, we've developed a simple ratings system that covers those things that vary from line to line—quality and size of the cabins and public spaces, decor, number and quality of dining options, gyms/spas (if any) and whether the line is a good choice for children or not. We've also rated enrichment programs, an important aspect for many river cruisers. We've given each line an overall **star rating** based on the combined total of our poor-to-outstanding ratings, translated into a 1-to-5 scale:

1	=	**Poor**	4	=	**Excellent**
2	=	**Fair**	5	=	**Outstanding**
3	=	**Good**			

In instances when the category doesn't apply to a particular ship, for instance no kids allowed, we've simply noted "not applicable" (N/A) and absented the category from the total combined score, as these unavailable amenities will be considered a deficiency only in certain circumstances (for instance, if you plan to travel with kids).

Now for a bit of philosophy: The cruise biz today offers a profusion of experiences so different that comparing all ships by the same set of criteria would be like comparing a Paris apartment to an A-frame in Aspen. That's why, to rate the ships, we've used a sliding scale, rating ships on a curve that compares them only with others in their category. Once you've determined

---

What You Should Know About Cruise Resellers

For the most part, river cruise resellers are totally legit. They literally repackage river cruises that are offered by many of the river cruise lines that are listed in these two chapters. The being said, you'll want to make sure the reseller is, in fact, a reliable operator. For one, you could call the river cruise line it is selling and check with them. If it's a tour operator (such as Collette, Classic Vacations, Gate 1, etc.) that is repackaging the river cruise, which is very common, make sure it's a reputable one. You could check with the American Society of Travel Agents (asta.org), or see if the tour operator is a member of the U.S. Tour Operators Association (ustoa.com), an organization that offers travelers protections in the event one of its members goes bust.

what kind of experience is right for you, you can look for the best ships in that category based on your particular needs.

Itineraries

Each cruise-line review includes a chart showing itineraries. We did this by river line rather than ship because river ships tend to move around—the same ship may do several different itineraries in a year and several ships may do the same itinerary. All itineraries are subject to change. Consult the cruise-line websites or your travel agent for exact sailing dates.

Prices: Don't Get Sticker Shock

We've listed starting brochure prices for cabins, and starting prices for cabins with balconies (including French balconies). If the starting price is for "cabins/balconies" that means it's an all-balcony ship, as many of them are in Southeast Asia, for instance. If there is no starting price for balconies that means there are no balcony cabins. Suites will be higher priced than the starting prices we have listed. We stress that all the prices listed reflect the line's **brochure rates,** so depending on how early you book and any special deals the lines are offering, you may get a rate substantially below what we've listed. Rates are all per person, per cruise, based on two people sharing a cabin (rates for a solo passenger in a cabin in many cases will be higher).

AMERICAN CRUISE LINES

www.americancruiselines.com. ℂ 800/460-4518.

Pros

○ **Upscale but homey.** These riverboats don't skimp on space or amenities, and have a comfy ambience with overstuffed couches, white wooden rocking chairs, a historic calliope, and a chart room full of river maps. They're like beautifully made, favorite quilts.

○ **Convenience for American vacationers.** Travelers can often get to the riverboats by car, train or short flights.

Cons

○ **No kids' programs.** There are no children's programs or facilities (which some undoubtedly find a plus).

○ **No bar or lounge.** There is a daily complimentary cocktail hour and wine and beer with lunch and dinner, but no place to buy a drink other times.

THE LINE IN A NUTSHELL   This small-ship line is growing fast with a fleet of newly built riverboats on the Mississippi River and on the Columbia and Snake rivers in the Pacific Northwest.

Frommer's Ratings (Scale of 1–5)

Cabin comfort & amenities	5	Public spaces	4
Decor	4	Dining	4
Fitness, spa and pool	2	Service	3
Family-friendly	2	Enrichment	4

THE EXPERIENCE   As its name suggests, this company exemplifies the red, white and blue—its Maryland-built fleet flies the U.S. flag and is staffed with an all-American crew. American Cruise Lines celebrates the U.S.A. by traversing its waterways to cities (like New Orleans, St. Louis, St. Paul and Memphis) and small river towns you've never heard of but will be charmed by (such as Madison, Ind.; Astoria, Ore.; and Hannibal, Mo.).

The newly built riverboats have huge staterooms with big bathrooms, cozy lounges, local entertainment and delicious, often locally sourced, food. These river cruises aren't inexpensive, but are a good value since fares include complimentary cocktail parties, beer and wine with lunch and dinner, service charges, wireless Internet and some shore excursions.

American Cruise Lines also operates four coastal ships that carry no more than 104 passengers.

THE FLEET   American Cruise Lines' river fleet includes the 150-passenger *Queen of the Mississippi* and *American Pride,* the 120-passenger *Queen of the West,* and the 185-guest *America.* The company is planning another ship to start sailing U.S. rivers in 2017. They all look like traditional Victorian-era riverboats with wedding-cake exteriors and working red paddlewheels. The *American Pride, Queen of the West,* and *America* all have calliopes, a keyboard instrument similar to an organ but with calliopes notes are produced by pressure generated by steam, creating a truly unique sound.

PASSENGER PROFILE   These river cruises attract affluent, highly educated and well-traveled guests typically 55 years and older. They love to travel, but perhaps at a slower pace. (Hint: A company selling point is "elevator service to all decks.") A good number drive or take the train to homeports in the heartland. Every riverboat has solo-occupancy staterooms, so there's usually a sprinkling of single travelers.

DINING OPTIONS   Seating is open in the main dining room, so guests sit where and with whom they wish. Generally, seating is allowed from 6:30 to 7:30pm, after the complimentary cocktail hour in the lounge. Complimentary wine and beer is served at lunch and dinner.

Since every entree is individually prepared, passengers fill out paper forms with their selections at the previous meal.

Meals are often made with locally sourced ingredients—for example, freshly caught salmon and Rainier cherries in the Pacific Northwest and certified Berkshire pork from an Iowa farm and Wisconsin artisan cheeses on the Mississippi River itineraries. The food is delicious but not overly fussy. Breakfast offerings are extensive both in the dining room as well as on the room service menu.

ACTIVITIES   As you cruise along America's inland waterways, American Cruise Lines will bring various local experts, guest speakers, authors and historians on board to provide passengers with more information about the destinations they are sailing to and through. Some of these experts might also join groups onshore to continue to provide relevant insights.

AMERICAN CRUISE LINES ITINERARIES

8-day Lower Mississippi ("New Orleans-New Orleans"), round-trip from New Orleans, $4,540, balconies from $5,875, Feb–July, Oct–Dec

8-day Lower Mississippi ("Lower Mississippi River Cruise"), New Orleans to Memphis, $4,540, balconies from $5,875, Apr–Dec

15-day Mississippi ("Grand Heartland Cruise"), St. Paul to New Orleans, $8,850, balconies from $11,515, Aug–Oct

22-day Mississippi ("Complete Mississippi River Cruise"), New Orleans to St. Paul, $12,800, balconies from $16,675, Aug

8-day Upper Mississippi ("Upper Mississippi River Cruise"), St. Louis to St. Paul, $4,540, balconies from $5,875, July–Oct

8-day Upper Mississippi ("Memphis-St. Louise Cruise"), Memphis to St Louis, $4,540, balconies from $5,875, July

8-day Ohio River ("Ohio River Cruise") from Memphis to Cincinnati, $4,540, balconies from $5,875, June–July

8-day Mississippi ("St. Louise-New Orleans Cruise"), St. Louis to New Orleans, $4,540, balconies from $5,875, July

8-day Mississippi and Cumberland ("Memphis-Nashville Cruise"), Memphis to Nashville, $4,540, balconies from $5,875, Sept

8-day Cumberland ("Cumberland River Cruise"), Nashville to St. Louis, $4,540, balconies from $5,875, Sept

8-day Columbia and Snake ("Columbia and Snake River Cruise"), Portland to Clarkston (Wash.), $4,055, balconies from $4,900, Apr–Oct

5-day Columbia ("**Highlights of the Columbia River**"), round-trip from Portland, $2,595, balconies from $3,030, Aug

11-day Columbia and Snake ("Northwest Pioneers Cruise"), Clarkston (Wash.) to Portland, $6,485, balconies from $7,580, Aug

Note on this chart: Itineraries may also be available in the reverse direction. The first price is the lowest available price for all cabin categories, and the second price is the lowest balcony price, including French balcony cabins.

CHILDREN'S PROGRAM There is no formal program, but the hotel director can organize customized activities for young travelers.

ENTERTAINMENT After-dinner entertainment is provided by locals who board and perform for about an hour or so. It might be a historian in period clothing who shares tales of patriots, fur traders, Indians and explorers on the Columbia River; or a vocal trio that performs classic patriotic songs during Mississippi River cruises. Throughout the cruise, river experts and naturalists share stories and interesting facts about the region. The low-key entertainment is in keeping with the quiet onboard atmosphere.

SERVICE Don't expect formal, European-style service from tuxedo-clad waiters. The American Cruise Lines riverboats have all-American crews that offer friendly, personal service. The welcoming attitude even extends to friends of passengers¡, who can board for dinner when the ship docks near their homes. Staterooms are cleaned twice a day. The hotel manager on board can make appointments in port for spa and hair treatments or tee times at local golf courses. Gratuities are not included in the cruise price.

TOURS   River cruises include a complimentary shore tour virtually every day. Some examples: In Madison, Indiana, a historic trolley tour visits a Greek Revival mansion and a restored saddletree factory. In Natchez, Mississippi, complimentary options include a historic district tour or a shuttle into town for shops and museums. Optional excursions are priced from $20 to $130.

PRE- & POST-CRUISE STAYS   American Cruise Lines offers discounted rates at hotels such as Marriott, Hilton or Red Lion at departure points. In some cases, complimentary parking is offered for the duration of the cruise.

American Pride & Queen of the Mississippi
The Verdict

The *American Pride* and *Queen of the Mississippi* have brought together modern-day amenities (such as private balconies) with an old-timey look and feel befitting the Ol' Miss.

Specifications

Passengers	150	Total cabins/balcony cabins	84/78
Passenger decks	4	Crew	50
Year entered service:			
Queen of the Mississippi	2015	*American Pride*	2012

THE SHIPS IN GENERAL   These almost identical sister riverboats accommodate 150 passengers in big, roomy staterooms, most with private balconies. The ships have a Victorian decor that brings to mind Mississippi riverboats of yore, all the way down to the bright red paddlewheel.

CABINS   The cabins are very large at 260-square-feet and up. Most have private balconies, but those that don't instead have a picture window that opens (allowing for some fresh air in the cabin). A main difference is that the *Queen of the Mississippi* has nine staterooms on the top deck (aka the Sun Deck) of the ship, giving them a unique vantage point high above the river. Staterooms are equipped with a satellite TV with DVD player and personal Keurig coffeemakers.

PUBLIC AREAS   The ships have a number of small lounges with a living room-like feel, where passengers gather to play cards, chat or read. The Chart Room is stocked with maps and navigational charts of the Mississippi River and its tributaries.

The Magnolia Lounge is the main gathering spot for the before-dinner cocktail hours, lectures and musical performances. It's comfortably furnished with plenty of couches and has large windows.

The Paddlewheel Lounge overlooks (you guessed it) the authentic paddlewheel that helps propel the ship. It features deep red carpeting and upholstered couches with stained-glass-style lighting fixtures.

On the fourth deck, the Sky Lounge is a bright and cheery spot with coffee, cold beverages and snacks available. The deck outside is lined with white wooden rocking chairs.

The Sun Deck features an expansive shaded area, lounge chairs, exercise equipment, a putting green and, of course, a calliope. The promenade goes all the way around the deck. The ships have complimentary wireless Internet.

DINING OPTIONS All meals are served in the windowed Dining Salon on the Main Deck. It is open seating and informal—resort casual. Breakfast, lunch and dinner are ordered off a menu and are cooked to order. There is a complimentary cocktail hour with full bar each evening before dinner, and complimentary wine and beer served with lunch and dinner. There is no real lounge or bar to buy drinks beyond that, but ice and mixers are always available, and additional beverages can be ordered through the hotel director or staff.

POOL, FITNESS, SPA, BIKES There is a small fitness area on the Sun Deck with pretty decent equipment. It varies by ship but might include an elliptical and exercise bikes or a chest press. There is no pool or spa. The hotel manager on board can make spa or hair salon appointments in ports along the way. The ships do not carry bicycles.

Queen of the West

The Verdict

The staterooms are not as large as the newly built riverboats, but the Pacific Northwest food, itinerary, and scenery win raves.

Specifications

Passengers	120	Total cabins/balcony cabins	70/40
Passenger decks	4	Crew	40
Year entered service	1995		

THE SHIP IN GENERAL American Cruise Lines purchased the *Queen of the West* from its former owner, Majestic America Line (a company that went belly up in 2008) in 2009. Over the course of the next 2 years, American Cruise Lines invested millions to increase the size of staterooms and make upgrades around the ship. The company increased staterooms from an average of about 160-square-feet to an average of about 240-square-feet. All told, the ship's capacity was reduced from 150 to 120 passengers. The company also added more private balconies to the *Queen of the West*, as it worked to bring the vessel to the higher standards of today's river cruiser (such a demanding bunch). The result was that there are still some itty-bitty cabins on board but plenty of roomier staterooms for those who don't want to squeeze. Beyond that, everything from the flooring to ceilings and lighting were replaced for the 2011 season. The dining room and lounges were redecorated and a new library was added. Needless to say, the *Queen of the West* sailing today has received some serious TLC.

CABINS The staterooms range in size from 135-square-feet for a single-occupancy cabin to 390-square-foot suites. Many have private balconies and fall into the 175- to 250-square-foot range.

PUBLIC AREAS In addition to the large main lounge on the Main Deck forward, the *Queen of the West* also has a lounge overlooking the big, red paddlewheel. There's a small library on third deck and a lounge area on the top deck near the calliope. The *Queen of the West* has complimentary wireless Internet.

DINING OPTIONS Breakfast, lunch and dinner are made to order in the Dining Salon, which is open seating. As with other American Cruise Lines vessels, there is a complimentary cocktail hour, and complimentary wine and beer with lunch and dinner, but that's it for booze served on board. The tasty meals incorporate local food such as fresh salmon and Rainier cherries.

POOL, FITNESS, SPA, BIKES On the Sun Deck there's a small fitness area with a few pieces of cardio and weight-training equipment but no pool or spa. The hotel manager on board can make spa or hair salon appointments in ports along the way. The ship does not carry bicycles.

America
The Verdict
Slightly larger than its predecessors, this newly built riverboat is slated to enter service in spring 2016.

Specifications

Passengers	185	Total cabins/balcony cabins	98/95
Passenger decks	4	Crew	60
Year entered service	2016		

THE SHIPS IN GENERAL The *America* is the third Mississippi paddlewheeler that American Cruise Lines built from the ground up, joining the company's *American Eagle* and *Queen of the Mississippi* (they have engines too, in case you were wondering). The *America* had not yet launched when this book went to publication but the company was making big promises about its features and amenities, including the seven planned lounges (we spotted four on the deck plan) and larger-than-average staterooms.

CABINS The cabins are expected to be rather spacious—American Cruise Lines has not released exact cabin dimensions yet but said the staterooms will be "the largest staterooms of any small cruise ship." We'll believe it when we see it. Some of the staterooms will have 60-square-foot private balconies, and suites are expected to be between 450 and 750-square-feet.

PUBLIC AREAS The *America* will have a main dining room that will be able to accommodate all passengers at once. It will have multiple lounges including one overlooking the paddlewheel and a library with maps and charts. The Sun Deck will feature a small putting green. There will be complimentary wireless Internet.

DINING OPTIONS The open seating Dining Room will be the heart of the meal-time action on the *America.*

POOL, FITNESS, SPA, BIKES There will be an outdoor fitness area on the Sun Deck, but no pool, spa or bicycles on board.

AMERICAN QUEEN STEAMBOAT COMPANY

www.americanqueensteamboatcompany.com. 📞 888/749-5280.

Pros

o **Authentic Americana.** Be transported back in time on one of American Queen Steamboat Company's two authentic paddle-wheelers. Although they aren't crazy vintage—the *American Queen* originally launched in 1995 and the *American Empress* in 2003—they were built as replicas of their Mark Twain-era predecessors and look and feel every bit the part.

o **Entertainment.** Witnessing Big Band, jazz and vibrant storytelling in the ornate and festive showrooms on board these throwback-to-another-era vessels is not to be missed.

o **Local cuisine.** American Queen Steamboat Company prides itself on infusing the cuisine on board with the culinary traditions of the destinations it sails through—gumbo or smoked salmon anyone?

Cons

o **Working with older vessels.** The American Queen Steamboat Company offers its passengers the opportunity to sail on pieces of living history, but the disadvantage of these slightly older ships is that they have older hardware and layouts that don't always have the types of amenities that the modern-day river cruiser has grown accustomed to, like a plethora of private balconies and en suite bathrooms that don't feel like prefab motel bathrooms, for instance. Hey, you can't have everything, right?

THE LINE IN A NUTSHELL The American Queen Steamboat Company's *American Queen* and *American Empress,* with their historical look and feel, serve as the ideal vehicles on which to travel back in time and embrace the history and traditions along some of the most storied inland waterways in the U.S.

Frommer's Ratings (Scale of 1–5)

Cabin comfort & amenities	3	Public spaces	5
Decor	4	Dining	4
Fitness, spa and pool	3	Service	4
Family-friendly	3	Enrichment	4

THE EXPERIENCE When the American Queen Steamboat Company purchased the *American Queen* and relaunched it in 2012, it effectively resuscitated overnight passenger cruising on the Mississippi River, which had slowed to a near halt after the vessel's previous owner, Majestic America Line, ceased operations in 2008.

5-day Lower Mississippi ("Big Band"), round-trip from New Orleans, $799, balconies from $1,249, Feb

9-day Lower Mississippi ("Big Band"), round-trip from New Orleans, $2,149, balconies from $3,399, Feb

9-day Lower Mississippi ("Antebellum South"), New Orleans to Memphis, $2,149, balconies from $3,399, Feb.-Nov.

9-day Lower Mississippi ("Civil War"), Memphis to New Orleans, $2,249, balconies from $3,599, Mar and June

9-day Lower Mississippi ("Music of America"), New Orleans to Memphis, $2,249, balconies from $3,599, Mar

9-day Upper Mississippi ("4th of July Celebration"), Memphis to St. Louis, $2,149, balconies from $3,399, July

9-day Ohio, Tennessee and Cumberland ("Bourbon"), St. Louis to Cincinnati, $2,149, balconies from $3,399, July

9-day Ohio, Tennessee and Cumberland ("Presidents & Politics"), Cincinnati to St. Louis, $2,149, balconies from $3,399, July

9-day Upper Mississippi ("Life on the Mississippi"), St. Louis to St. Paul, $2,149, balconies from $3,399, July-Aug

9-day Upper Mississippi ("Mark Twain"), St. Paul to St. Louis, $2,249, balconies from $3,599, July

9-day Upper Mississippi ("Music of the 50s and 60s"), St. Paul to St. Louis, $2,249, balconies from $3,599, Aug

The purchase and restoration of the 436-passenger *American Queen* has been a labor of love for the Memphis-based company, which in 2014 relaunched the *American Empress* (formerly the *Empress of the North*), another vessel that had been laid up since the 2008 collapse of Majestic.

The American Queen Steamboat Company has invested heavily to bring these vessels up to contemporary standards (including having added flat-screen televisions and Egyptian cotton bedding to the staterooms, and having replaced curtains with mahogany shutters in its outward facing staterooms). But don't expect the super high-end sophistication that European river cruising has come to represent.

When you cruise with the American Queen Steamboat Company, you should really be ready to throw yourself into American history and folklore. In other words, to embrace the kitsch, embrace small town U.S.A., and embrace the people and traditions along the rivers.

The *American Queen* and *American Empress* (despite being only 21 and 13 years old, respectively) are a bit like floating museums of the country's rich river history. From the interesting American artwork on board the *American Empress* to the Grand Saloon inspired by Ford's Theatre on the *American Queen*, they just don't make vessels like these anymore. And what better way

9-day Upper Mississippi ("Good Old Summertime"), St. Louis to Memphis, $2,249, balconies from $3,599, Aug

9-day Upper Mississippi ("Big Band Swing"), Memphis to St. Louis, $2,499, balconies from $3,999, Sept

9-day Upper Mississippi ("Autumn Colors"), Memphis to St. Louis/St. Louis to St. Paul/St. Paul to St. Louis, $2,499, balconies from $3,999, Sept-Oct

9-day Ohio, Tennessee and Cumberland ("Five Rivers of the Heartland"), St. Louis to Nashville, $2,499, balconies from $3,999, Oct

9-day Ohio, Tennessee and Cumberland ("Music of America"), Nashville to Memphis, $2,499, balconies from $3,999, Oct

9-day Lower Mississippi ("Thanksgiving Festival"), New Orleans to Memphis, $2,249, balconies from $3,599, Nov

9-day Lower Mississippi ("Elvis"), Memphis to New Orleans, $2,249, balconies from $3,599, Nov

23-day Lower and Upper Mississippi ("Mighty Mississippi"), St. Paul to New Orleans, $5,949, balconies from $9,499, Aug-Sept

9-day Columbia River, round-trip from Portland, $2,649, balconies from $2,649, Mar and Nov

9-day Columbia and Snake Rivers, Portland to Clarkston (Wash.), $2,649, balconies from $2,649, Apr-Nov

Note on this chart: Itineraries may also be available in the reverse direction. The first price is the lowest available price for all cabin categories, and the second price is the lowest balcony price, including French balcony cabins.

to float between American classics like New Orleans and Memphis (hello Graceland!), or between the effortlessly charming port-town of Astoria in Oregon and the heart-stoppingly scenic views of the Columbia River Gorge?

THE FLEET River cruise ships in the U.S. are quite a bit larger than their European equivalents and thus they have many more staterooms but public spaces that are larger, too.

In 2015, the *American Queen* celebrated 20 years since it first set sail on the Mississippi River, and the 436-passenger paddle-wheeler remains one of the largest riverboats that was ever built stateside. From its steam engines to its two-deck-high chambers in the J.M. White Dining Room, from its Ford Theatre–inspired Grand Saloon to the Mark Twain Gallery with its large collection of Tiffany glass, there are features that make this vessel as much of an attraction as the rivers it sails. There are 12 cabin categories on the *American Queen*, ranging from a 132-square-foot inside cabin (not including the super-small single inside cabins for solo travelers) to 353-square-foot luxury suites. The majority of the staterooms open up to a public, wrap-around balcony.

Like a smaller cousin of the *American Queen*, the 223-passenger *American Empress* was rechristened in Portland, Oregon, in 2014. Originally built in 2003, the *American Empress* sailed Alaska's Inside Passage and the Pacific

Northwest until 2008, when it was laid up. In its latest incarnation, the River Grill on the fourth deck has received one of the ship's most intensive makeovers, having been transformed from a snack stand into a sophisticated dining experience, centered around a U-shaped bar. The *American Empress* has seven cabin categories, ranging from the 150-square-foot veranda staterooms to the 410-square-foot luxury suites with verandas.

PASSENGER PROFILE   U.S. river cruising tends to attract the retiree and boomer segments of the population, as well as American history buffs of all ages. Because you don't need a passport, the product is also attractive to passengers who prefer not to travel internationally.

DINING OPTIONS   Rest assured that you will taste the local flavors of the South, Midwest and Pacific Northwest while sailing with the American Queen Steamboat Company. So whether it's a jazz brunch on the *American Queen,* complete with crab cakes benedict, or smoked salmon on board the *American Empress,* you can expect some regional specialties on the menus. It's not a gourmet experience, especially compared to the fancy platings on the ships across the pond, but it is an inspired effort to immerse passengers into the destinations.

On the *American Queen,* breakfast, lunch and dinner are served in the grandiose J.M. White Dining Saloon, where passengers can expect to chow down on the cuisine of the Mississippi River region (think shrimp and grits or bananas foster). Here, breakfast and lunch are served buffet-style and dinners are served by a charming wait staff, many from the south. The Front Porch Café offers lighter meals and snacks with a view (the popcorn machine, soft serve and juices are big hits). There is also 24-hour room service available.

The recently updated and elegantly modern Astoria Dining Room on the *American Empress* is where passengers eat the majority of their meals on board, ranging from made-to-order eggs at breakfast to five-course dinners. All meals are served in the Astoria Dining Room, no buffet here, which makes it feel a bit fancier than the food service on the *American Queen.* Expect to find a great deal of the seafood and wines that the Pacific Northwest is known for woven into the daily menus. For those looking for a more intimate dining experience, the River Grill & Bar, with it's fun and social U-shaped bar, serves up handsomely plated bistro and seafood dishes. It has both inside and outdoor seating. Beer and wine are complimentary during dinner. And there is 24-hour room service on the *American Empress* as well.

On both vessels, there is an Early Riser's Coffee service, and there are two seating times for dinner. In between meals snacks such as sandwiches, ice cream and cookies are made available.

Note: A 15% beverage service charge is added to bar charges and to wine purchased in the dining room—there is complimentary wine and beer with dinner and the rest is on passengers.

ACTIVITIES   We have one word for you: "riverlorians." If you have never heard of them, you will become very familiar with the concept on board the *American Queen* or *American Empress.* These local experts are the lifeblood of the onboard activities, heading up lectures and presentations. They are people who are genuinely engrained in various aspects of U.S. river cruising, whether it's a steamboat historian who may offer up his/her services in the Chart Room (a popular space full of historical maps and river data), a Civil War expert or a nature enthusiast to talk about the wildlife along the rivers.

CHILDREN'S PROGRAM Children of all ages are allowed on board American Queen Steamboat Company's vessels, with children ages 2 and younger traveling for free and children 3 and older traveling at the standard rate. There are no onboard or onshore programs that are specifically geared towards children or families, and while there could definitely be some fun and educational aspects for kids, the generally older clientele on board and lack of kid-friendly activities could make these cruises a bit of a snooze for youngsters (however if a few families all decided to go together so their kids could have age-appropriate buddies to hang with, we could see this potentially working for the younger set, especially on the *American Queen,* which has a pool).

ENTERTAINMENT The lounges on European river cruise vessels ain't got nothing on *American Queen*'s two-deck-high Grand Saloon, fashioned after Ford's Theatre in D.C. (okay, a much smaller, and more ornate Ford's Theatre). Whether you grab a balcony seat or get a little closer at stage level, not only is the venue a delight but the shows are pretty awesome, too. *American Queen* will bring in various Big Band acts; singers and dancers performing well-known scenes from American musicals; and not to be overlooked is the Mark Twain impersonator (sure, it's no toe-tapping performance, but these guys are gifted storytellers and can really get you into the spirit and history of the Mississippi). After-hours entertainment includes live jazz, blues, country and rock in the Engine Room Bar with a view of the churning paddlewheel.

While the *American Queen*'s Grand Saloon steals the show, the *American Empress*'s intimate but lively Show Lounge also offers up topnotch music groups and cabaret performers. The Paddlewheel Lounge is a much more mellow bar scene where there might be just a singer or a piano player, and come late-night passengers might find some groove-able tunes being played in this comfy, local dive-esque bar.

SERVICE Service is not as highfalutin on the American Queen Steamboat Company vessels as it is on the river cruise ships in Europe. It's more that down-home American hospitality with a down-to-earth all-American crew. Think more approachable and less over-the-top white-glove treatment. For some people this may seem like a bit of a downgrade from the European experience but others they appreciate that it feels less stuffy and more social (waiters and bar tenders tend to be open and chatty). Gratuities of $16.50 per guest per day are automatically added to passengers' onboard accounts and passengers are welcome to adjust the amount at the end of the cruise.

TOURS The American Queen Steamboat Company has a unique shore excursion program that includes its signature hop-on-hop-off tours on its goofy but effective fleet of motorcoaches that feature large images of its ships along the sides (you kind of learn to love them). The motorcoaches serve as shuttle buses that follow a route along various points of interest in any given port. A guide on board will offer information about the destination as you travel along and you can either just stay on and enjoy the scenery or hop off at any of the stops to take a closer look at the sights. The tours will often include admission to select attractions, such as a museum or landmark. The motorcoach will usually continue to drive around in 15- to 20-minute intervals so that if you hop off, you can just catch the next one when it swings by. Each guest receives a map of the hop-on-hop-off route, and attractions with a gold star indicate those which passengers can enter for free with their boat ID. These hop-on-hop-off tours are included in the price of the cruise.

In addition to the included hop-on-hop-off tours, there are additional premium excursion options in most ports for an additional charge. Typically these are half-day tours or experiences that range from $25 to $100. There are a few pricier premium excursions, such as on the Columbia and Snake rivers where the *American Empress* sails, including a helicopter tour over Hell's Canyon for $200 and a fishing outing for $200 as well.

PRE- & POST-CRUISE STAYS   The American Queen Steamboat Company has pre- and post-cruise stays in the cities of Spokane, Wash., Portland, Ore., New Orleans, Memphis and Nashville, as well as one it calls the Headwaters of the Mississippi, which brings passengers to the Mississippi River headwaters at Lake Itasca, which includes a hotel stay in St. Cloud, Minn. These 2- and 3-day extensions typically include hotel accommodations, some meals, and some touring and are priced at between around $500 and $600 (Can you do better yourself, pricewise? Undoubtedly). Additionally, there is a selection of pre- and post-cruise shore excursions priced similarly to the premium shore excursions offered during the cruise itself.

American Queen
The Verdict
If you're up for a bit of kitsch, the *American Queen* is a fun and charming vessel on which to see the heartland of the country.

Specifications

Passengers	436	Total cabins/balcony cabins	222/25
Passenger decks	4	Crew	172
Year entered service	1995		

Note: *The American Queen has a wrap-around balcony, but we only included private balconies above.*

THE SHIP IN GENERAL   This Grande Dame of Mississippi river cruising truly represents a bygone era of steamboats and paddle-wheelers. They just don't make vessels like this anymore with its two-deck-high Grand Saloon (where shows are performed) and the J.M. White Dining Room reminiscent of a New Orleans restaurant. There are limited staterooms with private balconies but most other accommodations open up to the common wrap-around veranda that provides a front porch atmosphere. Since relaunching the vessel in 2012, American Queen Steamboat Company has invested boatloads to improve the amenities and features on board, from the bedding to the decor, and those upgrades show.

CABINS   There are 12 different cabin categories so we won't break down every single one here, but to get a sense of the full spectrum, the smallest are the teeny tiny inside single cabins at just 80-square-feet (intended for solo travelers). There are numerous cabins that are 140-square-feet (both inside and outside cabins), and there are 190-square-foot cabins, some of which have a private balcony. There are also 230-square-foot Suites with Open Verandas and Luxury Suites that are between 338 and 353-square-feet.

Cabins are outfitted with well-curated antiques, bathrooms with standing showers. The suites also feature Keurig coffee machines, and sitting areas with a sofa bed. Luxury Suites have a refrigerator as well. Guests staying in certain suites also have access to what the company calls "Commodore Services," which includes private check-in upon embarkation, a fruit basket upon arrival, and reserved balcony seating in the Grand Saloon. Those in Luxury Suites will also receive "River Butler" services, including unpacking and packing of luggage, laundry and ironing services, shoe shine, afternoon tea in their suite, and breakfast and dinner served on the balcony, if desired.

For families or groups of friends traveling together, there are several adjoining staterooms on the vessel as well.

PUBLIC AREAS   The Sun Deck features a small pool area and indoor fitness room with a handful of cardio machines. One deck down, the Promenade Deck (deck five) is home to the River Grill & Bar, an alternative dining venue which serves up a more casual atmosphere. The Observation Deck (deck four) houses the Chart Room, where passengers will find river maps, navigation equipment and references. On the Texas Deck there is the Front Porch Café where snacks are served throughout the day and passengers can choose between indoor or outdoor seating, including on the rocking chairs outside. The Cabin Deck is where the Engine Room Bar at the aft of the vessel is situated, the place to be for live music, drinks and possibly dancing to the view of the churning paddlewheel just a few feet away. This is also the deck where the main reception area is located, including the gift shop, the purser's office, and the excursions office. The Mark Twain Gallery, a Tiffany glass-filled sitting room, as well as the Gentlemen's Card Room and Ladies' Parlor, are here as well (don't worry, the card room and parlor aren't actually gender segregated). And finally, on the Main Deck is the J.M. White Dining Room, the Main Lounge and Captain's Bar (home to occasional tea service and a place to grab a drink to the soundtrack of live piano music), and the piece de resistance, the Grand Saloon, the main theatre, a two-deck-high opulent venue that showcases everything from Big Band acts to mini-musicals. There is also a spa treatment room on the Main Deck. Elevators connect all five lower decks but not the Sun Deck.

DINING OPTIONS   The main dining venue is the J.M. White Dining Room, where breakfast, lunch and dinner are served with an emphasis on both traditional entrees and regional specialties. For instance, dinner options can include a healthy salad or shrimp and grits, a classic chicken entree or fresh fish with shrimp creole. The Front Porch Café offers an Early Riser's Coffee service and serves up lighter meals and snacks (like cookies, ice cream and popcorn) throughout the day. There is also 24-hour room service available.

POOL, FITNESS, SPA, BIKES   The sun deck holds a small pool and gym; the spa treatment room is on the Main Deck. Spa services range from a 30-minute Memphis Express Massage for $75 to a $150 60-minute Tropical Indulgence Scrub & Wrap. The *American Queen* also has a small fleet of bright green bikes available for guests to use, free of charge.

American Empress

The Verdict

It doesn't have the same grandiosity as the *American Queen,* but the *American Empress* still has a vintage charm all its own, befitting the Western frontier Americana vibe in the Pacific Northwest.

Specifications

Passengers	223	Total cabins/balcony cabins	112/86
Passenger decks	4	Crew	83
Year entered service	2003		

Note: *The American Empress has a wrap-around balcony on its upper deck, and cabins on that deck were not counted as balcony cabins above.*

THE SHIP IN GENERAL   The *American Empress* was formerly owned by the Majestic America Line, a large U.S. river cruising operation that fell into shuttered in 2008. American Queen Steamboat Company purchased the vessel and put it back into service in 2014 after extensive renovations, including transforming the River Grill on the fourth deck from a snack stand into a sophisticated dining experience, centered around a U-shaped bar. There isn't a huge amount of public areas, but those that the ship has are classy and serve their purpose (more on that in the public areas section below). For art lovers, the *American Empress* is a surprising treasure trove of pieces evoking different themes such as local steamboat scenes, Native American images and marine life (the whale paintings are particularly memorable).

CABINS   The *American Empress* has seven cabin categories, ranging from the 150-square-foot Veranda Staterooms to the 410-square-foot Luxury Suites with Verandas. The vast majority are Deluxe Veranda Staterooms, which measure 180-square-feet and have a private balcony. Suites and staterooms are designed with an antique Americana vibe but with modern amenities such as flat-screen TVs and Keurig coffee makers (which are in the Deluxe Veranda Staterooms, Superior Veranda Staterooms, Suites with Verandas and Luxury Suites with Verandas). Bathrooms are stocked with fragrant Clarins bath products.

PUBLIC AREAS   The *American Empress* keeps it simple—there's the Astoria Dining Room, the River Grill & Bar, the Paddlewheel Lounge, the Show Lounge, the Purser's Office and a Gift Shop.

Though there aren't many public areas, the ones the *American Empress* does have are done well. The Paddlewheel Lounge has windows that look right onto the spinning paddlewheel and feels like a classy neighborhood bar. The Astoria Dining Room has been elegantly updated since it was purchased by the company and now feels like a civilized Pacific Northwest restaurant. The River Grill is an enticing upscale alternative to the Astoria, also serving up a fair amount of seafood, and the bar seating is a fun change of pace. The Show Lounge is a cozy live music venue hosting solid acts.

DINING OPTIONS For breakfast, lunch and dinner, menus are offered and selections are served to the tables (no buffet). As an alternative, the River Grill serves a slick dinner service with chef's selections. This is where you will also find the Early Riser's Coffee service. Seafood is a dominant ingredient on the menus due to the availability of it in the Pacific Northwest. You'll also find free-range chicken, artisanal cheeses and impressive regional wines.

POOL, FITNESS, SPA, BIKES Sorry, there's no pool, gym, or spa on board. Like the *American Queen,* the *American Empress* also has several bikes that passengers can check out for a ride along the river, free of charge.

AQUA EXPEDITIONS

www.aquaexpeditions.com. ℂ 866/603-3687.

Pros

o **Luxury all the way.** You will be cruising the exotic Amazon or Mekong but you'll be doing it from designer digs while eating cuisine created by a top chef.

o **Windows galore.** There's no missing any views on these ships. The ships have glass everywhere, giving them the look of floating glass houses.

o **Family-friendly.** Kids age 7 and up are welcomed and the ships even have rooms that sleep three or connect for families.

Cons

o **It's expensive.** This is an elite product; you'll pay upwards of $1,000 per person per night.

o **You'll be unplugged.** Expecting Internet access in the Amazon? Fuggetaboutit.

THE LINE IN A NUTSHELL This eco-conscious luxury line put cruising in the Peruvian Amazon on the map, providing a fancy way to see untapped landscapes. No roughing it in the jungle here. The line also expanded to the Mekong in 2014.

Frommer's Ratings (Scale of 1–5)

Cabin comfort & amenities	5	Public spaces	5
Decor	5	Dining	5
Fitness, spa and pool	4	Service	5
Family-friendly	4	Enrichment	3

THE EXPERIENCE Aqua Expeditions was founded in 2007 by Francesco Galli Zugaro, who previously worked in the cruise industry in the Galapagos. Zugaro, who also co-founded the clothing line Lonesome George & Company, wanted to bring an upscale African safari experience to the jungles of Peru.

AQUA EXPEDITIONS ITINERARIES

3-day Peruvian Amazon ("Discovery Cruise") round-trip from Iquitos, from $3,165 to $3,315, year-round, no balconies

4-day Peruvian Amazon ("Explorer Cruise") round-trip from Iquitos, from $4,220 to $4,420, year-round, no balconies

7-day Peruvian Amazon ("Expedition Cruise") round-trip from Iquitos, from $7,385 to $7,735, year-round, no balconies

3-day Mekong ("Discovery Cruise"), Phnom Penh to Ho Chi Minh City, from $3,315, year-round, from $3,810 (balcony)

7-day Mekong ("Explorer Cruise") between Ho Chi Minh City and Phnom Penh or Siem Reap*, from $4,420, year-round, from $5,080 (balcony)

7-day Mekong ("Expedition Cruise") between Ho Chi Minh City and Phnom Penh or Siem Reap*, from $7,735, year-round, from $8,890 (balcony)

* varies by season

The luxury river line has built a fine reputation for its two small all-suite ships, operating environmentally conscious, year-round cruises.

The custom-designed ships are akin to luxury B&Bs with refined spaces including oversized suites (though without separate rooms) and cuisine by acclaimed chefs. Yet it's a casual environment with families welcome. Fares include wine with meals and transfers, but not cocktails and gratuities.

During the day in the Amazon, you head off in 10-person aluminum skiffs with the ship's local naturalist guides to spot wildlife in the jungle and visit remote, and often impoverished, fishing villages. And that can be a startling contrast to the luxe life you're living on the boat. Shipboard you dine on fine cuisine from menus created by Chef Pedro Miguel Schiaffino, one of Lima's culinary darlings; drink topnotch South American wines (included) and rest your head in luxurious river-view accommodations.

The Mekong experience is similarly extravagant, featuring gourmet Southeast Asian cuisine overseen by Chef David Thompson, an Australian who has received acclaim for his Thai cuisine. Shore excursions on the Mekong are also in skiffs and led by experienced guides who lead cultural tours to places including Buddhist monasteries and are adept at spotting wildlife.

THE FLEET In the Peruvian Amazon the line operates the 24-passenger *Aqua Amazon* and 32-passenger *Aria Amazon,* both ships designed by noted Peruvian architect Jordi Puig and refurbished in 2015 with new floors, furniture and amenities in the suites. Luxury tour operator Abercrombie & Kent sometimes charters the vessels on the Amazon. Cruising the Mekong through Cambodia and Vietnam is the 40-passenger *Aqua Mekong,* designed by Vietnamese architects.

PASSENGER PROFILE These ships are geared towards well-heeled, adventure-minded travelers looking for a laidback yet luxurious river cruise experience. About half of the passengers are American, the rest from South

America and other parts of the world (most English-speaking). Because kids 7 and up are allowed, families are sometimes on board and the demographic tends to be more diverse than on other river lines—not everyone on board will be 55 and up. None of the ships have elevators, and with getting into and out of a skiff sometimes tricky, the ships are not recommended for those with physical limitations.

DINING OPTIONS   In the Amazon, Chef Schiaffino, who has two top-rated restaurants in Lima (Malabar and Amaz) sources about 70% of the ingredients on the ships from Amazonia. Your Peruvian ceviche will feature fresh fish from the river, with the local ingredients also showcased in dishes such as hearts of palm soufflé. The wine collection has a South American slant (wine, beer and soft drinks are complimentary with meals). You have the option of sitting at a table for two or dining with others. On the Mekong, menus feature the talents of Chef Thompson, an Australia native whose Nahm restaurant in The Halkin hotel in London received a Michelin star, the first Thai restaurant to win that award. His second branch of Nahm, at the Metropolitan hotel in Bangkok, has been recognized as one of the top 50 restaurants in the world. Again, local ingredients are a focus including in flavorful curries. Breakfast and lunch are buffet style, while dinner is a sit-down affair.

ACTIVITIES   Much of each day involves exploration on tours with the line's experienced local guides/naturalists. An option on the Mekong only is biking (the ship carries a fleet of 10 bikes). When not touring, most passengers socialize, sit with a good book, watch the scenery or play games. The naturalist guides also lead informal forums on topics as varied as a discussion on saving endangered turtles or how to mix a perfect *pisco* sour, the Peruvian national cocktail.

CHILDREN'S PROGRAM   Though there is no specific kids' program, the naturalists in the Amazon are adept at introducing wildlife at a child's level of understanding (ditto for sights on the Mekong). The guides also do little classes for kids such as cooking or towel origami.

ENTERTAINMENT   Evening entertainment may involve a movie screening (on the Mekong ship there's a special screen room with comfy chairs) or music in the lounge.

SERVICE   Expect pampering. The ships have nearly as many crew as passengers, and they are expert at getting to know your name, wants and needs. Crew pool tips, and the suggested amount $20 to $30 per passenger, per day. There's also a suggested tip of $7 to $10 per passenger, per day, for the guides.

TOURS   Daily tours (sometimes two a day) are included in the fare. Most of the tours are in 10-passenger skiffs, though some are on foot. Note that passengers are not allowed to tour on their own in the Amazon (where exploration is mostly in the jungle) though can go off on their own in some locations on the Mekong.

PRE- & POST-CRUISE STAYS   Aqua Expeditions does not offer pre- or post-cruise stays.

Aqua Amazon

The Verdict

This fancy little ship, with its suites and fine cuisine, was the first to put the Peruvian Amazon on the cruise map.

Specifications

Passengers	24	Total cabins/balcony cabins	12/0
Passenger decks	2	Crew	21
Year entered service	2008		

THE SHIP IN GENERAL The line's first ship on the Amazon made a splash with modern decor by internationally renowned Peruvian architect Jordi Puig and a luxury vibe. Yet it's a casual environment.

CABINS Everyone stays in a suite with large picture windows. Cabins are big at 230-square-feet and all have sitting areas. Four Master Suites bring the benefit of forward-facing views. Some suites can be interconnected for families, a cruise ship rarity. Updated bathrooms have slate walls and marble floors and are equipped with rainforest showers and organic bath products.

PUBLIC AREAS Hangout spaces on the top deck include a big-windowed indoor lounge with a bar at one end, cushy furnishings and a few library shelves and an outdoor lounge equipped with day beds in the sun and shade. You can walk around for more views from the observation deck. Shopaholics will find temptations in the tidy little boutique including quality Peruvian handicrafts and 14k gold Aqua Expeditions jewelry and a special waterproof Enigma timepiece designed by Gianni Bulgari exclusively for the launch of the *Aria Amazon* (proceeds from the sale of the limited edition items go directly to social projects in the Amazon).

DINING OPTIONS In the polished wood-floored dining room with panoramic windows, the cuisine is overseen by Chef Pedro Miguel Schiaffino, one of Lima's culinary stars. The menu includes such Amazon-influenced dishes as scallops with wild almonds and *umari* fruit and gnocchi made with plantain and yucca, served with complimentary South American and European wines. You can snag a table for two or dine family-style.

POOL, FITNESS, SPA, BIKES There are none.

Aria Amazon

The Verdict

Walls of glass ensure the Amazon is always in view on this intimate, tony ship, a pumped-up version of the *Aqua Amazon*.

Specifications

Passengers	32	Total cabins/balcony cabins	16/0
Passenger decks	2	Crew	24
Year entered service	2011		

THE SHIP IN GENERAL   This contemporary ship with its walls of glass, designed by Peruvian architect Jordi Puig, was actually built in the jungle. In no easy feat, materials were hauled in from around the world—custom-made furniture from Brazil, wallpaper from Malaysia, lighting fixtures from Spain, bath fixtures from Italy. The result is splendid but casual luxury.

CABINS   The 16 Design Suites all have views through a wall of glass and are a generous 250-square-feet, with a river-facing California King-size bed (which can also be configured as two twins), done up in Peruvian cotton linens, and sitting area with day bed (which can double as a bed for a child). Suites are located on the first and second decks (be aware those on the first deck may hear engine noise). The designer used Peruvian fabrics, natural wood flooring, soft lighting and a purposefully calm color scheme. Bathrooms are equipped with rain showers and organic bath products. Four suites can interconnect for families.

PUBLIC AREAS   On the Sun Deck you can sit in a cushioned lounger (an awning provides shade) or in the Jacuzzi, sipping champagne or a *pisco* sour while keeping an eye out for Amazon pink dolphins. Or relax in the indoor lounge, on cushy couches or stools at the bar, catching views through floor-to-ceiling windows. You can walk around for more views from the observation deck. There's also a nice boutique selling upscale handicrafts.

DINING OPTIONS   In the sleek contemporary dining room, you can admire Peruvian art, while sampling Chef Schiaffino's Amazon-influenced creations, served on fine china. Accompanying complimentary South American and European wines are served in crystal glassware. Choose a table for two or dine family style.

POOL, FITNESS, SPA, BIKES   There's an outdoor Jacuzzi in the bow and a small exercise area equipped with a treadmill and stationary bike. There's also a small massage room (a 55-min. Swedish massage is $55).

Aqua Mekong

The Verdict

Cruise the Mekong in high style on this designer ship.

Specifications

Passengers	40	Total cabins/balcony cabins	20/8
Passenger decks	2	Crew	32
Year entered service	2014		

THE SHIPS IN GENERAL   This luxurious little ship was designed with an Indochine-meets-contemporary vibe by acclaimed Saigon-based architects Noor Design. The idea was to bring to the river the aesthetic of a five-star boutique hotel. The designers accomplished this task using sustainable local materials and natural fibers. Plus it's the only river ship we know of where there's a games room equipped with a crystal foosball table. Other niceties include complimentary laundry service.

CABINS   Everyone stays in a 320-square-foot Design Suite with polished wood floors and river views. Eight of the suites have floor-to-ceiling windows leading to balconies furnished with daybeds. Suites without balconies have big panoramic windows that open and a sofa that converts to a single bed if there's a third person in the suite. Some of the suites connect, and can be configured for those who want a separate bedroom and living rooms (with his and her bathrooms). All the suites have King-size or twin bed configuration options. Bathrooms have double sinks, a large walk-in rainforest shower and all-organic bath products.

PUBLIC AREAS   The ship has indoor and outdoor bars and even the option of indoor and outdoor dining. Other spaces include a theater-style screening room for movies (movies are also sometimes shown outdoors on the back deck). In the outdoor lounge, you can sip a cocktail while lounging on a single or double daybed. The indoor lounge has barstools around the carefully lit bar, cushy sofas and panoramic windows. Southeast Asian antiques and handicrafts are for sale in the ship's boutique. As mentioned above, the little games room has foosball.

DINING OPTIONS   Michelin-starred consulting Chef Thompson incorporates culinary traditions along the river and fresh ingredients in dishes such as river prawns with ginger, shallots, tamarind and palm sugar served on betel leaves, or Cambodian green curry of fresh catfish. But there's European fare too including a gourmet pizza night. Tables in the dining room are decorated with fresh flowers, complimentary wines served in crystal glassware. You can get a table for two or dine in a larger group.

POOL, FITNESS, SPA, BIKES   The ship carries 10 bikes and kayaks for passenger use, on a complimentary basis. It also has a plunge pool with private cabanas and a small gym. Massages ($55 for an hour) incorporate such local ingredients as coffee and lemongrass and are available in two treatment rooms, one large enough for two to be soothingly pummeled side by side.

CENTURY CRUISES

www.centuryrivercruises.com. *C* 86-23-6232-8976.

Pros
o **Newer ships.** Century Cruises has a younger—and arguably flashier—fleet of vessels than its competitors. So, if you like that newer carpet and fresher paint smell and feel, Century might be the Yangtze River cruise line to book.
o **Amenities.** Century's newest generation of river cruise ships ushered in fancy onboard amenities—the *Century Paragon* and *Century Legend* each boast a 2,153-square-foot indoor pool area and a 150-seat movie theater.

Cons
o **Foreign-owned.** Century Cruises caters to a discerning Western market, but some people may find the fact that it is Chinese-owned and operated frustrating from a customer service and communications point of view.
o **Multiple languages.** Century welcomes a mix of both Chinese and foreign passengers on board. The result is a mix of languages (announcements

made in several languages for instance) and cultures on board that can enhance the experience for some but can be a bit alienating for others.

THE LINE IN A NUTSHELL Century Cruises vessels, specifically the two newest ones—*Century Paragon* and *Century Legend*—are the newest and flashiest on the Yangtze. With their massive staterooms and sprawling indoor pool complex, there's a reason why Century ships have picked up a lot of high-profile clients (including Uniworld).

Frommer's Ratings (Scale of 1–5)

Cabin comfort & amenities	4	Public spaces	4
Decor	3	Dining	2
Fitness, spa and pool	4	Service	3
Family-friendly	3	Enrichment	3

THE EXPERIENCE Century incorporated European engineering and design to its newest generation off vessels (the *Century Emerald, Paragon,* and *Legend*) to bring them much closer to a Western interpretation of what high-end river cruising should look like. They didn't quite arrive to that level of detail-oriented sophistication, but they certainly got much closer.

These newer ships have clean, modern interiors and larger cabins. But unlike the ships in Europe, vessels on the Yangtze are larger and have more public space, which means that Century vessels feel like a hybrid between river and ocean cruising, with amenities such as an indoor swimming pool and a cinema.

Century has inked charter deals with several big players in the river cruising world, such as Avalon Waterways and Uniworld.

THE FLEET In 2013, Century Cruises launched two sister ships, the 398-passenger *Century Legend* and *Century Paragon,* which together brought the company's fleet size to seven. The *Paragon* and the *Legend* have some pretty fancy bells and whistles like a more than 2,000-square-foot indoor swimming pool area and a 150-seat cinema. The oldest vessel in the fleet is the 186-passenger Century Star, which launched in 2003. There are also two 306-passenger ships, the *Century Sky* and *Century Sun,* and two 264-passenger ships, the *Century Diamond* and *Century Emerald.*

PASSENGER PROFILE You can expect a mix of both Asian and non-Asian passengers and a bit of a younger demographic, from age 45 and up.

DINING OPTIONS It's all buffets all the time on the Century vessels, which serve breakfast and lunch buffets that have both Western cuisines and Asian favorites. And for dinner it's what the company calls a "Chinese banquet" which is basically a slightly more elaborate buffet with a stronger emphasis on Chinese dishes. It's a good thing Yangtze river cruises tend to be relatively short otherwise the buffet thing would get kinda old. All meals are served in the main Dining Hall, although passengers staying in the Executive Suites on the *Century Paragon* and *Century Legend* also have access to an exclusive and more intimate *a la carte* restaurant, which is perhaps reason

Note: *Century Cruises itineraries are intended to be booked through a travel agent or tour operator, so the company does not provide retail pricing. Prices are available through partner river cruise lines, such as Uniworld and Avalon.*

enough for the splurge (the Dining Hall can get a bit loud and hectic). There is also an early risers' coffee and tea service at the Sundeck Bar.

ACTIVITIES   It's a relatively short cruise and there are excursions each day but for the remaining sailing stretches, activities are centered around optional Tai Chi, lessons in Mahjong (the popular Chinese card game), maybe some Chinese language lessons and just relaxing on board. Individual tour and river cruise lines may offer additional talks and lectures.

CHILDREN'S PROGRAM   Children are not prohibited, but there are no programs specifically geared towards kids offered by Century.

ENTERTAINMENT   There are nightly live shows and they can be quite the productions. From impressive magic shows to elaborate folk troupes, these acts are more than you might expect out in the middle of the Yangtze River. Also, there are some serious giveaways. Passengers who participate in some of the interactive shows may find themselves the owner of a brand new iPad. The whole thing takes on a very Chinese game show feel and it can get loud, boisterous and pretty hilarious. There are also karaoke rooms but when and whether they are open for use is a bit of a mystery.

SERVICE   With a few hundred passengers, all part of different tour groups, the service on board is really just about managing passenger flows rather than about anything truly hands-on. Gratuities are based on whichever river cruise line the cruise was booked with. So, for instance, Uniworld includes gratuities with its prices (so you can assume they take care of them for you on their Century sailings), but Avalon does not, so they will likely provide some guidelines. If they don't provide guidelines, feel free to ask your Avalon guide or crew manager who will be with you on the cruise. If you want more personalized service, book one of the 34 Executive Suites, which include butler services such as unpacking, shoe polishing, in-room dining service, laundry, daily snacks and fruit, and a bottle of red wine at embarkation.

TOURS   There will be at least one excursion offered each day—it could be something walking distance from the vessel, like the riverside Shibaozhai Pagoda, or a trip via smaller motorboats to see some of the smaller, narrower gorges along tributaries of the Yangtze River.

PRE- & POST-CRUISE STAYS   Century Cruises does not offer pre- or post-cruise extensions. Those can be arranged with the individual tour operator or river cruise line with which the Yangtze river cruise was booked.

Century Legend & Century Paragon

The Verdict

An attempt by Century Cruises to bring Yangtze river cruising up to the standards of European river cruising, the *Century Legend* and *Century Paragon* certainly raised the bar in China.

Specifications

Passengers	398	Total cabins/balcony cabins	196/196
Passenger decks	6	Crew	150
Year entered service	2013		

THE SHIPS IN GENERAL   One of the biggest selling points of the *Century Legend* and *Century Paragon* is that they are the newest vessels sailing the Yangtze.

As part of a larger effort to bring the Yangtze river cruising experience up to European standards, Century Cruises hired European engineers and architects to assist with the design and construction of the *Century Paragon* and *Century Legend,* and it shows—these ships definitely brought Yangtze river cruising squarely into the 21st century and put pressure on the entire Yangtze river cruise market to step up its game.

These ships are quite a bit larger than those in Europe, with about three times the capacity. That allows for more and larger staterooms and public areas.

Indeed, one area where these vessels particularly excel is the stateroom size. The vast majority of the cabins, which are also the smallest cabins, are the 301-square-foot (not too bad for the *smallest* cabins), river-view Deluxe Cabins, so really there isn't a bad room in the house. And the largest accommodations are the two 1,140-square-foot Presidential Suites with a 323-square-foot balcony (the balcony alone is bigger than most staterooms on European vessels). All of the staterooms have balconies and are outfitted in very respectable decor, reminiscent of a classy business hotel.

Other impressive spaces are the 2,153-square-foot indoor swimming pool area and the 150-seat movie theater, which sound and look great, but in fact don't get as much play as they should/could. Century Cruises also invested in a propulsion and rudder system designed to reduce vibrations on these vessels—sometimes those less glamorous upgrades actually do more to improve the overall experience than the fancier-sounding ones.

The downside to these larger vessels with more passengers is that service is much less attentive than in Europe and the dining experience is average, at best, with all three meals served buffet-style. For those who like the idea of a little more exclusivity from the masses, there are two dedicated Executive Levels that serve the passengers in the Executive Suites, with an exclusive a la carte restaurant, reception area and bar.

CABINS   In addition to the two massive 1,140-square-foot Presidential Suites, there are 34 Executive Suites at 415-square-feet each, four Junior Suites at 323-square-feet each, and 156 staterooms at 301-square-feet each. As mentioned, all the staterooms have balconies, separate sitting areas, LCD satellite televisions (including HBO and CNN), individually controlled air-conditioning, and bathrooms with a separate tub and shower (done in this weird side-by-side setup, which makes you wish they were actually just combined).

PUBLIC AREAS The *Century Paragon* and *Century Legend* have an impressive five-deck-high open atrium that is the focal point of the vessels. Beyond that there is the swimming pool and cinema, as well as two spa treatment rooms and a clinic on the Bottom Deck. The main Dining Hall is two decks up on the Upper Deck. Three decks up on the Observation Deck is a multipurpose lounge and bar area—this is where the crazy evening shows take place. And the Sun Deck is home to the executive club restaurant, an outdoor bar area, a shaded lounge area, a gym and library. There is no ship-wide wireless Internet, but there is a 24-hour Internet cafe with computer stalls passengers can use. An elevator travels to all decks except the lowest deck.

DINING OPTIONS As we've mentioned, all three meals are served in the large Dining Hall (also known as the Panoramic Restaurant), with its massive central buffet display and large round tables—so prepare to get friendly with your fellow passengers; whether you want to or not, you are going to be sitting at round tables for six or eight people. The buffets are stocked with plenty of Chinese cuisine alongside lots of Western choices—so there will be eggs and bacon available for breakfast and salads at lunch. And dinner is pretty much an all-out Chinese banquet, complete with Peking duck, steamed bok choy and other Chinese specialties. If you like Chinese food, you're in luck.

POOL, FITNESS, SPA, BIKES Guests flock to the large indoor pool, a gym, and a couple spa treatment rooms (that serve up massages and facials). There aren't any bikes on board but you wouldn't really have any opportunities to use them if there were.

Century Star, Century Sky, Century Sun, Century Diamond & Century Emerald
The Verdict

This slightly older generation of Century vessels still has some nice features such as large staterooms but definitely doesn't have the freshness in style and design the *Century Legend* and *Century Paragon* have.

Specifications

Passengers:			
Century Star	186	Century Sky, Century Sun	306
Century Diamond, Century Emerald	264		
Total cabins/balcony cabins	67/53	Passenger decks	5
Crew:			
Century Star	128	Century Sky, Century Sun	152
Century Diamond, Century Emerald	138		
Year entered service:			
Century Star	2003	Century Sky	2005
Century Sun	2006	Century Diamond	2008
Century Emerald	2010		

THE SHIPS IN GENERAL   These ships cater more to the domestic Chinese market, so expect to see lots of Chinese passengers on board. And while they have some of the same comforts as the newer *Century Paragon* and *Legend,* such as spacious staterooms, they don't have as many amenities. The public spaces are all adequate but don't have the nicer details and design of the newer ships. All told, these five vessels are by no means slumming it, but if you want the best of the fleet, the *Century Legend* and *Century Paragon* are where it's at. The one slight advantage for some people who just don't like the large size of the *Legend* and *Paragon* is that these are smaller ships and don't carry as many passengers, so in that way the experience is perhaps more similar to the intimacy you grow accustomed to on European river cruise ships.

CABINS   There are three categories of staterooms on the *Century Star, Sky,* and *Sun,* and four categories on the *Century Diamond* and *Emerald.* The majority of cabins on the *Century Star* are either 237- or 285-square-feet with a couple 797-square-foot Presidential Suites. The Deluxe Cabins on the *Century Sky* and *Sun* are 279-square-feet; the four Junior Suites are 323-square-feet; and the six Deluxe Suites are 383-square-feet (no crazy-big Presidential Suites here). And on the *Century Diamond* and *Emerald,* the majority of staterooms are 269-square-foot Deluxe Cabins, with suites ranging from 301 to 840-square-feet. There aren't bathtubs in all the staterooms but select suites do have tubs. All staterooms have balconies, small sitting areas (on the smallest cabins this might be just an extra chair and small side table), and satellite TV. These cabins still feel like business hotel rooms but definitely feel more dated than the staterooms on the *Paragon* and *Legend.*

PUBLIC AREAS   Standard public areas on these vessels are one main restaurant, two or three bar and lounge areas, including one on the Sun Deck, a gift shop, gym, and spa treatment rooms. Internet is available in the 24-hour Internet cafe with computers that passengers can use.

DINING OPTIONS   As with the *Century Paragon* and *Legend,* all three meals are served as a buffet in the main restaurant and the food is nothing to write home about. The *Century Emerald* also features the additional *a la carte* restaurant for guests staying in suites, otherwise to the main dining hall you go.

POOL, FITNESS, SPA, BIKES   There is no pool on these vessels, but they do have a gym and several spa treatment rooms. There are no bikes on board.

CROISIEUROPE

www.croisieuroperivercruises.com. ℂ 800/768-7232.

Pros

- **Value.** If you're on a super tight budget, it's hard to get much lower than the low cost of CroisiEurope's river cruises.
- **European experience.** CroisiEurope attracts a mix of Europeans and English speakers and the onboard experience has a decidedly French flavor. For some, having that international interaction enhances the experience.

o **Original rivers/itineraries.** One way that CroisiEurope is trying to better compete in the dog-eat-dog river cruise industry is by charting new and unique rivers in Europe, including recently the Loire River. It also often goes further along certain popular rivers than other lines, such as further up along the Seine River.

Cons

o **Older vessels.** CroisiEurope is a 40-year-old river cruise line so the company has a fair amount of aging ships in its fleet. The decor, furnishings, and over-all look and feel of some of the vessels are dated. At the company's very attractive prices, passengers likely won't mind, but for anyone who has been on some of the industry's sparkling new builds, you will feel the difference.

o **Lack of choice.** CroisiEurope famously has traditionally offered only one entree option for dinner (though it's working to add more choices), and it has a single dining venue per boat. It also does not have the same variety of shore excursions and activities as other lines.

o **Melting pot.** As mentioned above, while some might love the fact that they're sailing with people from France, Germany, the U.K. and Spain, others might find the announcements in multiple languages annoying and the inability to necessarily converse or connect with the other passengers limiting.

THE LINE IN A NUTSHELL CroisiEurope's main competitive selling points are lower prices and finding new and unique rivers to cruise. The company is able to keep its pricing below standard U.S. market rates because all of its operations are done in-house (as opposed to contracting things such as food and beverage services, or nautical operations, out to third parties). And it's able to sail some unique and new rivers because of a recent idea the company and its shipbuilders had to construct vessels powered by paddlewheels that allows them to have lower drafts and thus sail in shallower waters—the company has already launched its small, sleek paddle-wheelers on France's Loire River and Germany's Elbe River, and has plans to do the same on other rivers that it is still keeping hush-hush.

Frommer's Ratings (Scale of 1–5)

Cabin comfort & amenities	3	Public spaces	4
Decor	3	Dining	3
Fitness, spa and pool	N/A	Service	3
Family-friendly	4	Enrichment	3

THE EXPERIENCE This is river cruising Euro-style, which is a different experience than river cruising built for Americans by American companies. If river cruising is compared to a floating hotel, CroisiEurope is like staying in a floating European bed-and-breakfast. Meals are European in taste and delivery, service is of a European standard, and entertainment has a European flare. You have to be up for the different way things are done across the pond.

CroisiEurope is run by three generations of the Schmitter family who founded the Strasbourg, France-based company in 1976. The Schmitters know river cruising and the European waterways well. And they also know they have some changes to make if they are going to continue to successfully court the U.S. market.

Since turning its focus more seriously towards the American market, Croisi Europe has been building and renovating ships that are more in line with the higher-quality interiors and amenities that Americans expect from European river cruises. The company starting building a new generation of vessels that kicked off in 2014 with the launch of the 84-passenger Lafayette on the Rhine—this new class of CroisiEurope ships feature sleek and modern interiors with colorful accents such as Missoni-printed blankets strewn across the beds and eclectic decor such as funky chandeliers and colorful furnishings. The new generation includes the 96-passenger *Loire Princesse* and the 80-passenger *Elbe Princesse* that launched in spring 2016. CroisiEurope is also investing in offering greater variety in its onboard meals and giving passengers more choice in general, such as with some new included excursions.

PASSENGER PROFILE   Perhaps because of its more accessible pricing, CroisiEurope tends to attract a younger clientele, passengers in their 40s and 50s with the average age being about 50 years old. As mentioned, it's an international mix, with about 20 percent coming from North America, 30 percent being English speakers from elsewhere (such as Brits and Australians), and 50 percent European passengers, mostly French and German speaking.

DINING OPTIONS   CroisiEurope vessels have one main dining room, which serves French and European cuisine. Breakfast is buffet style, and lunch and dinner served as sit-down, three-course meals paired with complimentary wine. In fact, all beverages including water, juice, coffee, tea, beer and wine are complimentary. The food on Croisi ships has been notoriously so-so compared to other river cruise lines The company traditionally offered one entree at lunch and dinner, compared to the overabundance of options on other lines. But CroisiEurope has acknowledged that it needs to step up its food and beverage program game and is beginning to offer more options and (hopefully) at a higher quality, too.

ACTIVITIES   CroisiEurope offers lectures and demonstrations during its cruises. When groups that speak different languages are traveling on the same vessel lectures will be provided according to language (so a Spanish speaking group will be offered a presentation or demonstration on a given topic at one time, and an English speaking group will be offered a lecture at another time).

CHILDREN'S PROGRAM   CroisiEurope allows children as young as infant and toddlers on board but does not provide cribs or any special equipment, so passengers are encouraged to bring their own. The company offers a discounted cruise price for kids under 10, and also has several family-friendly cruises during the summer months in Spain, Portugal and Italy—there are kid-friendly menus on these sailings, and active excursions such as hiking trips.

ENTERTAINMENT   Similar to other river cruises, CroisiEurope often has live music in its onboard lounge. Some itineraries may include a folk dance troupe or local musicians that come on board for a livelier evening in the

CROISIE'S fleet

CroisiEurope has 29 vessels, all of which are of various designs and sizes and cannot be grouped together to create convenient ship specification charts. So we're going to do you and us a favor and just provide a thorough overview of the fleet here rather than break down each of the 29 ships.

CroisiEurope divides its vessels into two categories, what it calls "Four-Anchor" and "Five-Anchor" ships. Similar to hotels in Europe, what they consider Four-Anchor or four-star, would probably qualify more as a three- or four-star product according to U.S. standards, and what they consider a Five-Anchor or five-star ship would probably qualify as more of a four-star ship or four-star-plus ship.

Many CroisiEurope vessels are showing their age, especially the Four-Anchor ones. But as the company races to catch up to the other cruise lines in Europe, its most recent ship launches and renovations are improving those boats significantly….and *almost* bringing them up to the quality of their main rivals.

Four-Anchor Ships: There are 20 ships in CroisiEurope's Four-Anchor category. Out of these, eight were built in the mid- to late 1990s, and the rest were built in the early 2000s. The oldest is the 162-passenger *La Boheme*, which launched in 1995 and sails the Rhine and Danube rivers, and the youngest is the 180-passenger *L'Europe*, which launched in 2006 and also sails the Rhine and Danube. The vessel with the smallest capacity is the 98-passenger *Victor Hugo* (launched in

2000), which sails the Rhine and Danube, and the vessel with the largest capacity is the *L'Europe* as well as the 180-passenger *Beethoven*, which launched in 2004 on the Rhine and Danube.

Half of the four-anchor ships sail on the Rhine and/or Danube rivers (**Beethoven, La Boheme, Douce France, L'Europe, Leonard da Vinci, Modigliani, Mona Lisa, Monet, Symphonie,** and **Victor Hugo**). Of the remaining vessels, three sail on the Seine River (**Botticelli, France,** and **Renoir**), three sail on the Douro River (**Fernao de Magalhaes, Infante d'Henrique,** and **Vasco de Gama**), two on the Rhone (**Mistral** and **Van Gogh**), and one sails the Po River (**Michelangelo**).

These are all two- or three-deck ships with tiny staterooms. On most of these, all of the staterooms are the same size, and can be as small as 108-square-feet (as on the *Victor Hugo, Symphonie, Mona Lisa, Douce France,* and *La Boheme*), and are no larger than 145-square-feet (as on the *Beethoven* and *L'Europe*). Many feature staterooms that are 118-, 129-, or 135-square-feet. Again, that's one size for all the staterooms on one ship—no classism here!

On these ships, what CroisiEurope calls French balconies are larger sliding glass windows with railing outside, but the windows are large and almost hit the floor in most cases, so we'll let it slide. Though they definitely aren't as welcoming as the newer French balcony concepts on the rivers—there isn't a sitting

lounge. There are also themed dinner events that feature regional specialties. Entertainment is not a forte of CroisiEurope's, though the eclectic mix of passengers on board can sometimes make evenings more dynamic compared to lines that cater predominantly to North American travelers.

SERVICE Service on board CroisiEurope is attentive but low-profile. Crew are polite and helpful but also largely work in the background. There is definitely less hand holding than on other European lines. Gratuities are not area or somewhere to chill so this is more like something you would poke your head out of to catch a breeze. The public spaces on these ships are pretty simple. You'll most likely find a single restaurant, a bar and lounge, and a Sun Deck. There might be a little additional library space here or there. There aren't any pools or gyms or spa rooms. Nor are there multiple dining venues. Bottom line: These are relatively comfortable transport vehicles.

Five-Anchor Ships: These represent the newer vessels in CroisiEurope's fleet, vessels that were either built or renovated between 2012 and 2016, with the exception of the 176-passenger *Vivaldi,* which was built in 2009 and sails the Danube River. The 138-passenger *Seine Princesse* was built in 2001 and renovated in 2012 and sails the Seine (of course), and the 176-passenger *Gerard Schmitter* was built in 2012 and sails the Rhine. One year later, the 174-passenger *Cyrano de Bergerac* launched in Bordeaux. The 131-passenger *Lafayette* launched on the Rhine in 2014 and the 96-passenger *Loire Princesse* set sail on the Loire in 2015. The 146-passenger *Camargue* originally launched in 1995 on the Rhone and was renovated and relaunched there in 2015. The 132-passenger *Gil Eanes* launched in 2015 on the Douro. And the 80-passenger *Elbe Princesse* was christened in 2016 on the Elbe.

As mentioned above, the *Loire Princesse* and the *Elbe Princesse* represent

CroisiEurope's clever new paddlewheel concept (don't think the huge paddlewheels as on the U.S. river vessels, just small guys on the sides of the ship or at the rear), which allow the ships to have a lower draft as the paddlewheels help to propel them and reduce the need for larger, lower hanging engines below. This introduces the possibility of sailing on some never before cruised rivers with lower water levels, so it will be interesting to see where CroisiEurope takes this.

Generally speaking, these Five-Anchor vessels arrive at something much closer to what is being offered by the rest of the river cruising market, and their interior design is pretty sleek. The staterooms are not huge but are mostly in a more comfortable range than those on CroisiEurope's Four-Anchor vessels. Aside from the *Camargue,* which has 108-square-foot tastefully designed staterooms, the smallest staterooms on these ships are 135-square-feet (as on the *Cyrano de Bergerac*), with most being between 145- and 156-square-feet. On these vessels you see proper French balconies, with floor-to-ceiling sliding glass doors, such as on the *Camargue, Gil Eanes,* and *Lafayette.* And the *Loire Princesse* actually has full, step-out balconies. Staterooms on these vessels all have a standard en suite bathroom with shower, satellite TV, a hair dryer and safe. Public spaces include the restaurant, a bar and lounge, the Sun Deck and possibly one additional outdoor terrace area.

included, and CroisiEurope's policy is that it divides up any tips received by passengers equally among crew members. The company suggests 5 to 10 euros per day, per person. There is an envelope in the cabin for tips and a designated box to drop it into in the reception area, so cash is the way to go.

TOURS Up until 2016 CroisiEurope had a unique excursion model whereby none of its tours were included in the price. So passengers could either go out exploring on their own or book optional tours. But beginning in

8-day Lower Danube ("Along the Danube, the Danube Delta, the Balkan Peninsula and Budapest"), Tulcea (Romania) to Budapest, $2,322, balconies from $2,573, Apr–Oct

7-day Upper Danube ("The Beautiful Blue Danube"), round-trip from Vienna, from $2,076, balconies from $2,458, Apr–Oct

6-day Upper Danube ("The Baroque & Picturesque Danube"), Budapest to Passau (Germany), from $1,772, balconies from $2,248, Apr–Oct

5-day Douro ("Porto, the Douro Valley, and Salamanca"), round-trip from Porto, from $1,490, balconies from $1,862, Apr–Oct

8-day Elbe ("From Prague to Berlin: Cruise on the Elbe and Vltava Rivers"), Prague to Berlin, from $3,087, balconies from $3,372, Apr–Oct

7-day Dordogne and Garonne ("Two Mighty Rivers, the Gironde Estuary and the Arcachon Basin"), round-trip from Bordeaux, from $2,208, balconies from $1,759, Apr–Oct

5-day Dordogne and Garonne ("The Gironde Estuary and the Garonne River"), round-trip from Bordeaux, from $1,407, balconies from $3,794, Apr–Nov

4-day Dutch and Belgian Canals ("Holland and Tulips"), Antwerp (Belgium) to Amsterdam, from $992, balconies from $1,284, Mar–May

7-day Loire ("The Loire, a Royal Legacy"), round-trip from Nantes (France), from $2,806, balconies from $3,318, Apr–Oct

5-day Loire ("The Loire, a Royal River"), round-trip from Nantes (France), from $2,085, balconies from $2,467, Apr–Oct

6-day Po ("Venice and the Lagoon islands—Chioggia, Padua, Verona, Ferrara, Bologna, Venice"), round-trip from Venice, from $1,878, balconies from $2,105, Feb–Oct

4-day Po ("Venice and its Lagoon"), round-trip from Venice, from $1,100, balconies from $1,273, Feb–Oct

8-day Rhine ("From Amsterdam to Basel: The treasures of the celebrated Rhine river"), Amsterdam to Basel, from $2,643, balconies from $2,877, Apr–Oct

6-day Rhine ("Holland and the Romantic Rhine Valley"), Amsterdam to Strasbourg, from $1,499, balconies from $2,231, Apr–Oct

9-day Rhine and Rhone ("Across Europe: The best of the Rhine and the Rhone"), Amsterdam to Avignon, from $2,427, balconies from $2,774, Apr–Oct

6-day Rhone ("The Camargue and the gateway to Provence"), Chalon-sur-Saone to Martigues (France), from $1,634, balconies from $1,856, Apr–Oct

7-day Rhone and Saone ("From the Saone to the Rhone passing through Burgundy and Provence"), round-trip from Lyon, from $1,969, balconies from $2,461, Apr–Oct

7-day Seine ("The Seine Valley and the Normandy Beaches"), round-trip from Paris, from $2,168, balconies from $2,371, Apr–Oct

5-day Seine ("The Most Picturesque Ports of Call in the Seine Valley"), round-trip from Paris, from $1,602, balconies from $1,779, Apr–Oct

2016, excursions on CroisiEurope ships are included in the cruise fare, some-thing North American travelers have come to expect from river cruising vaca-tions. These new included tours range from panoramic tours of major European capitals or excursions that focus on a particular theme or attraction.

PRE- & POST-CRUISE STAYS   CroisiEurope does not offer pre- or post-cruise programs. But the company said it can help clients arrange hotel accommodations before or after the cruise if they want to extend their trip.

EMERALD WATERWAYS

www.emeraldwaterways.com. ✆ 855/222-3214.

Pros

o **Value-priced.** This Australian line (a sister line to Scenic) is geared towards budget-conscious river cruisers.

o **Amazing swimming pools.** The infinity-style indoor/outdoor pool on the line's "Star Ships" is a "wow" feature—and even converts into a movie theater at night.

o **Fun entertainment.** Maybe it's because there are Australians on board, but this line has more of a late-night scene than you'll find on other river ships.

Cons

o **The food is just eh.** The cuisine is not what you'll be bragging to friends about. Still, it's plentiful and filling.

o **All ships the same.** The line's "Star Ships" are new and hip and cool, but they are pretty much look alike.

THE LINE IN A NUTSHELL   This Australian-owned and value-focused line debuted in 2014 as the first new river line in Europe in 6 years to cater to English-speaking passengers. Looking to up the hip factor in a market that mostly caters to the age 55-plus crowd, the line operates five sleek, 182-passenger, Dutch-built ships it calls "Star Ships."

Frommer's Ratings (Scale of 1–5)

Cabin comfort & amenities	4	Public spaces	4
Decor	4	Dining	3
Fitness, spa and pool	5	Service	4
Family-friendly	1	Enrichment	4

THE EXPERIENCE   This sister company to fancier Scenic brings river cruisers a value-focused proposition: Fares include most tours (even smartly programmed full-day tours with lunch ashore), pre-cruise hotel nights, trans-fers, wine, beer and soft drinks with meals, unlimited coffee drinks, port charges, and internet access (you can borrow an iPad from reception if you didn't bring your own) Also included are all gratuities (which in effect means that Emerald is more inclusive than competitors such as Viking).

The line also stands out in terms of design innovation; the five nearly identi-cal "Star Ships" boasting a modern decor (the lounge may have an ebony bar that lights up like at a club) and the standout feature of a glass-enclosed swimming pool that converts into a movie theater at night. There's innovation in terms of cabins as well: The line's Panorama Balcony Suites have a glass wall that converts to a French balcony at the push of a button.

The ships are friendly and social and offer more nightlife than you'll find on some competing lines—which may very much be due to the fact there are likely to be fun-loving Australians and Kiwis among passengers on board. The company has its U.S. headquarters in Boston.

THE FLEET   The line's five 182-passenger "Star Ships," *Emerald Belle, Emerald Dawn, Emerald Sky, Emerald Star,* and *Emerald Sun* have a surprising dose of hip. All launched between 2014 and 2016; it's the newest fleet on the rivers. For 2016, Emerald Waterways also chartered the 192-passenger A-Rosa Stella (from German line A-Rosa Cruises) for a few summertime sailings in France. In 2017, Emerald will launch the 138-passenger *Emerald Liberté* on France's Rhône and Saône rivers (replacing the charter) and the 112-passenger *Emerald Radiance* on the Douro in Portugal, both ships smaller versions of the "Star Ships." For exotic itineraries, Emerald charters the 56-passenger *Irrawaddy Explorer* for some cruises in Myanmar, and the 64-passenger *Mekong Navigator* for a few departures in Vietnam and Cambodia.

PASSENGER PROFILE   Passengers come from English-speaking countries including Australia and New Zealand and the U.K.—the value-pricing and aggressive marketing attracting a lot of older Brits (who also get free air from the U.K.). Americans and Canadians are in the minority. Most, but not all passengers are age 55 and up, often way up. Those from "Down Under" tend to liven the scene, while the British passengers are quieter and Americans and Canadians can go either way.

DINING OPTIONS   Breakfast and lunch are buffet-style, with hot and cold options; dinner is from a four-course menu with choices including Continental and regional specialties, and always available items such as steak, grilled chicken and salmon. In a bit of an oddity, during the evening cocktail hour in the lounge, the chef proudly presents his featured dish of the day: a plate of, say, venison, passed around for everyone to see and smell. Preparations are okay (you won't go hungry), if not particularly memorable. Vegetarians may be disappointed by the daily veggie entree, which seems to get short shrift in the creativity department. On the other hand, if you like Baked Alaska, you'll be thrilled to find the dessert menu goes there.

In building new ships, Emerald had the opportunity to adopt features already popular on competitors, so as an alternative to the main restaurant you can do a light breakfast or lunch from a buffet selection on The Terrace and eat al fresco while catching forward-facing views from the ship's bow (just like on Viking's "Longships"). Room service is only available in top-suite accommodations, and even then is limited to continental breakfast. House wine and beer and soda are served at lunch and dinner, but if you order drinks during cocktail hour or other times you pay extra for them.

CRYSTAL CRUISES adds rivers

Last year, upscale ocean line **Crystal Cruises** (© 866/446-6625; www.crystalcruises.com) announced that it wants in on the river action too. So, the company purchased a classic river cruise ship and relaunched it in the summer of 2016. The **Crystal Mozart** underwent an extensive redesign, which included increasing suite sizes and transforming the 203-passenger vessel into a 160-passenger one.

After that there are four newly built Crystal river cruise vessels, which the company is calling "river yachts", on the way in 2017—the 110-passenger **Crystal Bach** and **Crystal Mahler** and the 84-passenger **Crystal Ravel** and **Crystal Debussy.**

Accommodations will range from 220-square-foot windowed staterooms on the lower decks to 750-square-foot two-bedroom suites on the second deck.

Crystal's "river yachts" will have their public areas and dining venues all located on one level—the third deck—including a Palm Court with a stage, dance floor and a glass-domed roof; a library; a fitness center and spa. There will be sporting equipment available for use such as electric bicycles, kayaks and water scooters.

Crystal also plans on switching the sailing schedule up a bit and will dedicate a portion of each cruise to sailing during daytime hours, giving guests the opportunity to enjoy the nightlife in various destinations. The company plans on offering onshore culinary experiences at Michelin-starred restaurants, evening events and cultural entertainment during these evening stopovers.

The five vessels will be sailing the Rhine, Main, Danube, Seine, Garonne, and Dordogne rivers on itineraries ranging from 5 to 16 nights.

ACTIVITIES The most creative feature on these ships is the infinity-style, heated swimming pool, which is surrounded by loungers so you can linger, and has a retractable glass roof that lets in sunshine on warm days—and stays closed on other days so that you can swim in any weather. At night, a crew member pushes a button and a wooden floor covers the pool, the room becoming a 25-seat cinema showing newish and classic movies. If there's a flick you want to see arrive early as the seats fill up fast. Yes, there's even popcorn.

Other activity offerings are of the low-key variety. There are not guest lecturers on board, but we like the fact that Emerald has members of its crew do sessions where they talk from their personnel experiences—on a Lower Danube sailing, for example, the cruise director, who grew up in Romania during Communist times, talked quite candidly about what that experience was really like. The wheelhouse is always open for those interested in navigation and locks and hanging out with the officers.

CHILDREN'S PROGRAM There is none. Kids must be 12 years of age or older to cruise on Emerald Waterways (though exceptions may be made on Christmas cruises).

ENTERTAINMENT With party-loving Aussies and Kiwis on board there is a bit of a late-night disco scene. Folks hit the dance floor to a nostalgic playlist that includes the Village People and Gloria Gaynor. When the DJ plays Olivia Newton John, the crowd goes wild. After 10pm, the crew serves snacks to keep everyone energized. Some nights there are also movies. Early evening a keyboardist plays tunes during cocktail hour. Not to be missed is the crew show, held one evening of the sailing. We've all seen the waiter who thinks he can sing, but on one cruise we listened to a hotel director who sang like a professional, and laughed hysterically as several members of the crew performed skits that were well rehearsed and well delivered. Folk troupes and other performers come on board, such as a Bavarian band on Rhine and Upper Danube itineraries, and exuberant dancers in Serbia.

SERVICE The international crew (from various countries in Eastern Europe, Asia and elsewhere) tries hard, is very efficient and is for the most part quite friendly. But we did encounter some situations where our American English was not quite understood. Tips are covered in the cruise fare, though you are welcome to give extra if you like, say to your favorite bartender. There's also a box at reception where you can slip in a few dollars if you want at the end of the cruise (the money is divvied up among the crew).

TOURS Daily shore excursions are led by local guides who do a particularly good job highlighting local history and culture. Some are half day, others full day (with lunch included). There is opportunity to interact with locals on some tours. On the Lower Danube, itineraries include lunch in the home of a local family in a small village in Croatia, where the topic of discussion includes the Yugoslav Wars of the 1990s (passengers are divided into groups of about eight, so you get quality time with your host family, which also prepares your meal). In Bratislava, Slovakia, you may be invited to sit down with a local family for a home-hosted afternoon tea. In addition to included tours there are premium, "Discover More" tour offerings such as an exclusive evening concert in Vienna ($100) or an excursion to the Danube Delta on Lower Danube itineraries, for an extra charge. New in 2016 are guided bike tours on several itineraries, for an extra fee.

PRE- & POST-CRUISE STAYS Emerald Waterways offers the option of extending your vacation with 2-day hotel stays, on a bed-and-breakfast basis, at centrally located properties.

Emerald Belle, Emerald Dawn, Emerald Sky, Emerald Star & Emerald Sun

The Verdict

These new "Star Ships" bring a welcome dose of hip to river cruises, and they are affordably priced to boot.

Specifications

Passengers	182	Total cabins/balcony cabins	92/74
Passenger decks	3	Crew	47
Year entered service:			
Emerald Star, Emerald Sky	2014	Emerald Dawn, Emerald Sun	2015
Emerald Belle	2016		

THE SHIPS IN GENERAL The line's "Star Ships" were designed, in terms of river cruise standards, to be trendy. How trendy? Given the older demographic, Emerald Waterways showed off the "contemporary" flair by having 1960s fashion icon Twiggy as godmother of the *Emerald Sky*. If not quite edgy, the ships, with features including a swimming pool that converts to a movie theater, are certainly cool.

CABINS Everyone gets a view from their cabin and most staterooms are in the well-designed and generously sized (180 sq. ft.) Panorama Balcony Suites category. The key feature in these rooms is a wall of glass, the top half of which opens with a push of a button for a balcony effect (it's a new way of doing a French balcony). A few fancy suites have glass doors leading to real step-out balconies, plus the French balcony feature. Those in one-bedroom Owner's Suites (315 sq. ft.) get a bedroom that closes off from the living room, a spacious bathroom, a walk-in closet, and such niceties as a Nespresso coffee machine, an iPad to use throughout the cruise and a complimentary minibar that gets stocked daily. The Grand Balcony Suites (210 sq. ft.) have a real balcony (though not a separate bedroom) and comes with beefed up amenities. Standard staterooms (called Emerald Staterooms) come with a long rectangular window positioned high on the wall and are 162-square-feet. There are also a couple of 117-square-foot cabins designed and priced for solo travelers (with a single bed). Everyone gets a flatscreen TV, iPad/iPod docking stations, a safe, minifridge, and hairdryer. The beds are quite comfortable. Bathrooms have nice-size showers; minibars have drinks and snacks for a fee. You can turn on an electronic switch to indicated "Do Not Disturb" (just don't forget to turn it off or your cabin might not get cleaned). The decor is chic in the staterooms accented by Eames-esque chairs and details such as grey or beige padded headboards and modern-design reading lamps.

PUBLIC AREAS Among the innovations on the "Star Ships" is the decor, which is nicely contemporary and streamlined and kind of cool, using mirrors, and polished metal and glass for a different take than the more subtle, Scandinavian decor on some competitor's' river ships. As we said, the big "wow" is the glass-enclosed, heated pool with its own lounging area. Walls of glass in the pool space assure you don't miss views and especially when the weather isn't great up on the Sun Deck, this is a preferred hangout spot—there's even a self-serve espresso machine in one corner. The pool converts into a movie theater at night; with the push of a button the water gets covered by a wooden floor, and the crew then sets up 25 chairs.

Also impressive is the main lounge with its floor-to-ceiling windows and glass bar with twinkling lights and surrounded by barstools—you can belly up to the bar for a martini as you would at a hip club on land. The reception area has video screens displaying places and sights en route.

Elevators access all decks but the sun deck. The Sun Deck is set up with lounge chairs and tables both in the sun and shaded under canopies, and the fun feature of a giant Tic-Tac-Toe board.

EMERALD WATERWAYS ITINERARIES

Itineraries may also be available in the reverse direction. First price is the lowest available price for all cabin categories, and the second price is the lowest balcony price, including French balcony cabins.

9-day Rhone ("French Waterways"), with 7-day cruise, round-trip from Lyon, $4,490, balconies from $4,890, Apr–Oct

9-day Rhone ("A Taste of France"), with 7-day cruise, Paris to Lyon, $5,590, balconies from $5,990, May–Oct

13-day Rhone and Saone ("French Escapade: Monte-Carlo to Paris"), with 9-day cruise, Monte Carlo to Paris, $5,990, balconies from $6,390, Apr–Oct

9-day Seine ("Rendezvous on the Seine"), with 7-day cruise, round-trip from Paris, $4,290, balconies from $4,690, Apr–Oct

14-day Seine ("Cruising the Seine, plus Versailles, Paris & London"), with 9-day cruise, round-trip from Paris, $6,490, balconies from $6,890, Apr–Oct

23-day Seine, Rhone and Saone ("Belle Epoch: London to Monte-Carlo"), with 18-day cruise, London to Monte Carlo, $11,990, balconies from $12,790, Apr–Sept

13-day Rhine and Moselle ("The Rhine and Moselle"), with 11-day cruise, Amsterdam to Basel, $4,890, balconies from $5,440, Apr–Oct

10-day Rhine ("The Rhine, Swiss Alps & Amsterdam"), with 7-day cruise, Amsterdam to Basel, $4,690, balconies from $5,090, Apr–Oct

8-day Rhine ("The Romantic Rhine: Amsterdam to Basel"), Amsterdam to Basel, $3,590, balconies from $3,990, Apr–Oct

12-day Danube ("The Blue Danube"), with 7-day cruise, Regensburg (Germany) to Budapest, $4,490, balconies from $4,890, Apr–Oct

12-day Danube ("Musical Magic Along the Blue Danube"), with 7-day cruise, Budapest to Regensburg (Germany), $5,690, balconies from $6,090, June–Oct

12-day Danube ("Danube Reflections"), Vienna to Regensburg (Germany), with 7-day cruise, $4,690, balconies from $5,090, May–Sept

15-day Rhine, Main and Danube ("Amsterdam to Budapest by Riverboat"), Amsterdam to Budapest, $5,690, balconies from $6,340, Apr–Oct

8-day Belgian and Dutch Canals ("Belgium & Holland in Spring"), Brussels to Amsterdam, $2,890, balconies from $3,345, Apr

12-day Danube ("Budapest to the Black Sea"), with 7-day cruise, Budapest to Bucharest, $4,890, balconies from $5,290, May–Aug

24-day Rhine, Main and Danube ("Grand European Cruise"), with 22-day cruise, Amsterdam to Bucharest, $10,090, balconies from $11,140, May–Aug

8-day Danube ("Blue Danube: Family Riverboat Adventure"), Budapest to Regensburg (Germany), $3,690, balconies from $4,090, July

10-day Rhone ("Bon Voyage! France Family River Cruise"), with 7-day cruise, Paris to Lyon, $4,690, balconies from $5,090, June–July

8-day Rhine ("Castles on the Rhine: Family Riverboat Adventure"), Basel to Amsterdam, $3,790, balconies from $4,190, June–July

In the dregs of the ship is what the line bills as a boutique, but it's just a few glass cases with sunglasses and jewelry.

DINING OPTIONS   All meals are served in the Reflections Restaurant. Lighter fare for breakfast and lunch (including a soup, salad and sandwich buffet) is also available in the al fresco cafe, The Terrace. All meals are open seating, with breakfast and lunch served buffet-style. There are more tables for two on these ships than on some other lines (though another couple may be seated close by your side). If the weather is nice there may be a barbecue one day on the Sun Deck, where you'll also find a Sky Bar open on warm weather days. In deference to the British crowd, the ship serves afternoon tea in the lounge, featuring cakes and little sandwiches you choose from a buffet. Wine, beer and soft drinks are complimentary with meals, and you can upgrade to premium wine for a fee.

POOL, FITNESS, SPA, BIKES   Okay, we know, we've raved about the pool already and it is fab—really one of our favorite features to be found on any river ship, and we didn't even mention yet that there are stacks of fluffy fresh laundered towels on shelves so you can cozy up with several in a lounge chair after your swim (there's also a shower you can use before or after your swim). There is also attention paid by this line to other wellness facilities. The ships have a jogging/walking track on the Sun Deck, where you'll also find a 3-hole golf putting green. The small fitness room is equipped with two stationary bikes, weights and a rowing machine—plus, you will find yoga mats by the pool. The ships also have a masseuse on board offering massages (about $70 for a full-body massage) and doubling as a hairdresser.

Breaking News

As this book went to press, a fire had broken out on board the *Emerald Belle* while it was being worked on in the shipyard. The damage was said to have been "significant," and at press time it was unclear whether the *Emerald Belle* would be launching as planned in 2016.

HAIMARK

Important note: At press time, the sales and operations of all of the river cruise vessels that previously had been marketed and chartered by Haimark Travel Ltd. had been taken over by local shipbuilders. The Haimark Travel website was no longer functioning, nor was Haimark responding to requests for bookings. That doesn't mean that the boats reviewed below are off the market—far from it! If you wish to cruise on any of the ships mentioned in this section, contact:

o **Lotus Cruises Co.** (bookings@lotuscruises.com) for the *Mekong Navigator*

o **Abercrombie & Kent** (see p. 212) for the *Mekong Princess*

o Myanmar-based **Ayravata Cruises** (www.ayravatacruises.com) for the Irrawaddy Explorer

○ Peruvian company **Delfin Amazon Cruises** (amazondiscovery@delfinamazoncruises.com) for the *Amazon Discovery*

And **Avalon Waterways** continues to manage all sales of the *Avalon Myanmar* and *Avalon Siem Reap*. Similarly, **Uniworld Boutique River Cruise Collection** is proceeding with all its planned sailings on the *Ganges Voyager II* in India.

THE LINE IN A NUTSHELL   If you like the idea of sailing past floating villages in Southeast Asia, through rural India and along the Amazon jungle in style, the boats of the former Haimark are the way to go.

Frommer's Ratings (Scale of 1–5)

Cabin comfort & amenities	5	Public spaces	5
Decor	4	Dining	4
Fitness, spa and pool	5	Service	4
Family-friendly	3	Enrichment	4

THE EXPERIENCE   For a lot of travelers, there's something indulgent about being able to visit truly fascinating and unfamiliar places but with some of the creature comforts of home, such as plush bedding and safe-to-eat foods. Haimark gets that and built up an entire river and small-ship cruising business based on that concept—the idea is to visit the unique and colorful splendor of places like Vietnam, Cambodia, Myanmar, India and the Peruvian Amazon with the welcome relief of returning at the end of each long, often hot, sightseeing day to an air-conditioned, luxury river cruise vessel with upscale service and amenities.

Having learned the ins and outs of the business at Southeast Asia river cruise trailblazer Pandaw River Expeditions, the executives at Haimark know a thing or two about working in exotic markets and how to deliver a good customer service experience in emerging destinations, despite the challenges those destinations can pose (such as different standards for everything from safety to hygiene). This is not like operating in Europe, not by a long shot. And Haimark works a lot of magic behind-the-scenes to bridge the gap between what travelers have come to expect from the river cruising experience in Europe and their high-end version of river cruising in exotic locales.

THE FLEET   Haimark's fleet consists of seven vessels, all built within the last 2 years. There are two on the Mekong River in Southeast Asia; the spa-themed, 24-passenger *Mekong Princess* and the 68-passenger *Mekong Navigator.* There is also the 44-Passenger *Amazon Discovery* that sails the Peruvian Amazon; the 56-passenger *Irrawaddy Explorer,* which sails in Myanmar; and the 56-passenger *Ganges Voyager I* and *Ganges Voyager II,* which sail in India.

PASSENGER PROFILE   The Haimark passenger base is aged 55-plus and have often been on river cruises before (which makes sense given that Haimark's focus is exotic rivers—these people have probably done some rivers in Europe and are looking for more). They are physically active and are up for soft adventure luxury travel.

HAIMARK ITINERARIES

7-day Mekong ("Upstream/Downstream"), Ho Chi Minh City to Siem Reap, $2,499, balconies from $2,899, Jan–May, Aug–Oct, Dec

9-day Irrawaddy ("Yangon/Mandalay"), Yangon to Mandalay, cabins/balconies form $3,499, Jan, Mar–Apr, Aug–Sept, Dec

7-day Ganges ("Upstream/Downstream"), round-trip from Kolkata, cabins/balconies from $2,799, Sept, Dec

Note for this chart: Itineraries may also be available in the reverse direction. The first price is the lowest available price for all cabin categories, and the second price is the lowest balcony price, including French balcony cabins.

Note: Haimark charters many of its vessels and departures to other river cruise lines and tour operators, so these are the sailings it has directly available for sale through Haimark. All other departures are available through its partners.

DINING OPTIONS   Unlike the larger river cruise vessels in Europe, Haimark's boutique riverboats have less public space, which means dining is limited to the one main dining room on board. But lack of variety in venues doesn't mean lack of variety in terms of cuisine or choices. Haimark does an expert job churning out high quality meals. Breakfast and lunch are buffet style and include both Western and local standards. Dinners are multicourse sit-down affairs. When sailing through a part of the world where one can't always be sure about what is safe to eat and what isn't, Haimark passengers can be sure they have good meals waiting for them back on the ship—a tour of a galley run by a Haimark chef revealed a common trick for cleaning raw vegetables in countries like India or Cambodia involving an anti-bacterial pellet that is thrown into the water with the vegetables when they are being washed and works to disinfect them, making raw produce such as that used in salads safer to eat.

Cuisine hygiene aside, you can expect Indian dishes such as various curries on the Ganges, and plenty of Asian cuisine on the Mekong and Irrawaddy as chefs from the region are very often incorporated into the kitchen and share their local recipes.

ACTIVITIES   There isn't much down time on exotic river itineraries. Mornings and afternoons are usually spent out exploring, often in hot and humid climates, so that when passengers get back to the ship, they are ready to rest, relax and cool off for a bit. That being said, these are also fascinating places with layers of history and culture. So, often there will be an educational discussion in the evening before dinner in an air-conditioned lounge, during which passengers can learn about a given topic such as Hinduism in India or details about the Pol Pot regime in Cambodia. These are usually led by the guides who are with the cruise group for the duration of their journey; unlike in Europe where there are different local guides in each port, on exotic itineraries there is usually a guide or several guides depending on the size of the vessel that will sail along with the passengers and will serve as their educator both on and off the ship.

CHILDREN'S PROGRAM   Haimark does not allow children under 12 and does not have any programs specifically geared towards children.

ENTERTAINMENT When you're in colorful parts of the world, the entertainment is often colorful, too, and Haimark makes sure that passengers experience the dynamic music, dance and art of the destinations by bringing local acts on board to perform for guests, usually on a makeshift stage area on the sun deck. These intimate shows can be anything from a solo singer to an instrumental concert to a decked out dance troupe. Sometimes crew members reveal hidden talents. Whatever the act, they make for a funny and lively break from the otherwise quiet nights out on these far-flung rivers, because unlike in Europe where you're often docked in a city, on exotic rivers nights are often spent somewhere seemingly a long way from society.

SERVICE If you're going to build fancy-schmancy boutique river cruise vessels, you'd best have the service to match. From shoe cleaning services and refreshments waiting for passengers when they return from their daily excursions, to accommodating crew and friendly wait staff, the service on board Haimark vessels is in line with the look and feel of the ships themselves.

TOURS All excursions are included and there are at least two outings daily. Depending on what is available to visit, those two outings could be two different village visits, or one outing could consist of going out on smaller motorboats to visit a floating village. An excursion could consist of a short motorcoach drive to a local landmark, such as a Buddhist temple or important religious shrine. There are also usually some fun surprises in the form of a bicycle rickshaw ride or getting pulled along by an oxen cart.

PRE- & POST-CRUISE STAYS Haimark does offer land extensions for all of its river cruises, which could range from one or two options to as many as four different options for extending the journey. In Peru, for instance, there's a pre-cruise option for 2 nights in Lima as well as a 4-night and 3-night post-cruise option in Machu Picchu and Lake Titicaca, respectively.

Mekong Navigator

The Verdict

The *Mekong Navigator* was the first vessel in the former Haimark fleet to set sail, setting a high bar for the company's ambitious exotic-luxury river cruising model.

Specifications

Passengers	68	Total cabins/balcony cabins	34/30
Passenger decks	3	Crew	36
Year entered service	2014		

THE SHIP IN GENERAL Haimark came out of the gates with an all-suite Mekong cruiser with spacious accommodations (the smallest suites are 256-square-feet each) and a look and feel reminiscent of Indochina's colonial era glamour. Furnishings are lush and luxurious antique-style pieces accented by subtle and tasteful Southeast Asian art and decor.

CABINS The vessel features two 584-square-foot Grande Suites (grand indeed!); two 387-square-foot Prestige Suites; 16 Signature Suites at

291-square-feet each; 10 Vista Suites at 276-square-feet each; and four Superior Suites on the lower deck at 256-square-feet each. The top three categories of suites have their own private verandas, and the Vista Suites have French balconies. The Super Suites have porthole windows. Unique for river cruise vessels, the Grande and Prestige Suites are outfitted with king-size beds and marble spa soaking tubs in the bathrooms. These two categories of suites also benefit from daily butler service, a complimentary, 1-hour, spa treatment per person, complimentary laundry service and complimentary evening canapés. Passengers in the Signature Suites can request continental breakfast on their balcony.

PUBLIC AREAS Public areas include Le Salon, the bar and lounge; Le Marche, the onboard restaurant; La Vie, the spa and fitness center; La Biblioteque, the library; a boutique; a reception desk and a sun deck.

DINING OPTIONS The *Mekong Navigator* has one dining room, Le Marche, which serves Western cuisine alongside local dishes in a casually elegant environment (think: sophisticated wood finishings and plush seating to the backdrop of large scenic murals). Breakfast and lunch are served buffet style and dinner includes complimentary wine during the nightly single, open seating service. Tables seat two and four passengers.

POOL, FITNESS, SPA, BIKES The onboard La Vie Spa offers a menu of massages, wraps, and aromatherapies, in two private spa rooms located on the sun deck. There is a fitness center also located on the sun deck, adjacent to the spa area, that features equipment such as stationary bicycles, a rowing machine and an elliptical. There is no pool or bikes on board.

Mekong Princess

The Verdict

Haimark kicked it up a notch with its second Mekong vessel, the *Mekong Princess,* an all-suite, spa-themed intimate vessel with an emphasis on wellness and luxury.

Specifications

Passengers	24	Total cabins/balcony cabins	12/12
Passenger decks	2	Crew	18
Year entered service	2015		

THE SHIP IN GENERAL With the river cruise boom ramping up on Southeast Asia's Mekong River in recent years, Haimark came up with a way to potentially stand out from the growing Mekong pack—an entirely spa-themed river cruise ship, featuring Southeast Asian spa therapists and healthy culinary options on board. While many Mekong vessels have spa treatments available, the *Mekong Princess* takes the concept a bit further with a spa menu that includes massages, facials, scrubs and body wraps using all-natural products native to the area, and each guest receives one complimentary, 1-hour treatment of their choice during the sailing. There is also daily yoga, tai chi and meditation classes offered either in the fitness center or on the open-air observation deck.

CABINS   The *Mekong Princess* has four categories of suites (12 suites total), all of which are outfitted in French colonial decor, with floor-to-ceiling windows, private balconies and marble baths with rainfall showerheads and spa bath amenities. The two largest suites are the 496-square-foot Angkor Suites located at the bow of the upper deck and have private outdoor verandas and marble tubs. Guests staying in the Angkor Suites will also have complimentary laundry service, evening canapes and a special spa-bath preparation. There are also two 306-square-foot Tonle Suites, four 234-square-foot Apsara Suites, and four 234-square-foot Saigon Suites. All but the Saigon Suites, which are located on the Main Deck, are located on the Upper Deck. There is daily butler service available to passengers in all suite categories.

PUBLIC AREAS   A stylish elegance abounds throughout the *Mekong Princess* public areas, which are rife with rich textiles and antique-style furniture. A subtle and soft gold and cream palate threads its way throughout the vessel, including in the reception area, on the observation deck and in the Ramvong lounge, in the Indochine dining room, Princess library and Internet lounge, in the fitness center and spa.

DINING OPTIONS   The *Mekong Princess*'s sole dining room is the Indochine restaurant, where the focus is on spa cuisine that fuses traditional Southeast Asian cuisine and Western dishes. Sample dinner menu items include spiced yellow mango, Burmese crab noodle soup, Cambodian fish stew, beef tenderloin Bordelaise and honey banana mousse. Breakfast and lunch are served buffet-style and dinners are a multicourse affair that includes wine.

POOL, FITNESS, SPA, BIKES   Not surprisingly, a spa-themed vessel has a spa on board with an extensive menu of treatments (massages, facials, scrubs, body wraps and custom treatments) and each guests receives a complimentary 1-hour treatment. There is also a small fitness center with a couple cardio machines. Daily yoga, Tai Chi, and meditation classes are offered either in the gym or on the upper deck. There is no pool or bikes on board.

Irrawaddy Explorer

The Verdict

Haimark entered the Irrawaddy frenzy with an all-suite, luxury vessel similar in concept to its Mekong vessels, but with its own unique Burmese flavor and details.

Specifications

Passengers	56	Total cabins/balcony cabins	28/28
Passenger decks	2	Crew	56
Year entered service	2014		

THE SHIP IN GENERAL   With ever more options for river cruising along Myanmar's Irrawaddy River, the *Irrawaddy Explorer* is definitely at the higher end of those choices (though it's not alone in this segment). If you have an eye for highly curated design details and a taste for upscale service and amenities, this vessel should at the very least be on your short list of options for cruising from Yangon to Mandalay.

CABINS The all-suite vessels feature four categories of suites ranging from 280- to 400-square-feet each. The Mandalay Suites (400 sq. ft.), Kipling Suites (270 sq. ft.) and Orwell Suites (280 sq. ft.), all feature step-out balconies and the Maugham Suites (280 sq. ft.) feature French balconies. Regardless of which suite category, you can expect fine linens, a flat-screen television with an on-demand movie system, an individual climate control system, and spa robes, slippers, and bath amenities. The two Mandalay Suites also have round bathtubs, and include complimentary laundry service, daily butler service, and in-room dining upon request. The decor marries Burmese antique-style furnishings, printed-silk cushions and throws, and colorful paintings and locally inspired artwork such as Burmese script or scenes from along the Irrawaddy. It all seems like it's meant to transport us back to the Irrawaddy's 19th-century heyday when countless cruisers were sailing up and down the river.

PUBLIC AREAS With intricately carved wood pieces throughout the ship, the public areas on the Irrawaddy Explore pays a subtle homage to the rich and colorful Burmese culture. There is a reception area, the Customs House Dining Room, the Writer's Lounge (the indoor bar and lounge area, reminiscent of a classy hotel bar), an observation deck, spa and fitness room.

DINING OPTIONS Burmese cuisine, with influences from Chinese, Thai and Indian kitchens, is served alongside Western food in the *Irrawaddy Explorer*'s Customs House Dining Room. There is open seating at every meal, with a majority of the tables seating four diners. Breakfast and lunch are served buffet style, and the wait staff serves a multicourse, seated dinner each night. You can expect a quality and colorful culinary experience at each meal.

POOL, FITNESS, SPA, BIKES On board is a small spa with a menu of treatments, including some using products containing the popular Burmese cream Thanaka, which comes from the bark of several local tree varieties (Burmese women all over the country can be seen wearing it, as it is meant to act as a sunscreen and all around skin protection agent). And there is also a small fitness room. There is no pool or bikes.

Ganges Voyager I & Ganges Voyager II
The Verdict

With these two sister ships, Haimark not only effectively helped introduce a new river cruising destination to the world but did so with its trademark high-end ship-building style.

Specifications

Passengers	56	Total cabins/balcony cabins	28/28
Passenger decks	2		
Crew:			
Ganges Voyager I	30	*Ganges Voyager II*	36
Year entered service:			
Ganges Voyager I	2015	*Ganges Voyager II*	2016

THE SHIP IN GENERAL   Again Haimark took an all-suite approach with these Ganges river vessels, bringing together spacious staterooms with somewhat limited but relatively well-executed public spaces (there are reports that the recently launched *Ganges Voyager II,* which is being chartered by Uniworld, is in need of some workmanship upgrades). In an exotic destination such as India, it's less about what there is to do on the ship and much more to do with exploring off the ship. But the *Ganges Voyager I* and *II* certainly make for a comfortable floating hotel to return to after fascinating excursions along the Ganges.

CABINS   There are four categories of suites: a 400-square-foot Maharaja Suite, two Viceroy Suites at 360-square-feet, two Heritage Suites at 280-square-feet, and 20 Standard Suites at 260-square-feet each. All the suites have a French balcony, sitting area and flat-screen TV. The bathrooms feature a rain shower, robes and slippers. Guests staying in the Viceroy and Maharaja Suites will have daily butler service, laundry service, one complimentary spa treatment per person, and a complimentary bottle of wine upon embarkation. Guests in the Maharaja Suites will also be offered daily, in-room breakfast and accented bath preparation the deep-soaker bathtub, upon request.

PUBLIC AREAS   The formula for Haimark's public areas continues on its Ganges vessels with several well-appointed and efficient spaces for eating, lounging and entertainment. With a nod to Indian high-style throughout, there is a reception desk, the East India Dining Room, the Governor's Lounge, and observation deck, the Voyager spa, and a fitness room.

DINING OPTIONS   The East India Dining Room seats tables of two and four passengers, who will be offered a buffet breakfast and lunch and a served, multicourse dinner to the backdrop of passing Ganges views. You can expect the menu to be infused with Indian favorites such as Naan bread, samosas, curries and masalas, alongside Western dishes, allowing guests to either go comfort food or for a more immersive experience.

POOL, FITNESS, SPA, BIKES   There is a small spa that offers both regional Indian and Western spa treatments using all-natural products. There is also a fitness room on board, but no pool or bikes.

Amazon Discovery

The Verdict

There is no shortage of river cruise vessels on the Peruvian Amazon, but the *Amazon Discovery* brings a distinctive sophistication to the unique and adventurous Amazonia experience.

Specifications

Passengers	44	Total cabins/balcony cabins	22/0
Passenger decks	2	Crew	29
Year entered service	2015		

THE SHIP IN GENERAL   A distinctly more modern feeling vessel than the rest of the Haimark fleet, the *Amazon Discovery* features sleek decor, roomy suites, and some of the bonus services and amenities the company likes to throw in for its highest category of suites. Like with its other river cruise ships, the *Amazon Discovery* was designed to fit into its environment, with details that evoke the flora and fauna and the spirit of well, discovery, that the Amazon evokes (for instance there are telescopes in every suite).

CABINS   The four categories of suites include the 237-square-foot Flora Suites; the 237-square-foot Fauna Suites; the 253-square-foot Estuary Suites; and the one 597-square-foot Amazonia. None of the suites have balconies (it's the Amazon, there are bugs), but instead they all feature floor-to-ceiling windows for viewing the lush rainforest. Guests staying in the Amazonia or Estuary suites also receive one complimentary 60-minute spa treatment per guest, the services of a personal butler and complimentary laundry service, among a few other perks. All suites include individual air-conditioning, nice linens, robes and slippers, and all-natural bath amenities.

PUBLIC AREAS   There are four main areas to rest, refresh, and relax on board. The Open-Air Deck features a shaded lounge area and a small plunge pool. The indoor Canopy Lounge hosts evening performances, naturalist talks and Peruvian cooking classes. Meals are served in the Andes Dining Room. The small Rainforest Spa room offers massages, wraps, and scrubs.

DINING OPTIONS   In the Andes Dining Room, meals are prepared from local ingredients with both Peruvian and international influences. Guests can help themselves to a buffet breakfast and lunch; dinner is served as a multi-course meal. Most tables seat parties of four and meals are open seating.

POOL, FITNESS, SPA, BIKES   There is a spa room and a plunge pool. No fitness area or bikes on board.

PANDAW RIVER EXPEDITIONS

www.pandaw.com. ℂ 800/729-2651.

Pros

- **Experience.** Scotsman Paul Strachan, founder of Pandaw River Expeditions, has been operating ships up and down the Myanmar's Irrawaddy River for 20 years. Strachan knows the region and its rivers better than anyone and because of that is constantly pushing the envelope with new itineraries that explore ever more exotic and uncharted inland waterways of Asia.
- **A focus on the destination.** Strachan himself will admit that he is no innovator. The ships the company is building today are much the same as the ships it built 20 years ago—classic, steamboat style vessels. Instead the company is focused on immersive destination experiences and creating a fun and engaging atmosphere on board.

Cons

o **No frills.** Unlike other river cruise operators that are trying to bring a version of luxury, European-style river cruising to Southeast Asia, Pandaw is all about keeping Southeast Asian river cruising true to its original self. The company is not big on fancy public spaces or amenities such as pools.

THE LINE IN A NUTSHELL If you prefer destination knowledge over marble bathrooms, if you're more interested in authentic local experiences than in creature comforts, you'll probably fit in perfectly with the Pandaw product and with the other, laid-back passengers on board.

Frommer's Ratings (Scale of 1–5)

Cabin comfort & amenities	4	Public spaces	4
Decor	4	Dining	4
Fitness, spa and pool	3	Service	4
Family-friendly	4	Enrichment	5

THE EXPERIENCE In 1998, Pandaw Founder Paul Strachan acquired the Pandaw, a steamboat built in Scotland in 1947. He renovated the vessel and operated it up and down Myanmar's Irrawaddy River for several years, and ultimately sold it. In 2001, the company built its first company-owned riverboat, which was almost an exact replica of the original Pandaw. Today, Pandaw River Expeditions operates a fleet of 15 such vessels, all colonial-style, three-deck ships with wraparound balconies, despite the fact that newcomers such as AmaWaterways, Sanctuary Retreats, and Aqua Expeditions have all emerged on the Southeast Asia river cruise scene with larger vessels, indoor hallways, sprawling suites, spas and swimming pools.

Instead, Strachan is focused on remaining true to a Southeast Asia river cruising model that fosters a more social atmosphere by drawing people out of their staterooms and into the public spaces. The wraparound balconies, for instance, encourage guests to mingle and also facilitate the movement of fresh air as the vessels sail, something Strachan has said is both a comfort and safety issue, offering stability to vessels that have more shallow drafts.

While the design of the Pandaw vessels hasn't changed much in 20 years, recently the company has been pushing the envelope with new river cruise routes. Last year, Pandaw introduced a Mekong River sailing through Laos on the newly constructed, 20-passenger Laos Pandaw. Additionally, Pandaw recently introduced a new Halong Bay and Red River itinerary that inaugurated a new route along Vietnam's Red River.

Recently, Pandaw also unveiled a new itinerary that includes all six countries through which the Mekong River flows: Vietnam, Cambodia, Thailand, Laos, Myanmar, and China. Getting permission to sail across the border into China has proven the biggest challenge in achieving that goal.

Pandaw has been testing the waters beyond Southeast Asia, as well, having chartered some vessels in India recently and with the hopes of perhaps introducing its own vessels there in the near future.

THE FLEET   As mentioned above, the Pandaw fleet is pretty consistent in style and design. They are divided into two, relatively simply groups: Pandaw's K Class of vessels, which are the company's two-deck ships, and its P Class of vessels, which are its three-deck ships. There are 15 vessels in the Pandaw fleet, nine in its K Class and six in its P Class. The vessels sail in Myanmar, Vietnam, Cambodia, Laos and China, and Pandaw also partners on charter cruises in India, and on the Peruvian and Brazilian Amazon.

All Pandaw vessels follow the same format. For the most part, all the staterooms are the same size (all passengers are created equal). They do not have private balconies but instead open up to the common wrap-around balconies not unlike those on steamboats like the *American Queen* in the U.S. There is one dining room, one bar and lounge, and an outdoor lounge and seating area. And that about does it. Simple is as simple does.

There is tons of wood everywhere, the walls, the furniture, the floors, everything is done in wood, which actually keeps the vessels looking pristine. They are no-fuss but in a way that totally works and doesn't feel dingy—they remind us of nice, homey local B&Bs that are simple but very clean and charming. You realize on ships like this just how few amenities we really need to have a good vacation.

PASSENGER PROFILE   From its Scottish roots to its strong Australian and British customer base, you can expect to hear a lot of accents throughout the Pandaw experience. Whether sailing Myanmar's Irrawaddy River or the Mekong River through Vietnam and Cambodia, you're likely to be among a more adventurous bunch of more seasoned travelers than you'll find on Europe's rivers. According to Strachan, these are travelers who are "not coming for the pool or the Jacuzzi." Which is a good thing because Pandaw doesn't have those things.

DINING OPTIONS   Pandaw seeks to introduce its passengers to the wide variety of tastes and flavors of Southeast Asia on board its ships. Breakfast is served as a buffet and during lunch there is a soup, salad and dessert buffet but the main course is served to the table. Dinner is waiter service only. Passengers will have the opportunity to taste some of the more exotic and spicy foods Asia is known for or will be offered European alternatives. There are always vegetarian options, as well. Pandaw also prides itself on offering diners the choice of eating inside or outside (it's dining room windows also open up) so that they don't always feel cooped up in an air-conditioned spaced and removed from the fresh air and scenery. Only at night does it shut its dining room windows entirely to avoid unwanted visitors, aka insects.

7-day Chindwin ("A Voyage to Nagaland"), Kalewa (Myanmar) to Homalin (Myanmar), from $2,975, Sept

8-day Irrawaddy ("Burma Highlights"), Mandalay to Bagan, from $4,995, Mar

11-day Irrawaddy ("Classic Burma and the Golden Rock"), Mandalay to Yangon, from $2,465, Feb–Mar

20-day Chindwin and Upper Irrawaddy ("Chindwin and the Upper Irrawaddy"), from 7,055, Aug

18-day Irrawaddy ("From Rangoon to Kalay"), Yangon to Kalay (Myanmar), from $4,737, Aug

10-day Irrawaddy ("Inle lake and the Irrawaddy"), Yangon to Bagan, from $2,370, Jan–Aug

10-day Irrawaddy ("Mandalay Pagan Packet") Bagan to Mandalay, from $1,550, year-round

7-day Chindwin (Irrawaddy tributary) ("The Chindwin") Monywa (Myanmar) to Kalewa (Myanmar), from $3,500, year-round

10-day Irrawaddy ("The Golden Land"), Yangon to Mandalay, from $2,723, year-round

14-day Irrawaddy ("The Irrawaddy"), Yangon to Mandalay, from $5,720, year-round

10-day Red River ("Halong Bay and the Red River"), Halong Bay to Hoa Binh (Vietnam), from $2,600, year-round

10-day Mekong ("The Laos Mekong"), Vientiane (Laos) to Chiang Khong (Thailand), from $3,900, Jan–Feb

7-day Mekong ("The Mekong to China"), Chiang Saen (Thailand) to Jinghong (China), from $3,500, Jan–Mar

14-day Mekong ("The Mekong: From Laos to China"), Vientiane (Laos) to Jinghong (China), from $6,930, year-round

Note on this chart: Itineraries may also be available in the reverse direction. First price is the lowest available price for all cabin categories, and the second price is the lowest balcony price, including French balcony cabins).

Note: All Pandaw vessels have wrap-around (not private) balconies, so these are the starting prices for all cabin categories.

ACTIVITIES During Pandaw itineraries, the guide will host daily briefings and will also offer insights into what passengers will be visiting and experiencing each day. In addition to these cultural discussions, there are cooking demonstrations, fruit carving lessons (Southeast Asians are particularly adept at this art), and themed movie nights such as playing "L'Indochine" while sailing in Vietnam or the very uplifting 1984 drama *The Killing Fields,* while sailing in Cambodia. Otherwise, it's a good book on the sun deck or in the lounge, and/or a good drink at the bar.

CHILDREN'S PROGRAM Pandaw welcomes children on board and has also begun offering a handful of sailings designed specifically for families, including cruises in Myanmar, in Halong Bay and on Vietnam's Red River, and on the Mekong River in Vietnam and Cambodia. On designated family departures, kids under age 4 travel for free if they sleep on a cot in the same cabin as their adult companions, and children ages 4 to 18 travel at a discounted rate. To accommodate younger passengers on these sailings, Pandaw will feature more kid-friendly cuisine, will have cooking lessons on board, offer more active excursions, have bike tours at larger port calls, and will feature movie nights on board.

ENTERTAINMENT   During each expedition there will be at least one cultural performance on board; on longer cruises passengers can expect at least two performances per cruise. The shows might be an elaborate puppet show, as is custom in Myanmar, or a traditional folk dance performance. Otherwise, it's colorful conversations and cocktails with your fellow passengers.

SERVICE   Pandaw has been doing this for a long time. The company is intimately involved with the region, knows its people and has a solid system for training crew members. They execute extremely polite and courteous service, and it's all done with bright smiles on their faces. Many of the crew have been with Pandaw for a long time, so they know what they're doing, they know the destination and they provide comfort in their expertise.

TOURS   Daily excursions are the whole reason for taking a Pandaw cruise, to witness the people and the traditions along the river. Pandaw offers daily excursions (at least one or two) that could be a walking trip through a village or to a unique landmark, or something a bit more adventurous such as a horse cart ride or a cycling trip—Pandaw recently brought mountain bikes on board its vessels for use on such excursions or for passengers to take out on their own. The bikes are available to book for $25 per person, and Pandaw crew will advise guests on the best routes to follow and, if needed, a member of the crew will accompany the guests on their cycling trip. Some excursions take place via motorboat as passengers visit remote river jungles or fishing villages. In larger ports, a more comprehensive tour will be offered, such as in Phnom Penh, Cambodia or in Mandalay, Myanmar. During excursions, Pandaw crew bring water along to help hydrate while out and about. There are also usually opportunities to visit various charity programs Pandaw is involved with in the region, as well as to head to a local market with the ship's chef.

PRE- & POST-CRUISE STAYS   Pandaw does offer a variety of pre- and post-cruise options. It can be a 1-night stay on board a Pandaw vessel in the Burmese capital of Yangon (with its recent explosion in tourism since opening up more to the rest of the world in 2011, Myanmar is notoriously short on hotel rooms), or a 3-night extension on Thailand's River Kwai, made famous by the 1957 British World War II film, *The Bridge on the River Kwai*. There are also extensions available in Vietnam's Ho Chi Minh City, and Cambodia's Siem Reap and Phnom Penh.

K Class—Angkor Pandaw, Kalaw Pandaw, Kalay Pandaw, Katha Pandaw, Kha Byoo Pandaw, Kindat Pandaw, Laos Pandaw, Yunnan Pandaw & Zawgyi Pandaw

The Verdict

These two deck ships are intimate, with only 10 to 36 passengers on board, but their smaller size allows them to go farther up certain rivers and navigate truly unique passages in Southeast Asia, such as the Red River in Vietnam and the Mekong River into Laos and China.

Specifications

Passengers:			
Kalay Pandaw	10	Kha Byoo Pandaw, Laos Pandaw, Zawgyi Pandaw	20
Yunnan Pandaw	28	Angkor Pandaw, Katha Pandaw	32
Kalaw Pandaw, Kindat Pandaw	36		
Total cabins/balcony cabins:			
Kalay Pandaw	5/0	Kha Byoo Pandaw, Laos Pandaw, Zawgyi Pandaw	10/0
Yunnan Pandaw	14/0	Angkor Pandaw, Katha Pandaw	16/0
Kalaw Pandaw, Kindat Pandaw	18/0		
Passenger decks	2		
Crew:			
Kalay Pandaw	7	Zawgyi Pandaw	8
Angkor Pandaw	22	Katha Pandaw	16
Kalaw Pandaw, Kindat Pandaw	27		
Year entered service:			
Katha Pandaw	2011	Angkor Pandaw	2012
Kalay Pandaw	2013	Kalaw Pandaw, Kindat Pandaw, Zawgyi Pandaw	2014
Kha Byoo Pandaw, Laos Pandaw	2015	Yunnan Pandaw	2016

Note: Pandaw vessels have wrap-around balconies, which the company considers as balconies, but since they are not private balconies we did not include mention of them here. Also, crew counts were not available for all the vessels as some vessels are chartered out to other companies the majority of the season.

THE SHIPS IN GENERAL   Pandaw's ships are simple and effective. Fashioned after the steamboat vessels of the 19th-century Irrawaddy Flotilla Company, these two-deck vessels represent a kind of peaceful effortlessness that suits the destinations they sail through well. These vessels are built from teak wood and brass and the teak is ever-present throughout—on the walls, the floors and in the furniture. Additional outdoor furniture tends to be wicker chairs and wooden loungers. The decor is muted, with understated regional artwork here or there. It's a serene and straightforward way of just letting people enjoy the views without any fuss.

CABINS   Staterooms are either 170- or 180-square-feet each (except on the *Zawgyi Pandaw*, where they are 150 each), and whichever they are, all staterooms are the same size on each vessel and the only difference is whether they are on the upper or lower deck—but even the lower deck cabins are above water level so they receive adequate light and have access to the balcony. They all have doors that open up to the wrap-around balcony with deck seating provided for each cabin. There are in-suite bathrooms with showers, and cabins are outfitted with air-conditioning, mineral water, a safe, and a hair dryer. Beds can be configured as two twins or combined into one larger bed for two. There is storage under the bed, and a small writing desk and mirror, as well.

PUBLIC AREAS   Public areas include the main dining room with indoor and outdoor seating, the indoor/outdoor bar and lounge area with shaded outdoor seating and often times a small library room.

DINING OPTIONS   Pandaw passengers will head to the dining room for a buffet breakfast and for lunch service which is a combination soup and salad buffet with a served main course. They can eat inside in the air-conditioned restaurant or take their meal to the outdoor seating area. Dinners are served by the wait staff. Food on board is a mix of local cuisine (so passengers get a taste of the regional specialties), as well more familiar offerings for less adventurous eaters. Beverages are included in the cruise fare, save for drinks from the espresso bar and wines.

POOL, FITNESS, SPA, BIKES   There is no pool or gym on board these vessels, but various massages are available for booking and are performed in a small treatment area on board. Also these vessels carry mountain bikes for passengers to rent out for $25 per person.

P Class—Bassac Pandaw, Indochina Pandaw, Mekong Pandaw, Orient Pandaw, Pandaw II & Tonle Pandaw
The Verdict
These slightly larger vessels tend to sail some of the more traditional itineraries, such as the vastly popular Mekong and Irrawaddy rivers.

Specifications

Passengers:			
Mekong Pandaw, Pandaw II	48	Tonle Pandaw	56
Bassac Pandaw, Indochina Pandaw, Orient Pandaw	60		
Total cabins/balcony cabins:			
Mekong Pandaw	24/3	Pandaw II	24/2
Tonle Pandaw	28/0	Bassac Pandaw, Indochina Pandaw, Orient Pandaw	30/0
Passenger decks	2		
Crew:			
Mekong Pandaw	20	Pandaw II	25
Tonle Pandaw	26	Bassac Pandaw	28
Indochina Pandaw, Orient Pandaw	27		
Year entered service:			
Pandaw II, Tonle Pandaw	2002	Orient Pandaw	2008
Indochina Pandaw	2009	Bassac Pandaw	2012
Mekong Pandaw	2013		

Note: *Pandaw vessels have wrap-around balconies, which the company considers as balconies, but since they are not private balconies we did not note them here (except on the two vessels where there will be actual private balconies).*

THE SHIPS IN GENERAL   These larger vessels have many similarities to their smaller counterparts, but with a bit more room to play with, Pandaw is starting to experiment with additional features and amenities. For instance, Pandaw has built two suites on the front section of the upper deck on the *Pandaw II,* and three suites on the front section of the upper deck on the *Mekong Pandaw.* Some of these vessels have larger library rooms or proper lecture rooms, as well. But again they are steeped in that hallmark teak wood construction with a simple, steamboat-style look.

CABINS   All of the staterooms on Pandaw's P Class of vessels are 170-square-feet each and feature en suite bathrooms with showers, air conditioning, and beds that be configured into two singles or one double. They all open up onto the wrap-around balcony deck. The suites on the *Pandaw II* and *Mekong Pandaw* will be approximately 360-square-feet each and will feature a private balcony, a lounge area with sofa, a minibar with included local soft drinks, beer and spirits, tea and coffee making facilities, an in-room espresso machine, and the option of having a third bed in the lounge area. Additionally, suite guests will have included wine with lunch and dinner.

PUBLIC AREAS   In addition to the dining room and bar and lounge, both with indoor and outdoor seatings, these ships feature additional areas to meet and greet other passengers, including a library, shop, and a lecture and meeting room. There is Wi-Fi available on board but given the remoteness of the vessels at times, its reliability is questionable.

DINING OPTIONS   Meals are served in the dining room where passengers come for a buffet breakfast a semi-buffet lunch with a soup and salad bar and served entrees and a sit-down dinner. Don't be surprised to see Vietnamese, Cambodian, and Burmese specialties on the menus.

POOL, FITNESS, SPA, BIKES   There is no pool or fitness room, but the Mekong Pandaw has a spa treatment room that offers a variety of massages. Massages are also available on the other ships but are executed in a small massage area. Pandaw vessels now carry mountain bikes on board for rent at 25 bucks a pop.

UN-CRUISE ADVENTURES

www.un-cruise.com. © 888/862-8881.

Pros

o **Inclusions.** Included-in-the-fare wines, beers and spirits, all taxes, a complimentary massage and excursions visiting museums, nature centers, wineries and other points of interest

o **Proper viewing.** Unlike many cruise ships, the S.S. *Legacy* has forward observation terraces and two promenades (one fully encircling) that provide ideal vantages for scenic cruising.

Cons

o **No balconies.** The S.S. *Legacy* has no balcony cabins but there are open decks that are literally steps away from every stateroom.

THE LINE IN A NUTSHELL Seattle-based Un-Cruise is the post-2013 amalgamation of popular adventure cruise line InnerSea Discoveries and its luxe American Safari Cruises division. The company operates a fleet of small expedition ships and yachts that ply some of the most remote waters and coastlines of Alaska, the Sea of Cortez, Costa Rica, and even the Galapagos. In 2013, Un-Cruise began offering a new Columbia and Snake River cruising program with its largest ship, the 88-guest S.S. *Legacy,* a charming replica Victorian-era coastal liner.

Frommer's Ratings (Scale of 1–5)

Cabin comfort & amenities	5	Public spaces	3
Decor	4	Dining	5
Fitness, spa and pool	4	Service	5
Family-friendly	N/A	Enrichment	5

THE EXPERIENCE In contrast with Un-Cruises fleet of zodiac- and kayak-equipped, wilderness-exploring expedition ships, the S.S. *Legacy* offers a port-intensive Heritage-focused cruising experience. With April through November weekly departures from Portland, Oregon, the S.S. *Legacy*'s 7-night itineraries include the charming Oregon coastal city of Astoria with its Victorian-era waterfront; cruising through the spectacular Columbia River Gorge; transiting numerous locks and stops in pastoral river towns and/ or passage through the semi-desert terrains of Eastern Oregon and Washington as well as Northern Idaho. Throughout the voyage, Un-Cruise guests are treated to a wide variety of shore excursions as well as in-depth enrichment presentations covering the geology, history, flora and fauna of one of the world's most beautiful river systems while being wined and dined in low-key but elegant style.

THE FLEET In addition to the S.S. *Legacy,* Un-Cruise has a fleet of eight ocean-going and inner sea-cruising adventure ships, five of which offer an all-inclusive, deluxe experience (spirits, massage, daily turn down service, more spacious cabins and more overall space per guest): *Safari Quest* (22 guests); *Safari Explorer* (34 guests); *Safari Voyager* (64 guests); *Safari Endeavor* (84 guests); and the chartered *La Pinta* (48 guests). Three Un-Cruise adventure ships are not all-inclusive and have smaller staterooms: *Wilderness Adventurer* (60 guests); *Wilderness Explorer* (74-guests); and *Wilderness Discoverer* (76 guests).

PASSENGER PROFILE With an emphasis on enrichment versus wilderness hikes, kayaking and wildlife-seeking adventure, the S.S. *Legacy* caters to a less physically active demographic than the typical Un-Cruise adventure guest. This is also not a ship for those seeking mainstream cruise entertainment and diversions such as casinos, big production shows and swimming pools.

7-day Columbia and Snake ("Ameritage! Four Rivers of Wine & History"), round-trip from Portland, from $3,695, Apr, June, Aug, Oct

7-day Columbia and Snake ("Legacy of Discovery"), round-trip from Portland, from $3,395, Apr-Nov

Note on this chart: Itineraries may also be available in the reverse direction. The first price is the lowest available price for all cabin categories, and the second price is the lowest balcony price, including French balcony cabins.

The target market is middle-aged to elderly, well-traveled, affluent and enrichment seeking. Families are welcome but no guests under 8 years are allowed.

DINING OPTIONS Un-Cruise cuisine is delicious and tends to be more health-conscious and lighter than mainstream cruise ship fare, using locally sourced ingredients with an emphasis on regional specialties. Lunch and dinner entrees are paired with complementary wines and vegetarian options are always available.

ACTIVITIES Un-Cruise has guides and local historians come on board to bring to life the stories and natural history of the rivers. You can also expect a representative of a local Native American tribe to share that part of the region's history with guests. Other activities include onboard wine tastings and/or pairings for experiencing the area's rising-in-acclaim wine varietals. It's not back-to-back activities though, and in between presentations and excursions, there is downtime for socializing and relaxing on board.

CHILDREN'S PROGRAM There are no separate, organized children's activities but all tours, on board presentations and shore tours are kid-friendly.

ENTERTAINMENT Other than a crew talent show, there are no production shows or guest singers/musicians. Instead, the ship's team of three heritage guides provide in depth enrichment presentations, sometimes taking on the roles and sporting the vintage garb of legendary regional characters, such as road-building magnate Sam Hill and sugar heiress Alma Spreckles.

SERVICE Extremely friendly and attentive all-American staff and crew.

TOURS Excepting 1 full day of river cruising, morning and afternoon tours are offered every day. Highlights include a Hell's Canyon jet boat adventure and picnic, visits to Multnomah Falls and the Columbia River Gorge Lookout, wine tastings and a morning at the Maryhill Museum with its collection of world class artwork and sculptures.

PRE- & POST-CRUISE STAYS Un-Cruise offers stays at the Hotel Rose near the Willamette River (from $165.00 per night) as well as pre- and post-cruise 8-night train journeys (from $7,895) into the Canadian Rockies, starting in Seattle and ending in Vancouver, British Columbia.

S.S. Legacy

The Verdict

Two thumbs up for a unique river cruising experience that captures the nostalgia of a bygone era while providing most of the creature comforts of contemporary cruising.

Specifications

Passengers	88	Total cabins/balcony cabins	44/0
Passenger decks	4	Crew	34
Year entered service	1984		

THE SHIP IN GENERAL   Despite its designation, the S.S. *Legacy* is not an actual steamer but rather an elegantly designed, diesel-powered avatar of an early 20th Century coastal liner. Built in 1983 as the Pilgrim Belle for Coastwise Cruise Lines, it was also known as the Colonial Explorer and Victorian Empress before joining the now-defunct Cruise West's fleet in 1996 as the Spirit of '98. When Cruise West floundered in 2010, the ship was laid up in Seattle until it was purchased and refitted by Un-Cruise as the S.S. *Legacy*. The 88-guest vessel has four passenger decks, starting at the top with Bridge, Upper, Lounge and Main Decks. An elevator provides access to Upper, Lounge and Main Decks.

The Bridge Deck has plenty of sunning space, two whirlpools and a sheltered fitness area at the stern. On the Upper Deck, there is a forward observation terrace that continues aft via a fully encircling, sheltered promenade leading to cabin accommodation. The Lounge Deck has an open viewing area on the bow that is reached via the Lounge and sheltered promenades on either side access the accommodations, meeting at the stern. The Main Deck has an interior passageway leading to the accommodations followed by the reception area and dining room, culminating at the Pesky Barnacle Saloon and a sheltered terrace at the stern.

CABINS   The *Legacy* has 44 all-outside staterooms in six categories, ranging from a palatial Owner's Suite to cozy Master Staterooms. Depending on the category, all staterooms have queen, double or twin bedding; a flat-screen TV/DVD player; iPod docking station, air conditioning/heat; plenty of under-bed storage space and private bath with shower. An especially nice touch are the brass framed windows that open up to the promenades on the Upper and Lounge Decks. Wheelchair guests, please note that the Owner's Suite can accommodate wheelchair guests but there is no elevator service to its location on the Bridge Deck. Also, Admiral Stateroom 309 has been refitted with a bench and handles in the shower and a ramp entry outside the door to get over the lip-entry but it is not fully ADA-certified.

PUBLIC AREAS   The ship has vintage decorative elements such as hammered tin ceilings, floral upholstery and sturdy, brass-framed picture windows but the emphasis is on spaciousness and comfort versus over-the-top poshness and the ersatz Victoriana of some river cruise boats. Located on the Lounge Deck, the Grand Lounge is divided into fore and aft sections and seats up to 70 guests. It has access to the open bow, features large brass-framed windows, a self-service coffee and tea area, AV equipment for presentations, a boutique and the ship's largest bar. The Pesky Barnacle at the aft of the Main Deck is a saloon that seats 18 guests, and offers round-the-clock, unlimited whiskey, scotch and on-tap beer as well as card tables and board games.

DINING OPTIONS   The S.S. *Legacy* has a single, 96-seat dining venue that can accommodate all guests in one leisurely seating. It has booth seating for four or round tables accommodating up to six guests and picture windows on either side that offer near-water-level views. There is an early riser's breakfast with fresh fruit and tasty, baked-on-board pastries as well as a full breakfast with eggs, cold cuts, cereals, yogurt, pastries and daily options such as a broccoli and cheddar strata or eggs benedict. Lunches usually include a salad, sandwiches and home-made soups, while dinners have a choice of entrees, including fresh, local seafood and meats, and desserts that are made from scratch, be it a tiramisu or homemade gelato. Special dietary requirements can be accommodated when made in advance.

POOL, FITNESS, SPA, BIKES   There is a tiny sauna and two Jacuzzis but no pool. The enclosed fitness area has two ellipticals, a pair of stationary bikes and a stretching area with yoga mats. Daily free fitness classes are provided.

VANTAGE DELUXE WORLD TRAVEL

www.vantagetravel.com. ☎ 888/514-1845.

Pros

o **Aggressive prices.** Vantage is all about throwing out the 2-for-1 deals and free airfare to motivate bookings.

o **Nice new ships.** The company has some older as well as newer vessels in its fleet and the new vessels are totally respectable, modern river cruise ships.

Cons

o **Gimmicky.** The onslaught of 2-for-1 sales and free-airfare deals have a pushy and gimmicky feel and leave you wondering, "What's the catch?" And once you sail with Vantage you can expect a never-ending supply of said deals.

THE LINE IN A NUTSHELL   Vantage Deluxe World Travel is a decent four-star (though don't expect anything very ritzy) river cruise line that caters to older and solo travelers—similar to Grand Circle but with newer, shinier ships (the two companies are actually owned by members of the same family but they are completely separate entities).

Frommer's Ratings (Scale of 1–5)

Cabin comfort & amenities	4	Public spaces	4
Decor	4	Dining	3
Fitness, spa and pool	3	Service	4
Family-friendly	5	Enrichment	5

THE EXPERIENCE   Vantage is a perfectly middle-of-the-road river cruise line. It's definitely nothing crazy fancy but its newer ships especially shouldn't be ruled out and present a great value for what you get—they provide many of the amenities that have become common on the rivers, such as French balconies on the majority of staterooms, and Wi-Fi and bicycles on board.

Vantage was founded in 1983 and relies almost entirely on a consumer database of several million potential travelers that it markets and sells its river cruises to. The company has an aggressive customer-referral program, offering customers a discount off their next trip if a referral books, and about two-thirds of its business comes from repeat clients. So if you haven't heard of Vantage, it's probably because you're not in the system yet.

Because of the deals and incentives, a lot of people who sail with Vantage get hooked and become Vantage loyalists. Vantage is also big with solo travelers as it sets aside a handful of cabins on each vessels as dedicated single cabins with no single supplement, and has a cabin share program whereby it will pair up solo passengers willing to room with other solos.

Like several other river cruise companies Vantage was a tour operator first and foremost, and then its river cruising business began to take off, which means that it knows how to handle the logistic of group travel. It provides mostly inclusive river cruise packages (often bundled with appealing air deals, in fact some of its river cruise pricing is only offered as such if air is purchased together with the cruise) comprised of most meals, excursions and transfers.

THE FLEET Vantage began chartering river cruise ships in the late 1990s (it still charters the 5-year-old, 130-passenger Douro Spirit) and began building its own river cruise vessels in the 2000s. Today, the company owns and operates five river cruise ships in Europe, including its latest that is launching this year, the 176-passenger MS River Voyager.

Vantage christened one of its first new builds, the 134-passenger River Voyager, in 2002 (the vessel was then refurbished in 2012). Ten years later the company launched the 176-passenger MS River Discovery II in 2012, followed by the 176-passenger MS River Splendor and 134-passenger MS River Venture in 2013.

The layouts of the 176-passenger and 134-passenger vessels are very similar and there is a subtle variation in the onboard themes and color schemes. For instance, there tends to be a musical theme on many of the ships. The latest ship, the River Voyager, will have a jazz theme throughout with a "Bourbon Street Dining Room," "Cotton Club Lounge" and Blue Note Lounge," and the suites are named after jazz greats like Louis Armstrong and Miles Davis. The River Navigator has a Rat Pack theme, with a lounge named after the dynamic group and a jukebox that plays their hits. Suites on the Navigator are named after some of the Rat Pack members. And artwork on board evokes the themes as well.

Vantage has incorporated environmentally friendly aspects into its river cruise vessels, including energy-efficient engines and water- and energy-saving elements on board such as LED lighting.

Don't expect marble bathrooms or anything like that, just regular, relatively uninspired hotel-style furniture that is neither memorable nor disagreeable. The vessels also feature free Wi-Fi on board.

6

Vantage Deluxe World Travel

OTHER RIVER CRUISE LINES

PASSENGER PROFILE Vantage markets itself to the 55-plus crowd and is firmly planted there. As mentioned above, they also cater to solo cruisers, with both single cabins set aside for solo passengers as well as a roommate share program for single passengers willing to bunk up with other single travelers to avoid a single supplement. Vantage is definitely a river cruise company by Americans for Americans. A big selling point of theirs, for people who prefer that sort of thing, is that you will be cruising with your fellow countrymen and women with service and amenities, such as food options, geared towards the American palette.

DINING OPTIONS Speaking of palette, Vantage definitely makes sure to have "safe" options on its menus, items that are familiar and perhaps not too exotic, something its customers appreciate. It does offer local specialties as well, but always alongside food that we would know or can get in the U.S. too (such as dinner salads and steak, for instance).

Meals are served in the main dining room, where both breakfast and lunch are served as a buffet—the lunch buffet will always have a salad bar. The dinner menu typically includes an appetizer, soup and/or salad, choice of entree, and choice of dessert. Don't expect a ton of variety, and food is adequate but nothing overly memorable. Wine is included with dinner.

ACTIVITIES Vantage offers a wide range of onboard and on-shore programs intended to inform cruises (in an insightful fashion) about the destinations its ships sail through. There are often themed talks and lessons on board, which could be an art history lecture during a Seine sailing (an itinerary that includes visits to Monet's studio and the Giverny Museum of Impressionism during a port call in Giverny) or a Portuguese language lesson on a Douro river cruise. You can feel will feel like you're back in school again when you find yourself taking copious notes about European royalty during a presentation on the topic in the lounge. Vantage also offers local craft-making workshops (you know you have always wanted to try your hand at making your very own santon doll, the terracotta figurines that are popular in Provence).

CHILDREN'S PROGRAM Vantage requires all travelers to be above 8 years of age, but for children ages 8-18, Vantage offers several family-friendly river cruise departures and kids 8-18 can cruise for free when their traveling companions reserve a category B or higher stateroom (subject to availability). All of its "Family Cruise" sailings take place either during the summer or winter holidays and include kid-friendly activities such as arts and crafts and local school visits, and kids will receive a complimentary travel journal. These sailings also feature kid-friendly menus.

ENTERTAINMENT You can expect the usual: various acts brought on board that reflect the more well-known as well as lesser known talents of the region you are sailing through. There won't necessarily be live music nightly in the lounge, but Vantage often features a jukebox-generated soundtrack for the after-dinner mingling scene. There may also be the occasional movie night, during which a film relevant to the destination will be aired.

204

20-day Seine and Rhone ("Grand River Journey Through France: Normandy, Paris & Provence"), Avignon to Paris, from $4,199, balconies from $5,399, Mar–Oct

10-day Rhone ("Best of Burgundy, Beaujolais & Provence"), Chalon-sur-Saone to Tarascon (France), from $1,999, balconies from $2,599, Mar–Nov

10-day Rhone ("Culinary French Waterways: Best of Burgundy, Beaujolais & Provence"), Chalon-sur-Saone to Tarascon (France), from $2,599, balconies from $3,199, Oct

10-day Seine ("Paris & Highlights of Normandy"), round-trip from Paris, from $2,199, balconies from $2,799 Mar–Oct

10-day Seine ("Art Along the Seine: Paris & Normandy") round-trip from Paris, from $2,999, balconies from $3,599, Apr–Oct

9-day Dutch and Belgian Canals ("Springtime in Holland & Belgium: Tulips, Windmills & Canals") round-trip from Amsterdam, from $2,999, balconies from $3,499, Mar–May

24-day Rhine, Main and Danube ("Grand European River Cruise: Rhine Valley to Bucharest"), with 23-day cruise, Bonn to Ruse, from $6,499, balconies from $7,699, May–Oct

15-day Main, Rhine and Danube ("Classic Rivers of Europe: Castles, Cathedrals & Fairytales"), Bonn to Budapest, from $2,999, balconies from $3,899, May–Nov

9-day Danube ("Gateway to Eastern Europe"), Budapest to Ruse, with 8-day cruise, from $3,099, balconies from $3,699, May–Oct

14-day Rhine and Moselle ("Crossroads of Europe: Cruising the Rhine and Moselle"), Arnhem to Basel, from $2,599, balconies from $3,299, May–Oct

10-day Douro ("The Douro: Portugal's River of Gold"), Lisbon to Porto, from $3,199, balconies from $3,399, Mar–Oct

11-day Elbe ("The Magnificent Elbe: Berlin to Prague"), Berlin to Prague, from $4,599, balconies from $4,749, Apr–Oct

7-day Seine ("Classic France Along the Seine"), round-trip from Paris, from $1,999, balconies from $2,599, Nov

Note on this chart: Itineraries may also be available in the reverse direction. The first price is the lowest available price for all cabin categories, and the second price is the lowest balcony price, including French balcony cabins.

SERVICE Vantage has a 4:1 ratio of crew to passengers—so this is where you kind of have to know what you want or expect from a service standpoint. The industry average is probably around 3.5 passengers for each crew member, with higher end lines getting closer to 3 passengers per crew member and even 2.5 passengers to crew member (on some of the Asia river cruises it can get close to 1:1). But service isn't cheap (neither is the cabin space to accommodate crew) and not everyone needs that level of attention. A company like Vantage isn't really about coddling its customers. And when you're paying these kinds of prices, you really shouldn't expect it. You should expect a very friendly staff that is busy making sure food is being served on time, itineraries are running smoothly and cabins are being refreshed. And for some people, that's really all that matters (butlers schmutlers).

Gratuities are not included and Vantage provides passengers with a 9-to-11-euros per person per day guideline for tipping which includes all of the onboard ship staff, save for the cruise director and concierge. The recommended gratuity for him/her is between three and six euros per person, per day. Five euros per person per day are automatically applied to passengers' onboard accounts, but it is optional and guests can adjust the amount. All gratuities can be charged to your onboard account. The company also recommends one to two euros per person, per day, for local guides and drivers.

TOURS   Since Vantage was a tour operator before it was a river cruise line, you can expect the company to reliably operate one excursion per day throughout its river cruises. Excursions are generally local guide-led sightseeing tours either of a specific landmark or museum, or an overview tour of a port town. Then passengers might be given free time to explore on their own. While some river cruise companies offer two and sometimes even more touring options per day, Vantage really sticks to the one and either gives guests free time beyond that or it's back on board for some lectures and interactive demonstrations.

PRE- & POST-CRUISE STAYS   Vantage has plenty of options for extending your river cruise. For one, you can combine river cruises (for a discount, of course), or you can tack on 3- to 5-day city stays the include hotel accommodations, breakfast, a panoramic city tour, transfers and the services of a local host. The 3-day Paris extension, for instance, is priced from $599 per person. A 5-day Prague extension is priced from $899 per person. In most cases these suggested extensions are close enough to the embarkation or disembarkation point that Vantage can arrange a coach transfer between the river cruise ship and the hotel.

River Voyager, River Discovery II, River Navigator, River Splendor & River Venture
The Verdict

These vessels are basic and contemporary and get the job done. The younger ones are slightly sleeker than the older ones—and no, that isn't meant to be a metaphor for life.

Specifications

Passengers:			
River Voyager, River Discovery II, River Splendor	176	River Navigator, River Venture	134
Total cabins/balcony cabins:			
River Voyager	92/65	River Discovery II, River Splendor	92/72
River Navigator	69/61	River Venture	69/58
Passenger decks	3		
Crew:			
River Voyager	45	River Discovery II, River Splendor	46
River Navigator	40	River Venture	41
Year entered service:			
River Voyager	2016	River Splendor, River Venture	2013
River Discovery II	2012	River Navigator	2002

THE SHIPS IN GENERAL   Vantage has definitely been stepping up its game little by little ultimately offering up ships that most passengers will be perfectly pleased with given the reasonable prices and never-ending deals parade. There's nothing overtly right with these vessels and there's nothing overtly wrong with them either. These aren't "wow" ships, these are ships that provide most things that an average traveler would want in terms of amenities—a solid selection of cabin sizes; French balconies; cleanliness; decent food, and some wine and beer with dinner.

CABINS   The majority of cabins on Vantage vessels are 165-square-feet each, with a handful of smaller single cabins on the lower decks that measure 125-square-feet. There are also between 4 and 12 Deluxe Suites that measure 225- to 250-square-feet each, and an Owner's Suite that is 300- to 330-square-feet. With the exception of the *River Navigator,* which has large windows on the second-deck staterooms, cabins on the second and third decks have French balconies. All Vantage staterooms have queen-size beds that can be converted into two twins, bathrooms with glass showers, a hair dryer, one U.S. outlet, a safe, individual climate control, flat-screen TVs with movies and international news channels and L'Occitane bath products. Some staterooms also have a stocked minibar, suites also have a coffee machine and the Owner's Suite has a Jacuzzi tub.

PUBLIC AREAS   There is one main dining room and one main bar and lounge area on these vessels. Most of these ships also have on additional smaller lounge, the Captain's Club, at the aft of the vessel, which serves as an alternative dining venue with healthier, spa cuisine options and has a retractable roof that can be pulled back when the weather is nicer for an outdoor dining experience. There is also a fitness room as well as a walking track on the top Solaris Deck (where between 27 and 54 laps—depending on the vessel—is the equivalent of a mile). The ships also have a massage treatment room and/or salon. There is an elevator between the three passenger decks and a hydraulic chairlift up to the Solaris Deck.

DINING OPTIONS   Meals are served at set times and are open-seating in the main dining room (a restaurant that has different names on each ship, such as the Bourbon Street Bistro on the *River Voyager* and the Compass Rose on the *River Splendor*). As we mentioned previously, meals are intended to have both American and European options whether during the buffet breakfast and lunch or during the sit-down dinners. For a change of pace, the lounge at the aft of the vessels serves up lighter fare. There is also an early riser's breakfast option; tea, coffee and hot cocoa available all day; and cookies and snacks offered in the afternoon.

POOL, FITNESS, SPA, BIKES   There is no pool on board, but passengers can hit the fitness room or walking track to get their heart rates up a bit. Massage services are available in a spa treatment room. There are no bikes.

6 | VICTORIA CRUISES

www.victoriacruises.com. ✆ 800/348-8084.

Pros

o **U.S.-owned.** Victoria Cruises likes to boast about the fact that it is a U.S.-based river cruise line on China's Yangtze River. That's due in large part to the fact that its main competitor, Century Cruises, is a Chinese-run operation. Self-pumping aside, there is something to be said for dealing directly with an American company that knows the wants and needs of the U.S. consumer.

o **Frequent updates.** Victoria Cruises has been building river cruise ships for the Yangtze for some time, which means that its vessels range in age from 7 to 22 years old. But the company is constantly investing in upgrades and overhauls to keep its fleet feeling fresh.

Cons

o **Older vessels.** Despite the investments in its fleet, Victoria's ships are older and for some passengers who really prefer the latest and greatest, that could be a drawback no matter how much the company keeps spending on refurbs.

THE LINE IN A NUTSHELL Victoria Cruises has been bringing passengers up and down the Yangtze River for more than 20 years. This isn't Victoria's first Yangtze rodeo. So if you like the idea of an experienced, U.S.-based river cruise line taking charge of your Yangtze River vacation either directly, or through the numerous tour operator partners that charter Victoria vessels, this is probably going to be your pick.

Frommer's Ratings (Scale of 1–5)

Cabin comfort & amenities	4	Public spaces	4
Decor	4	Dining	4
Fitness, spa and pool	4	Service	4
Family-friendly	3	Enrichment	4

THE EXPERIENCE The Yangtze river cruise market is much evolved from its pre-2009 self, and the changes that Victoria has undergone are representative of that. Prior to the global economic downturn, Yangtze River cruises were more of a mass-market, lower budget experience. But when the numbers of travelers opting for Yangtze River cruises dropped dramatically with the downturn, the model shifted from high-volume to higher quality cruises, and Victoria Cruises has been investing millions in its product in recent years to successfully embrace that transition. A major component of Victoria's aggressive fleet enhancement program has been the addition of what the company calls its Executive Amenities Program, a premium option that includes access to an executive lounge, concierge service, upgraded cabin categories, private small-group shore excursions, complimentary Internet access, laundry and shoe shine services, and reserved seating for evening entertainment.

Additionally, the fleet investments will come full circle this year when the company relaunches the *Victoria Jenna,* the largest and newest vessel in the Victoria fleet, having launched in 2009. With the renovation of the *Victoria Jenna,* Victoria Cruises will have completed upgrades and renovations on its entire fleet of Yangtze River cruise ships.

THE FLEET   There are seven vessels in the Victoria fleet ranging from the two oldest, the 208-passenger *Victoria Sophia* and the 218-passenger *Victoria Selina,* which both launched in 1994, to the youngest and largest, the 378-passenger *Victoria Jenna,* which was built in 2009 and is being relaunched for the 2016 season.

But age is (almost) irrelevant when it comes to these ships, as Victoria has been investing millions to update them, sometimes more than once. At this point, all seven ships have been renovated within the last 3 years and all of them now have additional bells and whistles, like the Executive Amenities Program mentioned above, or the full-service spa and salon the *Victoria Katarina* received in 2014.

The ships all have a similar look from the outside, like some kind of river/ocean hybrid given that they are much larger than river cruise ships in Europe. Their exteriors are not super modern or sleek but the interiors are, in fact, getting ever more stylish over time.

PASSENGER PROFILE   Victoria Cruises' target audience is the affluent Boomer and retiree market, people with the time and money to not just do a whirlwind tour of China's highlights, but to tack on an additional 3 or 4 days on the Yangtze. But it's not strictly an older crowd, just predominantly one. Victoria works with a large variety of tour operators and that means passengers can be all ages, come from all over the world and have all kinds of career and education backgrounds.

DINING OPTIONS   Along with beefing up its ships' interiors, Victoria Cruises has also been working to offer more and better options in its dining rooms, including a larger selection of Western favorites alongside Chinese cuisine. Meals are served buffet-style in the main restaurant, and there is also daily afternoon tea and early morning coffee and tea. In addition to the main dining room, the *Victoria Anna, Victoria Jenna, Victoria Katarina, Victoria Lianna,* and *Victoria Selina* all have a second a la carte dining venue, which passengers staying in Suites and upgraded Superior Cabins on the Executive Decks have complimentary access to. Passengers staying in Superior Cabins on other decks can pay an additional fee to eat at the a la carte restaurant.

ACTIVITIES   In between excursions, Victoria offers several activities that passengers can participate in during their Yangtze cruise. Some options include Tai Chi in the morning, various craftwork demonstrations such as

3-day Yangtze ("Three Gorges Highlights"), Chongqing to Yichang, cabins/balconies from $880, Mar–Dec

4-day Yangtze ("Three Gorges Highlights"), Yichang to Chongqing, cabins/balconies from $880, Mar–Dec

6-day Yangtze ("Grand Yangtze Discovery"), Chongqing to Shanghai, cabins/balconies from $1,610, Apr–May, Sept–Oct

8-day Yangtze ("Grand Yangtze Discovery"), Shanghai to Chongqing, cabins/balconies from $1,610, Apr–May, Sept–Oct

7-day Yangtze ("Three Gorges Explorer"), round-trip from Chongqing, cabins/balconies from $1,610, Mar–Dec

Note on this chart: Itineraries may also be available in the reverse direction. The first price is the lowest available price for all cabin categories, and the second price is the lowest balcony price, including French balcony cabins.

calligraphy or kite making lessons, and lectures about Chinese history or culture and life along the Yangtze River. There might also be some lessons in Chinese language (in case you want to try to learn Chinese in a couple days—we hear it's a very easy language to pick up).

CHILDREN'S PROGRAM Victoria Cruises does not have any policies barring children on its vessels, and the company does offer special rates for children. But the company does not offer any kids programs and is not focused on courting the family market.

ENTERTAINMENT After dinner, evening entertainment in the lounge includes cultural performances, maybe a crew show or a traditional fashion show.

SERVICE It's not always easy to ensure personalized service on a larger vessel (large for river cruising, at least). But with about one crew member for every two passengers, there are plenty of hands on deck to help Victoria's passengers should they need it. And service is definitely amped up on the Executive Decks, where passengers get concierge service and complimentary laundry and shoe shine services, among other little bonuses. Victoria Cruises includes a small service charge in its prices, which is intended to take the place of tipping. The charge, however, does not include a tip for a guide that might join the group specifically during the Yangtze River cruise or tips for special services such as a spa treatment.

TOURS You can expect to be offered at least one excursion each day as you sail along the Yangtze River. An example of some of the excursions Victoria offers includes visiting a relocation village for families who were forced to move as a result of the raised water levels created by the Three Gorges Dam, or a small-boat excursion to weave through the smaller or "lesser" gorges of the stunning Three Gorges area of the Yangtze River.

PRE- & POST-CRUISE STAYS Victoria Cruises does not offer pre- or post-cruise extensions but its Yangtze river cruises are booked by numerous tour operators who often package the cruise as part of a larger China itinerary. Some of the tour operators and packagers that Victoria works with Gate 1 Travel, Odysseys Unlimited, Orient Flexi-Pax Tours, Overseas Adventure Travel, Pacific Delight Tours, Ritz Tours, smarTours, Travcoa, and Wendy Wu Tours.

Victoria Jenna
The Verdict

Victoria's newest and largest vessel, the *Jenna* is getting spiffed up for the 2016 sailing season with a new spa area.

Specifications

Passengers	378	Total cabins/balcony cabins	189/189
Passenger decks	5	Crew	180
Year entered service	2009		

THE SHIP IN GENERAL The *Victoria Jenna* could be the most stylish vessel in the Victoria fleet. It was being relaunched as we went to press but renderings of the upgraded staterooms promise a clean and modern look with subtle Asian design touches—think contemporary furniture coupled with Asian-inspired printed wallpaper.

CABINS The *Victoria Jenna* has 189 staterooms, of which 149 are Superior Cabins that measure 225-square-feet each, 35 are Executive Suites that are 333-square-feet each, three are Deluxe Suites at 428-square-feet each, and two are the 588-square-foot Shangri-La Suites. All of the staterooms are out-fitted with private balconies and TVs with satellite cable channels. The bath-rooms also all have tubs.

PUBLIC AREAS The *Victoria Jenna* has two restaurants, the main dining room and an a la carte restaurant (aka the VIP Café) on the top deck (for Executive Suite guests). The ship's entrance is highlighted by a bright, three-deck atrium lobby. There are also two lounges, three bars, a fitness center, two lecture rooms, a library, a beauty salon, and a gift shop. Victoria provides Wi-Fi access on board.

DINING OPTIONS Passengers can either head to the main dining room where breakfast, lunch and dinner are served as a buffet of Chinese and West-ern food, or there is also the a la carte restaurant on the top deck (aka Pinnacle Deck). The a la carte restaurant serves a buffet breakfast and lunch as well and an a la carte dinner service, and is complimentary for Executive Suite, Deluxe

ABERCROMBIE & KENT
☎ 888/611-4711. www.abercrombiekent.com.

One of the world's largest luxury tour operators, A&K offers a European river cruise program, Connections, on all the main rivers, using the vessels of Amadeus Waterways and bolting on its own extras to create inclusive packages. Groups are limited to a maximum of 24, using tour leaders who live in the destinations. A lot of departures are themed, from art to World War II, food and wine or music.

Hotel stays are added to each cruise (for example, a Danube cruise might include a night in Munich and a night in Budapest at either end), as are private 'experiences', from concerts to cooking demonstrations, and private drinks receptions on board. As such, the cruises cost a lot more than the basic Amadeus offerings; upwards of $400 per day, but with everything taken care of. Fellow passengers in the A&K group are likely to be well-heeled, inquisitive Americans, although the mix on board the ships will be international.

Abercrombie & Kent also sells luxury barge vacations on the French canals, using the luxurious barges of Belmond and European Waterways (see p. 146).

AMADEUS CRUISES
☎ 888/829-1394. www.amadeuscruises.com.

Based in Austria, Amadeus Cruises offers seven ships to international guests on all Europe's major rivers. The ships vary greatly in age—from ten years old (and refurbished) to brand new—and the newest, the flagship *Amadeus Silver II*, is especially elegant, with enormous cabins, walk-in closets, gorgeous bathrooms and, on the top two accommodation decks, all balcony cabins. Cuisine is of a high quality, with table service at both lunch and dinner, and wine is included with meals. Where this line differs from its rivals is in shore excursions, which are sold on an a la carte basis, meaning the base price for the cruise is less—around $180 per night.

Amadeus sells through a lot of tour operators so fellow travelers may be in groups. Who you sail with is the luck of the draw but English is spoken on all sailings.

A-ROSA CRUISES
☎ 855/552-7672. www.arosacruises.com.

German-owned A-Rosa Cruises operates 11 contemporary ships on the Rhine, Main, Danube, Moselle, Rhone, and Saone, five of which are designated for international guests, with English spoken on board on those sailings. Distinguished by pouty, red lips and a red rose splashed across the bow, the ships appeal to a younger, more active audience, with facilities including a pool, organic sauna, spa, gym with personal trainers, bicycles and indoor/outdoor dining. Food is classy buffet style, with an emphasis on healthy Mediterranean dishes, and prices, from around $340 a night, include all drinks and a choice of excursions. A few cabins can accommodate families, a rare find on river cruises.

BLOUNT SMALL SHIP ADVENTURES
☎ 800/556-7450. www.blountsmallship adventures.com.

Blount offers a unique product; two shallow-draft ships that can sail in the ocean as well as exploring canals, rivers, lakes and coastal waterways, with an informal, friendly lifestyle on board. The ships, *Grande Caribe* and *Grande Mariner*, are neither new nor luxurious but offer destination-intensive itineraries, reaching small ports and anchorages other ships can't access.

The 88-passenger *Grande Caribe*, for example, makes its way from Boston to Montreal via a string of bays, sounds, rivers and canals, while sister ship *Grande Mariner* works its way east from Chicago to Rhode Island via some of the USA's most iconic waterways. Other destinations include Lake Michigan, the Canadian Maritimes, and the Atlantic coastal waterways. Expect to pay from around $285 a night including meals and drinks with dinner.

Blount's cruises are about cultural immersion and exploring. Each ship carries kayaks and bicycles and most voyages are accompanied by a naturalist, or historian. Guests are also offered wine tasting, cooking demos and photography seminars. Expect fellow travelers to be empty-nesters with an interest in discovering their homeland.

LINDBLAD EXPEDITIONS-NATIONAL GEOGRAPHIC

✆ 800/EXPEDITION (397-3348).
www.expeditions.com.

Soft adventure ocean line Lindblad Expeditions does cruises on the Peruvian Amazon on the 28-passenger *Delfin II*, year-round. The ship itself is a pretty sight, done up in varnished wood inside and out. Accommodations are in spacious cabins with picture windows, with all the amenities you'd expect at an upscale hotel. Passengers spend days exploring on comfortable skiffs or on foot, and the ship also has a few kayaks for passenger use (when you go off on your own you are quietly followed by crew for safety reasons). Peruvian-influenced meals with complimentary wine are served. You can hang out, listen to good biology lectures and catch views in the cushy open-air lounge with bar—with Peruvian *pisco* sours on the house. Lindblad's 8-day itinerary on the *Delfin II* begins at $6,690 per person.

SANCTUARY RETREATS

✆ 630/725-3449. www.sanctuaryretreats.com.

Sanctuary Retreats, a brand of Abercrombie & Kent, offers luxurious cruises in China, Egypt and Myanmar. The ships are all top-end; in China, the 124-passenger Yangzi Explorer has a crew-to-guest ratio of 1:1, the largest cabins on the river (its Celestial and Imperial Suites at 1,184 sq. ft. just beat out the *Century Legend*'s and *Century Paragon*'s 1,140-sq.-ft. Presidential Suites), a la carte dining and an enormous (for a riverboat) spa. Itineraries are 3 or 4 nights, with numerous bolt-on options.

Sanctuary Ananda, launched in Myanmar in 2014, is an all-balcony, contemporary ship featuring a pool, superb Thai and Burmese cuisine and a shallow enough draft to carry 42 passengers in style on the Chindwin and the northern Irrawaddy as well as the more tried-and-tested stretch of the river between Mandalay and Bagan.

In Egypt, the company operates four luxurious ships on the Nile (and these really are luxurious in a destination where every operator claims its ships to be five-star). The 64-guest *Sanctuary Nile Adventurer* sails between Luxor and Aswan. The *Sanctuary Sun Boat III* can sail all the way from Cairo to Aswan, accommodating 36 guests on an opulent boat modeled on the styles of the 1920s and 30s.

Sister ship *Sun Boat IV* is bigger, with 36 cabins and four suites; a typical Aswan-Luxor voyage on this ship will cost around $290 per night, including excursions. Finally, there's a traditional *dahabiya*, the *Zein Nile Chateau*, available for charter for up to 12; a *dahabiya* is a traditional sailing boat dating from the Victorian era of exploration, although this one has been done up in lavish style, with each room presenting a different theme.

Sanctuary's passengers tend to be from all over the world, younger, stylish, wealthy and generally well-traveled.

VOLGA DREAM

✆ 800-884-1721. www.volgadream.com.

Volga Dream, a Russian company that operates one ship (also called the *Volga Dream*), has an office in Florida that handles U.S.-based bookings. The 100-passenger *Volga Dream* was relaunched in 2007 after being renovated. It carries 50 cabins ranging from the 101-square-foot standard cabins on the lower deck to the 260-square-foot Owner's Suite. There is also a 69- and an 81-square-foot single cabin for solo travelers. The majority of staterooms are in the 100- to 126-square-foot range. There are no private balconies, but as on ships in the U.S. or in Southeast Asia there are wraparound balconies on all decks. Cabins aren't big but have a unique Russian Art Deco vibe to them. They come with the bare necessities: bathrooms with showers, a closet, air-conditioning, and a minifridge. The public spaces include a restaurant, a lounge and bar, another smaller bar, a fitness room, boutique, hairdresser and a small coffee station. Meals are Russian-influenced, and the colorful entertainment on board is definitely locally sourced. Prices for a 12-day cruise from Moscow to St. Petersburg (or the reverse) range from $3,095 to $8,895.

Suite and Shangri-La Suite guests or available for an additional fee to Superior Cabin guests.

POOL, FITNESS, SPA, BIKES   There is a fitness room and hair salon on the *Jenna* but no pool or spa, and no bikes.

Victoria Anna, Victoria Katarina, Victoria Grace, Victoria Lianna, Victoria Sophia & Victoria Selina

The Verdict

This group of six Victoria ships illustrate the evolution of the Victoria brand, from much less interesting overnight passenger cruise ships to much more dynamic vessels with flashier features and amenities on board.

Specifications

Passengers:			
Victoria Anna	266	Victoria Katarina	264
Victoria Grace	198	Victoria Lianna, Victoria Selina	218
Victoria Sophia	208		
Total cabins/balcony cabins:			
Victoria Anna	133/133	Victoria Katarina	132/132
Victoria Grace	99/99	Victoria Lianna, Victoria Selina	108/108
Victoria Sophia	104/104		
Passenger decks:			
Victoria Anna	5	Victoria Katarina, Victoria Grace, Victoria Lianna, Victoria Sophia, Victoria Selina	4
Crew:			
Victoria Anna	138	Victoria Katarina	128
Victoria Lianna, Victoria Sophia, Victoria Selina	121	Victoria Grace	117
Year entered service:			
Victoria Anna	2006	Victoria Katarina	2004
Victoria Grace	1996	Victoria Lianna	1995
Victoria Selina	1994		

THE SHIPS IN GENERAL   What started out as much simpler river cruise vessels with small staterooms and limited public spaces have grown into more sophisticated ships with more suites, exclusive-access amenities (like the a la carte restaurant available only to some guests—see below) and more.

CABINS   All of these vessels have a mix of Superior Cabins and two or three categories of suites. Superior Cabins range from 157- to 226-square-feet, and suites range from 236- to 646-square-feet. All the staterooms have balconies and are outfitted with bathtubs in the bathrooms. They all also have satellite TV. There are either two twin beds or one double and a seating area in each stateroom.

PUBLIC AREAS As is standard now throughout the Victoria fleet, these vessels feature two dining venues—the main restaurant and the a la carte alternative—one or two lounges, and one or two bars, a gym, lecture room, library, beauty salon, massage room, and gift shop on board.

DINING OPTIONS The majority of passengers eat all three meals a day in the main restaurant, which features buffets for breakfast, lunch and dinner. As an alternative, Executive Suite guests are invited to eat at the a la carte restaurant, a smaller venue on the upper deck where breakfast and lunch are buffet service and dinner is a la carte.

POOL, FITNESS, SPA, BIKES Most of these vessels have a fitness room, hair salon and spa treatment room. They don't have a pool or bikes on board.

BARGE CRUISING

7

I f a river ship is a small hotel on the water, barges are more like fancy little B&Bs—intimate, casual travel with such luxuries as a wonderful private chef preparing meals accompanied by endless wine.

The barges, some quite elaborately outfitted, are small, flat-bottomed boats, most of which were originally built for carrying freight and renovated to carry guests. These small craft explore the historic canals, rivers and lakes of France and other European countries in spring, summer and early fall.

It's a decadently slow form of travel, so slow (you may only go 70 miles in a week) that you may be able to keep up jogging, walking or biking on towpaths alongside the canals. Or you can opt to sit on the deck sipping wine or champagne as you pass towns with stone houses and beautiful countryside, admire birdlife and trees and flowers and watch lockkeepers turn big wheels by hand (or the push of a button), raising and lowering locks so your barge can float through. Included tours take you to scenic villages, medieval cities, castles, wineries and other nearby attractions.

One of the most appealing things about barges is the scale. There's typically room for no more than 24 passengers and the boat may carry less than a dozen guests. Hangout spaces will include a cushy lounge, dining area and outdoor sunning area (sometimes with small Jacuzzi). Cabins and suites tend to be small, even tiny. In these intimate surrounds you will get to know your fellow passengers quite well. Renting an entire vessel for a family or a group of friends is an option, if you can afford it.

Pricing typically includes accommodations, meals (in addition to your boat chef's preparations there may even be a dinner at a Michelin-starred restaurant on shore), drinks (wine with lunch and dinner and cocktails) and all excursions and transfers.

Food is a big deal. Your chef may head to shore early every morning to buy fresh croissant or gather supplies at a local market. In France, you'll linger at both lunch and dinner, which will both include elaborate cheese courses.

As with river cruises, you get to see and experience a variety of places but you only have to unpack once. And for those who worry about seasickness, it's virtually nonexistent on a barge.

Most cruises are 6 nights (though may be packaged with a 1-night hotel stay). Fares start at about $2,500 and are typical upwards of $5,000 per person per week. The crew-to-passenger ratio is usually high, ensuring everyone gets pampered and the staff is normally fluent in English. There is also the far cheaper, and very fun option, of driving your own barge (see box, p. 219).

WHERE TO BARGE CRUISE

France

France is by far the top place for barge cruises, with destinations including the **Canal du Midi,** a tree-lined, UNESCO-listed canal built in the 1600, and an engineering marvel of its time. Cruising in Southern France, you'll catch views of medieval towns, Roman ruins and rolling countryside, while sampling local Corbières wines and locally produced olive oil.

In the **Champagne region,** you'll visit big-name producers such as Moet & Chandon, where you can marvel at the numbers of bottles stored, in the approximately 17.4 miles of cellars. Chateaux and champagne are the prime attractions. Other highlights include the mighty French Gothic cathedral in Reims, where 25 French kings were crowned.

Barge cruises on the **Rhône** explore the picturesque towns of Provence, where the light and scenery inspired impressionist and post-impressionist artists, including in Arles, where Vincent Van Gogh lived and painted. Your itinerary will also include Avignon, with its famous bridge and Palais des Papes (Pope's Palace) and may include wine tasting at Chateauneuf-de-Pape.

Itineraries on the **Upper Loire** explore the quaint towns and natural beauty in an area known as the "Garden of Paris." French royalty came here to escape the hustle and bustle of Paris, building Fontainebleau and other legendary chateaux. Wine lovers will want to do some sipping in Sancerre. Other attractions include an aqueduct designed by Eiffel.

Barge cruises in the **Alsace Lorraine** region in easternmost France afford opportunity to try Alsatian wines while embracing a fascinating mix of French and German culture. You'll cruise past half-timbered villages and storybook castles, forests and rolling vineyards.

Burgundy is home to more vineyards than you can even attempt to visit, barge cruises exploring either northern/central Burgundy, where hillside vineyards produce Chablis; or southern Burgundy, heart of the famed Cote d'Or region, with stops in a who's who of wine villages including Nuits St. Georges, Pommard, and Montrachet.

England, Ireland & Scotland

The British Isles is an increasingly popular barge destination. In **England,** on the River Thames, you can stop by barge to see Henry VIII's Hampton Court, explore the English countryside, visit the college town of Oxford and spend time at local pubs (an eight-person barge called the Magna Carta also does sailings themed on the TV show *Downton Abbey* that include a visit to High-clere Castle, the gorgeous estate seen on the show).

Search for the Loch Ness Monster as you cruise the Caledonian Canal and lakes of **Scotland,** passing scenery that includes spectacular mountains. Along the way, sights include Cawdor Castle, inspiration for Shakespeare's Macbeth, and visits to whiskey producers.

In **Ireland,** a barge cruise on the River Shannon involves visiting pubs, quaint towns and whiskey distilleries (the 10-passenger Shannon Princess also has some golf-themed itineraries).

BARGE COMPANIES

You can book a barge through an agency that represents operators, directly with a barge company, or through your travel agent. Unlike with river ships, the actual owner of the barge may be a private individual, sometimes even your captain. For this reason, you may find the same barge sold through several different companies. Here we list some of the top barge companies (entities that own the barges they book) and agencies (which book from individuals and barge companies).

French Country Waterways

This American-owned company (based in Massachusetts) has a fleet of five 8- to 18-passenger barges which travel to Burgundy, the Champagne region, Alsace/Lorraine and the Upper Loire (sold through the company and travel agents). Everything from drinks to daily four-course dinners (paired with premium French wines) is included. One time each cruise, a dinner ashore is arranged at a Michelin-starred restaurant, a highlight for many cruisers. Six-night deluxe canal cruises depart every Sunday from April through October. Accommodations include private baths. Rates start at $4,195 per person for a 6-day cruise. © **800/222-1236;** www.fcwl.com.

Belmond Afloat in France

Luxury travel specialist Belmond owns five barges carrying 4 to 12 passengers, exploring France, including Burgundy, the Canal du Midi, the Franche-Comté region, and the Rhône. With over-the-top touches like a grand piano (on one of the barges), antique Louis XVI furniture, and five-course meals prepared by Cordon Bleu–trained chefs and accompanied by fine local wines, these are uber-luxurious experiences. Cruises are available April through October. Rates start at $4,872 per person for a 6-night cruise. Rent the smallest barge from $20,832 (for two to four guests). © **800/524-2420;** www. belmond.com/afloat-in-france.

European Waterways/Go Barging

Representing 17 barges, carrying between 6 and 20 passengers, European Waterways has a large variety of destinations including France, Germany, Holland, Scotland, England, and Ireland. In addition to gourmet meals and

CAPTAINING YOUR own ship

If you'd rather be the captain of your own canal boat (no experience necessary), you can rent one and navigate the canals of France or other countries on your own. It's a much cheaper choice, though you do need to do your own cooking and fetch your own wine. Included is a pre-cruise briefing and demonstration on how to drive the boat, and then you're off. Prices vary wildly depending on boat, cruise, time of year and services, and a specific boat you see listed on a website may not be available when you want to travel (though there may be a comparable option). Your best bet is to take a look online, figure out what you're interested in (number of cabins, and so forth) and then call to speak with a representative (or your own travel agent) about your options.

LE BOAT

Le Boat owns and operates a fleet of 40 self-drive cruisers in eight European countries. You can book a barge for 2 to 12 passengers. ℂ **800/734-5491;** www.leboat.com.

BARGE CONNECTION

This California-based tour operator has been specializing in barge vacations since 1998. It can help you book barge cruises, self-drive barges and riverboats in Holland, France, England, Ireland, Scotland, Germany, Belgium, and Italy. ℂ **888/550-8580;** www.bargeconnection.com.

drinks, the cruises include use of bicycles, and daily escorted excursions "off the beaten track" to wineries, castles, markets or to see craftsmen at work. Decor throughout features antiques, wood paneling, carpets for a cozy feel. Each barge has a library, games, and a CD player/iPod dock. Depending on the barge, there may be a spa pool on the sun deck, computer with Internet access, and a telescope for star-gazing. Trips run between March and October. Rates start at $3,790 per person for a 6-night cruise. ℂ **877/879-8808;** www.gobarging.com.

CroisiEurope

A big name in river cruising in Europe for decades (see chapter 8), CroisiEurope operates five barges, each with 12 cabins (24 passengers), which travel on various canals in France, including in Provence, Burgundy, the Alsace-Lorraine and the Loire Valley. CroisiEurope may be one of the most affordable barge cruise options you can find, but service and food are still stellar. All the ships feature a much more modern decor than many other barges and a hot tub on the sun deck. The all-inclusive price includes transfers, meals, drinks and excursions. Trips run between April and October. Rates are from $2,444 per person for a 6-night cruise. ℂ **800/768-7232;** www.croisieuroperivercruises.com.

Abercrombie & Kent

Luxury tour operator Abercrombie & Kent (see also chapter 6) has a portfolio of some 25 handpicked 4- to 24-passenger barges that cruise on the Canal du Midi and in Provence, Burgundy, the Upper Loire, Alsace, Bordeaux, and the Champagne region of France; Holland; Italy; and Ireland, Scotland, and

England. Pre- and post-trips can be customized, as can every detail of the trip, from flights to car service. A & K works with various barge companies but promises that each ship meets its high expectations of luxury. Rates are from $3,640 per person for a 6-night cruise. ℂ **888/785-5379;** www.abercrombie kent.com.

7 The Barge Lady

It can be daunting to figure out which cruise is best for you and an individual or you and a group. Specializing in just barges for more than 35 years, the Barge Lady has experts who can help with a match based on your desires, expectations, interests, and budget—they represent some 50 barges. The small staff makes recommends from experience; they've actually been on the barges. Pricing varies depending on what level of luxury you desire. ℂ **800/880-0071;** www.bargeladycruises.com.

EUROPEAN RIVER CRUISES

I n this chapter we cover highlights of the main rivers in Europe, by far the world's largest river cruise destination.

You'll notice we first detail the most popular riverways, the Danube and Rhine and their tributaries. That's because these are by far the most popular stretches—taking you past castles and vineyards and to such world-class cities as Amsterdam (via the Dutch canals), Budapest and Vienna. This is not at all to say these are the only itineraries in Europe. In this chapter you'll also find sought after options in France, including cruises through French wine country and to see the World War II Landing Beaches in Normandy, itineraries through the beautiful Douro region of Portugal and sailings deep inside Russia (these itineraries we have listed in alphabetical order, by river).

UPPER DANUBE

Also known as the Blue Danube, after the composer Johann Strauss II's waltz of the same name, the Upper Danube is a journey through some of Europe's most important history, carving a path from Western to Eastern Europe through Germany, Austria, Slovakia and Hungary.

In river cruising, the Upper Danube constitutes the part of the Danube that runs from Regensburg, Germany (the Danube itself does flow a bit further west past Regensburg, but river cruises tend to either end here or continue north towards the Main-Rhine-Danube Canal), to Budapest, Hungary, passing through the Austrian capital of Vienna and the Slovakian capital of Bratislava along the way.

In between these cultural hubs, it's as if each smaller city along the Danube were trying to outdo the next in terms of beauty and charm (it can actually get a bit ridiculous how pretty these places

---

Activity Listings in This Guide & Chapter

Our destination write-ups include a **Top Activity** and an **Off-the-Beaten-Path** option. The former describes what you will do on the tour your cruise line will provide (though you may also be able to do parts of the experience on your own). Our **Off-the-Beaten-Path** option (sometimes two) is for those who want to skip the included tour, who have been there, done that, or otherwise want an alternative experience.

The Danube

are). From the castle ruins built atop a craggy hill in Durnstein, to the colorful waterfront buildings in Passau, you may start to recognize some of these locations simply because their picture-postcard quality often make them the stars of many a river cruise brochure. It is said that a river cruise vessel sailing past the stunner that is the Hungarian Parliament Building in Budapest is among the most widely used and most effective marketing images in river cruising (not surprising if you have seen said Parliament Building).

There's good reason that year after year, river cruise lines will say that the Danube River, and in particular the Upper Danube, continues to be a top-seller—and it's not just because of the photos (but the photos probably help).

The Danube was an important waterway for the many empires that came and went in Europe over the centuries, from the Romans to the royals, from the Ottomans to the Austro-Hungarians. And you will see monuments large and small representative of all of them along this journey. You will also be able to trace the routes of the many religious movements that have risen and fallen throughout Europe.

The rich musical history along the Danube is a strong draw for lovers of classical music, including cities such as Salzburg, the birthplace of Mozart (which while not on the Danube itself is just 70 miles southwest of Passau and is sometimes included in Upper Danube itineraries), and of course Vienna, which was home to so many greats including Schubert, Strauss (I and II), Liszt, Brahms, Mozart and Beethoven, among others.

And while the wines in Central Europe may not be as well known or renowned as that of France, Portugal, Spain or Italy, you will be surprised at just how vibrant the vintner culture is in the Wachau Valley along the Upper Danube River (see chapter 12 for more on the wines you'll encounter).

This region also provides an idyllic backdrop for bike riding. One of the most popular river cruise biking excursions is the 20-mile ride from Durnstein to Melk. River cruise ships will drop off passengers that want to do the ride near Durnstein (often giving them an adorable lunch box to refuel along the way), and will literally meet them upriver in Melk. There is no better way to see and experience the river than from the vantage point of the winding riverside bike trails, zipping past rows of vines, passing through tiny riverside towns, waving to the locals and working up an appetite for another indulgent dinner on board.

Ports of Embarkation: Regensburg & Budapest
REGENSBURG

Regensburg is a German city located on the banks of the Danube River. Most river cruise vessels will dock within walking distance to the center of town, where the Tourist Information office is located (Rathauspl. 4; www.regensburg.com).

This Bavarian city that dates back to the Roman Empire has been designated a UNESCO World Heritage Site for its noteworthy number of structures that represent numerous eras throughout European history, including Romanesque and Gothic buildings. But the era that most defines Regensburg is the Middle Ages, with many of the buildings dating to between the 11th and 13th centuries.

It's almost impossible to pull up to Regensburg and not notice one of its most significant landmarks, the towering **Regensburg (or St. Peter's) Cathedral** (Domplatz 1, admission free), a stark example of Gothic architecture with its tall, pointed towers. It's worth a closer look at both its exteriors and interiors as there are tons of impressive details both inside and out. Dedicated to St. Peter, the majority of the cathedral as we see it today was built between the 14th and 16th centuries, and features an exquisite collection of stained glass windows, and a massive organ with 5,871 pipes that hangs (yes, hangs) from the center of the cathedral, held up by four steel ropes.

You are now conveniently situated to start roaming the lovely streets of the historic city center. Start weaving your way towards the **Old Town Hall (Domplatz),** which dates back to the 13th century. All around this square you'll find plenty of little shops to peer into. Either before or after visiting the colorful square, grab a bite at the more than 500-year-old tavern **Historiche Wurstkuchl** (Thundorferstr. 3; www.wurstkuchl.de), a haven of bratwurst, mustard, sauerkraut and beer. Prices range from $1 for a pretzel to $16 for a

RECOMMENDED food & drink

We've already mentioned the Bavarian **bratwurst,** usually a lighter colored sausage made from veal, pork or beef, which you should definitely try in Regensburg, and of course there will be **wiener schnitzel** (typically breaded and fried veal, chicken or pork) on offer in Austria (though other nearby countries have embraced this simple but delicious dish, too). In Budapest, you can expect to see the classic Hungarian stew **goulash** on the menu. And Slovak cuisine is big on different variations of **potato dumplings.** There will be no shortage of solid local beers to sample along the way, but you can also expect great Rieslings and white wine varietals from the up-and-coming Wachau wine region. Overall, expect hearty, meat-heavy cuisine to be the norm throughout this trip (those who prefer lighter fare, not to worry, there are usually plenty of healthier options on board the river cruise ships, such as fruit and yogurt for breakfast and salad buffets for lunch). If you have a sweet tooth, you should definitely try the crispy, flaky, chocolate cake **sachertorte** while in Vienna.

plate of 10 brats. Beers range from $3 to $12 for a two-person bottle. Many purchase a small container of house-made mustard as a souvenir (it's delish and in the restaurant's shop).

If you're not rushing to get back to the ship and if the weather is nice, head to the 12th-century **Old Stone Bridge,** which is just a "stone's" throw from Wurstkuchl. The lasting power of the bridge itself is impressive, as are the views of Regensburg.

BUDAPEST

Budapest was the resulting city when Buda on the west bank of the Danube united with Pest on the east bank of the Danube in the 19th century. If you're lucky your vessel will be docked on the west bank (as many of them are) with views of the Parliament Building on the east bank. If you're even luckier, your stateroom will be facing east. There are several Budapestinfo Points throughout the city, the most central of which is at Suto u. 2, near Erzsebet Square.

If your river cruise starts or ends in Budapest, it would not be a bad idea to add a day or two in this dynamic city.

While many of the former communist countries of Eastern Europe still show scars from their stark communist and World War I and II pasts, Budapest somehow maintained its glory through all the wars and oppressive regimes that made their way through this part of the world. Today it is a large urban hub of nearly two million, which ranks it in the top 10 largest cities in Europe.

You'll likely feel overwhelmed by everything there is to see and do in Budapest (and there's a lot), but most river cruise lines cover these basics with their sightseeing tours. You'll likely get a closer look at that stunning **Hungarian Parliament Building** (Kossuth Lajos Square 1-3; tickets to go inside are $5 for adults, $3 for students, and free for children under 6), in addition to hitting up **Fisherman's Bastion** (Szentharomsag Square), a unique neo-Romanesque terrace with seven towers; **St. Stephen's Basilica** (Szent Istvan Square 1), a huge Roman Catholic church finished in 1905; **Heroes' Square** (Hosok Square), a

19th-century tribute to the Magyar tribes; and the **Buda Castle** (Szent Gyorgy Square 2) for a view of the river and the twin cities of Buda and Pest.

Once you have seen the requisite landmarks, you can now chart your own path. Would you rather head towards the hilly, winding streets of **Buda,** perhaps go back to **Castle Hill** (take the funicular from Chain Bridge; $5 round-trip for adults, $4 round-trip for kids) where Fisherman's Bastion is located and do some more roaming among the UNESCO World Heritage-worthy cobblestone streets? Or maybe you would rather head to the grand boulevards of **Inner Pest.** Here you will find a treasure trove of museums, including the **Hungarian National Museum** (Muzeum krt. 14-16; hnm.hu/en; tickets are $5.50 for adults, $3 for children and seniors, and $2 for students) and the **Holocaust Memorial Center** (Pava St. 39; hdke.hu/en; tickets are $8 for adults, and $6 for seniors and students), a 1920s synagogue memorializing Hungarian Jews killed during World War II.

All of this culture vulture-ing aside, we know what you really came to Budapest to do—to simply spend a day pruning away in the **Szechenyi Thermal Baths** (Allatkerti krt. 9-11; www.szechenyibath.hu; full-day admission with a changing cabin is $18; full-day with just a locker is $16; 2 hr. with a changing cabin is $17). This more than 100-year-old bathhouse is supplied by two thermal springs, which the facility has divvied up into countless dipping pools of varying temperatures, some cool, some very hot. From the tiny wooden changing/locker rooms, to the incredibly entertaining variety of visitors, who range from elderly locals to backpacking 20-somethings, this place is a world unto itself. From swimsuits to food concession stands, the bathhouse has just about everything you need (or might have forgotten) to spend a full day here soaking and lounging.

Key Ports
PASSAU

Passau is a small but delightful German town in Lower Bavaria formed by the confluence of three rivers: the Danube, the Inn, and the Ilz. River cruise ships dock up and down the Passau waterfront, anywhere along which provides walking access into the city. There is a Tourist Office in the City Hall Square (Rathausplatz 3; tourism.passau.de/home).

Top Activity   Exploring Old Town: The main game in town is Passau's **Old Town,** with its baroque 17th-century architecture, one of the best examples

highlights OF THE UPPER DANUBE

Vienna. It's the music, the cafes, the museums, those adorable trollies. Vienna is just so many cool things all in one place, it hurts.

Biking the Danube River Valley. What better way to connect sightseeing in Durnstein with that of Melk Abbey than with a 20-mile bike ride past vineyards, villages, through forests and along the Danube River.

Budapest. There's a reason that the Parliament Building is in all those river cruise brochures. Wow.

of which is the gaudy **St. Stephen's Cathedral** (Domplatz; free admission but noontime concerts cost about $4.50) with its ornate columns, intricate carvings and the largest organ in Europe with more than 17,000 pipes. And you thought the hanging organ in Regensburg's St. Peter's Cathedral was cool.

Off-the-Beaten-Path   River Walk: For a quiet walk along a river that is not the Danube, head to the southern edge of the Old Town peninsula for a short but sweet jaunt along the **Innpromenade,** a walking trail that runs along the Inn River with views of the much less developed south side of Passau.

LINZ

This lovely-yet-quirky Austrian city is often used more as a hopping off point for excursions than it is for visiting Linz itself, but don't let that stop you from heading into town. Ships dock just slightly northeast of the town center along Donau Park, about a 10- to 15-minute walk to the central Hauptplatz Square, where the Linz Tourism office is located (Hauptpl. 1; www.linz.at/english/tourism).

Top Activity   Salzburg: Often times river cruises offer their passengers two full-day excursion options from Linz—**Salzburg in Austria** and **Cesky Krumlov in the Czech Republic.** Neither one is a bad option, but if we had to advise one way or the other, and if you haven't been to either, we would say go for Salzburg (sorry Cesky Krumlov, we love you too! See below). It's just hard to beat the magic of Wolfgang Amadeus Mozart, who was born in Salzburg. Head to No. 9 Getreidegasse, the house where the wunderkind was born and lived until he was 17, which is now a museum (entrance fee is $18 for adults, $6 for youths age 15-18, and $5 for kids 6-14). And then there's the "Sound of Music" connection, with scenes from the iconic musical having been filmed in and around the city. One of our favorites is the **Mirabelle Palace and Gardens** (Mirabellplatz; free admission) where Maria and the children sang "Do-Re-Mi" in the movie.

Off-the-Beaten-Path   Cesky Krumlov: Honestly, this city is really cool, too. There are a lot of fairytale towns on this itinerary but **Cesky Krumlov** just might be the fairy-tale-est of them all. This 13th-century castle and peninsula-cum-island city, surrounded almost entirely by the winding Vltava River has a recreational vibe due to the ever-present shallow river on which people go rafting. Do a short tour (usually included with the river cruise excursion) of the expansive **Cesky Krumlov Castle** (Zámek 59; if not included there are three optional guided tours in English, priced from $10; www.zamek-ceskyk-rumlov.eu), then head into town for some shopping and bopping. The **Egon Schiele Art Centrum** (Siroka 71; www.schieleartcentrum.cz/en; admission is $6.50 for adults, $3.50 for students, $5 for seniors, and free for kids under 6) in town hosts decent contemporary art exhibits on occasion.

VIENNA

Unfortunately, river cruise ships can't get right into the heart of Vienna as they are too big for the city's smaller network of canals. They usually dock on the Danube River near the Reichsbrucke Bridge, about 3 miles from the center of the city. A taxi or a bike into the city would be your best bet if you're going it alone. Tourist Info Vienna (www.wien.info/en), Vienna's main tourist information office, is located at Albertinaplatz/Maysedergasse.

Top Activity Schonbrunn Palace: If you've been in Austria for more than a few minutes, you've probably heard mention of the Hapsburg Monarchy, which ruled the country for nearly 400 years, from the early 1400s to the early 1800s. This powerful and fancy family had a lot of real estate, and one of their most important pieces of it is located in Vienna, the **Schonbrunn Palace** (Schonbrunner Schloss-strasse 4; www.schoenbrunn.at/en.html; tickets are $13 for adults, $10 for kids ages 6–18; and $12 for students), a sort of Viennese Versailles, a visit to which is included in many river cruises that stop in Vienna. The royal summer residence has more than 1,400 crazy ornate rooms, a massive expanse of manicured gardens and the requisite royal drama to get sucked into during the tour. Learning about the complicated lives of monarchs is tiring, so we highly recommend you refuel at the **Court Bakery** beneath the Cafe-Restaurant Residenz in the palace courtyard to the left of the main entrance. They do a touristy but ridiculously tasty apple strudel-making demonstration every hour on the hour that will give you new appreciation for this Viennese treat.

Off-the-Beaten-Path Biking Vienna: With the increasing popularity of having bikes on board river cruise ships, your vessel is likely to have them (if not, Vienna has a convenient Citybike rental program). So hop on two wheels and take on the city by cycle. There is a convenient sightseeing bike path called the **Ringstrasse** that winds around central Vienna and will take you right past the **Vienna State Opera,** the **Austrian Parliament Building,** and the **Austrian National Theatre or Burgtheater.** Just slightly off of the Ringstrasse is the lively **Naschmarkt** (kitty-corner to the contemporary art museum **Secession,** Friedrichstrasse 12) a stretch of food stalls and chic eateries where you can pick up everything from regional snacks and ice cream scoops to Asian and Middle Eastern plates (the falafel guys are indefatigable).

BRATISLAVA

Most ships dock directly south of the city on the Danube River, a short 5- to 10-minute walk into the heart of the Slovakian capital. Visit Bratislava, the city's tourism marketing organization, has a Tourist Information Centre in the center of town (Klobucnicka 2).

Top Activity Exploring Old Town: Your cruise tour will head straight into the **Stare Mesto** (Old Town), and so should you if you want to explore on your own. There you'll find the **Old Town Hall** (located at Hlavne namestie, the city's Main Square), which houses a museum about the history of Bratislava and also serves as a central starting point for tooling around the town.

Off-the-Beaten-Path Castles: Take your pick of castles. Are you more into cool castle ruins? Then head to the **Devin Castle** on the outskirts of the city (but take note this will require a 15-minute cab ride to and from the center of town). Or are you more into palacelike castles? Then head to the **Bratislava Castle** (Vajanskeho nabrezie 2; $7.50 for adults, $4.30 for seniors and students) conveniently located right in the center of town. Not into castles at all? Then just go for a beer at the brewpub **Richtar Jakub** (Moskovska 16; www.richtarjakub.sk/en/).

8

EUROPEAN RIVER CRUISES | Upper Danube

Optional Add-Ons on the Route

The Upper Danube is such a rich itinerary that we could barely fit it all in above. Thus, we want to make sure we mention a few key additional ports and highlights here. First and foremost is **Melk Abbey,** a Benedictine abbey high above the Austrian town of Melk that dates back to the 11th century. You will be offered an in-depth tour of the abbey, the centerpiece of which (at least in our opinion) is the absolutely gorgeous **library** that houses equally gorgeous antique manuscripts. If you're feeling energized (perhaps by that 20-mile bike ride we mentioned), opt for a hike up to the hilltop **Crusades-era castle ruins** in **Durnstein, Austria.** And of course we would be remiss if we didn't mention that some Upper Danube river cruises actually begin or end in **Prague,** which is a 2.5- to 3-hour drive from the Danube river port of Regensburg. We have an entire write-up of Prague in the Elbe River section (p. 255), so if your Danube river cruise includes this Czech gem, please check out what to see and do in Prague there.

LOWER DANUBE

The lower part of the 1,775-mile Danube flows from Budapest to the Black Sea (vast Danube Delta) through the countries of Hungary, Croatia, Serbia, Bulgaria and Romania (in some places there's one country on one bank and another on the opposite bank) and two locks at the Iron Gates. The eastern stretch of the river is dramatic both scenically and historically, displaying remnants from the Celts, Greeks, Romans (who called the river "Danuvius"), the Hungarian Empire, the Hapsburg Dynasty, Ottoman Turks, World War 1, World War II and Communist times. Sights connected with Romania's Dracula (or the fictional character's inspiration, Vlad the Impaler) are among the attractions.

The most scenic passage is a 62-mile gorge through national park land between the Balkan Mountains and Carpathian Mountains, at the border of Serbia and Romania, known as the Iron Gate. Don't miss being on deck as your ship captain navigates some of the deepest sections of river found anywhere in the world (up to some 50 feet deep) through narrowing passages past towering white cliffs. There are other sights here too including a beautiful Orthodox church built at river's edge (where it perfectly catches the light on a sunny day) and a haunting, mountainside carving of Decebalus, the last king of Dacia.

Most cruises are for 10 days or more, including hotel nights in Bucharest and sometimes Budapest (it's worth lingering a day or two in both cities). Cruisetour options may take you to Transylvania or as far as Istanbul.

In general, you'll encounter more full-day tours on this itinerary than on the Upper Danube because many key sights, such as the Rocks of Belogradshick, are inland. This means you'll also spend more time on motorcoaches, but on the Lower Danube you'll also spend more time walking over uneven surfaces (including rocks and cobblestones). Also be forewarned Bucharest is considerably south and it can get hot in that direction in summer.

The Eastern Europe route is very different than Western Europe in other ways, too. Instead of viewing castles and vineyards you'll learn about what life was like in a war-torn land and during Communist times. You'll see natural beauty you may not have expected, spot birds including storks and partake in lively cultural exchanges—including watching exuberant local dance troupes that may come aboard your ship for performances. But in places such as Osijek or Vukovar, Croatia, you'll also hear about and see evidence of tumultuous times during the Yugoslav Wars of the 1990s (Osijek was also in the news in 2015 as being on the route of refugees fleeing Syria). In Belgrade, you'll still see remnants of the NATO bombing campaign of 1999 that ended the Kosovo War.

Bulgaria may be the biggest surprise, a fascinating country with natural and manmade beauty, and a place your friends probably haven't seen.

Ports of Embarkation: Budapest & Bucharest, Romania

BUDAPEST

(The Upper and Lower Danube itineraries share this port. See the write-up above.)

BUCHAREST

Embarkation places vary but all are more than an hour outside the city, such as in Turnu Magurele or Giurgiu. You need transport to Bucharest (a cab from the Bucharest Airport to Giurgie, for instance, will cost about 150€/$161). Visit www.romaniantourism.com for more information.

Bucharest surprises not only with its intriguing history—everything from Vlad the Impaler, inspiration for Bram Stoker's fictional Dracula, to more modern bad guy, dictator Nicolae Ceausescu—but also for its Eastern take on Paris, displayed in broad boulevards with Belle Époque palaces, parks and even a Romanian version of the Arc de Triomphe (Arcul de Tiumf). The ambience in Romania's capital city is at the same time bustling and charming.

Not to miss sights include **The Palace of Parliament** (at Calea 13 Septembrie 1; if your cruise ship isn't getting you there put in a request in advance for a tour at http://cic.cdep.ro/en; or prepare to line up for a guide). No matter how much you prepare yourself for it, your first glimpse of this square concrete bulk with its classical facade will make your jaw drop. Ceausescu's palace is the second largest public building after the Pentagon, and the dictator had a sixth of the city flattened so he could build it—the project involving 20,000 workers and 700 architects, working around the clock for 5 years. The money came from public coffers at a time much of the country was in poor circumstances. In the few rooms you'll visit, you'll see lots of marble and gold and tapestries and polished woodwork—no expense was spared in this huge tribute to a leader's huge ego. Ceausescu was overthrown and assassinated in 1989 before he would see the finished project, however.

Elsewhere in the city you will encounter stories of Vlad the Impaler... whether you want to or not. The 15th-century Prince of Wallachia, also known

highlights OF THE LOWER DANUBE

The Palace of Parliament in Bucharest. Ego-maniacal impulses turned into stone and wood—that's what you'll see at the massive, ostentatious structure built by Romanian dictator Nicolae Ceausescu.

Dracula. Intriguing stories about Vlad the Impaler (inspiration for the fictional Dracula) abound in Romania, and you'll have opportunity to visit some of his haunts.

Iron Gates. The natural beauty will surprise you as you cruise through this 62-mile gorge, past towering cliffs. You also go through two locks with the same

name and have opportunity marvel at the engineering know how.

The Rocks of Belogradshik. These red, naturally shaped peaks will remind you of the American West, but with the addition of surrounding Roman and Ottoman ruins.

Poignant firsthand accounts of war. On some itineraries you will find opportunity to have lunch at the home of a local Croatian family to hear about their lives and their personal take on the Yugoslav War of the 1990s.

as Vlad Tepes, inspired Bram Stoker's character Dracula, and Vlad's rather nasty looking likeness is on a statue in Bucharest's Old City (standing outside the remains of the court complex) and on countless t-shirts and other souvenirs. The narrow streets of the Old City are good place to head for dining and nightlife. If you're lingering a few days, Bucharest also has some outstanding museums including **The National Art Museum** (Calea Victoriei 49-53; admission to all the galleries about $3.50 ($2 if you only do the Gallery of European Art; www.mnar.arts.ro) with a 100,000-piece collection of Romanian and European art dating from the 15th to 20th centuries and located in a beautiful neoclassical former royal palace. Highlights of the collection include a room full of early Brancusi sculptures.

Key Ports
BELGRADE

The pier on the Sava is just downhill from downtown. You can walk to the main shopping area in about 30 minutes, but twists and turns and stairs make the trek somewhat confusing. Your ship will also likely have complimentary shuttles, which is a better bet. Right at the pier are some decent restaurants and cafes. Tourist Organization of Belgrade: www.tob.rs.

Top Activity Belgrade Tour: A city tour will cover the main sights of Serbia's vibrant capital city, including the park grounds of the imposing **Kalemegdan Fortress,** a defensive structure that occupies a hill overlooking the Sava and Danube rivers; and a visit to the world's largest Orthodox cathedral, **St. Sava Church.** You'll view ornate palaces, Art Nouveau buildings and relics of the Ottoman period, but most startling will be remaining reminders of the NATO bombing campaign that ended the Yugoslav Wars in 1999—there are blocks where buildings are missing like teeth in a mouth, the bombing that precise.

The city was settled by Romans, ruled by all kinds of folks including the Bulgarians, Hungarians, Serbs, Ottomans, and Hapsburgs, and occupied by Austrians and then Germans in the two World Wars. Belgrade became capital of the Federal People's Republic of Yugoslavia in 1944, and was made capital of Serbia in 1992.

To get into the vibe of modern Belgrade, you might want to linger where the shuttle bus will leave you off in the pedestrian-only Ulica Kneza Mihaila, where you can mingle with locals at stores and cafes, with a number of the buildings former mansions built by wealthy Serbians in the late 19th century.

Off-the-Beaten-Path   National Museum: Occupying a red facade building near Republic Square, the **National Museum** (Trg Republike 1A; www.narodnimuzej.rs; admission $1.75 for adults) is the place to learn about Belgrade and Serbian history and the complexities that led to the Yugoslav Wars. The exhibits cover archeology, history and fine arts (with objects ranging from ancient times to Picasso). Among the museum's treasures are the 12th-century Gospel of Miroslav a beautiful Cyrillic manuscript protected as a UNESCO "Memories of the World" treasure.

Also   Off-the-Beaten-Path   Skadarlija: This curved, cobblestoned street is treasured as Belgrade's version of Paris's Montmartre, a bustling Bohemian-style artist's quarter that dates to the 19th century and has long served as a hangout place for writers, actors, artists and journalists. It's a charming place, its restaurants and outdoor cafes drawing both visitors and locals. There are also a few art galleries and antique shops.

VIDIN, BULGARI

The rocks (see photo on p. vi) are worth the 30-mile, 1½-hour bus ride from Vidin. Official Tourism Portal of Bulgaria, http://bulgariatravel.org.

Top Activity   The Rocks of Belogradshik: Millions of years of being exposed to the elements have sculpted these towering red rocks, occupying a hilltop in the Balkan Mountains, into natural works of art. It doesn't take much imagination to see the pinnacles known as "Madonna with Child" and

RECOMMENDED food & drink

The food heritage in the Balkans includes Ottoman influences, such as in the popular *cevapcici* (ground meat kebabs) with garlicky Tzatziki dip. Bulgarians love their *banitsa*, a flakey pastry stuffed with meat, vegetables or cheese, and you'll find several dishes that will remind you of Greek cuisine, including *sarmi*, stuffed grape leaves. You'll have opportunity to sample several varieties of *goulash*, en route, not just Hungarian. In Serbia, *muckalica* is a stew made with barbecued meat and vegetables. In Bucharest, look for *mamaliga*, a polenta-type pottage made from cornmeal, and *sarmale*, parcels made with cabbage or vine leaves, stuffed with rice or meat. In all the countries you'll have opportunity to sample local beer. In Croatia choices include Osjecko beer, brewed in Osijek, a city you'll be visiting on your cruise. All the countries en route produce wine, with Romania among the world's top 20 wine producers. You'll also encounter various fruit-based brandies en route including Serbian *rakija*.

"the Monks," and various animal shapes. There's even a pyramid. All this might remind some of the American West but the hilltop also holds Roman ruins and a surrounding wall built under Sultan Mahmud II in 1850. A UNESCO World Heritage site, the rocks were nominated as one of the "New 7 Wonders of Nature" in 2007. Don't miss this excursion.

Off-the-Beaten-Path   Vidin: Your port city, Vidin, is one of the oldest cities in Bulgaria. If you're not too exhausted after seeing the Rocks, take a walk around the fortress of **Baba Vida** (Kraidunavski Park; admission about $2.25; www.museum-vidin.domino.bg/eng/index2.htm), built in the 10th century and the best-preserved medieval castle in Bulgaria (there's even a moat). The ruins of the once grand **Vidin Synagogue,** built in 1894 by a Jewish community that had flourished in Vidin for 5 centuries, is another key sight. Seized by the communist government after World War II, a restoration project was put in place in the 1980s and the roof was removed. Alas, the fall of the government placed the project in limbo. But there have been plans announced recently to turn the synagogue complex into a museum and spaces for prayer in commemoration of the Holocaust.

RUSSE, BULGARIA (OR OTHER PLACES NEARBY)

This city is about a 90-minute drive from the hilltop towns of Veliko Tarnovo and Arbanassi. Included excursions are typically for a full day. Official Veliko Tarnovo tourist website, www.velikoturnovo.info/en/#.

Top Activity   Visiting Veliko Taronvo and Arbanassi: Expect a full-day tour as you travel through the North-Central Bulgarian countryside to the cliff top town of Veliko Taronvo, the medieval capital of Bulgaria. Sights here include medieval churches, 200-year-old houses, Tsarevet's Fortress and a needle-shaped monument that pays tribute to Bulgarian kings. But the highlight attraction is the historic village of Arbanassi, a few miles north on a plateau overlooking the Yantra Valley. The town is lined with traditional houses and many 16th- to 18th-century buildings, including churches. It looks so perfect in its mountain location you may feel as if you've landed in a Bulgarian version of Epcot. Your tour will likely include an Ottoman-built home with traditional furnishings and one or more small churches festooned floor-to-ceiling with intricate religious murals and icons. (*Note:* On a few itineraries you may alternatively visit the amazing Rock Churches of Ivanovo, carved into steep cliff-sides and decorated inside with stunning medieval frescoes. Some mildly challenging walking is involved).

Off-the-Beaten-Path   Craft shopping: Shoppers will want to eat lunch quickly in Veliko Taronvo to make a beeline to Stefan Stambolov street. It holds shops and artisan's workshops for fine copperware, textiles, pottery, jewelry and even Soviet-era antiques (Stalin bust, anyone?).

KALOCSA, HUNGARY

You travel to Kalocsa by bus, the town is about 3 miles from the river.

Top Activity   Paprika and horses: On a tour, at the **Paprika Museum** on the outskirts of town you will get a lecture on paprika production in Kalocsa, one of Hungary's oldest towns and unofficial "paprika capital." But the big attraction here is a journey into the **Hungarian Puszta** (also sometimes spelled Pusta) region to visit a horse farm, and see a performance of amazing riding skills by Magyar horsemen (who do such things as stand on two horses by leading two others by their reins).

Off-the-Beaten-Path **Craft shopping:** If you have free time in Kalocsa it's a good place to gather souvenirs, not only paprika but also locally embroidered placemats and garments and objects decorated by the "painting women of Kalocsa," who do floral motifs on ceramic jugs, mugs and wooden furniture.

Optional Add-Ons on the Route

If not included on your itinerary, it's worth it to spring for an excursion to **Snagov Monastery** (Snagov Island, Snagov, admission about $4; www.snagov.ro/ro/) outside of Bucharest, where Vlad the Impaler is supposedly buried—though what was thought to be his remains turned out to be those of a horse. In a beautiful country setting, you'll hear about the Prince's atrocities. Your cruise line may also offer a well worthwhile, full-day excursion to the **Danube Delta.** The Danube disintegrates into this swampy delta where a massive nature preserve is home to some 300 species of birds including pelicans, eagles, ibises and various waders, among other wildlife attractions.

As for pre- and post-cruise experiences: In addition to exploring Budapest and Bucharest, you might consider renting a car and traveling into the beautiful, mountainous Romanian countryside to **Transylvania,** where the drama is not in the form of Dracula but rather in medieval towns, deep forests and hilltop citadels, such as Sighisoara, where Vlad was born. There are wolves in the Carpathian Mountains (considered protectors by the locals) but what you'll encounter in Transylvania will not be monsters but fairy-tale sights and warm locals. As another option, while you are in Bucharest you might head farther south, say, to the **Greek Isles,** combining your river cruise with a Mediterranean ocean experience. You can get from Bucharest to **Athens** on a nonstop flight in 1½ hours.

RHINE (& MOSEL)

The Rhine, together with one of its longest tributaries, the Mosel, encompasses one of the most popular rivers for cruising in Europe, coming in second only to the Danube. The route offers cruisers a mix of historic cities, medieval villages, gloriously steep slope-side vineyards, mountains, and the famous Castles on the Rhine. We're talking fairy tale landscapes, so it's no wonder nearly every major river cruise company offers sailings on the Rhine.

The second longest river in Europe, and the largest in Germany, the river sometimes referred to respectfully by Germans as "Father Rhine," starts in the Swiss Alps and ends in the North Sea in Holland some 820 miles later. Most 7-day river cruises traverse the waterway between Basel and Amsterdam, stopping at key cities and towns along the way in France and Germany. You'll

The Rhine & Mosel Rivers

also find longer itineraries that connect the Rhine with the Danube (via the Main-Danube Canal).

Scenery is the main attraction of this river. The upper Rhine Valley itself is a UNESCO World Heritage Site for about 40 miles (between Rudesheim and Koblenz). You will want to be well positioned on your ship's Sun Deck or at least near a window in the lounge to see this impressive stretch. Sights include **Stahleck Castle,** a 12th-century fortification overlooking the Lorelei Valley (which has been a youth hostel since 1926) and **Marksburg Castle,** built in 1117, which is the only Rhine fortress that has never been destroyed. But there are many more castles to come as your river ship sails through the picturesque **Rhine Gorge** past the legendary **Lorelei Rock,** a 394-foot cliff where legend has it a maiden (read, mermaid) mesmerized sailors with her song, luring them to their demise at her feet.

Wine first came to the Rhine with the Romans (through Southern France) and today's world-class production is another attraction, your cruise taking you through 9 of Germany's 13 wine districts including into prime Riesling territory. Find more about the region's wine in chapter 12.

One thing you might not expect to find on the Rhine is the amount of traffic. This is a major river for transport between Basel and the North Sea, and your river ship will share the inland passageway with freight barges, leisure craft (including rowboats and canoes) and other passenger river ships. In summer, you'll also pass swimmers. It's hardly a sedate waterway, and the activity can be as fascinating as the gorgeous countryside views.

While there isn't the cache of a Vienna on the route you do visit such places as the fairy-tale-esque French city of **Strasbourg** and **Heidelberg,** with its 6,000-year-old university and 13th-century castle. Life in Heidelberg was the inspiration for the Sigmund Romberg's opera "The Student Prince." The Moselle is arguably one of the most beautiful waterways in Europe, taking you through mountains and picturesque villages. And you can linger pre- or post-cruise to explore the canals and other sights in the world-class city of **Amsterdam,** one of those places where there's always something awe-inspiring, beautiful or at least unusual to discover.

Ports of Embarkation: Amsterdam & Basel
AMSTERDAM

Locations vary, but your ship is likely to be near the Amsterdam Passenger Terminal, about a 20-minute walk from the 15th-century De Nieuwe Kerk church; or at De Ruijter-kade, about a 10-minute walk from the Central Train Station. A fun way to get around the city is by bike, with rentals available in many locations. For tourist information visit www.iamsterdam.com.

With its canals and gabled homes, the Dutch capital of Amsterdam provides cruisers with the perfect way to start or end a 7-day Rhine cruise. Its impressive museums, unique architecture and juxtaposition of the modern with the old create a city that is at once quite contemporary and intriguingly historic.

Visitors can take a canal boat excursion or explore the city's darker side in the Red Light District, which also is home to the infamous Coffee Shops selling different forms of marijuana.

With a population of roughly 750,000, Amsterdam feels at times more like a village with all of the attributes of a major city. There are scores of concerts every day, summertime festivals and a well-known party scene. And then there are some 7,000 officially recognized historic monuments (you practically trip over them when you walk around town), many of which are located on 160 man-made canals, traversed by more than 1,500 bridges,

Among the fascinating attractions are the **Rembrandt House Museum** (Jodenbreestraat 4; adult admission about $14; www.rembrandthuis.nl/en/), which the artist bought in 1639 and where he lived and worked until 1656 when he went bankrupt. It can be a heartrending experience visiting the **Anne Frank House** (Prinsengracht 263-267; adult admission about $10; buy tickets online to avoid what can be long lines for tickets; www.annefrank.org), knowing this is where the young Jewish author hid from the Nazis during World War II in occupied Amsterdam, as she wrote her famed diary. There's also an insightful exhibit at the house about the occupation and current human rights crises.

The Netherlands' most popular art museum, the **Rijksmuseum** (Museumstraat 1; admission $19 for adults; www.rijksmuseum.nl) recently underwent a 10-year-long and multimillion euro overhaul (including moving works to new locations) so even if you've been before it's worthwhile to visit again. The museum is home to Rembrandt's *Night Watch,* Vermeer's *The Milk Maid,* and hundreds of other world-famous Dutch and European masterpieces. The **Van Gogh Museum** (Museumplein 6l adult admission $19; www.vangogh museum.nl) is home to more than 700 works by the famed artist, the largest collection anywhere. And if you want to go beyond arts, culture and history, the **Heineken Experience** (Stadhouderskade 78; admission $20; www. heinekenexperience.com) takes you through the process of making the famed Dutch beer—with free samples at the end.

BASEL

There are several possible docking locations, the Rhine running right through the city, the left bank and right bank connected by a half dozen bridges and ferries. For tourist information visit www.basel.com.

Wedged between France and Germany, the third largest city in Switzerland and a hub for the Swiss pharmaceutical industry, Basel is also on the art world map for its more than 30 museums, including the world-class **Kunstmuseum** (St. Alban-Graben 16; www.kunstmuseumbasel.ch) which reopened after a major renovation in the spring 2016. In 1967, the city's citizens voted by referendum to purchase two well-known works by Picasso, *The Seated Harlequin* and *The Two Brothers.* Picasso was so moved that he donated four other paintings to Basel, and they are part of the museum's collection.

Baselworld in spring and **Art Basel** in summer are the world's premier fairs for watches and contemporary art, respectively. Basel has Switzerland's oldest university (1460) and has been patron to some of the world's finest minds. It nurtured the painters Konrad Witz and Hans Holbein the Younger, as well as the great Dutch scholar Erasmus, the Dutch humanist and writer, who in 1513 published here the first edition of the New Testament in the original Greek (Eramus is buried in the city's cathedral). Other notable residents included the German philosopher Friedrich Nietzsche, who taught at the University of Basel, and Theodor Herzl, who addressed the first Zionist World Congress here in 1897.

Top sights include the **Mittlere Rheinbrücke,** Basel's most historic bridge first built around 1225; the **Basel Münster** cathedral (Münsterplatz, free admission), which offers superb examples of late Romanesque and early Gothic style from the 12th and 13th centuries, as well as late Gothic style; and the **Rathaus** (town hall), a bright red building located in the Marktplatz (Market Square), built as a symbol of power and to honor the city's entry into the Swiss Confederation in 1501. **Brauerei Fischerstube** (Rheingasse 45; http://uelibier.ch) is a famous local brewery that produces its own lagers and ales in the copper tanks in the back of the room. It has a range of food on offer, everything from oven-fresh pretzels to steak or sour beef liver with Rösti. And shopping is a sport in Basel, the alluring options including art, antiques, watches and chocolate.

highlights OF THE RHINE

Castles on the Rhine. You can view a spectacular array of castles and forts perched on hills along the banks of the Rhine during the nearly day-long cruise from Koblenz to Rundsheim, as well as the famed Lorelei Rock.

Amsterdam's Art Museums. Visit the famed Rijksmuseum, home to iconic Dutch masterpieces, as well as the Van Gogh Museum, both located in the Museumplein (which is also where the much photographed and marketed "I Amsterdam" sign is located).

Gothic Cathedrals. Cologne in Germany and Strasbourg in France both have some of the finest examples of Gothic cathedral architecture in Europe.

Regional Wine. Sip and learn. Rundesheim, Breisach, and other towns serve great examples of regional German wines in their wine bars.

Key Ports
COLOGNE

Your ship will dock right in the city. For tourist information log on to www.cologne-tourism.com.

Top Activity City Tour: Cologne, the largest city on the Rhine, dates back to Roman times and has a full dozen Romanesque churches and one of the largest Gothic cathedrals in Europe. During World War II, bombings destroyed 90 percent of the city, with only the cathedral remaining relatively unscathed. But like many other German cities, Cologne was completely restored. Top attractions include the **Dom** (Domkloster; admission to the cathedral free, admission to the treasury and tower about $5.50; www.koelner-dom.de), the landmark Gothic cathedral that dominates the city's skyline; and the **Römisch-Germanisches Museum** (Roncalliplatz 4; admission about $7.50; www.museenkoeln.de), a cultural landmark built in the early 1970s around the famous Dionysius mosaic discovered here during the construction of an air-raid shelter in 1941. The huge mosaic, more than 800-square-feet, once formed the dining-room floor of a wealthy Roman trader's villa.

The city is also renowned for its art museums, so if you feel like going off on your own without the ship's tour, Cologne is a good place to do so as it will allow you to linger in such first-class art museums as **Museum Ludwig** (Bischofsgartenstrasse 1; admission about $14; ww.museum-ludwig.de/en.html), dedicated to 20th-century and contemporary art and home to one of the world's largest collections of Picasso paintings, ceramics, and works on paper; or the **Wallraf-Richartz Museum** (Obenmarspforten; admission about $13; www.wallraf. museum/), with its extensive collection spanning art from Middle Ages to the 19th century. And fans of medieval art should make a beeline for the **Schnütgen Museum** (Cäcilienstrasse 29, admission about $6.50; www.museenkoeln.de).

Off-the-Beaten-Path Beer Tasting: To, ahem, learn more about local culture, why not sample the famed Kölsch beer at one of Cologne's congenial brew houses? There's **Früh am Dom** (Am Hof 12–18; www.frueh.de), a

RECOMMENDED food & drink

former brewery in the shadow of the Dom decorated with old frescoes on vaulted ceilings; or **Päffgen Kolsch** (Friesenstrasse 64; www.paeffgen-koelsch. de/kontakt), a brewhouse that features typical Rhenish fare like sauerbraten, pork knuckle and potato pancakes. In both places, you'll find ordering a beer means getting several beers in small glasses that are constantly replenished—until you say "uncle"!

KOBLENZ

You will dock in town. For tourist information visit www.koblenz.de.

Top Activity   **Exploring Koblenz:** The ancient city of Koblenz is located in an area known as the Deutsches Eck (German Corner) in the heart of the Mittelrhein region. Rivers and mountains converge here: The Moselle flows into the Rhine on one side, while the Lahn flows in on the other a few miles south; and three mountain ridges intersect. Founded by the Romans, this was a powerful city in the Middle Ages, when it controlled trade on both the Rhine and Moselle. Air raids during World War II destroyed 85 percent of the city, but extensive restoration has done much to re-create its former atmosphere. **Festung Ehrenbreitstein** (www.festungehrenbreitstein.de), Europe's largest fortress, is high above the left bank of the Rhine and offers a magnificent view over Koblenz to where the rivers meet. The earliest buildings date from about 1100, but the bulk of the fortress was constructed in the 16th century. In 1801 the fort was partially destroyed by Napoléon (the French occupied Koblenz for the next 18 years). A cable car carries you from the street Konrad-Adenauer-Ufer over the river to Ehrenbreitstein, with spectacular views of the Deutsches Eck below.

Off-the-Beaten-Path   Rüdesheim: If your ship visits Rüdesheim (in the late afternoon or for an overnight), do yourself the favor and skip your nap in favor of exploring the cobblestone streets of this small wine town. The pedestrian-only Drosselgasse is the place to sample one of the locally produced wines at one of the wine taverns; from April to October there's even live music.

MANNHEIM

River ships dock at this city, on the mouth of the Nekar River, as a gateway for a tour of Heidelberg, Germany's oldest university, founded in 1386. For tourist information visit www.tourism-heidelberg.com/.

Top Activity   Heidelberg Castle: A tour of the ruins of Heidelberg Castle, which dates from the 15th century, though most of it was built during the Renaissance in the baroque styles of the 16th and 17th centuries. The architectural highlight remains the Renaissance courtyard. Visitors also can see the Grosses Fass (a giant wine cask) in the cellar, which may be the world's largest wine barrel, made from 130 oak trees. During a tour of the castle, you can take in wonderful views of Neckar River Valley and the city's many red rooftops. Your ship tour may also include the town of Speyer, where the Romanesque cathedral is a UNESCO World Heritage Site. Built in the 11th century on the site of a former basilica, the building's design influenced Romanesque architecture for centuries to come, and is the final resting place of eight German monarchs.

Off-the-Beaten-Path   Christmas Store: Worth a look if you have free time is the **Haupstrasse,** Heidelberg's main shopping street, stretching over a mile, with shops (and restaurants and bars) including **Kathe Wohlfahrt** (Haupstrasse 124; http://wohlfahrt.com/en/christmas-stores/heidelberg), one of most lavish Christmas decoration stores in the world. Above all, Heidelberg is a university town, with students making up some 20 percent of its population. That's reflected in the lively restaurants and beer halls in Altstadt (Old Town).

STRASBOURG

Your ship will dock in the city. For tourist information, visit www.otstrasbourg.fr/en/.

Top Activity   City Tour: This famed French city is now one of headquarters of some of the European Union's governmental institutions, including the European Parliament and the European Court of Justice. But the real reason to visit Strasbourg is the **Old Town,** which has canals, churches, medieval covered bridges, large parks, and Art Nouveau and modernist architecture. In the Petite-France District, half-timbered houses decorated with bright baskets of flowers line the canal. The magnificent Gothic **Strasbourg Cathedral** (Cathédrale Notre-Dame, Place de la Cathédrale, admission about $5; www.cathedrale-strasbourg.fr) located at the heart of the Old Town, features a great tower to climb for magnificent views of the city, as well as an astronomical clock with a mechanical procession of high figures of Christ and the Apostles occurring every day at half past midday while the life-size mechanical cock crows three times.

THE DUTCH & BELGIAN rivers & canals

You may notice that your river cruise isn't actually on one of the main rivers we mentioned in this book. And if you're cruising in Belgium or the Netherlands, you might be right. Here, the Rhine River links up with the Meuse and Scheldt rivers in the Netherlands to ultimately form the Rhine-Meuse-Scheldt Delta as the waterways flow out into the North Sea. So, if you're sailing into and out of Amsterdam, you might be on the Rhine, but you may also be sailing along the vast networks of rivers and their tributaries created by the delta. If you're staying within the Netherlands and Belgium, as some itineraries do, you'll be sailing along these smaller rivers as well as along the many (and seriously impressive) man-made canals that wind through these countries. It can be confusing so rather than specify all the different canals and smaller rivers on the itinerary, river cruise lines often just refer to them as **"the Dutch and Belgian canals."**

So, what will you see along these smaller rivers and canals? Because this is a big shipping region for Europe, sometimes the scenery can get a bit industrial (that happens on the bigger rivers as well as you approach larger cities). But these smaller canals and rivers can be every bit as charming as their big-river brethren and sometimes even more so. Their smaller size allows passengers to be closer to and feel even more connected to the passing scenery, and they are the lifeblood of Dutch and Belgian life, providing access to those famous **Dutch windmills** and the uber-hip Belgian town of **Antwerp.** So don't be turned off by these complicated canals and rivers—they are no lesser an inland waterway than any other.

Off-the-Beaten-Path Cafes: Stroll the square in front of the cathedral and land at a cafe or restaurant for an Alsatian meal (such as chicken or veal kidneys cooked in white wine) or just a glass or two of *vin d'Alsace.*

Optional Add-Ons on the Route

While in Switzerland, you might want to explore some of the country including **Lucerne,** one of the most beautiful Swiss cities. Located at the north end of Lake Lucerne, it's a place of cobblestone streets, monuments, fountains, public squares, frescoed buildings and covered bridges, including the famed Kapellbrucke (Chapel Bridge) with its iconic tower in the center of the town. Efficient Swiss trains make it easy to get around the country, including from Basel to **Zurich,** only 53 miles away.

THE MAIN

The Main River is the longest tributary of the Rhine, and the longest river flowing entirely in Germany. It flows through the German states of Bavaria, Baden-Württemberg and Hesse. Many river cruise lines combine a cruise along the Main with the Rhine, or do the Main-Danube Canal and Danube, though a few also offer cruises that focus just on the quintessentially German Main itself.

The attraction for visitors is Frankfurt, Germany's fifth largest city, as well as traditional medieval Bavarian towns where wine and leather goods are

The Main River

manufactured. Views include forests, small towns, hilltop castles, palaces, vineyards and churches—a travel-poster-worthy panorama of beautiful landscapes.

Some of what you'll see en route was destroyed during World War II bombing and rebuilt. This fact does not distract from views such as the architectural masterpieces of 18th-century German architect and military engineer Balthasar Neumann, such as the Bishops' Residenz in Würzburg.

AmaWaterways, Avalon Waterways, CroisiEurope, Tauck, Scenic Cruises, Uniworld Boutique River Cruises and Viking River Cruises all have itineraries that include the Main, combined with other waterways.

While the cruises are year-round, a particularly popular time to visit Central Germany is in late November and December, when the country's renowned Christmas Markets are in full swing, including the massive markets in Frankfurt and Nuremberg.

A bit of geography: The river begins near Kulmbach in Franconia at the joining of its two headstreams, the Red Main and the White Main. The Red Main originates in the Franconian Jura mountain range and runs through

Creussen and Bayreuth. The White Main originates in the mountains of the Fichtelgebirge, and runs through the valleys of the German Highlands.

The lower section crosses the Lower Main Lowlands to Wiesbaden, where it discharges into the Rhine. There are 34 dams and locks along the 236-mile navigable portion of the Main, from the confluence with the Regnitz near Bamberg to the Rhine. The river runs through several cities including Frankfurt, Offenbach, Wertheim and Würzburg. In fact, it is the primary transportation artery of the industrial region around Frankfurt—in addition to being a scenic route for European river cruises.

8 Ports of Embarkation: Frankfurt, Nuremburg

FRANKFURT

Your ship will likely dock right in town near the Iron Bridge (Eisemer Steg) off the Main Kay. For tourist information visit www.frankfurt-tourismus.de.

Some people make the mistake of dismissing Frankfurt as just a modern business center and a European gateway (because of its large airport). But the city, sometimes referred to as "Mainhattan" for its skyscrapers and river location, is not without historic and cultural attractions.

Standing in the center of the **Römerplatz,** the medieval town square, in the Altstadt (Old Town) you can see the city's striking contrasts—restorations of 14th- and 15th-century half-timbered houses on the square, while just beyond them are modern skyscrapers (some of which replaced buildings bombed during World War II).

Frankfurt is the headquarters of the German Central Bank (Bundesbank), as well as the European Central Bank (ECB), which manages the euro. Some 300 banking institutions have offices in Frankfurt, including the headquarters of five of Germany's largest banks. The city's stock exchange, one of the most important in the world, was established in 1585, and the Rothschild family opened their first bank here in 1798.

The banks are one of the reasons Frankfurt has become Germany's most international city (there are a good number of ex-Pats in town). The city also has world-class ballet, opera, theater, and top-flight museums, including the **Städel Museum** (Schaumainkai 63, admission about $11, www.staedelmuseum.de/en) known for its expansive collection of German and European art. The city's hosts frequent art exhibitions, one of the world's largest annual book fairs, and has young vibe thanks to its large university (with 43,000 students).

Among Frankfurt's visitor attractions is the **Fressgass,** a pedestrian street whose proper name is Grosse Bockenheimer Strasse, nicknamed "Pig-Out Alley" or "Munch Alley" because of its wide array of food stores, wine bars, cafes and restaurants—sample everything here from boiled beef, pork schnitzel and sausages to Asian dishes. The nearby, highly ornamented **Kaiserdom** (Imperial Cathedral, Domplatz), officially known as the Church of St. Bartholomew, but called "The Dom" by locals, was built between the 13th and 15th centuries and survived World War II mostly intact.

The **Alte Oper** opera house (Opernplatz; www.alteoper.de) has been reconstructed to reflect its 19th-century glory, and hosts classical music performances. Other attractions include the **Paulskirche** (Paulsplatz 11), a restored church that remains a symbol of Germany democracy since it served as the meeting point for the first all-German parliament in 1848, and the **Alte Nikolaikirche** (Römerberg 11), a small red sandstone church built in the late 13th century as the court chapel for emperors of the Holy Roman Empire.

NUREMBERG

You will dock outside of town, buses taking you into the city. Tourist information log onto http://tourismus.nuernberg.de/en/home.html.

With a recorded history stretching back to 1050, Bavaria's main city is also among the most historic in Germany. The Old Town, through which the Pegnitz River flows, is still surrounded by its original 13th-century medieval walls. Located in the central marketplace, the "Beautiful Fountain" is crested with 40 colorful figures representing the Holy Roman Empire's worldview.

Nuremberg has always taken a leading role in German affairs. The Holy Roman emperors traditionally held the first Diet, or convention of the estates, of their incumbency here. And it was in Nuremberg that Hitler staged his rallies for the Nazi Party. After World War II, the Allies held landmark war trials where 21 top-ranking Nazis were charged with crimes against humanity—a tour of the city typically includes a visit to a memorial at the actual courthouse that sheds light on the trial (Justizgebäude, Bärenschanzstrasse 72, admission about $6). *Note:* Visiting the actual Courtroom 600 isn't guaranteed, as it's a functioning courtroom.

As a major intersection on medieval trade routes, Nuremberg became a wealthy town where the arts and sciences flowered. Albrecht Dürer

RECOMMENDED food & drink

Frankfurt is one of Germany's foodie capitals, but while fancy restaurants abound you'll eat well for less, especially when you try *real* Frankfurters: smoked sausages made from pork and spices (the oldest known recipe dates to 1487) and always served in pairs. At the *Apfelwein* (apple wine) taverns in Sachsenhausen, on the south bank of the Main, one can sample traditional Hessian dishes such as *Rippchen mit Kraut* (pickled pork chops with sauerkraut) and boiled beef or poached fish with the uniquely Frankfurt condiment *grüne Sosse*, a green sauce made from seven herbs and other seasonings, chopped hard-boiled eggs, and sour cream. In Nuremburg, the **Historische Bratwurst-Küche Zum Gulden Stern** (Zirkelschmiedsgasse 26, www.bratwurstkueche.de) is where you can find the famous **Nuremberg bratwurst** freshly roasted on a beech-wood fire. In Bramberg, you'll want to visit one or more of the brewpubs. **Schlenkerla** (Dominikanerstrasse 6) has been serving beer inside an ancient half-timbered house since 1405. In addition to the culinary specialty of Zamberger Zwiebel, an onion stuffed with pork, the reason to visit is Aecht Schenkerla Rauchbier, a beer brewed with smoked malt.

highlights OF THE MAIN

Eating on the Fressgass. This pedestrian street in Frankfurt is nicknamed "Pig-Out Alley" because of its wide array of food stores, wine bars, cafes, and restaurants.

Germanic National Museum in Nuremberg. This national museum showcases the country's cultural and scientific achievements, ethnic background, and history.

Touring Würzberg's Palace. Visit the Residenz, a spectacular baroque palace once inhabited by German bishop-princes.

Bamberg's Cathedral. See the spectacular 11th-century cathedral, the Bamberg Dom, which contains the tomb of Pope Clement II.

(1471–1528), the first genius of the Renaissance in Germany, was born here. Other leading Nuremberg artists of the Renaissance include painter Michael Wolgemut (a teacher of Dürer), stonecutter Adam Kraft, and the brass founder Peter Vischer. Among Nuremberg's famous products are Lebkuchen (gingerbread of sorts) and Faber-Castell pencils.

While in Nuremberg, visit the **Germanic National Museum** (Kartäusergasse 1, admission about $10), Germany's largest museum of arts and culture (it's the German equivalent of the Smithsonian). The museum is in a former Carthusian monastery, complete with cloisters and monastic outbuildings. A tour begins before you even get inside the door with the Way of Human Rights, 29 columns inscribed in different languages, with the Universal Declaration of Human Rights, adapted by the U.N. General Assembly in 1948 (haunting in a city that once so ignored human rights). An indoor highlight is a collection of Renaissance German paintings by Dürer, Cranach, and Altdorfer.

Altes Rathaus, the old town hall on Rathausplatz abuts the rear of St. Sebaldus Kirche; it was erected in 1332, destroyed in World War II, and subsequently reconstructed. Its intact medieval dungeons, consisting of 12 small rooms and one large torture chamber, provide insight into the gruesome applications of medieval law.

Key Ports
WÜRZBERG

You'll dock in town. For tourist information visit www.wuerzburg.de/en/.

Top Activity Bishops' Residenz: The baroque city of Würzberg is located on Germany's so-called "Romantic Road," at the junction of two age-old trade routes in a valley of beautiful vineyard-covered hills. A highlight attraction is the **Bishops' Residenz** (INFO), one of the most massive baroque palaces in Germany and one of the most lavish in Europe. It's where Würzburg's powerful prince-bishops lived after moving down from the hilltop **Festung Marienberg,** a fortified castle on the steep hill across the river. Construction of the Bishop's Residenz started in 1720 under the noted German architect Balthasar Neumann. Most of the interior decoration is credited to Italian stuccoist Antonio Bossi and Venetian painter Giovanni Battista

Tiepolo—inside is a gallery of paintings, Tiepolo frescoes and lots and lots of ornamentation, outside some impressive gardens. Würzburg was all but obliterated by Allied saturation bombing in 1945, but reconstruction has returned most of the city's famous sights to their former glory.

Off-the-Beaten-Path The **"Romantic Road":** Another option offered by your cruise line may be a ride along Germany's scenic "Romantic Road" to visit **Rothenburg,** a well-preserved medieval town with fairy-tale-like half-timbered buildings and cobblestone lanes. This is the place to load up on Bavarian souvenirs including cuckoo clocks. **Friese-Kabalo Kunstgewerbe OHG** (Grüner Markt 7) sells clocks along with Hummel figurines, pewter beer steins, music boxes, and dolls. Käthe Wohlfahrt's **Weihnachtswerkstatt** (**Christmas Workshop;** Herrngasse 1) is the place to stock up on Christmas ornaments. There's also a **German Christmas Museum (Deutsches Weihnachtsmuseum,** Herrngasse 1, admission about $4.50, www.weihnachts museum.com), with display cases filled with historic memorabilia including Santas (some looking quiet grim), toys, ornaments and nutcrackers.

BAMBERG

You'll dock near town at the confluence of the Regnitz River and Main. The city rises on a hill, and shuttles will get you to the top. There's a tourist office near the cathedral (Geyersworthstrasse 5; www.bamberg.info).

Top Activity **Exploring Bamberg:** Founded in 902, Bamberg is now a UNESCO World Heritage Site with attractions including a spectacular 13th-century, four-towered cathedral, the **Bamberg Cathedral** (Domplatz, admission free), which contains the tomb of Emperor Heinrich II, who erected the place, and his wife, Kunigunde (a suspected adulteress as depicted in the stonework). Also in the cathedral is the only papal tomb north of the alps, that of Pope Clement II. Few towns in Germany survived the war with as little damage as Bamberg, and you can walk cobblestone streets to see ornate mansions, palaces and churches in a variety of styles—Romanesque, Renaissance, Gothic and otherwise. The city tried not to play favorites between its ecclesiastical and secular sections and as a result the picturesque Gothic city hall, **Altes Rathaus,** is one of the strangest in Germany, located on an island in the middle of a river (from the island you get a wonderful view of the town's half-timbered fishermen's cottages lining the river banks).

Off-the-Beaten-Path **Drinking Beer:** The other major attraction in Bamberg has to do with barley and hops. The town has been called "a beer drinker's Eden" (there are more breweries here than in Munich) and the average Bamberger drinks 190 liters of beer a year. Choices include Bamberg is *Rauchbier,* a smoked beer first brewed in 1536.

Optional Add-Ons on the Route

Worthwhile optional shore excursions may include, in Würzburg, a visit with a glassblower and opportunity to get to learn about his craft or further exploration of the "Romantic Road."

While you are doing Germany, considering continuing your tour to visit other key cities, having such experiences as sipping beer in a **Munich** beer garden, visiting Beatles haunts in **Hamburg** and discovering the amazingness of the new **Berlin.** Or head into the Black Forest to **Baden-Baden** (www. baden-baden.com) for a quintessential German spa experience involving bathing, steaming, *schvitzing,* and swimming.

BORDEAUX

A river cruise in Bordeaux is different than other destinations in that you don't do quite as much cruising—we're not talking a long river. Your cruise is on the Dordogne and Garonne rivers and Gironde estuary of Southwest France, but really the focus is what's beside the rivers of the Aquitaine—one of the world's most celebrated wine regions as the home base for Médoc, Margaux, Saint-Émilion, Pomerol, and Sauternes (among Bordeaux' 57 wine appellations). For wine enthusiasts, it's the equivalent to letting a kid loose in a candy store, the only issue being how much wine can you possibly drink in a week.

Itineraries always include at least 1 night in the city of Bordeaux, which well deserves its title as a mini-Paris. Wandering the lovely riverfront and streets past medieval landmarks and grand 18th-century buildings, visiting markets, shopping for antiques and tippling at wine bars is sheer pleasure.

On a typical 1-week cruise you will see breathtaking châteaux (perhaps with an extravagant wine dinner at one), quaint villages with stone houses, fortresses and many vineyard-laden fields. You'll walk the medieval lanes in Saint-Emilion before a tasting at a nearby winery; and your ship will also cruise up to Cadillac, the city that gave the American car brand its name, to taste Sauternes—the precious, golden dessert wine.

The season for Bordeaux cruises is March to December with September and October during the harvest a particularly spectacular time to visit. But be aware the short route on the river is not without challenges—tides on the Bordeaux, Garonne and especially the Gironde can be tricky. You may find your ship stays in Bordeaux longer than planned and that rather than cruising to Blaye, for instance, you may be bussed. Also, for those who like long days of just cruising, you won't find that here.

Note: If your idea is to come to Bordeaux and pop in at say, Châteaux Lafite-Rothschild in Pauillac, be aware that wine estates are typically only open by appointment. In the case of Lafite-Rothschild, visits are only weekdays, 2 p.m. to 3:30 p.m., November through July, and you need to send a written request well in advance to visites@lafite.com.

Port of Embarkation: Bordeaux
BORDEAUX

Your river ship will dock on the lovely and active riverbank, and you can walk to some city sights. There is an excellent tourist office near the Place des Quinconces, 12 cours du 30-Juillet, www.bordeaux-tourisme.com.

The city at the center of arguably the world's greatest wine-growing region is often a big surprise to visitors, in a very good way. Once known as a rather

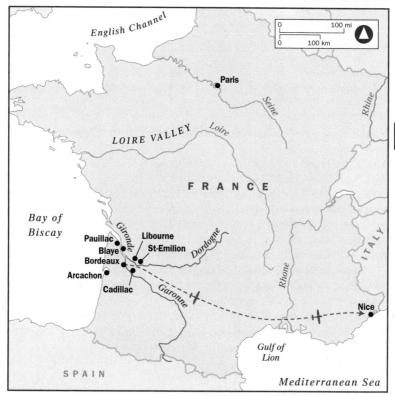

sleepy, industrial place, it's been cleaned up and fancied up and feels very much like a less daunting version of Paris. You'll find yourself oohing and aahing at beautiful squares, 18th-century buildings, enticing shops, and beautiful people at indoor and outdoor cafes and wine bars. The left bank of the Garonne is a UNESCO World Heritage Site. There's also a youthful vibe thanks to the city's 70,000 college students (about one-third of the population is under age 25).

Your ship will dock on the pretty riverfront, lined with public gardens, fountains and playgrounds, where locals stroll, jog, go for bike rides, admire the flowers and even skateboard, and kids splash with glee in a large reflecting pool, Miroir de'Eau, at the 18th-century Place de la Bourse.

From there, you can head off on foot or trams (cars are banned in much of the city center) to explore more wonderful squares including the **Place des Quinconces,** one of the largest squares in Europe; see the city's grand monuments (Bordeaux is second only to Paris in French historic monuments); and admire architecture including the neo-classical **Grand Théâtre,** on elegant streets and narrow cobbled alleys including in the medieval quartier

highlights OF BORDEAUX

The city of Bordeaux. You're in for a treat exploring this mini version of Paris, with its broad squares, monuments, beautiful architecture and cobblestone alleyways.

Wine. Come on a Bordeaux river cruise because you love wine and want to continue your wine education, or simply do some tasting.

Vineyard views. Sure, you may have seen vineyards before, but probably not miles and miles of them and accompanied by such extravagant chateaux.

Eating. Local product includes foie gras and truffles and meats that pair well with red wine.

St-Michel, home to the second tallest medieval stone tower in France (climb up 228 steps for breathtaking views of the city).

The city's history is reflected in several sights including **The Musee d'Aquitaine** (20 cours Pasteur; admission about $4.50; www.musee-aquitaine-bordeaux.fr), which tells the story, among others, of Aquitaine moving to British hands when, in 1154, Eléonore of Aquitaine married the future Henry II of England (the city returned to France in 1453 after the Hundred Years' War).

Shoppers will enjoy hunting for antiques on rue Notre-Dame in the Chartrons district (you will also find shops in the city representing the top French designer brands). See also Food & Wine below for more shopping opps.

And then there's the wine. Stop by any of the many wine shops for a quick lesson, and at wine bars where you'll quickly discover Bordeaux wine does not need to be expensive (you can drink a decent glass for under $5).

Key Ports
LIBOURNE

You disembark in this market town for tours to Saint-Émilion, about 6 miles away. The website for the Libourne tourist office is www.tourisme-libournais.com/en/pratique/tourist-office.html.

Top Activity Saint-Émilion Tour: Saint-Émilion is a quaint hillside town with wonderful (and steep) medieval lanes and views of the surrounding vineyards. The Saint-Émilion region was the first historic wine-growing region recognized by UNESCO. But the most fascinating attraction in town is a 12th-century **Monolithic Church,** carved out of limestone and partially underground. Wine is in the picture too, of course. At the heart of the town is the medieval **place de l'Eglise Monolithe,** which is brimming with outdoor cafes and the streets are full of wine shops. Plus, your tour will likely include a visit to at least one nearby winery for a tasting.

Off-the-Beaten-Path Hanging out in Libourne: Roughly at the center of the St-Emilion, Pomerol, and Fronsac wine districts, Libourne is a market town with a picturesque city square, lined with 16th-century buildings including the **Hôtel-de-Ville** (town hall), which has two rooms open to visitors and antiques on display. You can also explore the remains of 13th-century ramparts. Another attraction is the town's covered market (closed on Tuesdays) where

RECOMMENDED food & drink

You're not that far from the Atlantic, so you'll find fresh fish and shellfish. But meat is king here, pairing well with red Bordeaux. There's locally raised beef and lamb, which you can sample *a la bordelaise* (a rich wine sauce). You'll find local duck including duck confit and foie gras on many menus. Truffles and mushrooms are a specialty of the region as well. Other local delicacies include canelés (the chewy and sweet French pastry).

In Bordeaux, food hounds can find lots of yummy things at the upscale **Marché des Grandes Hommes** (12 Place des Grands Hommes) and its surrounding streets. Across the way, opening the door of the **Jean d'Alos cheese shop** (4 Rue Montesquieu), the aroma itself is the stuff that dreams of France

are made of. Not far from the Grand Théâtre, chocolate lovers should not miss a stop at **Cadiot-Badie** (26 Allée de Tourny), an extraordinary sweets shop founded in 1826. Creations include chocolate high heels. In the back are samples, so you can compare the Mexican chocolate with the Peruvian, and so forth.

Wine lovers should not miss a visit to Bordeaux's **L'Intendant wine shop** (2 Allée de Tourny). The famous shop looks small, but walk inside and a circular staircase leads to four floors and thousands of bottles of regional wine. The staff are as friendly as they are expert, and do not scoff at all when asked for a recommendation in the, ahem, reasonably priced range.

you can admire cheeses, charcuterie and wonderful local produce brought to market by area farmers.

BLAYE

Your ship will dock on a small pier below the citadel. For tourist information go to www. tourisme-blaye.com.

Top Activity **Visiting the Citadel:** Walk around the 17th-century **Blaye Citadel,** built by Sébastien Le Prestre de Vauban, considered one of the greatest military engineers of all time). Dramatically set on a rock above the Gironde estuary, the fortress was commissioned by Louis XIV to protect the waterway (where the Dordogne and Garonne rivers meet) and Bordeaux, located further upstream on the Garonne. The citadel, city walls and two nearby forts are collectively a UNESCO World Heritage Site.

Off-the-Beaten-Path **Shopping or Hiking:** If you have free time, explore some of the art and craft galleries located in what was once the citadel barracks. Or head off on trails above the riverfront for views.

PAUILLAC

You dock in the neat little harbor of this quiet city. Find more information at www. pauillac-medoc.com.

Top Activity **Tasting Wine:** You've landed in the main city in the Médoc wine region, the most prestigious wine region in the world. From here, a tour will take you past the elite wine houses such as Châteaux Lafite Rothschild, Latour and Mouton Rothschild, among others. There will likely be some tasting involved.

Not a lot of river cruise companies offer cruises on Italy's Po River. While it provides access to Italy's famous canal city **Venice,** and the surrounding towns of northern Italy, it is a tidal river, which makes navigation tricky. In actuality the Po becomes a network of rivers that form the Po Delta, which is where sailings actually occur, along the channels that fan out towards the Venice Lagoon. It's said that because of water level problems on the Po, river cruises here often turn into bus tours, with the vessel simply serving as a stationary hotel. Not that Uniworld's River Countess, a boat that plies this river, is a shabby hotel (CroisiEurope is the other operator on this stretch of water).

Despite the challenges, a Po River itinerary has some pretty sweet highlights, not least of which is Venice itself. The Po also provides access to the walled city of **Padua,** to **Bologna** (mmm, pasta) and Italian Renaissance beauty **Ferrara.** Po River cruises usually include a visit to the quaint fishing village of **Chioggia,** as well.

Did we mention it stops in Venice, too? That magical floating (or sinking, depending on how you look it) Italian city. Enough said.

Off-the-Beaten-Path   Explore Pauillac: Take a stroll in the wonderfully quiet town past sights including Plaza Lafayette, where the Marquis de Lafayette set sail to the New World.

Optional Add-Ons on the Route

Optional day tours may include a full-day trek to learn about truffles on a farm in Southwest France's Dordogne region, or a half-day trek to Arcachon, an oceanside resort town on the Atlantic, with Victorian architecture and a famous local product—oysters. Your cruise may offer an optional tour to visit the charming medieval town of cognac to learn about the history of the world's best-known bandy. At a Cognac house you may even be able to try your own hand at blending. There may also be an opportunity for bike tours in Bordeaux or the vineyards, with tastings involved.

Your cruise may include a hotel stay in **Paris** or be combined with a visit to the **Loire Valley** or both. You can get to Paris on your own via high-speed train in less than 4 hours. Another option is heading farther south, catching a direct flight from Bordeaux to **Nice** (with cheap flights on Air France discount carrier Hop!).

DOURO

The Douro, one of the major rivers flowing through the Iberian Peninsula, has become a popular, if off-the-beaten-path, European river cruise destination, with almost every major river cruise company doing sailings out of Porto, Portugal following the river as it winds through the hillside vineyards of the UNESCO-recognized Douro River Valley, and often including a foray by bus across the border into Spain.

The Douro River

Cruising on the so-called "river of gold," which begins in northern-central Spain before passing through Portugal to its final outlet in Porto (and the Atlantic), can be an unforgettable experience and a pleasant surprise to those previously unfamiliar with the region. That's especially true when you're gliding along the narrow stretches of the upper Douro between the steep slopes where thousands of acres of port wine grapes are cultivated. Most are awed by the scenery and gain a new appreciation for port wine.

One of the chief attractions is **Porto** itself, also recognized by UNESCO, and known for its historic center, spectacular bridges and world famous port wine houses.

On a Douro sailing, cruisers can wander around medieval hilltop villages virtually unchanged over the centuries. You can visit the cellars of some of the big port-growing wineries and see—in huge letters—the names of famous port brands on the steeply terraced vineyards along the river. Most cruises also include a day across the border in the Spanish medieval city and university town of **Salamanca,** one of the best-kept secrets in Europe.

River companies such as AmaWaterways, CroisiEurope, Scenic Cruises, Viking River Cruises and Uniworld Boutique River Cruises offer cruises on the Douro March to December (including during the September grape harvest) with ships slightly smaller than those on more popular routes such as the Rhine and Danube, due to the Douro's shorter and narrower locks, and often with the feature of a pool on top so that cruisers can take advantage of the often sunny climate.

Port of Embarkation: Porto

PORTO

The ship docks on the river, the city rising above on a hillside. You will want to take the shuttle bus downtown. For tourist information log on to www.visitporto.travel.

As capital of northern Portugal and the epicenter of port wine, Porto has a number of attractions worth pursuing including the imposing **Porto Cathedral** (Terreiro da Sé), one of the city's oldest and most impressive monuments, and the **Sao Bento Railway Station,** renowned for its blue and white tile panels depicting scenes from Portuguese history. Of course, one of the main visitor activities is also visiting the many port wine storehouses that line the Douro River, each offering free guided tours that end in a tasting.

Cruisers can tour past its well-preserved baroque buildings and cutting-edge architecture or opt to see the sites from a local's perspective on foot. Be sure to peek inside the **Livraria Lello bookstore** (Rua das Carmelitas 144), to admire the lavish Art Nouveau design. The most intriguing neighborhood is the UNESCO-designated **Ribeira,** with its old buildings and cobbled streets lining the riverbank (and hiding surprises, including arcaded markets).

The river has influenced the city's development since pre-Roman times, when the town of Cale on the left bank prospered sufficiently to support a trading port, called Portus, on the site of today's city.

Port wine has, for centuries, been known as the Englishman's wine. In 1703, England gave commercial preference to Portugal's wines and provided Douro Valley vineyards with a new market. It was in Porto that the local Douro wine was first mixed with brandy to preserve it during the journey to England. Even today, port is big business here, the hub of activity across the river from Porto in Vila Nova de Gaia. From vineyards along the Douro, wine is transported to "lodges" (warehouses), where it is matured, bottled, and eventually shipped around the world. More than 25 companies, including such well-known names as **Sandeman** (Largo Miguel Bombarda 3), maintain port-wine lodges here, each doing tours and tastings. One of the best to visit, in addition to Sandeman, is **Caves Ramos Pinto** (Av. Ramos Pinto, 400).

Porto also is a cultural hub, thanks to the **Serralves Contemporary Art Museum** and commercial galleries, many clustered along Rua Miguel Bombarda; and the Casa da Música (House of Music), designed by Dutch architect Rem Koolhaas.

Above the Douro in Porto, cruisers can view five spectacular bridges including the Maria Pia railway bridge, built by Gustave Eiffel in 1877.

highlights OF THE DOURO

Porto. Plan to spend time walking the main streets and back streets of this UNESCO-recognized city which gave a wine, country and language its name.

Tasting port wine. Stop by a port wine lodge for a free tour and tasting (there are more than 25 companies to choose from). You'll learn that the sweet, fortified wine takes on rich qualities as it ages. There will also be opportunity to visit vineyards en route.

The scenery. Rising above the river, the steep terraced vineyards are an awe-inspiring sight, as are mountain villages. There's a lot of scenery packed into this compact part of Europe.

Salamanca. Visiting this ancient Spanish city is like stepping back to the Middle Ages—though with the addition of the kinds of shops and cafes you'd expect in a university town.

Key Ports
REGUA

Your ship will dock in this cozy little town to get you to nearby wine-tasting opportunities. For tourism information visit www.dourovalley.eu/en.

Top Activity   Wine Tasting: This Portuguese town, renowned for its spectacular scenery, has port wine tasting at several different venues. Visitors can experience **Quinto do Seixo,** a 108-acre country estate that offers an interactive wine museum and great views of steeply terraced hillside vineyards, the Douro River and the nearby village of Pinhão. Your visit may also include a guided tour of the **Douro Museum** (5050-282 Peso da Régua, www.museu-dodouro.pt), which offers an in-depth look at the Douro wine-growing region; or **Vila Real** and the baroque Mateus Palace, with its rich interiors.

Off-the-Beaten-Path   Lamego: Historic and picturesque Lamego is home to one of the most important pilgrimage sites in all of Portugal, the **Nossa Senhora dos Remédios** (Sanctuary of Our Lady of Remedies). The shrine features a staircase of nearly 700 steps, beautifully decorated with white and blue tiles. Other attractions include a Gothic cathedral, a museum and charming cafes.

BARCA D'ALVA

This port call is simply a drop-off point for a full-day visit to Salamanca, Spain (on some itineraries the port town of **Vega de Terrón** is another drop-off port). For more information, visit www.dourovalley.eu/en/.

Top Activity   Visiting Salamanca, Spain: You will head off on a full-day tour to Salamanca, Spain, a UNESCO World Heritage Site located at the center of Spain's **Castilla y León** region. With perfectly preserved buildings constructed of golden sandstone, Salamanca is a "living museum,", and offers a chance to step back to the Middle Ages. You can tour Salamanca's university buildings, its twin-towered cathedral, the ornate **House of Shells,** as well as **Plaza Mayor,** considered one of the most magnificent main squares in all of Spain. After Salamanca, you'll rejoin your ship in the small port town of **Vega Terrón.**

RECOMMENDED food & drink

Portuguese cooking is based on olive oil and the generous use of garlic. If you select anything prepared to order, you can request that it be *sem alho* (without garlic), but why would you? A typical meal starts with soup such as **caldo verde** (green broth made with cabbage, sausage, potatoes and olive oil, and common in the north) or **sopa alentejana** (garlic soup) and then a fish or meat course. You may be offered **courverts**, which are little appetizers of bread, cheese and olives (note that they may be free, or not, so ask). The main, main dish you'll encounter is **bacalhau** (salted codfish), either served boiled with vegetables and then baked; fried in olive oil with potatoes and garlic; or stewed with black olives, potatoes and onions and topped with a boiled egg. You may even find it barbecued. Another classic dish is **caldeirada,** the Portuguese version of bouillabaisse. Shellfish is a delicacy and priced accordingly. **Grilled sardines** are a delicious and cheaper option. Porto residents are known as tripe eaters, the local specialty **dobrada** (tripe and beans). You'll also find **cozido á portuguesa**, a beef, pork, vegetable and sausage stew. Stop by a pastry shop or tea salon for sweets including custard tarts. There will of course be plenty of opportunity to taste Port (find more in chapter 12) and other Portuguese wines including **Vinhos Verdes** (green wine). **Cerveja** (beer) is gaining new followers yearly. One of the best of the craft beers is Sagres, honoring the town in the Algarve.

Optional Add-Ons on the Route

Your cruise will likely begin with a hotel stay in **Lisbon** (195 miles to the south) and you'll fly between Lisbon and Porto. Spread over seven hills north of the Rio Tejo (Tagus River) estuary, the city of Lisbon is always a big surprise, in a good way, with its historic neighborhoods dating back to Moorish times and lined with pastel-color houses. In the grand 18th-century city center, black-and-white mosaic cobblestone sidewalks border wide boulevards. *Elétricos* (trams) clank through the streets, and blue-and-white *azulejos* (painted and glazed ceramic tiles) adorn churches, restaurants, and fountains. A rickety ride on vintage tram 28 provides a swell intro to Lisbon, providing views including of the **Alfama**'s labyrinthine Moorish alleys. Popular sites include the 16th-century Belém Tower (the city's famous landmark you've seen in photos), located on what was an island in the middle of the Rio Tejo, to defend the port entrance; and the 500-year-old **Jerónimos Monastery** (Praça do Império, admission about $11, www.mosteirojeronimos.pt/en/), a UNESCO World Heritage Site. For more visitor information on what to do in Lisbon, visit www.visitlisboa.com.

From Lisbon, you may also be offered the option of an excursion to **Sintra** (about $64), the tour combining time to explore the quaint streets of the charming hillside town (which Lord Byron likened to Eden) with a look at some of Portugal's famous beaches including Cascais and Estoril. The town is about 18 miles north of Lisbon, and you can also get there by train from Lisbon (it's a 45-minute ride costs about $4). Portugal is a fairly easy jumping off point to Spain (including **Madrid** and **Barcelona**) and other top cities in

Western Europe. A non-stop flight from Lisbon gets you to Madrid in 2½ hours (try a discount carriers such as EasyJet.)

ELBE

Despite running through eye-popping scenic landscapes, Central Europe's Elbe River is only offered by a few river cruise lines. That's in large part because of the challenges this river presents. Its lower water levels and narrower passages mean that river cruise ships on the Elbe are more restricted in size and in navigation—in recent years, dry drought weather in Europe has made water levels on the Elbe so low that river cruises simply cannot sail on all the scheduled dates.

But challenges aside, river cruise companies such as Viking River Cruises and CroisiEurope have still decided to put river cruise ships on the Elbe because of the uniqueness of the historic ports and eye-catching views along the way—they also benefit from a degree of exclusivity, since other river cruise companies have thus far shied away from taking the risk.

The Elbe River runs approximately 680 miles between the Czech Republic and Germany, but a typical Elbe River cruise itinerary traverses a 200-mile stretch between Prague in the Czech Republic and Wittenberg in Germany, with initial embarkation or final disembarkation in Berlin (depending on the direction of the cruise).

Along the way, passengers will have the opportunity to visit Prussian palaces in Potsdam just outside of Berlin and will travel through what is known as the Saxon Switzerland, a region defined by soaring sandstone rock formations located southeast of Dresden, Germany. The Elbe also winds through the Saxony wine region, known for its Muller-Thurgau, Riesling and Pinot Blanc varietals.

The Elbe River also played a critical role in post-World War II geography, forming part of the border between East and West Germany.

Viking operates four vessels on the Elbe, two of which launched in 2015—the Viking Asrild and Viking Beyla. The Viking Fontane and Viking Schumann are older Viking vessels that sail the Elbe. CroisiEurope joined them in 2016, launching the 80-passenger paddle-wheeler the Elbe Princess. The vessel's two smaller paddlewheels at the aft of the ship allow for a shallower draft, enabling it to sail the Elbe's low waters year-round, according to CroisiEurope.

Ports of Embarkation: Prague & Berlin
PRAGUE

Prague isn't actually on the Elbe River—it's on the Vltava River, which is one of the major tributaries of the Elbe. Some cruises dock directly in Prague and some don't, so check with your river cruise line about specific docking locations. There is a tourist information center located in Old Town Hall (Staromestske namestí 1; www.prague.eu).

You'll want at least a day or two to explore this well-preserved and enchanting Central European city, which managed to escape World War II unscathed. It offers an impressive display of art and architecture that span across centuries,

The Elbe River

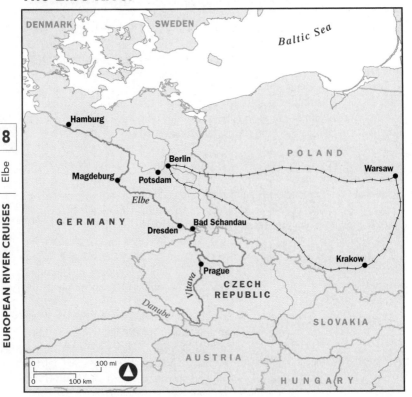

with all the major sights within walking distance from one another. There is the sprawling **Prague Castle complex** (119 08 Prague 1; www.hrad.cz/en; admission is $14 for adults, $7 for kids 6-16, students and seniors older than 65), which dates back to the 9th century (oldest intact castle in Europe), and the charming Medieval **historic town center,** which has been classified as a UNESCO World Heritage Site. You'll find most of the action along the cobblestone streets of the old town, where hordes of tourists can be found wandering among the souvenir shops and being tempted by *trdelnik,* or chimney cake, dough wrapped around steel rods, baked, then coated with anything from cinnamon sugar to chocolate to nuts. A popular gathering spot is the **Astronomical Clock** (Staromestske nam. 1) that sits alongside the Old Town Hall; on the hour it chimes and sends out enchanting figures to mark the passing of time.

A walk through and around Prague is a visual journey through many of Europe's most significant architectural movements. You will see important examples of Gothic structures (the **Charles Bridge** being among the most famous), and Baroque and Romanesque buildings that line the old town. Be sure to head to the **Jewish quarter,** the centerpiece of the city's newest wave of innovation and investment and home to ancient cemeteries and synagogues as grand and ornate as any European cathedral. One highlight is the 13th **Old-New Synagogue** (Maiselova 18; www.synagogue.cz; $8 for adults, $5.50 for children ages 6-15; free for children younger than 6), the oldest active synagogue in Europe, purposefully spared by Hitler who wanted to create a museum to the race he was determined to destroy. If you need a place to rest your feet and are looking for a solid snack, head to **Bakeshop** (Kozi 918/1; www.bakeshop.cz/en), which has bagels, spreads, salads and sweets, and is a short walk from the Old-New Synagogue.

BERLIN

Berlin is located 23 miles east of the Elbe River. River cruise passengers will usually overnight in a hotel in Berlin either at the start or end of their river cruise.

A fascinating capital city, Berlin is beloved as much for its triumphs as it is for its tragedies. Known around the world for the Berlin Wall that once separated East and West Berlin, today Berlin is a bustling modern metropolis as rich in foodie destination restaurants and chic design boutiques as it is in historical, cultural and national heritage institutions.

Like other major European cities Berlin is whatever you want to make of it. It can be a history buff's dream, an art lover's escape, or a fine diner's paradise. Some of the city's main tourist attractions include the 18th-century **Brandenburg Gate (Pariser Platz),** the East-West Berlin crossing point **Checkpoint Charlie** (Friedrichstrasse 43-45), and the **Memorial to the Murdered Jews of Europe or the Holocaust Memorial** (Cora-Berliner-Strasse 1; www.stiftung-denkmal.de/en, admission is free), a poignant outdoor memorial consisting of rows up rows of concrete slabs of various heights that evoke unmarked graves. Definitely worth a sobering stop. If you're looking to take a deep cultural dive, head to **Museum Island,** a collection of five art museums that occupy the northern half of an island in the Spree River. The most popular of the five is the **Pergamon Museum** (Bodestrasse 1-3; www.smb.museum; $13 for just Pergamon, or $20 for all Museum Island exhibitions), which houses astonishingly beautiful reconstructions of archaeological structures from ancient civilizations.

highlights OF THE ELBE

Elbe Sandstone Mountains. The Elbe River winds through this soaring and colorful range, which showcases a wide variety of rock formations due to erosion.

Potsdam. Need a palace fix? This UNESCO World Heritage Site serves up 1,200 acres of palaces and parks, a total of 150 buildings constructed between the 18th and 20th centuries.

Dresden. This resurgent city is often known more for what isn't there rather than what is due to the fact that Dresden's entire city center was destroyed by Allied Forces bombings during World War II (several historical landmarks since restored).

All told, Berlin is a city where pre-war glamour and post-war grit sit side-by-side. There is no shortage of creative energy, which means there is always some new exhibit or see-and-be-seen restaurant, bar or dance club that's worth checking out. Whether it's your first time to Berlin or you tenth, the city will likely have some unique surprises in store for you.

Key Ports

POTSDAM

Located 20 miles outside of Berlin, the palace and garden complex of Potsdam is not on the Elbe River—the closest Elbe port is in 80 miles east in Magdeburg (a bit more than 1-hr. driving), so this is a bus excursion.

Top Activity **The Sanssouci Palace and Gardens:** The palace (www. spsg.de/en/palaces-gardens/objekt/schloss-sanssouci/), built by Prussian king Frederick the Great in the 18th century, serve as a pristine example of German rococo architecture and its gardens are a destination unto themselves, the centerpiece of which are the terraced vineyards. Travelers can also visit Sanssouci's lavish interiors.

Off-the-Beaten-Path **Cafes:** Need somewhere to rest your tired feet after exploring the 700 acres of gardens at Sanssouci? One mile east of the palace complex is **Potsdam's Dutch Quarter** (www.potsdam-tourism.com/detail/id/10218/theme/a-z.html), where 130 Amsterdam-esque brick buildings house shops, cafes, bars and restaurants.

DRESDEN

Situated right along the Elbe River, ships can dock very close to the center of town in Dresden. Despite its history of destruction, Dresden has successfully been resurrected from its ashes with important historical landmarks having been restored since the Allied bombings of World War II took out much of the city, and a new Dresden has been building up right alongside it. There is a tourist information office (www.dresden.de) located at Neumarkt 2 in the center of town.

Top Activity **Exploring "Florence on the Elbe":** On your ship tour you will visit the 18th-century **Frauenkirche** (Neumarkt, free admission; www.

RECOMMENDED food & drink

A Berlin street-food specialty is **curry-wurst,** pork sausage with curry ketchup. But the food scene in Berlin offers as much choice and variety as any major European city, ranging from traditional restaurants to venues that serve unique spins on regional dishes, to international cuisine from around the world. As in much of Germany, there will be no shortage of good beers, **schnitzel** (breaded and fried veal, pork or chicken), 'wursts (sausages), **pretzels,** and **sauerkraut** on this journey. Many similar dishes will be found in the Czech Republic, but you will also begin to see a lot of **potato dumplings** (large dumplings made with a combination of flour and bread), as well as the popular Eastern European meat stew, **goulash.** In cooler months, you'll appreciate the wealth of hearty soups that are popular throughout the region.

frauenkirche-dresden.de/en/home), also known as the **Church of Our Lady,** with its distinctive bell-shaped dome. The church was a casualty of the Dresden bombings. After the reunification of Germany, the decision was made to rebuild the church and return it to its former glory, a decade-long endeavor that culminated with its reopening in October 2005. You will also have opportunity at the Residenzschloss, a former royal palace, to gape at the treasures in the collection known as the **Green Vault** (Sophienstrasse, admission about $10), ten rooms filled with gold jewelry, priceless porcelain and other royal extravagances.

Off-the-Beaten-Path A Brewery Visit: Get some Saxon brews and brats among the locals at **Watzke Ball und Brauhaus** (Kotzschenbroder Str. 1; watzke.de; entrees $8–$13), a historic restaurant, brewery and beer garden situated on the banks of the Elbe River.

BAD SCHANDAU

Bad Schandau is a German spa town just 4 miles north of the Czech border. It is located on the east side of the Elbe River and is the gateway to the Saxon Switzerland National Park within the Elbe Sandstone Mountains.

Top Activity Viewing the Bastei Rock Formation: The **Bastei** is a unique, 635-foot rock formation in the Elbe Sandstone Mountains and is one of the most popular lookout points within the Saxon range. Not only are the views themselves striking but the unique rock structures are reminiscent of the hoodoos of Utah's Bryce Canyon National Park—jagged, slim spires created by water erosion more than 1 million years ago.

Off-the-Beaten-Path Linger in Bad Schandau: The small town, with its medieval center and river waterfront, is a nice place to stroll, sit at a cafe or check out the shops. Or for something completely different, visit the warm, healing waters of the Toskana Therme spa (Rudolf-Sendig-Strasse 8a, admission from about $18; www.toskanaworld.net/).

Dnieper River

Remember Crimea? The region that was all over the news in 2014 when tensions flared up between Russia and Ukraine about the disputed territory? Well, ever since then, river cruises along the Dnieper (which heads through the heart of Crimea) have all but dried up. One small outfit is left running pretty basic cruises on the Dnieper. It's based in Huntington, N.Y. and called Imperial River Cruises, a river cruise reseller, which is offering a few Dnieper sailings on the 260-passenger General Vatutin, a German vessel built in 1976.

It's a shame because Ukraine's Dnieper River had much to recommend it. The cruise anchored in the storied capital Kiev and debarked the Black Sea city of Odessa. In between stops included several quirky riverside towns. Some itineraries also include Sevastopol and Yalta on the Crimean Peninsula. Let's hope the situation in the Crimea is resolved soon. Check with the US State Department website before booking a cruise here.

Optional Add-Ons on the Route

If not included on your cruise itinerary it's worth splurging on a 2-hour, $100 tour to visit the **Museum of Meissen or Art,** located in the German town of the same name. The museum houses the largest collection of Meissen Porcelain dating back to 1710. Visitors will also have the opportunity to experience the demonstration workshops, where they can learn about the materials and witness the craftsmanship that go into making the porcelain.

We also recommend, for pre- or post-cruise stays in **Berlin,** the **East Side Gallery** (Mühlenstrasse). This free, open-air gallery, located on the banks of the Spree River, comprises the longest still-standing stretch of the Berlin Wall, featuring a 4,300-foot stretch of paintings by more than 100 artists from 21 countries. It's located at Muhlenstrasse 1 in the city's east central Friedrichshain district.

RHONE & SAONE

Anchored by Lyon, the gateway to the south of France, the Rhone and Saone rivers provided an important navigational route throughout France's history, and thus today provide us with a route along which to witness much of that history.

Among other things, a defining feature of the Rhone River is just how rich with ancient Greco-Roman landmarks it is. From the Roman aqueduct Pont du Gard, 15 miles west of Avignon, to the Roman Amphitheatre in Arles, remnants of the all-powerful and long-lasting Roman rule are apparent throughout Provence.

Another defining feature is the sheer seduction of Provence itself with its lavender-filled landscapes dotted by those endearing Provencal farmhouses that will have you checking out real estate listings (because you never know, right?) throughout the route. The food (truffles, cheese and olives for days) and wine (you will get a better appreciation for the underrated quality of rosé) of the region are equally provocative.

This part of France was also a place of inspiration for some of France and Europe's most beloved artists, not least of which were Paul Cezanne, who was born in Aix-en-Provence, and Vincent van Gogh, who spent 15 very critical months in Arles.

Several years ago, there was renewed interest in river cruising in France in general, and along the Rhone and Saone rivers in particular. The region saw an uptick in new vessels as river cruise lines redeployed inventory here to catch up with what was growing demand. Whereas in the past, river cruising in France was always seen as sort of secondary to the big blockbuster river cruises on the Rhine and Danube, today the Rhone and Saone rivers really hold their own as a much sough-after river cruising destination. After a journey along these rivers, which couldn't provide a more attractive backdrop to a river cruise sailing, it's not hard to see why.

A bit of geography: The journey of France's 500-mile Rhone River begins high up in the Swiss Alps, from which the river heads west through Lake

The Rhone & Saone Rivers

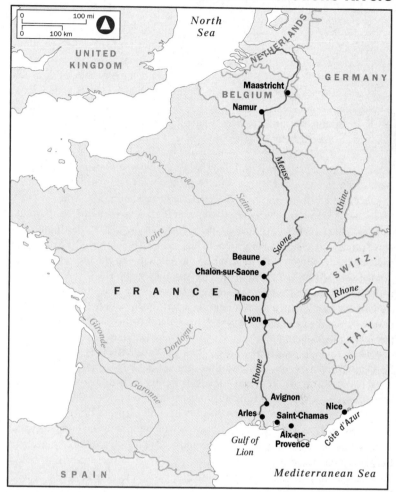

Geneva and into France. There it turns south from Lyon into the heart of the country's Provence region and out into the Mediterranean Sea. The Saone River is a 300-mile stretch of river that extends north from Lyon into the belly of Burgundy.

Ports of Embarkation: Lyon & Avignon
LYON

With Lyon situated on a small peninsula at the axis of the Rhone and Saone rivers, most river cruise ships dock within walking distance of Lyon's city center, making it easy for passengers to explore on their own, should they so choose. Lyon's Tourist Information Office is located on Place Bellecour.

Whether you stay an extra day or two, or simply use your embarkation or disembarkation day to roam the charming streets of Lyon, you'll find plenty to see, do and eat in France's third largest city.

The culinary culture is strong in Lyon, which sits at the axis of the Alps and France's Provence and Burgundy regions, all known for their rich gastronomy. This food is not for the meek eater. Head to a traditional Lyonnaise eatery (also known as a *bouchon*) and be prepared to encounter a menu chock full of sausages and cheeses, pates and terrines. **Daniel et Denise** (156 Rue de Crequi; www.daniel-et-denise.fr; main courses, $16-$28) and **Café des Federations** (9 Rue Major Martin; restaurant-cafedesfederations-lyon.com; standard menu, $21) are excellent options for those who want to experience some of the world-renowned local fare. Or picnic at the bustling **Les Halles de Lyon** food market (102 Cours Lafayette; www.halles-de-lyon-paulbocuse.com), which dates back to 1850, and where there is no shortage of culinary temptation.

Once fueled up on the hearty *Rhone-Alpes* regional food, you'll want to make sure you have your comfortable walking shoes on to start exploring a city with a vast amount of history and culture. In fact, Lyon was founded by the Romans in the 1st century B.C. and has been designated a UNESCO World Heritage Site. Begin with a stroll through **Vieux Lyon,** the city's largest Renaissance district, located in the 5th arrondissement.

Now it's time to cross the Saone River to the **Place Bellecour,** a large open square, the focal point of which is an equestrian statue of King Louis XIV, and conveniently the location of the tourist information office. It is also the heart of the city's main shopping district, much of which lies to the north of Place Bellecour en route to the **Hotel de Ville de Lyon** or **Lyon's City Hall (Place de la Comedie).** Here you will also find some of the city's most important cultural institutions, including the **Musee des Beaux-Arts de Lyon** (20 Place des Terreaux; www.mba-lyon.fr/mba; standard admission, $8, exhibitions, $10), an extensive European and French art collection displayed in more than 70 rooms of a former Benedictine monastery (with highlights including Egyptian coffins, Japanese ceramics and 19th-century paintings, including by Monet).

AVIGNON

River cruise ships dock right alongside Avignon on the Rhone River, and passengers are able to walk into the heart of the city. Avignon Tourisme's tourism office is located at 41 Cours Jean Jaures.

The ancient city of Avignon sets the tone for the sights and scenes along the Rhone River. Its extremely impressive 14th-century **Palais des Papes** or **Papal Palace** (located in the Place du Palais; $12 for entrance) is the largest Gothic palace in Europe. The light-colored stones with which the sprawling structure was built will be seen in various forms throughout Provence, where a hot Mediterranean climate offers a landscape with few trees, and thus mostly stones, for construction.

Most river cruise lines will include a guided tour of the Papal Palace complex. After visiting the palace, however, make sure to saunter around some of the cobblestone streets of **Old Avignon.** Here you're sure to find a charming

highlights OF THE RHONE & SAONE

Arles. See some of the now iconic locations that inspired some of Van Gogh's beloved works, including Café Van Gogh, the inspiration for Van Gogh's "The Cafe Terrace at Night." In a nearby town, you can also visit the hospital where Van Gogh stayed after he cut off part of his ear.

Côtes du Rhône. Wine lovers won't be able to pass through the Rhone and Saone regions without tasting their renowned varietals. Some of the most famous winemaking regions along the route include Hermitage and Châteauneuf-du-Pape in Provence, and Beaune in Burgundy.

Lavender fields. A stereotypical image from the Provence region is that of rows upon rows of lavender fields, and they are indeed stunning. Summer is the best time for viewing them.

bistro for a light snack or meal. If you're yearning to see a Van Gogh, an artist with whom many people associate the south of France, head to **Musee Angladon** (5 Rue Laboureur; angladon.com; tickets are $7 for adults; $3 for students; and $1.50 for children ages 4 to 18) where Van Gogh's "Irises" is housed alongside works by Picasso, Rousseau and Manet.

There are ample boutiques and shopping in and around central Avignon. Before heading back to the ship, try to get a glimpse of the **Pont d'Avignon,** a medieval bridge, part of which was destroyed. It has been left incomplete with four arches jutting out into the Rhone River, somehow making it all the more dramatic.

Key Ports
MACON OR CHALON-SUR SAONE

About 45 miles up the Saone River from Lyon is Macon, and about 80 miles up the river is Chalon-sur-Saone. River cruise lines typically use one or the other as their docking point from which to offer passengers excursions into France's Burgundy region.

Top Activity   Exploring Beaune: Twenty miles from the nearby port of Chalon-sur-Saone, or 36 miles from the port of Macon, is the evocative walled hilltown and wine capital of Burgundy, **Beaune.** And one of the most interesting wine attractions in Beaune is the **Hospices de Beaune.** Originally established in the 15th century as a hospital for those in need, the **Hospices de Beaune** (Rue de l'Hôtel Dieu; www.hospices-de-beaune.com; entrance fee is $8) now houses a museum about the charity hospital that occupied the building in the building from 1443 to 1971, and also hosts an annual charitable wine auction for wine produced in-house (back in the day that wine was made by monks).

Off-the-Beaten-Path   Tastings at Burgundy wineries: If you have time to get out of town, or if your river cruise line offers it, head for some of **Burgundy's famous wineries** in the **Côte d'Or,** which encompasses two of the most important winemaking regions in Burgundy, **Côte de Nuits** and **Côte de Beaune.** Pinot Noir and Chardonnay lovers will delight. If you're not sure

RECOMMENDED food & drink

We've already discussed the lauded cuisine of Lyon, but don't expect to be disappointed as you head further south into the heart of Provence, where the Mediterranean influences will become stronger. Local and rustic ingredients such as olives, market vegetables (ratatouille anyone?), wild boar, rabbit and *herbes de Provence*, a classic mixture of herbs such as rosemary, thyme and oregano now commonly used in kitchens throughout the world, often find their way into many of the dishes in Provence. **Bouillabaisse,** a rich seafood stew in a tomato broth, is a specialty of the seaside city of Marseille, but don't be surprised to find it in other areas of Provence. In Burgundy, expect traditional French dishes such as **escargot** and **frog's legs.** And of course, this is truffle country, so truffles and truffle oil will abound. Oh and cheese, there will be plenty of cheese, not least of which the popular and fragrant goat cheese, **chèvre.** For oenophiles, you will be passing through some of France's most delectable wine regions, including Côtes du Rhône and Côte d'Or, where Pinot Noirs, Chardonnays and Grenaches are some of the stronger players.

where to begin, follow the **Route des Grand Crus,** a wine-tasting route marked by brown signs on the road that say "Route des Grand Crus," and Beaune is along the route, so you can head out from there. You can just stop by wineries with an "open" sign, or if you have your sights set on a particular vintner, make reservations in advance.

ARLES

Located 25 miles down the Rhone River from Avignon, Arles is the very definition of all things Provence. You have the strong connection to Vincent van Gogh, who spent 15 months here from 1888 to 1889. And the town itself is a living monument to the Roman roots of the region. River cruise ships dock a hip, skip and a jump from the center of town.

Top Activity   Roman Ruins: Your guided sightseeing will focus on the Romans. Julius Caesar was here and the **Arles Amphitheatre** (1 Rond-Point des Arènes; admission about $6.50; www.arenes-arles.com) is the proof, a Roman Amphitheatre built in A.D. 90. For a great view you can climb three towers that remain from medieval times, when the place was turned into a fortress. Once able to accommodate up to 20,000 spectators, today the arena still houses bullfights and other major events. Another of the city's great classical monuments is the Roman theater Théâtre Antique (rue du Cloître), begun by Augustus in the 1st century (only two Corinthian columns remain). Also still standing from Roman times is the Place du Forum, with a cafe immortalized by the town's famous resident Vincent Can Gogh (see below).

Off-the-Beaten-Path   Van Gogh Haunts: Offered by your cruise line as an added-fee, add-on tour or doable on your own, is tracing Van Gogh's legacy. This includes visiting the **Mediatheque d'Arles** at Place Felix Rey to see the courtyard of the former hospital where Vincent van Gogh stayed after he cut off a portion of his ear. The courtyard was inspiration for the painting "Garden of the Hospital in Arles." Then go to **Café Van Gogh** (11 Place du Forum) to see the inspiration for "Café Terrace at Night." If you haven't got your Van Gogh fix yet, the modern **Fondation Vincent van Gogh Arles** (35 Rue du Dr Fanton; www.fondation-vincentvangogh-arles.org; entrance fee is $10 for adults; $7.50 for seniors age 65 and older; $4 for students and children ages 12–18; and free for children under 12) organizes exhibits of art influenced by Van Gogh.

Optional Add-Ons on the Route

Increasingly, river cruise lines are including an optional excursion to a truffle farm while sailing through the Burgundy and Provence region, and we definitely recommend the experience, especially for those who are truffle lovers. The process, which contrary to popular belief does not involve pigs, relies on trained dogs running around a given area in order to sniff out the unique and flavorful fungus from under the soil. Truffle season runs from November through March. Uniworld takes its passengers on select food-themed sailings to the Rabassière truffle farm in Saint-Chamas, 45 minutes southeast of Arles. It's actually not all that easy to arrange this on your own so check with your river cruise line concierge to see if they can help arrange it for you if it's not offered as part of the cruise.

Once you've already come as far south as Avignon for your river cruise, a pre- or post-cruise option (though somehow post-cruise seems more fitting) is to tack on a few days in the French Riviera to a southern France itinerary (a vacation from your vacation, so to speak, on the beaches of the Côte d'Azur). Plan on your own or go with one of the cruise line options. Viking offers a 3-day extension in Nice, starting from $799; and Tauck has a 14-day "French Escapade" itinerary that includes Nice and Monte Carlo on one end of a Rhone and Saone cruise, and Paris at the other end, with cruise prices starting at $5,990.

Meuse River

The Meuse River is a river that flows from France through Belgium and the Netherlands and into the North Sea. It is not offered on any river cruises—except one. In 2016, Avalon Waterways began sailing a small 60-mile section of the Meuse River between Maastricht in the Netherlands and Namur in Belgium, as part of its 9-day "Enchanting Belgium" itinerary. While most river cruises end in Maastricht, this slightly extended itinerary continues on to Namur, which is located at the confluence of the Meuse and Sambre rivers. Namur dates back to Celtic times and was an early Roman settlement. Avalon offers a guided tour of the city or passengers can roam the pedestrian streets on their own. There is a fortified citadel here that is in pretty impressive shape and the Jambes Bridge is a great vantage point from which some Meuse River views.

SEINE

Flowing from its source in Burgundy (about 20 miles from Dijon), through the heart of Paris, the Seine River meanders through the country for about 482 miles, finally joining the English Channel in an estuary between Le Havre and Honfleur on the Normandy coast. It is the longest and most-used inland river in France, carrying commercial traffic in addition to river boats. The stretch from Paris to the coast is about 240 miles, but this is one snaking river (as the crow flies the distance is only about 110 miles).

Its importance to the region dates back to the Iron Ages, when the Celts used the river to transport goods; later, Ancient Romans used it for trade, followed by the Vikings. The fertile center of its basin in the Île-de-France became the cradle of the French monarchy, and to this day is its heartland.

Many Seine river cruises depart from Paris, where so many of the city's famous landmarks are located beside the river, including Notre Dame, the Louvre, the Eiffel Tower and the Musée d'Orsay. In 1991, the Seine River in Paris was named a UNESCO World Heritage Site.

From Paris, cruises take passengers to both urban and rural towns and villages, including medieval sights, historic battlegrounds, and picturesque gardens. You can visit impressionist artist Claude Monet's home Giverny and historic Rouen, where in the height of the Middle Ages Joan of Arc was martyred. The Seine was a critical crossing in World War II and the beaches of Normandy are a profoundly moving sight to visit.

Cruises vary between 1 week and 10 days, and shore trips are usually split between full-day tours (such as to the Normandy Beaches) and half-day options, where you can tour a nearby site and visit the local town where you are docked afterward.

Port of Embarkation: Paris
PARIS

Most lines use either the Port de Javel Bas, about 2 miles from the Eiffel Tower, or the Port Quai de Grenelle (Quai André-Citroën), in the 15th arrond. Others use Quai Maurice Berteaux in Le Pecq, about 12 miles from the center of the city. For official tourist information for Paris visit the Paris Tourist Office website, http://en.parisinfo.com.

Most river cruises on the Seine begin and end in Paris, usually including at least 1 hotel night in the city. The City of Light, the City of Romance, or whatever you choose to call it, France's capital is a magical place to visit and to begin a river cruise.

The charms of Paris are legendary and a day or two won't be nearly enough time to explore, but there are some absolutely not-to-miss sights for any visitor. Wear comfortable shoes and get ready to walk, the easiest way to soak up the uniquely Parisian atmosphere. The city has 20 arrondissements (or neighborhoods), each with its own special character. With enough time, visiting several is a great way to explore the diversity of the city. But with limited time, there's plenty to see right in the center of town.

Of course, first-timers (and many repeat visitors!) will want to head straight to the iconic **Eiffel Tower** (Champs de Mars, 7th arrond; www.toureiffel. paris), built by Gustave Eiffel for the 1889 World's Fair. No other monument quite symbolizes the city as the tower does. Save yourself some aggravation and book tickets for the elevator to the top in advance online (rates at press time were 17€ or about $19). **The Cathédrale de Notre-Dame** (Place du Parvis Notre-Dame, 4th arrond; www.notredamedeparis.fr), one of the supreme masterpieces of Gothic art, built between 1163 and 1250, is another highlight. A visit to the **Musée du Louvre** (quai du Louvre, 1st arrond; www. louvre.fr), the world's most renowned art museum, home to the Mona Lisa, Venus de Milo, and Winged Victory, is another must-see. Adjacent is the **Jardin des Tuileries,** a wonderful place to catch your breath and enjoy the sculptures and ornamental ponds.

Other sights include the **Arc de Triomphe** (Place Charles de Gaulle–Etoile, 8th arrond), begun by Napoleon in 1806, modeled on ancient Roman arches, and is dedicated to the French army. Beneath is the Tomb of the Unknown Soldier. Try to make time for the **Musée d'Orsay** (1 rue de la Légion

highlights OF THE SEINE

The Eiffel Tower. Day, night, from afar, or up close, this iconic wrought-iron tower says Paris like nothing else.

Claude Monet. It's one thing to have seen the Impressionist Master's works. It's quite another to walk through his gardens and see what inspired him. Many Seine cruises offer an excursion to his long-time home in Giverny, where you also get to visit his long-time residence.

WWII Landing Beaches. Walking along the Normandy Beaches and visiting the numerous monuments and memorials is a poignant and humbling trek, which no visitor to Normandy should miss.

Joan of Arc. The riverside city of Rouen, the place where Joan of Arc lived, and died, offers a fascinating look into her past and what medieval life was like in the 1400s. Visit the marketplace where she was burned at the stake and other museums and monuments dedicated to her at this fascinating stop.

d'Honneur, 7th arrond), in a former railway station and now boasting an internationally renowned collection of 19th-century art, including important works by French Impressionist masters.

Before heading to your ship, take time to walk a bit on the Quays of the Seine, with some of the best panoramic views of Paris you can get. There are 37 bridges in Paris, many of them landmarks in their own right. Look for the Pont Neuf, the oldest and most evocative of Paris's 14 bridges.

Key Ports
VERNON/GIVERNY

Your ship will dock in the town of Vernon. Most passengers will head off on a tour to nearby Giverny.

Top Activity **Monet's Giverny:** Take a brief ride to **Giverny,** where Claude Monet resided from 1883 until his death in 1926. You can visit the beautiful gardens and picturesque stone farmhouse where he lived and worked. You'll recognize such sights as his water garden with its Japanese bridge, water lilies, wisteria and azaleas, which appeared in many of his works. Inside, you can view his collection of Japanese prints. For more on Monet, walk along the main street up the cemetery to visit the Monet family tomb and to the Musée des Impressionismes (99 rue Claude Monet; www.museedesimpressionnismesgiverny.com), to check out temporary exhibits that sometimes feature his works.

Off-the-Beaten-Path **Exploring Vernon:** If you have time, or have already been to Giverny, stroll through the charming town of town of Vernon, where you can visit the **Maison du Temps Jadis** (House of Past Times), Vernon's oldest house, and the 11th-century Church of Notre Dame. Your ship may offer a tour to the impressive **Chateau de Bizy** (www.chateaudebizy.com) built in 1740, once owned by King Louis XV and nicknamed "Normandy's Versailles." It's most known for its stables, which were inspired by those at Versailles and has beautiful grounds.

CAUDEBEC-EN-CAUX

Your ship may only dock briefly in this medieval city, all but destroyed in World War II and later rebuilt, to let people off on tours. For Caudebec tourist information visit http://en.normandie-tourisme.fr/normandy-tourism-109-2.html.

Top Activity   Visiting D-Day Sites: A little less than a 2-hour drive from this Norman city (depending on your itinerary, full-day tours may alternatively be offered from other cities, including Rouen) gets you to the historic Normandy Beaches, an absolute must for anyone visiting the area, and where the greatest invasion force of all time landed. Normandy's World War II D-Day sites, more than 30 memorials, cemeteries, and museums, range from coastal batteries to exhibits of underwater military finds. Visiting is an astonishingly moving experience.

The sites are spread out along a 31-mile-long stretch of coast. On a full-day tour you'll typically drive past Gold Beach, Courseulles sur Mer and Juno Beach on your way to visit such World War II landmarks as **Omaha Beach,** the **American Military Cemetery** (for a poignant moment of commemoration), and **Arromanches,** to see the remains of the floating harbor used for landings. You'll also see the jagged lime cliffs of the **Pointe du Hoc,** where a cross honors a group of American Rangers who scaled the cliffs using hooks to get at the gun emplacements. Farther along the Cotentin Peninsula is **Utah Beach,** where the 4th U.S. Infantry Division landed at 6:30 a.m. on June 6, 1944, and a U.S. monument commemorates their heroism. An alternative tour may visit the British and Canadian sectors including the **Pegasus Monument** in Ranville and Canadian cemetery at Beny-sur-Mer, as well as the **Juno Beach Centre,** Canada's WWII museum, with a stop as well at Arromanches.

Off-the-Beaten-Path   Bayeux Tapestry: If you've been to the beaches before, you may be able to book an alternative tour to Bayeux (about 92 miles from Caudebec) to see the most famous tapestry in the world, the Bayeux Tapestry, which is actually an elaborate embroidery on linen, depicting the story of the conquest of England by William the Conqueror. The 226-feet-by-20-inch masterpiece, housed in the **Musée de la Tapisserie de Bayeux** in Bayeux (14400 Bayeux; www.bayeuxmuseum.com) was likely created in Kent between 1066 and 1077. Other exhibits include maps, scale models, and a film about the Battle of Hastings. Your tour may also include a stop at a Calvados distillery, with a tasting of the strong apple brandy.

Also Off-the-Beaten-Path   Honfleur: Another option from Caudebec is a trip through the lush Normandy countryside to this charming little seaside town, once inhabited by pirates and seafarers and later by artists—including native son Eugène Boudin, Gustave Courbet and Claude Monet. Stroll along the **Vieux Bassin** (old harbor) and you can still see art students with their sketchbooks trying to capture the enchanting light that dances off the white boats and glistening water. The harbor is typically filled with fishing boats and pleasure craft, the scene overlooked by tall, 18th-century townhouses that today house cafes and restaurants. Among attractions is the **Musée Eugène Boudin** (Rue de l'Homme de Bois; www.musees-honfleur.fr), which has a

RECOMMENDED food & drink

It almost goes without saying that any river cruise along the Seine will highlight the fantastic wines and cheeses of France, and without a doubt, the breads and pastries you'll taste will have you daydreaming about them when you return home. There's just nothing better than a warm French baguette and it's nearly impossible to resist the smell of freshly made croissants as you walk by one of the many bakeries in the city (and why would you want to?). While in Paris, try bistro fare such as **Pot-au-Feu** (beef stew), with a good, crusty bread. Gorgeous displays of colorful **macarons,** also found in many bakery windows, are too tempting to pass up and are as tasty as they look. As you head from the city into Normandy, try the region's local cheeses, including **Camembert, Pont l'Evêque,** and **Boursin.** Normandy is famous for its **apples,** which are used to make Calvados, an apple brandy, as well as a strong cider. Apples are also be found in many sauces and desserts.

fine collection of artworks by Boudin and Monet, among others. Honfleur is about 32 miles from Caudebec.

ROUEN

Your ship will dock right in the city, with easy access to sights. For more information visit http://en.normandie-tourisme.fr/articles/rouen-217-2.html.

Top Activity   Exploring Rouen: Step off the ship and into the capital of Upper Normandy, where you can explore the medieval quarter with its half-timbered, glazed-tile houses; the intricate **Gros Horloge** astronomical clock, dating back to the 16th century; and the **Rouen Cathedral** (Place de la Cathédrale), a favorite subject of Claude Monet, one of the city's most famous residents (along with writer Gustave Flaubert and Joan of Arc). Joan of Arc was also imprisoned in Rouen and was burned at the stake in the city's marketplace in 1431.

The city's main sights are found on the Right Bank of the Seine. Most walking tours start next to the giant modernist Church of Ste-Jeanne, where Joan of Arc was executed for heresy on May 30, 1431. While the architecture of the church is from the 1970s, the rest of the area is medieval and the rue du Gros Horloge, or "Street of the Great Clock" is a favorite with visitors who love to browse along the pedestrians-only road. The ornate gilt Renaissance clock mounted on an arch over the street (how it got its name) is connected to a bell tower.

Off-the-Beaten-Path   Joan of Arc Museum: The excellent **Historical Jeanne d'Arc** (7 Rue Saint-Romain, www.historial-jeannedarc.fr/en/alive-history; admission 9.50€ or about $11) is a state-of-the-art experience that takes visitors on an interactive guide (audio tours available in English) through the life and times of Joan of Arc and offers an excellent look at the Middle Ages. In one exhibit, you'll be cast in the role of a witness to Joan of Arc's trials, where a hologram of Juvénal des Ursins, the ecclesiastic and judge, depicts her exoneration procedures.

Optional Add-Ons on the Route

Depending on your itinerary, there may be optional, for-a-fee excursions to the World War II Landing sites, to visit a Calvados distillery or to visit such Paris attractions as the Louvre.

If you're looking to extend your trip, consider adding on an excursion to **London** via the Chunnel on the high-speed Eurostar train (you can get from Paris to London in about 2½ hr.).

VOLGA

Russia's Volga River, at nearly 2,300 miles, is the longest river in Europe and conveniently connects two of the most significant cities in Russia—Moscow and St. Petersburg.

These two uniquely different metropolises provide both contrasting and complimentary windows into Russia's buzzing urban life, and the 444 miles of river between them offers a glimpse into Russia's simpler, more rural life.

It probably goes without saying that Russia is an incredibly dynamic destination, full of tension and contradiction. In some ways it is so grand, in other ways it is so poor; in some ways it is so modern, and in other ways so ancient. The depth and complexity makes it a very compelling experience. It is bound to introduce you to an array of emotions and experiences you weren't necessarily expecting to encounter.

And then there's our own country's tensions with Russia, which adds a whole other layer to the experience. Recently, those tensions have flared again and consequently demand for Volga river cruises dropped in 2014 and 2015 to the point that several river cruise lines, including Uniworld and AmaWaterways, stopped offering Volga river sailings. Uniworld has since reinstated a small handful of Volga sailings. And Viking, Scenic and the Russian line Volga Dream also sail the iconic Russian river. So it remains an option for those who still want to go.

The dominant themes and sights along the Volga River parallel the most important patterns and events in Russian history, from its long and intricate succession of monarchs and tsars, to its extensive roots in the Russian Orthodox Church, from its controversial role in World War II to its equally controversial fervent embrace of communism.

The Volga River isn't just a long river, it's vast, which means river cruise vessels on the Volga don't have the same long and narrow, bargelike look of river cruise vessels in the rest of Europe. Instead they tend to look a bit more like smaller versions of ocean-cruising vessels and carry between 100 and just over 200 passengers. Russian bureaucracy makes it all but impossible for river cruise companies to come in and build their own ships there. Instead, they are forced to use older Russian hulls and update them however they see fit.

Some companies, like Scenic and Uniworld have done a great job transforming the interiors of the ships so they feel really fresh and modern rather than stale and stodgy. On other vessels, you still get a glimpse into an older

The Volga

era of Volga river cruising, which in its unique way kind of has its charms too. In a destination like Russia, it's all about having the right attitude.

One other thing to note about the Volga is that unlike in the rest of Europe where the distances are relatively short between most river cruise ports and you usually end up in a new port each day, if not in two ports per day, on the Volga you will have some longer sailing stretches, including during the day. And the onboard amenities are relatively limited (there's no pool or casino, sorry). So, bring a couple great books (it can be fun to really immerse yourself into the destination with Russian classics such as Tolstoy or Dostoevsky), and/ or be prepared to really embrace the onboard activities no matter how cheesy. There are usually some engaging, if challenging, Russian language lessons on offer (Cyrillic is really complicated, people), some slightly more manageable cooking classes and probably a highlight (or lowlight, depending on how things turn out for you) of the onboard activities is the vodka tasting, during which you learn all the intricate steps Russians take to be able to maximize their vodka intake. Lard is involved. Consider yourselves warned.

Ports of Embarkation: Moscow & St. Petersburg
MOSCOW

River cruise ships are forced to dock really far from the center of Moscow along the Moscow Canal near the Metro stop Rechnoy Vokzal—30 minutes on the metro, and 30 minutes by car with no traffic. But anyone who has been to Moscow knows there is no such thing as no traffic, so it can often take quite a bit longer. This makes getting into and out of town a bit of a pain.

Moscow gets a bit of a bad rap, especially compared to the fetching St. Petersburg. Russia's capital city has more than 12 million residents and has a reputation for exorbitant prices and being overrun by Russian oligarchs. While those stereotypes aren't unfounded, they shouldn't take away from the fact that Moscow is actually chockablock with stunning sights.

Obviously, high on most visitors' lists is a pilgrimage to the defining landmark of Moscow, **Red Square.** The square's 16th-century **Saint Basil's Cathedral** or **Cathedral of Vasily the Blessed** with its trademark colorful spires is the backdrop to millions of Red Square selfies. A former Russian Orthodox Church, it now operates as a branch of the **State Historical Museum** (admission about $1.50; www.shm.ru/en).

Beyond the cathedral, Red Square connects so many important landmarks, the most significant of which is the **Kremlin** (www.kreml.ru; admission is $3 for Ivan the Great Bell Tower; $6 for Cathedral Square and current exhibitions; $9 for the Armory Chamber), a complex of five palaces and four cathedrals encompassed by the Kremlin Wall and its Towers. Today, the Kremlin is the residence of the Russian president and the country's executive offices. It's a huge and potentially overwhelming site to visit, but hopefully with the help of a good guide you will be able to properly take it all in. And if you're lucky, a military procedure might be on display, which makes for quite an attraction.

If you're a bit burnt out on Russian history after the Kremlin, we don't blame you. It's intense. Head to the east side of the Red Square to **GUM,** an ornate shopping mall that inhabits the former Upper Trading Rows building (Red Square, 3).

Now, it's time to experience one of the more unexpected highlights of Moscow—the subway system. The **subway stations in Moscow** are downright extraordinary. The uniqueness of each station, the cleanliness and the beautiful details, statues and decor, many of which are in a classic art deco style, put almost any subway station in the world to shame. Some standouts include the **Ploshchad Revolyutsii Metro Station** (opened in 1938), **Komsomolskaya Metro Station** (opened in 1952) and **Elektrozavodskaya Metro Station** (opened in 1944).

For a world-renowned performance, head to the **Bolshoi Theatre** (Theatre Square, 1; www.bolshoi.ru/en; ticket prices vary and should be purchased well in advance), which hosts concerts, opera and ballet performances—the ballet troupe is internationally acclaimed. The original theatre was constructed in the 1820s, a concert hall called **Beethoven Hall** opened a century later, and yet another performance venue, the **New Stage** was opened in 2002, adjacent to the historic theatre. Today, you can still attend performances on all three stages.

ST. PETERSBURG

River cruise ships don't dock super close to the center of town in St. Petersburg, either. They dock near the Volodarskiy Most or Volodarskiy Bridge (Neva River at Narodnaya ul.) at what is known as Salt Pier, which is about 10 miles into the heart of St. Petersburg or a 25-minute drive without traffic. Similar to Moscow, a no-traffic scenario is rare.

They say that Moscow is the economic capital of Russia and St. Petersburg is the cultural capital. And it's true: There's something softer and more artsy about St. Petersburg, starting with those captivating canals that wind through the city's network of islands.

Beyond that, St. Petersburg is a treasure trove of museums, palaces and cathedrals, the most famous of which is the **Hermitage Museum** (Palace Square, 2; www.hermitagemuseum.org; tickets cost $7.60 for entrance into the main museum and all its branches), a gargantuan museum that houses more than three million art and culture pieces in buildings that are works of art unto themselves. The centerpiece of the Hermitage is the **Winter Palace,** a former residence of the Romanov tsars, which ruled Russia for about 300 years from the early 1600s to early 1900s.

Tackling the Hermitage can feel like an insurmountable task. Thankfully, most river cruise itineraries will include a comprehensive tour of the museum's highlights—and if you wish to delve in deeper you can do so on your own.

Another feast for the senses is the **Church of the Savior on Spilled Blood** (the name isn't half bad either; Griboyedov Canal Embankment, 2A), a turn-of-the-century church that rivals the Saint Basil's Cathedral in Moscow in terms of colors and ornateness. Similar to Saint Basil's it is also no longer used a place of worship. Instead it houses a **museum of mosaics** (tickets cost $3; and it is operated by the State Museum St. Isaac's Cathedral Museum Complex: eng.cathedral.ru).

From here, you're in a great position to just roam the streets and canals of St. Petersburg a bit, to take in the intriguing architecture and the amalgamation of both exquisite and slightly crumbling buildings.

If you're looking for some evening entertainment, a night at the 156-year-old **Mariinsky Theatre** (Theatre Square, 1; www.mariinsky.ru/en; ticket prices vary and tickets can be purchased online) offers up concerts and ballet performances.

---

highlights OF THE VOLGA

St. Petersburg. Beyond the huge Hermitage, St. Petersburg and its ample waterways is a wonderfully pleasant city to get lost in.

Kizhi. The island village of Kizhi and its wooden houses and churches are a photographer's dream.

Red Square. Moscow's iconic square is reason enough on its own to come to the city.

Key Ports
UGLICH

Uglich, which is about 150 miles north of Moscow, is located right along the Volga River. Passengers will either walk or have a short motorcoach ride for their excursions here.

Top Activity   The Uglich Kremlin: The main attraction in Uglich is the **Uglich Kremlin,** a complex of historical buildings, the largest and most impressive of which is the **Transfiguration Church,** a large yellow structure with green spires and a goldmine of ornate icons within. When the weather is nice, the park grounds of the Uglich Kremlin make for a gratifying stroll.

Off-the-Beaten-Path   Colorful Church: Walk from the Transfiguration Church to the candy-colored **Church of St. Dmitry on the Blood.** While it's hard to take this building seriously with its candy red walls, bright green roofs and its brilliant blue spires, the well-preserved frescoes inside are beyond anything you would have expected from the almost Disney-eque exterior.

KIZHI

While river cruise ships generally dock a short distance from the main attractions of Kizhi village, the walk through the lush and wild landscape on this island in the middle of Lake Onega makes for a refreshing outdoor nature walk.

Top Activity   Visiting Landmark Churches: The UNESCO World Heritage Site **Kizhi Pogost,** which encompasses the two 18th-century wooden churches, the **Church of the Transfiguration** and the **Church of the Intercession,** and the wooden clock tower beside them, are often spotlighted in Volga river cruising brochures because the structures are remarkable (the spires look almost like cascades), both in appearance but also due to the fact they have survived for so long.

Off-the-Beaten-Path   Living Museum: Beyond Kizhi Pogost, the entire village of Kizhi operates as an **open-air museum,** similar to the concept of Colonial Williamsburg, where citizens demonstrate how people once lived on this isolated island. You can expect some impromptu demonstrations of various antiquated trades and houses set up the way they once were. There might be performances of folk music as well. All of this makes for a much more interesting and engaging visit.

MANDROGY

Your vessel will likely pull up within walking distance of the tourist village of Mandrogy.

Top Activity   Living History Museum: So whereas Kizhi is the real-deal open-air museum, **Mandrogy** is the fake deal. It's a replica of a traditional Russian village meant to showcase various crafts and traditions. It sounds gimmicky, and it is. And it's definitely more commercialized than Kizhi. And yet, it's not actually a terrible experience. This is a great place to get some souvenirs, like the hallmark **Matryoshkas** or **Russian nesting dolls,** and they have a great bakery that serves up **tasty sweets and *kvass,*** a Slavic fermented rye beverage, similar to kombucha. And since the area is also intended to be a recreational retreat for Russians and foreigners alike it has a very soothing

RECOMMENDED food & drink

In Russian cuisine, there is no shortage of starch, whether it's in the form of stuffed dumplings such as **pirozhki** or the pancakelike **blini.** Perhaps because of the country's long, cold winters, there is an impressive roster of soups in Russian cooking. You can also expect various varieties of fish and grilled meats, such as **kotlety,** which are cutlets made from minced meat. Pickled salads tend to be the norm for vegetables. Desserts usually consist of bready cakes and actual cakes. And of course there is never any shortage of vodka.

summer camp vibe. So if you can embrace some of the tackiness (a good ability to have in Russia in general), this stop is actually pretty fun.

Off-the-Beaten-Path   Vodka Museum: Along the lines of embracing tackiness, you may waffle on whether or not to pop into the **Vodka Museum** in Mandrogy, and we're here to tell you, go on in. It's worth it for some of the crazy vodka bottles on display and for the classic photo of President Vladimir Putin sporting a Canadian tuxedo.

Optional Add-Ons on the Route

Get your Scandinavia fix. Because St. Petersburg is located on the Baltic Sea, it's not uncommon for Volga river cruises (especially those ending in St. Petersburg) to be combined with **a trip to Scandinavia.** Viking offers a 3-day extension in **Helsinki, Finland,** which is just across the Gulf of Finland from St. Petersburg, with a train to Helsinki, 3 nights in the Radisson Blu Plaza Hotel (or similar), breakfasts, a guided walking tour and the services of a Viking tour guide, starting from $799. And Scenic has an 18-day "Jewels of Russia with Copenhagen" itinerary that kicks off with 3 days in **Copenhagen, Denmark,** priced from $13,490.

U.S. RIVER CRUISES

River cruises on the Columbia and Snake out west and Mississippi river in the south and Midwest give you an insider's view of the American landscape. Here we explore the top attractions.

COLUMBIA & SNAKE

The largest river in the Pacific Northwest, the 1,240-mile-long Columbia River begins in British Columbia's Rocky Mountains and flows out into the Pacific Ocean just west of Astoria, Oregon. The Columbia River forms much of the scenic border between Oregon and Washington, including the breathtaking Columbia River Gorge, which in and of itself makes the trip worthwhile. River cruises along the Columbia River are combined with a portion of the Snake River, which extends the cruises further east towards Idaho.

While most people are familiar with river cruising along the Mississippi River, cruises along the Columbia and Snake are rich with unique local history and culture, and the jaw-dropping views of the Columbia River Valley are not to be missed. Indeed, this fascinating stretch of the Pacific Northwest weaves through beautiful mountainous and forested landscapes, tells a vibrant Native American narrative and essentially follows along much of the final route of the Lewis and Clark westward expedition, which will be an ongoing theme throughout the cruise. Another added draw is the delectable local seafood, such as fresh salmon and crab, and the increasingly popular wines of the region. Not to mention, you get to start or end your cruise in the uber-fun and hip city of Portland.

There are three main players on the Columbia and Snake rivers—the American Queen Steamboat Company, which operates the 223-passenger paddle-wheeler the *American Empress;* American Cruise Lines, which operates two paddle-wheelers, the 120-passenger *Queen of the West* and the 150-passenger *American Pride;* and Un-Cruise, which operates its 88-guest S.S. *Legacy* there.

Ports of Embarkation: Portland, Oregon, & Clarkston, Washington

PORTLAND

Portland sits at the crossroads of the Columbia and Willamette rivers and ships that sail this route either dock right in the heart of Portland along the

The Columbia & Snake Rivers

Willamette River or just across the Columbia River in Vancouver, Wash., which is where the *American Empress* docks for instance. For more information about the destination visit the Portland Oregon Visitors Association at www.travelportland.com.

For some people (and perhaps even for its own residents), Oregon's biggest city has become a bit too cool for its own good. But there's a good deal of justification for the hype surrounding Portland these days. Aside from being a gateway to the incredible nature and scenery of Oregon's Columbia River Valley, Portland is booming with innovative cuisine, craft beers, and a strong sense of self. If you end up staying here for a couple extra days before or after your cruise, you won't be at a loss for restaurants to try and places to explore. While its somewhat easy to get around either walking or using public transportation, especially downtown, if you plan to stay awhile and roam some of the surrounding neighborhoods, you may want to consider renting a car.

It's hard not to lose an entire day alone lost inside the massive **Powell's Books** (1005 W. Burnside St.; ℅ **503/228-4651**) in downtown Portland. If you've worked up an appetite flipping through countless manuscripts, head to the block between SW 9th and 10th Avenues, and SW Alder and SW Washington streets where there is no shortage of food trucks to pick and choose from.

If the weather is nice, head to the **Portland Japanese Garden** (611 SW Kingston Ave.; ℂ **503/223-1321**) and **Hoyt Arboretum** (4000 SW Fairview Blvd.; ℂ **503/865-8733**) for beautiful trails and well-curated landscapes. If it's not (hey, this is the Pacific Northwest after all), check out what exhibits are on at the **Portland Art Museum** (1219 SW Park Ave.; ℂ **503/226-2811;** portlandartmuseum.org).

If you rented that car we mentioned, head to SE Division Street in Portland's Richmond neighborhood where a whole slew of interesting restaurants have cropped up, including **Bollywood Theater** (3010 SE Division St.; ℂ **503/477-6699**), for eclectic Indian fare, after which you should head straight over to **Salt & Straw** (3345 SE Division St.; ℂ **503/208-2054**) for crazy and unique ice cream flavors. In a city with endless solid craft brews, you can't go wrong with any number of local breweries, but we recommend **Ex Novo** (2326 N. Flint Ave.; ℂ **503/894-8251**), a family-friendly and charitable brewery in the slightly more industrial Eliot neighborhood.

CLARKSTON

Most vessels dock at the Port of Clarkston (849 Port Way), a short walking distance into the heart of this small town.

If Portland is the hip and happenin' urban hub along this river cruise route, then Clarkston is on the complete other end of the spectrum as the sleepy small town U.S.A. port with a population of less than 8,000. It sits across the Snake River from Lewiston, Idaho, and these twin cities are in the heart of Lewis and Clark country (Lewiston and Clarkston, get it?).

For a bit of history, and don't worry you'll be given plenty of recaps throughout the cruise, the early-19th-century Lewis and Clark Expedition, led by Meriwether Lewis and William first, was the first American-led expedition to cross what is now the western United States.

While Clarkston was named for Clark, neither of the two explorers actually ever visited the Clarkston side of the river. Nevertheless this region is full of Lewis and Clark lore.

Beyond history, one of the main draws of Clarkston is that it serves as a gateway to **Hells Canyon** a 10-mile wide canyon along the Snake River that hugs the borders of Oregon, Washington and Idaho. As the deepest river gorge in North America, Hells Canyon offers ample opportunities for recreational activities such as river rafting and hiking.

Key Ports
ASTORIA, OREGON

Your ship will dock just beyond the Columbia River Maritime Museum, which is located right along the waterfront at 1792 Marine Dr., walking distance to the center of town—though it's a pretty good walk.

Situated at the mouth of the Columbia River, Astoria, Ore., is the oldest American settlement west of the Rocky Mountains. It is located about 100

highlights OF THE COLUMBIA & SNAKE RIVERS

Astoria. A former fur trading hub, this lovable port town is now home to the Columbia River Maritime Museum and a burgeoning arts scene.

Vista House. It's hard to appreciate the majestic beauty of the Columbia River Gorge solely from the vantage point of water level. The Vista House in Crown Point, Ore., offers a breathtaking view overlooking the entire valley.

Multnomah Falls. If your river cruise line offers an excursion to this dreamy two-tiered cascade, don't ask questions, just sign up for it. You can thank us later.

miles northwest of Portland, so river cruises will travel to Astoria for a day then backtrack back through Portland before heading further east. But most passengers will find it's worth the 200-mile round-trip journey.

Astoria's history dates back thousands of years when Clatsop Indians inhabited the lands that are now known as Astoria. And in 1805, Lewis and Clark led their expedition through the town and spent the winter at Fort Clatsop. Today, Astoria is part industrial port city, part quaint and artsy port town.

Top Activity   The Columbia River Maritime Museum (1792 Marine Dr., admission is $12; ℗ **503/325-2323;** www.crmm.org): Located right on the bank of the river, the Columbia River Maritime Museum is a treasure trove of nautical history including an impressive collection of vessels, as well as paintings, clothing, weapons and instruments used in maritime operations.

Off-the-Beaten-Path   You've taken a stroll through Astoria's more official maritime past at the Maritime Museum, now sift through some of its less official artifacts at **Vintage Hardware** (101 15th St.; ℗ **503/325-1313;** astoriavintagehardware.com). Just be sure that whatever you buy isn't too big to bring back home with you.

STEVENSON, WASHINGTON

Although it's located on the Washington side of the river, Stevenson actually serves as the jumping off point from which to visit some of the most scenic attractions in the Columbia River Valley, to which you will likely be bused as part of an excursion by your river cruise line. Ships dock in the heart of the city just off Russell Ave.

Top Activity   City Tour: One of the most impressive waterfalls along the Historic Columbia River Highway is **Multnomah Falls** (53000 Historic Columbia River Hwy., Corbett, Or.), the highest waterfall in Oregon with a two-tiered 620-foot drop. And while Multnomah is definitely the most memorable and impressive, the 70-mile Historic Columbia River Highway, which runs from Troutdale to The Dalles, is truly a journey from one magnificent cascade to the next.

Off-the-Beaten-Path   Columbia Gorge: An ode to the centuries of history and life in the Columbia River Valley, the **Columbia Gorge Interpretive Center Museum** (990 SW Rock Creek Dr.; ℗ **509/427-8211;** www.columbiagorge.org)

documents everything from the lives of the Native American tribes that once occupied the region, to the timber and fishing industries that once thrived here. It's a great way to really get into the spirit of the destination and its rich and complicated past.

RICHLAND, WASHINGTON

You dock near the center of town in Richland, which constitutes one of three neighboring cities known as the Tri-Cities (the other two are Kennewick and Pasco). More information about the Tri-Cities can be found at www.visittri-cities.com. A Visitor Center is located at Richland City Hall, 505 Swift Blvd.

Top Activity   It's time to try some of these Pacific Northwest wines everyone keeps raving about. Head to the scenic **Red Mountain Viticulture Area** (redmountainava.com/theava) for tastings and wine pairings from regional producers. American Queen Steamboat Company offers this as a premium shore excursion for $69, per person. Un-Cruise offers an entire wine-themed sailing with several wine excursions, including in nearby Walla Walla, Wash.

Off-the-Beaten-Path   Head Underground: Opt for an excursion to Pendleton, Ore., 75 miles south of Richland (and yes, this is the town where the wool manufacturer Pendleton Woolen Mills was founded) for a **Pendleton Underground Tour** (www.pendletonundergroundtours.org), a guided tour through a network of basalt-rock tunnels under the city.

Optional Add-Ons on the Route

The Pacific Northwest can be so many different things to different people. For some it's lush forests and mountains, while others come to experience the vibrant Native American culture. Still others are consumed by the history and the links to the Lewis and Clark expedition. Indeed, there are many facets to the region. Here are some experiences that, whether or not they are included in your cruise, might add to or enhance your Columbia and Snake River journey in ways you may not have expected.

The **Western Antique Aeroplane and Automobile Museum, or WAAAM** (1600 Air Museum Rd., Hood River, OR; admission $14; ✆ **541/308-1600;** www.waaamuseum.org) features an over-the-top collection of vintage cars, motorcycles and airplanes and makes for a great excursion from The Dalles, Oregon. And if you're lucky, they'll even let you take a spin in one of their classic cars.

9

U.S. RIVER CRUISES | Columbia & Snake

RECOMMENDED food & drink

Fresh salmon, seafood and Pacific Northwest craft beers and local wines are the name of the game in this part of the world. Expect to find salmon of all kinds, from cold smoked lox to grilled or baked entrees on the menu. Seafood, too, finds its way into many of the dishes here, including tasty Dungeness crab. If seafood isn't your thing, don't worry, Pacific Northwesterners eat and serve a wide variety of meat and produce, with a strong emphasis on locally sourced products.

Are you totally sucked in to the whole Lewis and Clark saga yet? Well, whether or not you are, you will be after you visit, in Pasco, Washington, the **Interpretive Center at the Sacajawea State Park in Washington** (2503 Sacajawea Park Rd., admission free; www.stateparks.com/sacajawea_state_park_in_washington.html), which brings all the details of the Lewis and Clark expedition to light, and also houses a large collection of Native American artifacts. Sacajawea State Park is often offered as an excursion from the Richland area, so check your river cruise line's brochure to see whether it is.

LOWER MISSISSIPPI

(Due to the breadth and diversity of America's longest river we have divided the river into two parts. See also Upper Mississippi below).

When you think Mississippi River you may think Mark Twain and Huckleberry Finn, sleepy river towns and opulent paddlewheel-powered riverboats. Even today, views along "The Big Muddy" can take you back to a quieter time—serving up, what feels like not only the heartland but the heartbeat of America.

Surging north to south, the legendary waterway is one big river, 2,350 miles and the fourth longest river in the world—cutting down the middle of America. The name Mississippi derived from a Native Americans living on the shores (from either the Ojibwe or Algonquin tribes), and the word "Messipi, or "great river."

Though the geographic denominators for the 954-mile Lower Mississippi stretch are Cairo Point, Illinois to the Gulf of Mexico, river cruise itineraries, including on classic steamboats, follow the river from Memphis down to New Orleans, or the reverse, or do a shorter stretch round-trip from New Orleans. One surprise on this stretch may be it's not as muddy, not ferociously rolling as you might think from Mark Twain's depictions in *The Adventures of Tom Sawyer* and *The Adventures of Huckleberry Finn.* Twain lived upriver in Missouri.

While there have been earlier efforts to get more tourists onto the Mississippi for overnight cruises, there have been good times and bad in this regard. For a few years between 2009 and 2012 there were very few cruises (and none by paddle-wheelers) on the waterway. The river of late has seen a popular resurgence. Options now include exploration of the Lower Mississippi and Upper Mississippi by American Cruise Lines and American Steamboat Company. Europe cruise giant Viking River Cruises has plans to debut a version of its "longships" on the Mississippi in 2018. The cruises keep vacationers active, taking them to iconic river sights, towns and cities with a focus on Southern culture (classic and modern), antebellum mansions and Civil War battlefields, with shipboard historians filling in dramatic details. On excursions, local guides talk race, way of life, and floods (you may see areas abandoned or rebuilt as a result of Hurricane Katrina in 2005); some excursions may offer opportunity to sample local culture in the form of Cajun food, art and music.

Trivia Fact

Seven rivers in the Mississippi River system (www.nps.gov/miss) can handle boat traffic: the Atchafalaya, Arkansas, Ohio, Tennessee, Cumberland, Missouri, and Illinois.

The Mississippi River

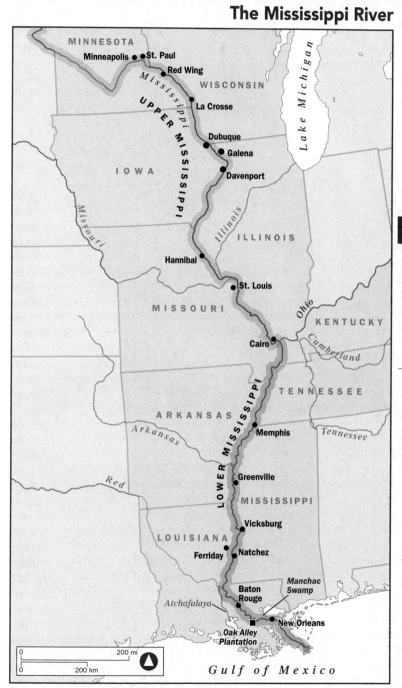

MINNESOTA

Minneapolis ● ●St. Paul

Red Wing

Mississippi

WISCONSIN

La Crosse

UPPER MISSISSIPPI

Lake Michigan

Dubuque

Galena

I O W A

Davenport

Missouri

Illinois

ILLINOIS

Hannibal

St. Louis

MISSOURI

Ohio

KENTUCKY

Cairo

Cumberland

LOWER MISSISSIPPI

TENNESSEE

ARKANSAS

Arkansas

Tennessee

Memphis

Red

Greenville

MISSISSIPPI

Vicksburg

LOUISIANA

Ferriday

Natchez

Atchafalaya

Baton Rouge

Manchac Swamp

New Orleans

Oak Alley Plantation

0 ——————— 200 mi
0 ——————— 200 km

Gulf of Mexico

The season is "year-round," but there are fewer cruises in the summer than in the spring and fall high seasons and there's a reason for that—the lines usually move their ships north to avoid super summer's super-hot temperatures and mosquitoes. There are also few cruises in winter beyond holiday sailings.

While the waters tend to be calm, as recent history has shown (Hurricane Katrina most notably), New Orleans and other parts of the Lower Mississippi are not immune to flooding, which can wreak havoc with itineraries during Hurricane Season, June through November (with the peak of hurricane season in September and October).

The lines take slightly different approaches to their itineraries. American Cruise Line provides a choice of complimentary excursions in every port and for-a-fee premium excursions in many; while American Queen Steamboat has the option of a continuing Hop-On-Hop-Off bus service allowing guests to visit and explore key attractions at leisure, as well as premium excursions for an additional fee.

Note: Theme cruises are popular on the Mississippi, including music (Elvis, Dixie) and Civil War history sailings. See our Theme Cruise chapter.

Ports of Embarkation: New Orleans & Memphis

MEMPHIS

The Beale Street Landing, where the American Queen docks, a short walk from downtown attractions, or you can take a shuttle. American Cruise Line docks at the Thalia Street Wharf (1350 Port of New Orleans Place) near restaurants and other attractions. For more information visit the Memphis Convention & Visitor Bureau website, www.memphistravel.com.

The "Blues City" and "Birthplace of Rock 'n' Roll is of course itself a major tourist destination for those interested in music in many forms, history, cuisine and Southern culture and, well, ducks—at the **Peabody Memphis,** one of the city's most popular attractions are the famous Peabody Ducks parading in the Grand Lobby. Must-do sights include **Beale Street** (and the Elvis statue), with a gander at the infamous **Sun Studio.** Don't miss the informative interactive exhibits at the **National Civil Rights Museum** (450 Mulberry St.; ✆ **901/521-9699;** www.civilrightsmuseum.org), located in The Lorraine Motel, the tragic site of the assassination of Dr. Martin Luther King in 1968, and a symbol for change in America. At the **Stax Museum** (926 E. McLemore Ave.; ✆ **901/942-7685;** www.staxmuseum.com; adult admission $13), where Otis Redding, Aretha Franklin, and The Rolling Stones recorded, you can learn how music changed the racial divide. Outside the city, you can get to **Elvis' Graceland** (✆ **800/238-2000;** www.graceland.com) either on tours offered for-a-fee by the cruise line or on your own by car, bus or taxi (American Cruise Lines offers Graceland as a Signature tour for $75 per person).

NEW ORLEANS

You dock at the Riverwalk or the Thalia Street Wharf, a short walk to Café Du Monde and the French Quarter. Go online for the New Orleans official guide, www.neworleansonline.com (✆ **800/672-6124**).

highlights OF THE LOWER MISSISSIPPI

The Oak Alley. The plantation looks straight out of *Gone with the Wind.* It's an iconic sight on the Mississippi.

Vicksburg National Military Park. Touring the battlefields is a must for history

and Civil War enthusiasts (and a poignant reminder of war for everyone else.

Natchez. This small, historic Mississippi city is full of southern charm and pre-war and antebellum mansions, many open for tours.

Your cruise may include a hotel night in the "Big Easy," but if not you'll want to do yourself a favor and spend a day or two absorbing the city's food, culture, and arts attractions. Plan to spend time exploring the historic and slightly risqué **French Quarter** including world-famous Bourbon Street, where you'll find shops, museums, jazz clubs and opportunity to sample Cajun cuisine. Don't miss a visit to the city's **French Market,** the country's oldest public market, for café au lait (coffee and chicory with half and half) and beignets (the state donut of Louisiana) at the landmark **Café du Monde** (800 Decatur St.; ☎ **504/581-2914;** www.cafedumonde.com), a coffee stand open since 1862. Among the city's 45 museums, we highly recommend a visit to the **National World War II Museum** (945 Magazine St.; ☎ **504/528-1944;** www.national ww2museum.org; admission from $24 for adults, $21 seniors, $16 students and military, free for World War II veterans), the country's official museum of the war, showcasing America's role both abroad and on the Home Front.

Key Ports
OAK ALLEY, LOUISIANA
Your ship will dock at the Oak Alley Plantation. You can walk to the main house (www.oakalleyplantation.com).

The walk from the shore to the Big House of this iconic Louisiana sugarcane plantation will stay in your memory—you pass under a quarter-mile canopy of 300-year-old oak trees. You'll tour the beautifully restored antebellum mansion and may have the option of visiting the barn which houses a collection of antique cars. We highly recommend sipping a mint julep on the porch.

VICKSBURG, MISSISSIPPI
The Levee Street Landing is near the Washington Street Shopping District, and a short walk from dining and casinos, as well. Vicksburg CVB (☎ **800/221-3536;** www.visit-vicksburg.com).

Top Activity   Vicksburg National Military Park (www.nps.gov/vick): This 1,800-acre national park is a must-see is for those really interested in Civil War history. Tours start at the visitor center where you can view artifacts including Confederate swords and uniforms. There's also a film on the 1863 Siege of Vicksburg, which is worth viewing as it sets the stage for a 16-mile drive to visit Union and Confederate siege lines and tombstones and markers conveying sobering statistics. A poignant recent addition is the Mississippi African American Monument, honoring black soldiers who served during

9

U.S. RIVER CRUISES

Lower Mississippi

RECOMMENDED food & drink

In New Orleans, sample Creole standards such as gumbo, crawfish *etouffee* and jambalaya, go for a variety of the favored sandwich, the po' boy, indulge in Gulf oysters (including Oysters Rockefeller which was invented at the classic Big Easy restaurant Antoine's, 713 St. Louis St.) and check out the increasingly lauded new cuisine scene. Beer lovers with find craft options including from the Abita Brewery in Covington, La. Cocktail lovers will want to go for the official state cocktail, the Sazerac (rye whiskey, Peychaud's Bitters, a touch of sugar, a hint of Herbsaint anise liqueur, and a tiny bit of lemon oil). Later in your cruise, as you explore the Mississippi, you'll have opportunity to sip mint juleps and dine on Southern standards as fried chicken and corn bread. In Memphis, do the BBQ (either dry, spice-rubbed ribs or sloppy-wet pulled pork) but save room for Soul Food such as fried catfish, black-eyed peas and sweet potato pie, washed down with craft beer such as the creations of the local Wiseacre Brewing Company (their Tiny Bomb American pilsner won a bronze medal at the 2014 Great American Beer Festival).

Vicksburg Campaign. Also on display is the U.S.S. Cairo, an ironclad gunboat recovered from the bottom of the Yazoo River (north of Vicksburg).

Off-the-Beaten-Path The **Biedenharn Museum of Coca-Cola Memorabilia,** 1107 Washington St. (© **601/638-6514;** www.biedenharncoca-cola museum.com/building.htm), is a fun, kitschy stop. Coca-Cola was first bottled in the building by the Biedenharn family in this very building in 1894, and the memorabilia-filled museum functions as a shrine of sorts—complete with an old-fashioned soda fountain and plenty of red-and-white memorabilia. Admission: $3.50 adults, $2.50 kids 6-12, kids under 6 free.

NATCHEZ

The city rises on a bluff from the water. If you don't want a work out and are not on a tour, you may want to take a bus up the hill (American Queen operates a hop-on, hop-off bus to get you to attractions).

Top Activity **City Tour:** This charming city, the oldest in Mississippi, is our favorite place to poke around on the route, including in boutiques, and admiring the wealth of antebellum homes. The **Natchez Visitor Reception Center,** 640 S. Canal St. (© **800/647-6724;** www.visitnatchez.com), provides a great introduction, with a film, and also a decent gift shop. If you're thinking mint julep, stop by the lush grounds of the 1859 Stanton Hall mansion where you'll find the **Carriage House Restaurant,** 401 High St. (© **601/445-5151;** www. stantonhall.com), open since 1926 (they have decent fried chicken too).

Off-the-Beaten-Path **Rosalie Mansion,** 100 Orleans St. (© **601/446-5676;** http://rosaliemansion.com): This bluff-top, Federalist-style pre-Civil War mansion is packed with authentic antiques and operated as a museum by the Daughters of the American Revolution. Tours are $12, $8 for under age 12.

BATON ROUGE

You dock in the heart of the city, between the Louisiana Art and Science Museum and the USS Kidd Veterans Memorial, a short walk from the Baton Rouge River Center and downtown attractions. For more info on surrounding attractions, head to the Baton Rouge Area Convention and Visitors Bureau (✆ **800/LA-ROUGE** [527-6843]; www.visit batonrouge.com).

Top Activity   **Louisiana State Capitol,** 900 N. Third St., Baton Rouge (www. nps.gov/nr/travel/louisiana/cap.htm). Sometimes referred to as the "new" capitol building, this dramatic, 34-story Art Deco structure is well worth a visit. The building was the brainchild of Governor Huey Long, and opened in 1932. The site of his assassination in 1935, it's the tallest state capitol building in the U.S. In addition to seeing the wonderful Art Deco details (including sculptures showing state history), you can get a great view of the Mississippi River from the visitors' observation deck on the 27th floor. Admission is free. When the legislature is in session you may be able to watch committee hearings on the ground floor.

Off-the-Beaten-Path   The **USS Kidd Veterans Memorial and Museum** (305 S. River St.; ✆ **225/342-1942;** www.usskidd.com) is a Fletcher-class destroyer now moored in downtown Baton Rouge as a memorial to those who served in the armed forces. Open to visitors, the ship has been restored to look like it did in 1945, with some 50 spaces on view. Museum displays include a P-40 Warhawk fighter plane. Admission is $10 adults, $8 veterans and seniors, $6 kids. It takes about 1½ hours to do the guided ship tour (you visit the museum section on your own).

Optional Add-Ons on the Route

Optional excursions include American Queen Steamboat's **B.B. King Tour,** from the port of Greenville to the modest brick Delta town of Indianola to learn about the legendary "King of the Blues," who passed away in May 2015. Included is a tour of the **B.B. King Museum** and **Delta Interpretive Center,** including a live, on-site gospel concert. As part of the organized tour you later hear local Blues performers at **Club Ebony,** an iconic southern juke joint King purchased in 2008.

Other add-ons to consider include a trip into the **Manchac Swamp,** for a swamp boat ride through mossy Cyprus trees you're likely to spot critters including such as nutria, ibis, turtle, herons, raccoons and egrets, and may get to pet a baby alligator.

Place Your Bets

For those who want to take a chance, there are several opportunities to hit easily accessible **casinos** on the Mississippi route, including in Vicksburg and Natchez. On some itineraries you also visit Greenville, home to the **Trop Casino,** 199 North Lakefront Road, Greenville, MS (✆ **800/878-1777;** www. tropgreenville.com) operated by Tropicana Casinos (your ship docks adjacent to the casino).

For a fascinating looking at cotton farming book an excursion to **Frogmore** (in Ferriday, La.). Touring the 1,800-acre farm you'll learn both about the life of plantation workers of the 1800s and modern cotton production. A walking tour includes slave cabins, among 18 restored antebellum structures, and focuses on the daily life on a cotton plantation and how that life was impacted by the Civil War. A rare original steam cotton gin is on display, and you'll also learn about today's computerized ginning.

UPPER MISSISSIPPI

From its one-time glacial origins at Lake Itasca, Minnesota to its juncture with the Ohio River near Cairo, Illinois, the Upper Mississippi laps at the shores of no fewer than five states in the American heartland. While its lower counterpart brims with Civil War heritage, epic plantations and Southern charm, the Upper Mississippi more than compensates with the variety and scope of its scenery and fascinating history. Its 1,250-mile length beckons with dense foliage, open prairies, limestone cliffs, three national parks, historic river towns and, of course, the lore of Mark Twain.

For a few bleak years, after the 2008 collapse of Majestic America Line, cruising here had all but dried up. Today, its waters churn with new vigor, thanks to rivals American Queen Steamboat Company and American Cruise Lines, both of which operate traditionally styled paddle-wheelers. Meanwhile, Viking River Cruises has announced plans to join the fray and will most likely put a new, unique spin on the experience.

Navigating the Upper Mississippi used to be fraught with rapids, hazards and wildly varying water levels but those days are long gone, thanks to 29 locks that dam its waters and lower or raise ships a total of 404 feet along its length.

With cosmopolitan St. Paul or St. Louis as starting and ending points, cruises in the region operate between July and October, when the weather and river conditions are most accommodating. Towards the end of that relatively brief season, the Upper Mississippi is at its grandest, painted in a spectrum of fiery Fall colors.

Key stops include Hannibal, Missouri, the birthplace of Samuel Clemons (Mark Twain) and semi-fictional home of Tom Sawyer, Huckleberry Finn and Becky Thatcher (all based on real life characters); Davenport, Iowa, voted one of America's most livable cities and home to numerous music festivals; Clinton, Iowa, known for its agriculture and lumber industries; Dubuque, Iowa, one of the oldest west-of-the-Mississippi settlements and rife with Victorian architecture; La Crosse, Wisconsin, celebrated for its breweries and river views and Red Wing, Minnesota, an artists' haven known for its ceramics industry.

In addition to the port visits, time spent cruising the busy river (on some American Queen Steamboat voyages, there is a full day of river cruising) provides a fascinating panorama of bridges, locks and hard-working tugs with grain, ore and cargo barges in tow.

Starry nights on deck can be especially enchanting, as your riverboat's searchlights dance through swarms of fireflies, moths and other fauna, illuminating oncoming vessels, while searching for potential navigation hazards and river markers.

Ports of Embarkation: St. Louis & St. Paul

ST. LOUIS

The St. Louis Port Authority pier is at 500 Leonor K. Sullivan Blvd. Find tourist information at Explore St. Louis, www.explorestourism.com.

First time visitors to The Gateway City tend to be pleasantly surprised, if not a bit overwhelmed by its myriad world class attractions, including its botanical gardens, the vast Forest Park, numerous art museums, the Science Center, the Anheuser-Busch Brewery, the Missouri History Museum and, of course, the famous arch. **St. Louis Gateway Arch** (✆ **877/982-1410;** www.gateway arch.com): Finnish architect Eero Saarinen's stunningly beautiful, 1965-built Gateway Arch is the largest manmade monument in the United States, towering 630 feet over the Mississippi waterfront. The steel and concrete arch was commissioned to commemorate Thomas Jefferson's vision of the United States' westward expansion. In one of its complimentary tours, American Cruise Line includes the tram ride to its enclosed observation platform, which provides a spectacular view of the river and downtown St. Louis. Steps away, there is the **St. Louis Courthouse,** perhaps best known for its role in the pivotal Dred-Scott case of 1857.

American Queen Steamboat itineraries that begin or end in St. Louis include an overnight at a deluxe hotel. American Queen guests have time to explore on their own or take The Gateway City Tour (5.5 hours/$69), which visits historic **Laclede's Landing,** a 9-block riverfront district with shops and eateries before heading to the **Cathedral Basilica of St. Louis,** where 84,000-square-feet of mosaics depict scenes from the Bible. Time to dine is provided in the Ballpark Village or Central West End near Forest Park before a visit to the Busch Brewery stables prior to arrival at Alton, Illinois, where guests embark the American Queen. On cruises ending in St. Louis, American Cruise Lines provides two complimentary excursions to choose from, the City Tour of St. Louis that explores several downtown neighborhoods, Forest Park and the historic stables of the Busch Brewery or The Arch Experience, which

highlights OF THE UPPER MISSISSIPPI

St. Louis Arch. The stunning structure is the largest manmade monument in the United States, towering 630 feet over the Mississippi waterfront.

Mark Twain Caves. The author/humorist spent is boyhood exploring in these

caves, a Registered National Historic Landmark since 1972.

The Fenelon Place Elevator. Dubuque's funicular railway is the shortest and steepest of its kind in the world.

RECOMMENDED food & drink

In St. Louis, make sure to try the famous toasted ravioli—deep-fried ravioli with parmesan and a side of marinara creating decadent gooey, crunchy goodness. Barbecued pork steaks in sauce are another favorite. Fitz's Bottling Company does amazing root beer. Craft beer lovers will want to check out Schlafy. Go with the local pork product in Iowa, including fried and served on a bun. Minneapolis/St. Paul are world-class foodie cities, but if you want to go local try the state fish, Walleye.

includes a tram ride to the top of the arch and a visit to the **Museum of Westward Expansion.**

ST. PAUL

Lambert's Landing is at 180 Shepard Rd. Find tourist information at Visit Saint Paul, www.visitsaintpaul.com, ✆ **800/627-6101.**

St. Paul and its neighbor Minneapolis are busting cities filled with fine restaurants, art galleries, parks, charming architecture and museums. American Queen Steamboat sells post cruise stays and both American Queen and American Cruise Lines offer tours on cruises that end in St. Paul as part of the transfer from Red Rock (where the ship berths) to St. Paul Airport. American Cruise Line provides an included walking tour past the mansions on Summit Avenue and a visit to Mounds Park overlooking the city. American Queen's The St. Paul City Tour (5 hours/$69), takes in **Minnehaha Falls,** the **Minneapolis Stone Arch Bridge,** and a drive past both cities' key attractions as well as a visit to the **Wabasha Street Caves,** once the hideout of gangsters and now an event hall. The tour concludes at a hotel or the Minneapolis-St. Paul International Airport.

Key Ports

HANNIBAL, MISSOURI

The Hannibal CVB has a free visitors guide you can download at visithannibal.com or ✆ **573/221-2477.**

Top Activity **Mark Twain Caves,** Hannibal, Missouri (✆ **800/527-0304;** www.marktwaincave.com): Both a natural and folkloric wonder, at Mark Twain Caves you can follow Twain's boyhood steps through the first cave to be opened to visitors way back in 1886. One of the stops on American Queen Steamboat's walk-on-walk-off tour, admission ($19) is extra. A proper visit takes 55 minutes and a light, waterproof jacket is recommended.

Off-the-Beaten-Path Known as "America's Hometown," many of Hannibal's key attractions are just steps away from the boat. American offers two complimentary excursions, a narrated trolley tour or admission to the Mark Twain Museum, while American Queen's Hop-On-Hop-Off shuttle calls at most of the town's highlights. Allow some spare time to climb up

Cardiff Hill to the lighthouse for its view of the river bend, and visit Becky's (as in Becky Thatcher) Butterfly Garden.

DUBUQUE, IOWA

The Iowa Welcome Center is located downtown at 280 Main St. (© **800/798-8844;** www.traveldubuque.com).

Top Activity National Mississippi River Museum and Aquarium (© **800/ 226-3369;** www.rivermuseum.com): The problem with Dubuque, Iowa's oldest town (established in 1833), is that there are just too many attractions for one visit, making it one of the richest and most popular stops along the Upper Mississippi. American Cruise Lines provides a can excursion to the National Mississippi River Museum and Aquarium, where interactive exhibits recount the trials and tribulations of its pioneers and earliest settlers. In addition, there are six large aquariums teeming with local wildlife.

Off-the-Beaten-Path The Fenelon Place Elevator (www.dbq.com/ fenplco): Despite its name, the Fenelon Place Elevator is actually a funicular railway that is considered the shortest and steepest of its kind in the world. The 296-foot-long railway, which is listed on the National Register of Historic Places, takes its passengers up a height of 189 feet from Forth Street to Fenelon Place, where there are views overlooking the river, historic Dubuque and three states. Rides cost $1.50 one-way, $3 round-trip (kids are half price and those under age 5 are free).

REDWING, MINNESOTA

Find information at the Red Wing Visitors & Convention Bureau website, www.redwing. org, or call © **651/385-5934.**

Top Activity Red Wing is 1 of just 12 towns in the U.S. featured on the National Trust for Historic Preservation's "Distinctive Destinations" list. Now a favorite get-away for residents of Minneapolis/St. Paul, it was founded in the 1850s by settlers who came to farm the fertile wheat plains nearby. Today it's best known for tanning (the leather kind) and shoe making as well as its world-renowned pottery. In addition to countless art galleries and antique shops, it is home to some 38 parks, many nestled among scenic bluffs overlooking the Mississippi. It's a fun place to explore on your own.

an alternate side trip TO GALINA, ILLINOIS

Not that there isn't plenty to do in Dubuque, but for those who have "been there, done that", it is well worth taking a taxi some 8 miles across the river to the town of Galena, which was established when Illinois was admitted to the Union in 1818. Of its hundreds of restored early-19th-century homes, 85 percent are on the National Register of Historic Places. The town has a wonderfully well-preserved and friendly Main Street with shops and restaurants and a number of homes that are open for tours.

There are also less common Mississippi River cruises that explore the tributaries, including the Ohio River through the heartland. You can cruise on American Cruise Lines on a 1-week itinerary in June or early July between Memphis and Cincinnati, including John James Audubon's hometown of Henderson, Kentucky and Louisville, which such popular sights as Churchill Downs and the Kentucky Derby Museum and the Louisville Slugger factory, where the famous baseball bats are produced—plus Clermont, Kentucky, where a Jim Beam distillery tour includes stopping by the Small Batch tasting room. American Queen Steamboat Company has 9-day cruises between St. Louis and Cincinnati including a July cruise that's themed on following Kentucky's Bourbon Trail

9 Optional Add-Ons on the Route

American Queen Steamboat tour options include opportunity to visit a **six-generation cattle farm** in Clinton, Iowa, for a behind-the-scenes look at livestock and American agriculture. Another tour gets you to Wasbasha, Minnesota, to observe and learn about American bald eagles at the **National Eagle Center.** American Cruise Lines' tour options include, in Missouri, a visit to **Trail of Tears State Park,** commemorating a tragic chapter in American history when 9 of the 13 Cherokee groups being relocated to Oklahoma were forced to cross the Mississippi River during harsh winter conditions in 1838 and 1839, with thousands dying in the process (paintings, maps and artifacts tell the story at the visitors' center).

EXOTIC RIVER CRUISES

River cruise lines, knowing many of their guests will like the experience and become repeaters, are studying maps and looking to spot every opportunity to expand. They are also hoping to attract new and more intrepid cruisers by offering cruises on such legendary waterways as the Mekong and Irrawaddy. But be aware the cruises in this chapter are very different than what you will experience in Europe. Yes, you will enjoy all the comforts of a nice hotel, but when you step off the ship you will land, in some cases, in muddy, impoverished villages, before returning to your ship for a fancy meal and a fluffy bed. It's a fascinating and to some a haunting dichotomy (though we like to believe tourism can in some way improve the lives of locals).

When visiting the countries in this chapter, we highly recommend you visit see a travel doctor to inquire about pills for malaria, any shots you might need and such (find information at wwwnc. cdc.gov/travel). Prone to stomach upset, Fran also puts herself on a regimen of Pepto-Bismol just in case (the CDC has recommendations in this regard at wwwnc.cdc.gov/travel/yellowbook/2016/ the-pre-travel-consultation/travelers-diarrhea). We also recommend you read any travel warnings at the U.S. Department of State website (www.state.gov/travel/).

PERUVIAN AMAZON

Experiencing the Peruvian Amazon firsthand, you quickly learn it matters not whether the mighty river, which runs more than 4,000 miles from the high Andes to the Atlantic, is in fact the longest river in the world—there is dispute with the Nile. In the Upper Amazon you are in one of the most isolated places in the world, and it's eerily beautiful, and full of amazing birds and other wildlife, and that's the experience you pay for.

Your cruise will begin with a flight from Lima to Iquitos, a city surrounded by water in Peru's Northeast. From there you'll board your ship, either in Iquitos or in the small city of Nauta, some 1¾ hours away over a bumpy jungle road. Every ship that explores here is small—the largest only 44 passengers.

The Amazon River

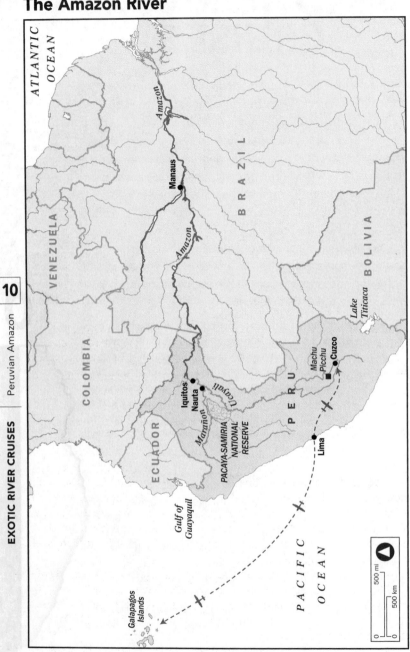

The area where you'll spend most of your time is the rivers, estuaries and lakes of the Pacaya-Samira National Reserve, a flooded forest covering millions of acres at the headwaters of the Amazon basin, some 2,400 miles from the Atlantic. You reach the actual Amazon where the Ucayali & Marañon rivers merge.

Before you imagine yourself in an adventurer in a canoe and start conjuring scenes from Teddy Roosevelt's "River of Doubt," rest assured you're Amazon trek will be more akin to "glamping." Your ship will have large cabins with picture windows, hot showers, good food and other creature comforts and serve as a basecamp for carefully guided exploration.

Taking you into the jungle will be naturalist guides from the Amazon, expert at explaining and sighting all sorts of surprises. Most days your included excursions will involve taking a cushioned seat in a skiff or *panga* (small boat) to head into the jungle, binoculars at the ready.

Cruising the legendary Amazon River and its tributaries brings you into one of the most unusual and bio-diverse places on the planet, a tropical rainforest region where 1 in 10 known species on earth can be found.

You'll find yourself having such experiences as being entertained by a group of monkeys following each other across tree limbs and screeching from treetops. You'll surprisingly easily spot protected Amazon River Dolphins in various shades of pink and gray and you'll see enough birds to keep an ornithologist enthralled. Each time your guide says "look" you may find your heart thumping. The jungle has many surprises.

Anacondas and red-eyed caimans float below the water's murky surface. Birds in colors that range from black to day-glow blue fly or sit in trees above. Focus your binoculars on that fuzzy ball high in the tree and you'll realize it's a three-toed sloth. When hanging logs or vines get in the way your guide may take out a machete to chop a path. You are in the middle of nowhere but know you are in capable hands.

Your cruise will also involve some relatively easy (though often muddy) hiking. Early morning exploration is likely, as the wildlife is most active at dawn and dusk.

You may have come to see birds and monkeys, and you'll find many species—this is a great place for birders to work on their Life List. But you'll know you're not in Kansas anymore when you hear, for instance, about the weird fish. There are piranhas in the Amazon, but fish with sharp teeth are just the beginning of the oddities. You'll hear about, if not see, fish that "walk" in the flooded forest, leaping into trees to eat wood and nuts, fish with hard-shell armor and even giant, air-breathing fish.

You will hear tweets, twerps, cracks, creaks, buzzes. The Amazon. Even the word sounds exotic, sexy—A-ma-zon. The cacophony of sounds made by birds, frogs, crickets, monkeys and others is so intense—especially at sunrise and sunset—that the forest sounds at times like a tape track is playing or a generator is running.

The cruises here are year-round and there is rarely a period with no rain— you are, after all, exploring a rainforest. But the area of exploration has drastic differentials in water level based on time of year. There are advantages to both the wet and dry season.

The official wet season is December to April, when many areas will be flooded, and you may spot fish able to leap into the waterlogged treetops to eat wood and nuts (there is such thing as air-breathing fish in the Amazon). The wet season is cooler and you'll have the advantage of your ship being able to get farther into the jungle.

The dry season is May to November, when you'll see the riverbanks and tree trunks rising into the sky and have better access to jungle hiking paths but you may find yourself hiking in 90-plus degree temperatures. Mosquitoes are always around (worse in wet season) so be prepared. The river lines typically provide rain ponchos, mud boots and insect repellent.

Be aware that on these cruises wildlife is very much the focus and becomes a bonding experience and a bit of a competitive sport—"Did you see the tamarind?" and "What, you mean you missed the howler monkeys?" is a typical dinner table discussion. While you will visit an isolated village or two, culture in the Upper Amazon is more allusive.

Note: Visiting a travel medical clinic before your trip for malaria pills and various shots is recommended.

10 Port of Embarkation: Iquitos
IQUITOS

Cruises embark from the city. There's a municipal tourism booth at the airport and a helpful tourism information office on the north side of Plaza de Armas. For tourist information visit www.peru.travel/en-us/.

Surrounded by water, including the Nanay, Italya, and Amazon rivers, Iquitos is a city of a half million people that can't be reached by road. Founded by Jesuit missionaries in 1757, and declared capital of Loreto (Peru's largest but least populated region) in 1840, Iquitos retains a unique tropical atmosphere, basically because it's so close to the rainforest and isolated from the rest of Peru. Rubber was the booming trade here in the late 1800s and early 1900s, and it shows. The riverfront along the Amazon is a long boulevard, **Malecón Tarapacá,** with a pedestrian walkway, and surprisingly ostentatious 19th-century mansions built by rubber barons and decorated with Portuguese tiles. The city's big tourist draw is access to jungle lodges and cruises in the Amazon, but in the city there's the **Plaza de Armas,** with the neo-Gothic, 1919 church **Iglesia Matríz,** which is worth a photo stop. And across the square is the oddity of **Casa de Fierro,** or Iron House, which was designed by Gustave Eiffel for the 1889 Paris Exhibition (it was shipped to Iquitos and re-built on site). On the edge of town is the downtrodden, but fascinating, **Belén district,** where families live on water-logged streets in ramshackle homes along the river, some on stilts and others floating, like you might find in Asia. The district also has a bustling open-air market. *Note:* For safety reasons it's not recommended you visit the **Belén** without a guide. Your tour may include a visit the **Manatee Rescue Center,** where injured or orphaned Amazonian manatees are rescued and treated before being released back into the wild.

highlights OF THE PERUVIAN AMAZON

Pink dolphins. Protected Amazon River Dolphins are surprisingly easy to spot especially where creeks or lakes and rivers meet. These playful, freshwater mammals show off various shades of grey and pink and can grow to up to 8 feet in length. You may even get a chance to swim with them (in an area your naturalists deem safe).

Monkeys. Swinging on vines, playing monkey/see, monkey/do following each other across tree limbs, and screeching from the treetops, you're likely to see (and/or hear) squirrel monkeys, capuchin monkeys, howler monkeys and tamarins.

Birds. It will come as no surprise that the Amazon is nirvana for birders, but it's still a shock to see entire flocks of kingfishers and egrets, parrots and macaws, vultures and hawks and such species as the plum-throated catinga, which is such a startling bright shade of blue it looks plastic.

Creepy crawlers. From anacondas (snakes!) that hang out in shallow waters to red-eyed caimans (alligators!) that can be spotted at night by their red eyes, to tarantulas (spiders!), to King toads the size of rabbits, the jungle is full of, well, creepy surprises.

Three-toed sloths. Maybe it's their cute little white faces or their legendary laziness, but among some 600 species of mammals in the Amazon, everyone gets particularly giddy when a three-toed sloth is spotted lounging on a tree.

Exotic plants. Your naturalist guides will share wisdom from jungle doctors involving medicinal purposes of various leaves, and seeds and fruits and roots (and you may even get to meet a shaman). Other fascinating plants on parade include strangling figs, stiltlike walking trees and giant water lilies.

Canopy walking. You don't always have to walk in the jungle, there may be opportunity on your itinerary to walk above it on platforms connected by swinging bridges, looking down on trees and wildlife.

NAUTA

There are two docking points, the fancier one an open-air building, the other involving a very steep climb down steps to a skiff (small boat) that will take you to your ship.

This isolated riverside city, with the look and feel of a one-horse town, was founded in 1830 by native chief Manuel Pacaya Irarica (namesake of the Pacaya-Samiria Reserve), and was the first river port in the region. A dirt road connecting Nauta to Iquitos was built in 1999 (before that, you had to get between here and Iquitos on the Marañón River, a trip that takes about 12 hours) and paved in 2005. Nauta is a meeting point for people who live in the rural Amazon villages, the place to come to sell fish and harvested products and to catch up on the latest news. The market is fascinating—you'll find fruits and vegetables you've never heard of and some fruit specifies too.

Key Ports
FISHING VILLAGES

Where you stop will vary, but you will likely get there via a skiff, with a dry or possibly wet (you'll want to wear the provided boots) landing.

Top Activity   Meeting Locals: In tiny communities along the Amazon, villagers fish (sometimes from dugout canoes), practice substance farming and may or may not have electricity. These are places that flood in wet season—what appears as a soccer field in dry season may be a lake in west season—and homes are often built on stilts to protect from the tides. Shy but friendly, the *ribereños* (those who live in villages on the riverbanks) greet visitors with smiles, and you may find yourself constantly followed by kids as you explore a village of 500. Your tour may include a visit to a local school. Communities have been encouraged by some of the river lines to make crafts as souvenirs, and you may find a little market where you can buy a rustic blowgun and colorful baskets.

Off-the-Beaten-Path   You won't have much opportunity to go off track in the jungle, an exception being if your ship is equipped with kayaks (such as on the *Delfin II* operated by Lindblad Expeditions-National Geographic), in which case you can do some paddling under the watchful eye of crew following in a skiff.

Optional Add-Ons

On the cruise, there may be opportunity to take part in such activities as piranha fishing or, in another stretch, to get in deep water for a swim, but there isn't typically any extra charge for such activities.

   As we mentioned, your cruise may include some overnights in Lima, but while in the region you may want to add-on a few days to see Machu Picchu, the fascinating 15th-century Incan city high in the Andes, one of the New 7 Wonders of the World. Cruise lines sell pricy packages, but you can also get there on your own from Lima. Flights run regularly between Lima and Cusco (fares from about $250). From there, you have 70 miles of sometimes rugged terrain to go—with getting-there options including multi-day hikes with camping on the Inca Trail or a nearly 4-hour train ride to the tourist town of Machu Picchu Pueblo, about 15 miles by bus below the ruins.

   Another option if you have the time is to fly from Lima to the Galapagos, continuing your nature quest on an ocean cruise to contemplate evolution on islands little touched by man.

RECOMMENDED food & drink

Two things you must try are a **pisco sour,** the national cocktail of Peru, and **ceviche,** the popular raw fish dish invented in Peru. On your cruise you will find opportunity to taste unusual Amazonian fruits that go way beyond the now familiar papaya and mango. Try Vitamin C-rich **Camu Camu,** the tomato-like **Cocona,** and spiky melonlike **Annona** (with a sweet, custardlike flesh). The chef on your ship will use other local ingredients including hearts of palm and you'll find bananas in both sweet and savory dishes. Menus will include fresh water fish and roasted meats, as well as dishes where fish or meat is wrapped in bijao leaves and either grilled or steamed. You'll have opportunity to sample South American wines. Look too for Peruvian beer brands including Pilsen, Iquiteña, and Cristal.

BRAZILIAN amazon

If you've already read our section about Amazon river cruises, you probably thought to yourself, 'That's odd. Isn't most of the Amazon River in Brazil?' And you'd be right to be a bit perplexed. Despite the fact that 60 percent of the Amazon rainforest resides in Brazil, which also houses much of the Amazon River Basin, including the Amazon River and its numerous tributaries, there has been much more development on the Peruvian Amazon than on the Brazilian Amazon.

But, there *are* in fact river cruises on the Brazilian Amazon, too, even if they do tend to be a bit more under-the-radar. Miami-based **Rainforest Cruises** sells a whole host of itineraries along the Brazilian Amazon, with inventory on about 10 different vessels, ranging from the super basic 8-passenger, ferrylike boat, *Lo Peix*, with few amenities (including no air-conditioning) to more high-end vessels such as **Iberostar's 150-passenger *Grand Amazon*** and the **24-passenger classic schooner *Desafio*.** Iberostar's *Grand Amazon* sails 4-, 5-, and 8-day cruises along the Solimoes section of the Amazon River and along Rio Negro, the largest tributary of the Amazon, with prices for a 4-day river cruise starting at $909 per person. Southeast Asia river cruise specialist **Pandaw River Expeditions** recently started offering Brazilian Amazon river cruises as well (an interesting leap to be sure) on the 21-passenger *Amazon Dream.* The *Amazon Dream* is a 90 foot-long, Brazilian vessel built of regional woods in 2006. Highlights of the cruise include seeing the confluence of the blue waters of the Tapajos River and the yellow waters of the Amazon River, excursions to Maica Lake and Lake Marai, visits to several Amazonian river villages, and in-depth exploration of the flora and fauna of the rainforest. The Pandaw departures are priced from $3,996 per person, and additional departures are available directly through Amazon Dream (www.amazon-dream.com).

Most journeys to the Brazilian Amazon begin or end in the capital of Amazonas, **Manaus,** a former river village that has grown into a vibrant city of two million. And while unique culture and heritage of the region is one draw, most visitors flock to the Amazon for its rich biodiversity—the Central Amazon Biosphere Reserve is considered to be the largest forest in the world.

GANGES & HOOGHLY, INDIA

When most people think of the Ganges River, they probably don't think of serene landscapes, nature viewing and quiet riverside villages. In truth, the Ganges River has more of a reputation for being dirty, polluted and full of dead bodies.

Well, it is a very brown river (a color that it derives from the soil). And there are undoubtedly areas of the Ganges, namely near urban centers and towns, that are pretty repellent. There is also an ancient tradition in Varanasi of throwing the remains of cremated bodies into what is considered by Hindus to be the most sacred river, Mama Ganga. So some of the stereotypes are not completely unfounded.

But there is also a whole other side to the Ganges River. The 1,569-mile river that spans across much of northeastern India takes on very different traits along different stretches of the river and its tributaries.

africa's CHOBE RIVER

Deepest Africa isn't a place normally associated with river cruising and the 30-passenger **Zambezi Queen** and its three smaller sisters, the **Chobe Princesses,** are essentially luxurious houseboats rather than cruise ships. All four ply the Chobe River, a sometimes mile-wide waterway forming part of the border between Namibia and Botswana and flowing into the vast Zambezi. The Victoria Falls is just 44 miles away and a stay in one of the many lodges at the Falls makes an ideal combination with a houseboat safari.

The boats actually cover very little distance, although the experiences here—the wildlife, the open spaces, the fiery sunsets—are extraordinary. The larger Zambezi Queen sails between moorings just 16 miles apart, while the Chobe Princesses have a wider range of around 32 miles. There are no ports of call and no river traffic; just hippos grunting and giant crocs basking on the sandbanks.

Zambezi Queen is stunning, all done up in tasteful neutrals with African artwork, zebra rugs and faux-leopardskin cushions. It is South African-managed with a friendly, well-trained Namibian crew. The ship has 14 air-conditioned suites, all with private balcony, and two with an extra bed. There's a plunge pool and sun deck, as well as a beautiful, airy communal lounge/dining room with board games, books and a fully stocked bar. Beer and wine are included in the cruise price, as is game viewing twice daily and other activities such as fishing (in season) and village visits, as well as transfers from Kasane International, the nearest airport. The ship offers 2- and 3-night itineraries, with three departures per week, year round.

The Chobe Princess houseboats, under the same management, are similar in set up but smaller; one has five suites and the other two four each, all air-conditioned. All three offer contemporary lounge areas and hot tubs and are available for private charter or on an individual basis, but with no fixed departures.

Fellow guests are likely to be South Africans and Europeans, adventurous and in river cruising terms, young (40-plus). If you book one of the departures packaged by AmaWaterways, which offers the Zambezi Queen as part of an extended tour of southern Africa, your shipmates will include Americans.

Days quickly settle into a pattern of early breakfast followed by game viewing ashore, by 4WD, in the Chobe National Park. Wildlife here includes more than 400 species of birds as well as zebra, plenty of giraffe, big cats, numerous antelopes and elephants; with 120,000 elephants in the park, estimated to be the greatest concentration anywhere in Africa, they are Chobe's biggest lure.

Afternoons are spent lazing on board, while evening game viewing takes place from the water, on a small tender boat laden with gin and tonics, in true safari style. These boats go right up to the riverbank, where hundreds of elephants emerge from the bush in the late afternoon and play for hours in the water.

After sundowners, it's dinner on board, washed down with chilled South African wines, and then early bed; the generator is switched off at 10pm and you fall asleep lulled by the sounds of the African night.

Zambezi Queen is sold by Ama-Waterways (www.amawaterways.com) as part of a longer touring holiday in Africa. All four boats are owned by The Mantis Collection (mantiscollection.com) which also promotes them on the dedicated website www.zqcollection.com.

—Sue Bryant

The Ganges & Hooghly Rivers

And along the 130-mile stretch of river between Kolkata and north through West Bengal to Murshidabad where several river cruise lines are introducing new itineraries (how far north up the river they go depends on the line), there are areas where the water looks downright pristine, the river banks are lined with lush, unspoiled vegetation and there are ample species of birds.

Here, a simpler way of life emerges, complete with unique local cultures and customs. Along this stretch of what is technically the Hooghly River, a tributary of the Ganges, passengers will encounter ancient Shiva temples and Islamic Imambaras. They will find crumbling British colonial palaces rising from the dense river foliage, and they will visit bustling riverside villages chock full of produce stands, bicycles, livestock and shrines.

In short, they will encounter countless experiences that have nothing to do with the clichés they have seen or heard about the Ganges.

So why has the Ganges suddenly been rediscovered? Blame modernization. This vast and legendary river, the longest in India, hasn't seen much overnight passenger traffic for centuries in large part due to the collapse of the profitable opium trade in the 1800s and the rise of a more efficient rail system that rendered the Ganges, and its tributaries, obsolete.

But since the early 2000s, there has been gradual rediscovery of the river, first by local outfits and more recently by international river cruise lines, with Haimark really paving the way with its high-end river cruise vessels there.

Passengers now have access to the rich waterways of West Bengal, to the Ganges and its tributaries, the Hooghly and Bhagirathi rivers, an area where there are refreshingly few tourists and all but no tourism infrastructure.

Port of Embarkation: Kolkata
KOLKATA
The swarming West Bengal city of Kolkata (formerly Calcutta) is located on the banks of the Hooghly River. Most river cruises along the Ganges and Hooghly rivers do a round-trip loop from Kolkata and back. There is a Tourism Centre in Kolkata located at 3/2 B.B.D. Bagh East (while there head to the impressive British colonial-era Writer's Building on the north side of the square).

Kolkata definitely gives visitors a boisterous welcome. India's second largest city is the quintessential chaotic Indian metropolis, with classic old yellow cabs crowding the packed streets, horns honking and pedestrians crisscrossing the roads every which way. The city's vibrancy is both frenetic and contagious.

Kolkata is home to the **Missionaries of Charity** (54A, A.J.C. Bose Rd.; www.motherteresa.org), the Roman Catholic congregation founded by **Mother Teresa** in 1950. At the Mother House, as its commonly known, visitors can see the room where Mother Teresa lived, as well as explore a basic but interesting exhibit that showcases her life and work.

Part of the charm and complexity of Kolkata are the remnants of British colonial architecture and the relics of the British Raj still present throughout the city. One such example is the imposing **Victoria Memorial** (1, Queens Way; www.victoriamemorial-cal.org), a grandiose marble building dedicated to the memory of Queen Victoria of England. Today, the Victoria Memorial houses a collection of artifacts from Kolkata's royal, political and military past. The building itself and its surrounding gardens are definitely the main attraction.

highlights **OF THE GANGES & HOOGHLY**

Varanasi. Most river cruise lines include Varanasi as a land extension, and there couldn't be a more fascinating start or end to your Ganges experience than this enchanting holy city, known for its theatrical spiritual rituals and the traditional cremations of dead (human) bodies that are conducted in huge bonfires blazing right out on the water's edge.

108 Shiva Temples. You can count them, they're all there, all 108 of them in the unassuming and lively riverside village of Kalna, home to this camera-ready temple complex.

The International Society for Krishna Consciousness. Remember the Hare Krishna movement? Shaved heads? Ponytails? Chanting? Well it's alive and thriving at the ISKCON headquarters in Mayapur. Here you will have the chance to learn more about the Hare Krishna beliefs and what the movement has been up to lately.

Ready for some more roaming? Head to **Jawaharlal Nehru Road** (formerly Chowringhee), one of Kolkata's main thoroughfares. Here you'll find the monumental **Indian Museum** (27 Jawaharlal Nehru Rd.; www.indian museumkolkata.org), which is worth a look whether you have it in you to go inside or not. Finally, pop into the nearby **New Market** (Lindsay St.) for your pick of trinkets and knickknacks to bring home.

Key Ports

KALNA

Once docked in the riverside town of Kalna, about 60 miles north of Kolkata, you will likely be offered a trishaw (a combination tricycle and rickshaw) ride to the town's famous temple complex.

Top Activity **Visiting the Shiva Temples:** Okay, it may not be a very original name for a temple complex, but at least you sort of know what to expect when you head to the **108 Shiva temples.** Just make sure your camera's memory card is unloaded and ready to roll. You'll want plenty of room to capture the beautiful repetition in these two concentric circles of sloped-roof temples, which date back to the early 19th century.

Off-the-Beaten-Path **Kalna:** A **trishaw ride** through a small but bustling town like Kalna isn't just a means to an end but an exhilarating experience unto itself. You'll find yourself weaving in between livestock, villagers carrying all sorts of interesting objects and any manner of other vehicles, including cars, bikes and other trishaws, all of which will miraculously come within millimeters of you without (hopefully) hitting you. It's a great way to get up close and personal with village life.

MAYAPUR

As in most ports along the Ganges and Hooghly, don't expect much in the way of infrastructure. Be prepared to possibly be boated to a small and rudimentary landing dock; and lots of random people, who may or may not work for your river cruise line, lending you helping hands as you disembark. It's all part of the experience!

Top Activity **Krishna Education:** There is one main reason for stopping in Mayapur, and it's to visit the Vedic temple complex of **The International Society for Krishna Consciousness (ISKCON).** (The Vedic belief system is considered the historical predecessor to Hinduism, though they are quite different, and is rooted in ancient Sanskrit texts.) There are so many interesting layers to this compound of worship. There is the link to Alfred Brush Ford, great grandson of Ford Motor Founder Henry Ford, who has reportedly poured tens of millions of dollars into the development of the Vedic Planetarium at Mayapur, a Vedic temple that promises to completely dwarf the current temple (a behemoth unto itself)—it will be larger than the Taj Mahal when completed. There are the followers themselves, of all ethnicities and nationalities. There is the chanting and dancing, if you're lucky enough to go on a day or at a time when it's on display. All told, you definitely shouldn't find yourself lacking of interesting buildings, shrines or events to take in here. And don't be surprised if Hare Krishna devotees offer visitors curious-looking sweets. It's one of their traditions.

Off-the-Beaten-Path   Golden Statue: Be sure to head inside the main Vedic temple at the ISKCON complex. Here you will see the gold statue of Srila Prabhupada, the founder of the modern-day Krishna movement. The temple itself and the rituals that take within place begin to give visitors a sense of the extreme level of devotion followers have.

MURSHIDABAD

Your vessel will likely pull up and dock right alongside one of the main attractions in Murshidabad, Hazarduari Palace.

Top Activity   Hazarduari Palace: This imposing and yet slightly neglected palace was constructed in the early 1800s. One of the oddest tidbits about Hazarduari Palace is that its interiors are said to contain 1,000 different doors (although we didn't count to make sure), of which 900 are false, intended to serve as a sort of trap or maze for unknowing intruders. Today, the palace is open to the public as a museum, which houses a collection of Nawab artifacts; this will also be an opportunity to learn more about Nawabs, India's Muslim rulers.

Off-the-Beaten-Path   Mosque Visit: Although Hazarduari Palace is arguably the most well-known landmark in Murshidabad, there's a strong case to be made for seeing the ancient **Katra Mosque,** which was built a century earlier in the early 1700s. Relatively undiscovered by tourists as of yet, you will likely find yourself roaming this impressive brick mosque complex all but alone with your fellow cruise passengers, which adds to the beauty and mystique. Added bonus: Some river cruise lines will transport you here by bumpy and exhilarating **horse and buggy cart.** We're not sure which gets our heart racing more, trishaw rides or horse and buggy rides. The mosque is no longer in use (it's in ruins in some places) and visitors can roam freely.

RECOMMENDED food & drink

Eating in India is a bit tricky. On the one hand, it all looks so colorful and delicious. On the other hand, you've probably heard of "Delhi belly" and might be a bit worried about getting sick. If you're really worried, stick to cooked dishes along with starches such as bread and rice, and you should be okay. Bengali cuisine is distinct from the better known (in the West, at least) Punjabi cuisine that is steeped in rich curry and masala dishes. Here in West Bengal, you can expect unique recipes and flavors that you may or may not recognize, such as *machher jhol,* a spicy fish stew; *luchi,* fried flatbread that poofs up with air; *cholar dal,* a dense lentil dish made with coconut, cloves, cinnamon and cardamom; and *aloo pasto,* potatoes with poppy seed paste. Also, Bengali cuisine is known for its sweets, so be sure to grab some *nolen gurer payesh,* Indian rice pudding; *sandesh,* cottage cheese-based sugar and cardamom cookies; and *mithi dahi* or *mishti doi,* Bengali sweet yogurt. Your best bet for trying some authentic Bengali cuisine will be in Kolkata. Head to **Kewpie's** (2 Elgin Lane; www.kewpieskitchen.com), a family-run restaurant not far from the Victoria Memorial.

Optional Add-Ons

Technically it's not *on* the route, but we'd be remiss if we didn't mention the overwhelmingly mystical and enchanting holy Ganges city of **Varanasi.** Most river cruise lines offer it as either an included or additional extension. Although it's along the Ganges, there are some navigational challenges in getting river cruises all the way up to Varanasi from Kolkata. Thus, you will likely arrive by airplane at the Varanasi International Airport, and be transferred to a local hotel. There are two rituals you will want to experience—the sunset Ganga Aarti ceremony, an over-the-top devotional ritual to the goddess Ganga, and the sunrise Ganges bathing rituals. A trishaw ride through the heart of Varanasi during the evening rush hour will step up the excitement even more—make that a lot more. Or top off your river cruise with a visit to the **Taj Mahal.**

IRRAWADDY (AYEYARWADY)

Largely closed off to visitors for decades, the Irrawaddy runs through the mysterious country of Myanmar (Burma), north to south from the glacial Himalayas to the Andaman Sea, some 1,350 miles. This is a once-rich country ruled by the British starting in 1885, independent since 1948, essentially shut down under a military dictatorship and only recently re-opened to western tourists. National elections in the fall of 2016 brought a landslide victory over military leaders by Nobel Peace Prize winner Aung San Suu Kyi's National League for Democracy, and much hope for optimism in one of the poorest countries in the world.

In the north, up near the Chinese border, where only a few specially designed river ships venture, the river is so shallow at times you could walk across, and you cruise through passages such as the Second Defile, where limestone cliffs narrow the waterway to 300 feet. At other times, the river's width spreads to a half mile.

The cruises bring beauty, including in the form of smiling people who greet tourists with the word *mingalabar,* an elevated form of hello. Gaggles of skinny children may follow you around dusty towns not because they want something from you but because they are as curious about you and your hair and eyes and belly as you are about them. Golden shines and pagodas and *stupas* (dome-shaped Buddhist shrines), monks in saffron robes, large golden depictions of Buddha, and local markets stocked with exotic goods will all leave you intrigued. Everything looks, feels and smells exotic.

Stretches of the river bring views of forests, rice paddies, small villages with houses on stilts, water buffalo. If you're lucky you may spot one of the endangered snub-nosed Irrawaddy dolphins—which in a rare symbiotic relationship actually help some fishermen on the river by leading them to schools of fish (the dolphins get to keep what falls out of the nets).

There is poverty among the people and you're best off leaving your western values at home. You'll find yourself on city roads clogged with cars or smelly Chinese motorbikes and dusty, bumpy one-lane stretches in the countryside.

The Irrawaddy River

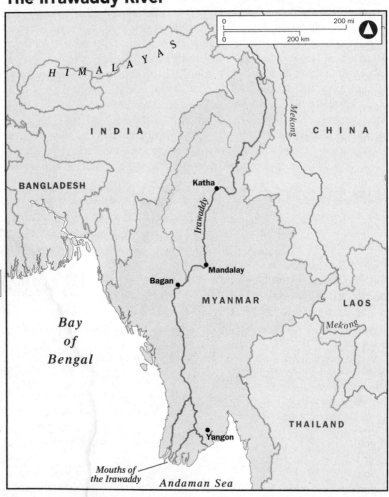

There may be pushy vendors (most notably in the popular tourist city of Bagan, where a pack may follow your group on motorbikes to all the sights your visit). You will have to walk barefoot, shoulders and knees covered into monasteries and temples, on floors that are not particularly clean. Toilets may be a hole in the ground, even at remote airports (bring your own tissue and lots of hand sanitizer).

All that said, the Irrawaddy is one of the most fascinating and untapped destinations you can visit.

The season is year-round. In fall and winter (especially November to March) temperatures are warm during the day and cooler at night, which some travelers will find a plus. The hotter season (in the height of which you might encounter 105 degrees in Mandalay) begins in March. The rainy season kicks in late May to September, though there are some advantages to cruising when the river is higher including easier access by water to some villages.

There are a variety of itineraries, most involving cruising, hotel nights and internal flights. Choosing which one works for you has a lot to do with whether you want to spend time in more developed tourism areas, maybe including a stay at a beautiful resort at tranquil Inle Lake; or want to get more into more untapped territory—and also how much time you want to spend on the river. Three- and 4-night cruises are between the more popular tourist cities of Bagan and Mandalay (you fly both ways from Yangon). One-week itineraries explore between Pyay (about a day's drive from the largest city, Yangon) and Bagan (you spend a day in a bus but only have one flight). Longer itineraries may start in Yangon and spend 2 days sailing to Pyay, and beyond to Bagan and Mandalay. In all cases you visit villages along the way. Rare cruises visit the north, such as Avalon Waterways' 14-day itinerary between Bhamo, near the Chinese border (a 2-hr. flight from Yangon) and Bagan (also including Mandalay). To us, this is the most authentic itinerary in terms of seeing areas where tourists are still a novelty.

Note that where you dock will depend on water levels, but you will frequently have to climb of steep backs (crew from your ship will help). Don't expect to find such luxuries as concrete steps or a pier.

Ports of Embarkation: Bagan, Yangon, Mandalay
BAGAN
You dock in Bagan on the eastern bank of the Irrawaddy.

This former Burmese capital and spiritual center is home to a massive, 26-square-mile archeological site that rivals Machu Picchu or Angkor Wat. There are 2,300 remaining temples, pagodas, stupas (dome-shaped Buddhist shrines) and monasteries, dating from the 9th to 13th centuries, many covered in gold, creating a magical landscape. Some of the relics are crumbling, but other still tower majestically above the dusty landscape.

You will visit the ornate Shwezigon Pagoda, one of the country's most important shrines and the beautiful Ananda temple, and view fresco paintings being restored at some sites. Your tour guide will typically also take you to a handicrafts market where you can buy fabrics and longyis (the traditional skirts worn by Burmese men and women) and a workshop where beautiful lacquer ware is created using ancient techniques. But for many, the must-do activity is climbing the steep steps of a tall temple to watch the sunrise or sunset over the scene (at sunrise, another option is views from hot air balloons).

YANGON
Most international flights land you at the airport, only about 10 miles from the city but up to a 2-hour drive based on traffic. Accommodations for river passengers are typically at the fancy Sule Shangri-La hotel, which has a wonderful pool and spa and several restaurants among attractions.

The largest city in Myanmar, this was the country's capital city until 2005—when the administrative capital was moved to Naypyidaw, about 200 miles to the north. On a walking tour from your hotel you'll pass fading British Colonial buildings and car-clogged streets, markets and gardens. By bus you'll visit such places as Sule Pagoda to see the luxuriously reclining 223-foot Buddha and take in the spiritual atmosphere of the 2,500-year-old Shwedagon Pagoda, the most important religious site in the country and home to many depictions of Buddha, some surprisingly accompanied by flashing lights. The main dome, the national symbol of Myanmar, is impressively covered in gold and diamonds.

If you have free time, visit the sprawling buildings of the Bogyoke Market, built in 1920, where you can find fabrics, jewelry and handicrafts galore (even a few art galleries featuring local artists including the Taw Win Art Gallery, Main Entrance to the market, www.tawwingallery.com). Right across from the Sule Shangri-La hotel, head to the 20th floor of the Sakura Tower and the **Thiripyitsaya Sky Bistro** (339 Bo Gyoke Rd.; www.sakura-tower-yangon. com/restaurant.php) for lunch or dinner with views.

MANDALAY
You dock along the river.

This legendary city was once home to a massive royal palace complex where King Mindon ruled from 1853 to 1878 until the royal family fled to India (some proud locals still claim royal blood). You will visit the Shwenandaw Monastery (also known as the Golden Palace Monastery), the only surviving building from the original complex. You may also visit the Sagaing hills, home to some 550 monasteries and thousands of monks and nuns, or stop by Mahamuni Pagoda, home to a Buddha covered in some 6 feet of gold—men only can pay tribute by adding small and inexpensive patches of gold leaf, which are for sale at the site.

A highlight is in nearby Amarapura, another former capital of Myanmar, watching fishermen pull in their catch at sunset at the rickety, ¾-mile teak

highlights OF THE IRRAWADDY

Visiting a Rustic Pottery Village. Mud from the river is used to make earthenware pots, including 50-gallon Ali Baba pots used to carry water and oil, and you visit a small village (such as Kya Hnyat) where you'll watch a potter hand-turn a pot, see the kilns and view landscapes of pots waiting to be fired.

Riding Elephants. On Avalon Waterways' 14-day cruises you visit a northern teak forest where wood-transporting elephants are being retrained to take visitors on short rides. You get to feed bananas to the babies.

Meeting School Children. Depending on your itinerary you may have opportunity to visit a rustic, one-room school and chat with local children, some of whom will have learned at least a few words of English but most of whom will never have met an American before. It's a heart-warming experience.

RECOMMENDED food & drink

Myanmar Beer is cheap, good, often fresh on tap or in red cans with the national symbol, the stunning Shwedagon Pagoda, on the label. Cuisine is influenced by the fact the country has some 135 ethnic groups, and you'll find Chinese, Indian and Thai influences. Fish is a staple and a salty fermented fish paste (ngapi) is the base for soups and other dishes. Rice is served at all meals, and because the climate tends towards hot, lots of salads are featured. It's fine to sample the exotic salads on your ship, where they will use purified water, but if you are dining off-ship you will want to exercise some caution—if you think they're using tap water (which is not potable to westerners) stick with hot cooked dishes. Dishes to try include *Mohinga*, a fish broth with rice noodles, Shan noodles (shan khao swé), topped with slightly spicy chicken or pork sauce, and tealeaf salad (*lahpet*), made with picked tealeaves.

U Bein Bridge, built of reclaimed wood from a palace in the late 1700s. You may subconsciously or not start reciting Rudyard Kipling's poem "Road to Mandalay." "On the road to Mandalay, Where the flyin' fishes play, An' the dawn comes up like thunder outer China 'crost the Bay."

Key Ports
KATHA
You tie up downhill from one of the small city's main streets.

Top Activity Exploring Katha: Only those cruises that venture north visit, but one of Fran's memorable experiences was just walking around this dusty city, which has the look and feel of a one-horse town—but with temples. There's a large food market area, vendors selling rice and fish and fresh fruit and vegetables and palm sugar candy, all ready with a smile when you take out your camera.

Off-the-Beaten Path Orwell House: Walk a little further and you'll find the red brick house where George Orwell resided, his time in Katha inspiring his book "Burmese Days." It's now the home of a local police officer, but has the look of a squatters place with a littered front yard and very little sign that this was a major outpost during the British Colonial period. The British Club still stands to, now housing business offices.

Optional Add-Ons
Your schedule is pretty tightly controlled so add-on day tours are rare. An exception may be that your river cruise company may be able to arrange a **hot air balloon ride** in Bagan. Ask your river line for details.

Some river cruises are packaged with stays in Bangkok. You might alternatively consider booking your flight from the U.S. to stop in another Asian hub for a few nights (a great way to break up what can be an excruciating long period of travel); options including Hong Kong, Singapore, Seoul and Tokyo.

MEKONG

The mighty Mekong begins in China with snow melt from the Himalayas of Tibet, flowing south to form the border between Myanmar (Burma) and Laos, then between Laos and Thailand. The river winds through Cambodia before reaching Vietnam's delta, draining into the South China Sea some 2,700 miles from its beginning. The waterway provides power, food, farm irrigation, transportation, and a link to each other for millions of people.

Cruising the Mekong gives travelers access to remote villages and to amazing temples and ruins that speak to the fascinating cultures of the past and present in Southeast Asia. It also brings you close to the people who live there, so you can learn first-hand about the long-term results of decades of war, especially in Cambodia, where the tragic lives and experiences of people you will meet carry a heavy emotional impact.

By far, the most popular and most served waters are between Cambodia's Siem Reap and the bustling, motorbike-crazed Vietnam metropolis of Ho Chi Minh City, which once was known as Saigon—and still appears that way on many maps and reports. Most river cruise companies ply this route, combining about a week on the river with tours at either end, highlighted by the famed and expansive ruins of **Angkor Wat,** the UNESCO World Heritage Site near Siem Reap.

Much of the river cruise between the two cities is rural, sometimes remote. Above the popular port stop at the Cambodian capital city of Phnom Penh, the Mekong and its tributary, the Tonle Sap lake and river, meander through the countryside on their journeys downstream without a hint of the kinds of industry that line most of the world's other major rivers. Rustic farm houses and occasional villages are set back from river's edges to protect them from the annual flooding that significantly raises the Mekong during the wettest season, which allows river vessels to cruise deeper into flooded forests and along other tributaries inaccessible to boats when the water is low.

The result is that during excursion stops along the river your vessel may be tied to a tree. You may step off the ship's ramp onto a temporary dock or no dock at all, merely a bare flat piece of land. At some sites, you may climb up dirt steps shoveled out of the riverbank for passengers by crew members who will help you up with one steady hand, carrying an open umbrella in the other to protect you from the sun. These paths to the river are temporary because more permanent steps and docks would be swept away with the next summer's floods.

In Cambodia, the river will take you to boat landings where no other form of transportation exists. Some villages are so remote from highways on land that they have no electricity, and they rely on the river for their link to the rest of the world. You may be transported from the riverbank to a local village by oxcart, serenaded by young girls showing off their limited English by singing, "If You're Happy and You Know It."

Your visit probably will include a rural school, where cruise lines make donations of school supplies. Passengers sometimes are encouraged to shop at markets in larger towns to buy pencils, paper, and elementary books to bring to a class learning English; in rural areas, supplies are lacking and trained

The Mekong River

teachers are nearly non-existent. Conversely, Passengers are dissuaded from giving money to children anywhere in Cambodia and Vietnam, as that might encourage their parents to keep the children home from school to panhandle. Buying shaved ice as a treat is okay.

Children are especially interested in older adults visiting Cambodia, as residents over the age of 60, particularly men, are few, following decades of warfare and the killing of educated citizens by the now out-of-power Khmer Rouge. "How old are you," a child may ask. Don't be surprised when they say, "That's really old," explained a tour guide. "The children mean respect."

Below Phnom Penh, the Mekong grows wider and busier, packed with vessels of various sizes and uses: fishing boats, ferries, sampans, barges bursting with rice, other food stuff, and building materials, as well as people maneuvering their small craft, steered by a long-tailed outboard motor. Tributaries reveal floating markets where you may see workers producing rice noodles and coconut candy or imperfect bricks to be shipped up or downstream for construction.

Excursions off the river ship use many modes of local transportation, including tuk-tuks, cyclos (a bike with a forward basket for a human), and

INTO laos

sampans. Local guides are essential for understanding the culture and etiquette at bustling local markets where little English is spoken and you may encounter, among more familiar fruits and vegetables, collections of sparrows and rats (skinned for cooking), grilled crickets, spiders, roaches, and fried tarantulas (reportedly containing proteins that help aching joints). Excursions also may include master artisans crafting works from silk and/or silver.

Cruising is available nearly year round with significantly fewer departures during the May and June monsoon season (when some lines offer no cruises at all). Most of the year, rain only falls about an hour a day, usually in the afternoons. High water season is from June into October, when conditions allow riverboats best access to tributaries; some can navigate shallow Tonle Sap Lake, which reduces transportation time between the river and hotels at Siem Reap. From mid-December to June, the river is shallower. When the Mekong is low, the Tonle Sap is a tributary; water flows from the lake and river into the Mekong. When the Mekong floods, the flow reverses; floodwaters of the Mekong flow up the Tonle Sap. Tropical temperatures across Southeast Asia generally fluctuate between 78°F and 86°F. The warmest months are March and April.

There are several itineraries for cruises between Siem Reap and Ho Chi Minh City. Some cruises spend slightly more time on the Mekong above Phnom Penh; others spend more time on the Tonle Sap. Some 2-week tours begin in Hanoi, in northern Vietnam. They may include overnights in other Vietnam destinations such as Ha Long Bay, a UNESCO World Heritage Site.

Ports of Embarkation: Ho Chi Minh City, Siem Reap
HO CHI MINH CITY
You dock downtown. For tourist information visit www.vietnamtourism.com.

This frenetic, modern city of 10 million people, and nearly as many motorbikes, is best enjoyed on a long walk, starting at the center of old colonial Saigon, near the Opera House and Hotel Continental Saigon (132-134 Dong

Khoi St.; www.continentalsaigon.com), which, during the Vietnam War, was a hangout for journalists. Its cafe still is a nice spot for coffee, a lunch, and a few thoughts about the 1960s and early 1970s.

Your city tour should include the ornate Central Post Office; the Reunification Palace (formerly known as Independence Palace and the place where tanks from the north stormed the gates on April 30, 1975); the Ben Thanh Market, for whatever souvenirs you might want to bring home; and the **Vietnam War Remnants Museum** (28 Vo Van Tan; www.baotangchungtichchientranh.vn), which houses a major collection of photographs, many by men and women who lost their lives in the Vietnam War, which Vietnam calls the American War.

You may want to ask for a lesson on how to cross the busy streets; it's a powerful moment when the traffic zooms around you as you walk purposely across, hand held for every motorist to see. If you have extra time, spend a few hours at the **Fine Arts Museum** (97 Pho Duc Chinh St., admission about 50 cents, closed Mondays) for its collection of sculptures from Champa (a civilization that flourished along the coasts of what is now Vietnam from A.D. 500 and 1500), paintings by leading Vietnamese artists past and present and lacquered works. The 1929, Colonial-era building is itself spectacular and out back there are wonderful galleries selling modern works by Vietnamese artists in a courtyard out back).

Outside the city, the highlight for tours is a visit to the **Cu Chi Tunnels,** where the Viet Cong hid during the early years of the war. You will have an opportunity to get on your knees to crawl through one of the Cu Chi tunnels (an experience that is somewhat terrifying). The tunnels, open daily, are part of a war memorial park, complete with a shooting range at which tourists can fire a variety of Vietnam War era weapons. Entrance fees start at about $5, but guided tours cost more. Visitors should not arrive after 3pm because the area is dark by about 5pm.

SIEM REAP

Transportation from city hotels is by motorcoach to river ships, which are outside the city. For tourist information visit www.siemreap.me.

This is a rather dusty city that once fit the description of backwater burg. But thanks to the key nearby attraction of Angkor Wat it is now expanding with gusto, fine hotels and restaurants as the resort gateway to the Angkor archeological site, drawing visitors from all over the world. There are several markets in town, including Psar Chas for Cambodian jewelry and other items. Shopping is a big thing here.

Downtown offers numerous opportunities for inexpensive meals, pub time and massages. A short walk away is a park along the narrow Siem Reap River.

Key Port
PHNOM PENH

You dock near downtown, near riverfront hotels, restaurants and shops.

Top Activity   Touring the city: Cambodia's capital shows off its French architecture from colonial days, the gold of the **Royal Palace,** Khmer artifacts in the **National Museum,** and **Silver Pagoda.** The dark side of Cambodian history is here, too, at the city's **Genocide Museum,** which details the not-so-recent past of the evil Khmer Rouge.

highlights OF THE MEKONG

Angkor Archeological Site. Home 1,000 years ago to a great Hindu empire, Angkor measures some 19 square miles of stone temples and tombs, now in various states of ruin and restoration. Tours typically spend at least a day or two, starting at the 12th-century Temple of Angkor Wat, a UNESCO World Heritage Site. Among the impressive sites are the fortified city of Angkor Thom; a 10th-century Hindu temple Banteay Srei; and Ta Prohm, a temple where the jungle growth has overtaken much of the ruins. Tour groups have the advantage of tickets and guide already reserved.

Bamboo Bridge across the Tonle Sap. Each year, residents of the island village of Koh Pen, Cambodia, rebuild a bridge during 3 weeks of December, after the end of the rainy season, from the mainland to their home. The bridge, made entirely of bamboo, carries wagons, cars, horse carriages and lots of people. It is dismantled in June, while torrents of water raise the river level with swirling currents, flooding the Mekong, which backs up to refill Lake Tonle Sap.

Wat Hanchey. A small riverside temple, dating back to the 8th century, draws hundreds of visitors on the Mekong. Its longevity is remarkable, because its bricks were made without fire. They were formed from limestone, termite mound clay, water, and palm sugar, held together with ... sticky rice and coconut milk. Nearby, passengers may partake in a traditional water blessing by local monks.

Off-the-Beaten-Path   The Killing Fields: Less than 10 miles south of Phnom Penh is a mass grave of perhaps 20,000 people, who lie barely underground in 4 acres, fenced off with walking paths and displays, including a tower with a glassed collection of skulls. This is one of more than 300 such Killing Fields and contains the bodies and clothing of some of the estimated two million Cambodians who died as "undesirable" during the murderous reign of Pol Pot and his Khmer Rouge. Bring a bottle of water to drink, and be prepared to walk away with a heavy heart.

Optional Add-Ons

While you are so close you may want to combine your Mekong excursion with a visit to frenetic **Hanoi** or **De Nang** and **China Beach.** We highly recommend taking a *junk* (boat) through the craggy and eerily misty limestone formations of **Halong Bay** and visiting the quaint, historical resort town of **Hoi An,** both a photographer's dream. Some river companies sell add-on options in **Bangkok.** Another idea is to recover from your adventure which some relaxing time on the beach in **Bali.**

THE NILE

It's an essential component of any Egypt itinerary—a Nile river cruise. And that's because the Nile River, arguably the longest river in the world at more than 4,200 miles (although there are debates about whether the Amazon is longer, depending on how you measure), serves as a convenient liquid highway that weaves right along some of Egypt's most significant archaeological sites.

Sailing along the Nile is also one of the most refreshing parts of any Egypt itinerary, a welcome relief from the traffic and crowds of Cairo. And after

RECOMMENDED food & drink

There are five principal ingredients in Cambodian cooking: *prahoc*, a pungent fermented fish paste; lemon grass; kaffir lime leaves, ground into paste and used like bay leaves to flavor soup or sliced into thin threads as a garnish; *galangal*, a cream-colored root that tastes like a subtle ginger; and tamarind paste. Rice dominates the Cambodian menu, with most dishes cooked in a wok. Given the number of rivers and the dominance of the Tonle Sap, you'll find plenty of freshwater fish. The typical breakfast is **rice soup** with lunch and dinner involving a number of dishes served simultaneously, almost always including a soup. Cambodia's signature dish is **amok**—fish cooked in banana leaves with turmeric and coconut milk. Another biggie is **lok lak,** diced, fried beef served with fried eggs, salad, and French fries or rice. If you like your food spicy (which Cambodian food is not) ask for hot sauce, and you'll get hot pepper combined with fresh lime.

The most popular beer to accompany your meal is Angkor Beer.

Vietnamese dishes such as **pho** (beef noodle soup) and **pho ga** (chicken noodle soup), fresh **spring rolls** and **green papaya salad** may be familiar—thanks to the many Vietnamese restaurants in the U.S.—but don't limit yourself there. Vietnamese cuisine relies heavily on fresh ingredients and the right combination of herbs and spices. Look for dishes featuring *mang* (tender young bamboo shoots), *bap chuoi* (banana blossom), *la chuoi* (banana leaves) and *kho qua* (bitter gourd). *Ot* (red chilies) are a common ingredient and add a zing while *Nuoc mam* fish sauce adds a pungent element. You'll find fresh fish everywhere and meat and poultry are locally farmed, as is rice. Accompany your meal with local beer (such as Saigon Beer), tea, whiskey or fruit juice, or try Vietnamese coffee, typically served with very sweet condensed milk.

long, hot days spent roaming temples and examining hieroglyphs in the Saharan sun, there are few sights more enticing than that of your trusty Nile river cruise vessel, an air-conditioned oasis, where you know there are cool libations awaiting you on board and a pool to dip in on the sun deck.

In its heyday, the Nile River had more than 300 river cruise vessels plying up and down its shores. It was a popular destination as much for North Americans making that bucket list trip to see ancient Egyptian archaeology dating back to 3000 B.C. (that's over 5,000 years ago, people), as it was for Europeans making a quicker, cheaper hop-over for a warm, relaxing vacation. The sheer number of vessels along the Nile to accommodate all these visitors often forced them to be docked in popular ports as many as five or six deep, or more.

Up until the Arab Spring uprisings of 2011, the iconic sites along the Nile were swarming with tourists, to the point there were legitimate concerns about the upkeep and preservation of those sites. But ever since then, Egypt's tourism industry has been struggling to recover and the number of Nile river cruises has dwindled to a much smaller number of operators.

Nevertheless, the Nile River and the remarkable ancient history it provides access to are still there, waiting with open arms. The crowds have all but vanished and the experience is no less extraordinary.

The Nile

From the Luxor temple with its defining obelisk structure to the countless royal tombs at the Valley of the Kings, from the endearing island temple Philae to the rich Nubian culture in Aswan, there is endless history and culture to explore. Here, having a good Egyptologist guide who can really take you back in time and help put together all the pieces is key. It's a lot of information to absorb and we've seen guides that brought it all to life in almost theatrical ways and guides that were totally phoning it in. How good the guide is will depend entirely on how well they're vetted by the river cruise line or tour operator. Abercrombie & Kent, for instance, has great guides.

And while it's all very fascinating, don't feel guilty if you experience some temple fatigue (hey, we've all been there) and need to take a day off and just

IS IT safe?

chill on board. It's a lot of walking in debilitating heat. Our advice is to be realistic, look at the itinerary in advance and decide which sites are total musts and which you could skip if you needed a break. We know, you want to do it all, and hopefully you can and will.

Another point: While much of your time will be spent diving deep into Egypt's ancient past, cruising the Nile is also a superb opportunity to see and experience the country's more recent history. You will get to witness what life is like outside the capital city Cairo. The Nile River, with its lush, palm tree-lined river banks, is a highway through the heartland of the country, where mosques will be amplifying the daily prayers and villagers dressed in more conservative garb and jelabiyas (the longer, "dresslike" garments worn by men) will be going about their daily tasks. It will, we guarantee you, be a feast for the senses.

Ports of Embarkation: Luxor & Aswan
LUXOR

River cruise ships dock up and down the length of the city of Luxor, but most end up within walking distance of the Luxor Temple. The Egyptian Tourist Authority, the country's official tourism marketing organization, has some helpful facts and information about Luxor on its website: www.egypt.travel/city/index/luxor.

Luxor is not just home to a fascinating temple unto itself, it also serves as the gateway to several other blockbuster hits of the Nile River. Most river cruises plan to have their passengers visit the **Luxor Temple** at night, and there's a good reason for this. Not only does an evening visit provide a welcome break from visiting temples in the glaring sun, but Luxor is incredibly well lit and visiting it during and after sunset offers a beautiful and unique perspective. The temple itself dates back to 1400 B.C. and is not just distinctive for its obelisk (which has a smaller counterpart in the Place de la Concorde in Paris), but also for the multiple eras of civilization represented throughout the temple. For instance, a part of the temple that had been converted into a Christian church at one point in time and you can still see Christian images alongside the ancient hieroglyphs. And perhaps even more fascinating is the **Abu Haggag Mosque,** built atop the temple when the temple was still buried under sand.

Most Nile river cruises begin with the largest and most complex ancient Egyptian site, the **Karnak Temple Complex.** Some 30 different pharaohs contributed to the construction of Karnak, which took some 1,500 years to complete and the result is a gargantuan complex, complete with its vast hall of columns and countless massive statues, which begin to give visitors a true sense of the outsized capabilities and ambitions of the ancient Egyptians.

Another important place to visit from Luxor is the **Valley of the Kings,** a burial site for pharaohs and ancient Egyptian nobles that houses some 63 tombs, the most well-known of which is that of **Tutankhamun** (aka King Tut), famously discovered by British archaeologist Howard Carter in 1922. The mostly intact findings from inside the tomb are now on display at the **Egyptian Museum** in Cairo—the sheer number and sophistication of the items are mind-boggling.

ASWAN

There is actually a pretty wide swath of docks along the river in Aswan, which means your ship might dock within walking distance to town or it might require a cab ride to get into town. If you plan to return to the ship on your own, make sure to have the crew write down the exact docking location and provide a phone number that you could give the cab driver as language barriers and providing directions can be a bit of a hurdle.

Aswan is the heart of Egypt's vibrant Nubian community, an ethnic group that hails from southern Egypt and parts of Sudan with a distinct look and demeanor (their characteristic slim and tall silhouettes and bright smiles are stunning). Like Luxor, Aswan offers a jumping off point for several noteworthy landmarks, and also provides a relaxing river oasis to call home for 1 or 2 nights. Here, the river is broken up by small, rocky islands, and the stretches of water between them are known as cataracts, providing a nice change of scenery from the picturesque yet homogeneous river scenery along much of the rest of the Nile. Another trademark of Aswan are the countless **feluccas,** wooden sailing boats that dot the riverscape. Most river cruise lines offer up a felucca ride as an excursion option and it's definitely a pleasant way to take in the views (the nice breeze on board is an added bonus).

While in Aswan, you will likely get the opportunity to swing by the **Aswan High Dam.** Although the dam in and of itself sort of pales by comparison to the beautiful temples and artifacts you see on the rest of the trip, the feat it accomplished in drastically reducing the amount of flooding along the Nile, as well as some of the complications it caused by threatening to submerge numerous archaeological sites (22 of which were relocated and saved,

highlights OF THE NILE

Luxor. It's hard to beat this buzzing axis of so many Nile big hits.

Abu Simbel. Sometimes included in a Nile cruise, sometimes offered as an extension, you will either have to drive (many, many hours) or take a charter flight to Abu Simbel. No matter how you get there, and no matter how burnt out you are on temples, go (and try to splurge for the flight). This temple was completely relocated in order to save it from being submerged in Lake Nasser.

Aswan. Perhaps it's those captivating cataracts, or just the effect the Nubians have on visitors, or the opportunities to get out on the water on smaller boats, but you instantly feel more relaxed being in Aswan.

including the incredibly impressive Abu Simbel and Philae), brings to light many of the more recent challenges in the region.

A boat ride to the island temple of **Philae** is a must. While the temple itself, devoted to the Egyptian goddess Isis and dating back to around 380 B.C., is a charmer, it's really the whole experience together that makes this excursion shine—the breezy motorboat ride past pretty islands of boulders, and approaching the island from the vantage point of the water. This is also a good opportunity to nab some trinkets from the Nubians.

But if you haven't had your fill of trinkets, and if you don't have plans to hit up the **Khan Al-Khalili,** or Grand Bazaar, in Cairo, head to the **bazaar in Aswan.** Even if you don't end up buying anything, it's just fun to poke around in all the spice, jewelry, rugs and trinket shops.

Key Ports
DENDERA

Dendera is located on the west bank of the Nile, about 50 miles north of Luxor. The Temple of Hathor, the main attraction here, is about 3 miles from the docking location and passengers are usually bused in air-conditioned motorcoaches to the temple.

Top Activity **Temple of Hathor:** Everyone has their favorite temple after cruising Egypt's Nile River, and the **Temple of Hathor** is often high on people's lists, not least because the nearly 2,400-year-old temple is so well preserved. Almost the entire facade is still standing, and there is a still intact roof over the temple, which has allowed for the preservation and restoration of actual colored hieroglyphics. Because of said intact roof, another treat is climbing an also intact staircase up to the rooftop and getting a view from above.

Off-the-Beaten-Path **Hieroglyphics:** Ask your guide or, if you're up a bit of adventure, some of the unofficial guides roaming the temple complex in their headdresses and *jelabiyas* to help you find a few points of interest at the temple, including what is claimed to be one of the few, or only, hieroglyphic depictions of **Cleopatra;** the location of the controversial **Dendera zodiac** (the original is in the Louvre); and to point you towards **the crypt.** They'll usually throw in some of their own colorful anecdotes and trivia, too. If you

RECOMMENDED food & drink

There is a lot of crossover between Egyptian food and certain Middle Eastern and Mediterranean dishes you may already be familiar with. For instance, Egyptians are all about the spreads and dips, such as **hummus, baba ghanoush** (an eggplant spread) and the very Egyptian dish **"foul,"** which is essentially a hearty bean spread that is eaten with any meal of the day. These are scooped up with Egyptian flat bread. **Grilled meats** also play a major role in Egyptian cuisine, anything from simple grilled beef, fish or chicken to something slightly more involved like grilled balls of meat, or **"kofta."** You'll also find plenty of kebabs, shawarmas and falafel. Food on board the Nile cruisers usually offer a mix of Egyptian and international cuisine.

go with unofficial guide, be prepared for him to ask you for a little *baksheesh*, or tip, afterwards (the equivalent of $1–$2 is plenty).

EDFU

Sixty-eight miles south of Luxor is the town of Edfu, located on the western bank of the Nile. The temple is only about a half a mile from the river, and it's not uncommon to be offered a horse carriage ride there.

Top Activity **Temple of Horus:** There's just something about Horus, that most awesome of ancient Egyptian gods most commonly portrayed as a falcon. If you think Horus is as cool as we do, then you'll definitely appreciate the temple named after him, the **Temple of Horus,** in Edfu. A very well preserved temple that dates back to around 200 B.C., highlights include the large statue of Horus in the courtyard and the detailed engravings and reliefs that tell his story in detail. Hopefully you will have a guide that properly breaks it all down for you. These stories will put any modern-day soap opera to shame!

YANGTZE

At 3,900 miles in length, the Yangtze River is up there with the other long rivers in the world. In fact, it's the third longest in the world after the Nile and Amazon, and the longest in Asia. But on a typical Yangtze River cruise, you will only sail about 365 miles between Chongqing and Yichang through southwestern China's Sichuan province on a cruise that will usually be 3 or 4 nights (the shorter length of the cruise combined with the long distance required to get to China is why many North American travelers often combine the Yangtze with longer land itineraries in China or elsewhere in Asia—there are longer Yangtze cruises too, though. See "Optional Add-Ons on the Route" at the end of this listing).

Sailing along the Yangtze River has been popular for decades, but more recently the Yangtze River has struggled to get out from under some of the negative publicity that surrounded the massive Three Gorges Dam project, which was completed in 2009. The 7,660-foot-long and 600-foot-high dam, the largest hydroelectric plant in world, caused hundreds of square miles of land along the river to be forcefully flooded, submerging entire cities and

adding on ABU SIMBEL

Located about 140 miles south of Aswan on the western edge of Lake Nasser the two temple structures of **Abu Simbel** date back to 1250 B.C. The construction was overseen by the very powerful pharaoh Ramesses II, whose power and ego are openly on display in the four 65-foot statues of him that adorn the larger temple. Abu Simbel tends to be a stop that some people waver on because of the added expense or travel time (it might be either included in your Nile cruise or offered as an optional excursion for an added charge), but if you have it in you for one last temple push, this is the temple to push for. You think by now that you've seen incredibly massive temples, and then you go to Abu Simbel, which seems to dwarf (in size not necessarily value) a lot of what you have seen up until then. And then you find out about how the temple was cut up into squares and relocated in its entirety in order to save it from being submerged in Lake Nasser, and you don't know whether the ancient Egyptians are more impressive or if modern technology is.

displacing 1.3 million people. The Chinese government relocated those communities further up the banks.

Despite some of the controversy surrounding the dam, and also in part because of it, the dam itself makes for a very compelling excursion, which is included in most Yangtze river cruises today. It's hard not to be amazed by the sheer engineering feat of the Three Gorges Dam project. There is a visitor center at the dam with a model to help better see the dam in its entirety and a guide should help break down all of its various components, such as its complicated system of locks and its ship elevator.

Among the scenic passageways the Yangtze River is most known for is the 120-mile stretch known as the Three Gorges. Here, the river narrows and ships are surrounded by soaring gorges on either side. And while they still soar quite high today, veteran Yangtze river cruisers say they were noticeably higher before the dam was built. Nevertheless, unknowing first-timers will be none the wiser and will still find that it's an incredibly scenic and impressive landscape to sail through.

One upside of the hardships that fell on the Yangtze river cruising market post-dam is that it spurred renewed investments in the vessels themselves with the hopes of attracting a more upscale clientele to the Yangtze than in the past, and of reinvigorating the market. The result is fancier digs from which to sail not just between those gorgeous gorges, but past curious pagodas and to witness what still remains of the strong cultures and traditions of the people who live along the Yangtze.

Ports of Embarkation: Chongqing & Yichang
CHONGQING

Chongqing is a very developed port city at the confluence of the Jialing and Yangtze rivers. There are numerous docks around the central peninsula area of Chongqing, and

The Yangtze River

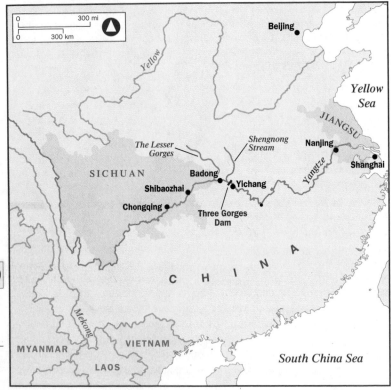

docking locations can change. Be sure to check with your river cruise line about your vessel's specific docking location.

Just like countless little-big cities in China, you may or may not have necessarily heard of Chongqing but it's actually a really massive metropolis of several million inhabitants. While some river cruise passengers may not spend much, if any, time in Chongqing other than to board their vessel, for those with a few extra hours or even a day or two to spare in the city, there are actually a fair number of interesting sights and attractions.

The best way to approach Chongqing is from a new-China-meets-old-China perspective. It is truly a city of contrasts (like much of the country) and it's fascinating to see the interplay between the ancient and modern.

To dive right into the heart of contemporary Chongqing, head to **Jiefangbei** or the **People's Liberation Monument** (177 Minzu Rd.), located right in the center of the city's bustling shopping area, complete with looming skyscrapers, dazzling neon lights and shopping galore. Once you have seen enough of Chinese consumer culture, head to charming **Ciqikou,** an ancient town located about 10 miles west of downtown Chongqing (you can either cab it or take the metro—Ciqikou has a dedicated stop on the Metro Line 1, and Chongqing has a very fast and reliable subway system). A one-time hub for producing and transporting porcelain, now Ciqikou is chock full of cute snack shops and trinket stores. It's not huge, but makes for a really sweet stroll through China's days of yore.

This last stop may be a little cheesy (okay, a lot cheesy), but we swear that the touristy **Hongyadong** (56 Cangbai Rd.), a sort of replica of old Chinese architecture clinging to the side of a cliff, is actually a decent place to get some Sichuan cuisine (see below), after a short shop-and-bop through the various tourist shops.

YICHANG

The two main ports used by Yangtze river cruise vessels in Yichang are located about 18 miles from downtown Yichang. If you need to go into Yichang, you will need to take a taxi.

Similar to Chongqing, many river cruise passengers simply use Yichang as the hopping on or hopping off point of their Yangtze river cruise. The reason most people come here is to visit the **Three Gorges Dam.** Most river cruises include a pretty extensive tour of the dam, including stopping at various vantage points to see the walls of the dam as well as the intricate locks system. As we mentioned in our section about locks (p. 54), the Three Gorges Dam has a five-tiered lock system that carries vessels 370 feet up or down through the graduated locks. There is also a 370-foot-high shiplift (like an elevator for ships) that can carry 3,000-ton vessels up or down in about 30 minutes. The regular five-step locks take about 2 hours and 40 minutes to pass through. Some Yangtze river cruise passengers will have the added bonus of actually passing through the Three Gorges Dam locks, and some won't. It all depends on which direction your cruise is sailing and whether it actually goes beyond the Three Gorges Dam. The dam also has a visitor center where you can see a model-size replica of the entire complex to better understand its size and scope.

Key Ports
SHIBAOZHAI

There is really one thing to see in the riverside town of Shibaozhai, the Shibao Pagoda. You will dock a short distance from the pagoda and walk there from the ship.

Top Activity You may already be able to see it from the ship, depending on your vantage point, but as you approach Shibaozhai, you may start to make out a red pagoda built into the side of a hill. This is **Shibao or Shibaozhai Pagoda,** a 12-story Buddhist pavilion dating back to the mid–19th century

RECOMMENDED food & drink

We have two words for you: hot pot. It's greasy and spicy and a bit of a mess, but the classic Sichuan hot pot meal is a must-try. Just imagine a big pot full of chili-spiced oil that you then proceed to throw any number of items into, could be meat, could be vegetables. You allow them to basically fry for a short time and then, gulp! Together with some marinated salads and rice, maybe a funky Asian soda to wash it all down, and you've got yourself a feast.

highlights OF THE YANGTZE

Three Gorges. This scenic stretch of the Yangtze River has been and likely always will be the main attraction.

Lesser Gorges. While the Three Gorges is the main attraction, you will also have the opportunity to get on a smaller boat

and wind through some of the lesser (in size only) gorges as well.

The Dam. Love it or hate it, the Three Gorges Dam has redefined the Yangtze River in profound ways and as such has become an important part of its story.

and worth climbing to the top of both for a closer look inside—where you will find a network of curious, seemingly abandoned chambers and rooms, some decorated with colorful wall paintings—as well as for the views of the Yangtze river landscapes from above. The hill itself makes for an attractive setting, with trees and shrubs jutting out from the rather dramatic rocky incline.

THE LESSER GORGES

As you may have already guessed, there isn't actually a port called "The Lesser Gorges," but about midway through your Yangtze River cruise in the Three Gorges area of the river, your vessel will either anchor mid-river or dock alongside a strip of shoreline to allow passengers to board smaller motorboats that will take them to and through some of the narrower passages and gorges of the Yangtze tributaries.

Top Activity   It's actually really great to be able to get out on the water and see the Yangtze, its tributaries and their attractive gorges more up-close on **a small boat excursion to the lesser gorges.** Some head to the **Shennong Stream** tributary of the Yangtze, others may head to the **Goddess Stream,** and still others may take passengers to another one of the smaller gorges. But as the rivers narrow and the gorges soar high above, the scenery truly comes to life. You may also be treated to a unique tradition whereby local villagers pull boats along harder-to-pass stretches by using ropes and tugging the boats from walkways along the cliffs.

Optional Add-Ons on the Route

For those who want to continue their Yangtze river cruise all the way to **Shanghai,** New York-based Victoria Cruises does offer that option on a 6-night sailing, starting at $1,610 per person. The cruise continues past the Three Gorges Dam in Yichang, with additional port stops in **Jiuhuashan,** where **Mount Jiuhua,** one of four sacred mountains in China, is located; **Nanjing,** the capital of China's Jiangsu province and home to a **Confucius Temple** that is known for the vibrant market outside; and finally ends up in **Shanghai,** China's huge international hub, defined by the **Bund promenade,** the skyline-defining **Oriental Pearl TV Tower** and those effortlessly delicious **Shanghai (or soup) dumplings.** Or add on Beijing, Shanghai and Xi'an: The classic tour of China will leave your camera's memory card empty and will not disappoint. You're also an easy flight away from **Hong Kong,** another pre- or post-cruise option.

THEME CRUISES

by Lisa Matte

Size. That's the biggest difference between a theme cruise on a riverboat and a theme cruise on an ocean liner: size of the ship, size of the passenger list, size of the theme roster, you name it—it all comes down to size.

What's right for you? The decision hinges on this: If you're intrigued by exploring a specific theme or topic in the company of people with similar interests, but prefer a more intimate setting, choose a river cruise. The choice of itineraries and routes may not be as expansive as on an ocean-going megaship, but the experience will match the setting—low key and personal with plenty of hands-on opportunities.

Cruising alone? Theme cruises are particularly attractive to solo cruisers, drawn to the idea of traveling with like-minded passengers. Shared interests ease social integration and options like roommate matches add to the appeal.

A wide select of theme cruises are available on river ships. The chart on the next page shows a sampling.

River cruise companies that include theme itineraries in their offerings usually list topics and sailing dates in a designated category on their websites. If your priority is to find a specific theme regardless of cruise line, **Theme Cruise Finder** (themecruisefinder. com) is a good place to start. Howard Moses, a travel agent and co-owner of Marietta, Ga.-based The Cruise & Vacation Authority (www.tcava.com), started the website on a lark in the early 2000s as a way to build a database of theme cruises around the world. Today, with more than 500 listings (for ocean and river theme cruises) it's among the most comprehensive guides to theme cruising available. There's no specific breakout category for river cruises—yet—so you'll have to do a bit of digging to narrow the field.

Sometimes ships are under full-ship charter to travel agencies and tour operators organizing cruises on a specific theme—which might be as diverse as golf cruises, classical music and adults-only party sailings. Again, you can find listings at Theme Cruise Finder. Given their relatively small size, river ships in some cases can also be chartered by those who want to do their own private events, such as a college reunion, corporate meeting or incentive group (contact the river line for information).

A Chart of Offerings

	ART	CULINARY & DRINK	CULTURE	FESTIVALS & HOLIDAYS	GOLF	COUPLES CRUISES	GAY AND/OR LESBIAN	HISTORY	MUSIC
Abercrombie & Kent				X				X	
AmaWaterways	X	X		X					
American Cruiseline		X	X					X	X
American Queen Steamboat Company		X	X	X				X	X
Avalon Waterways	X			X	X		X		
Crystal Cruises	X			X					
Emerald Waterways				X		X	X		
Tauck				X					X
Un-Cruise Adventures	X			X					X
Uniworld	X		X	X					
Vantage				X					
Viking River Cruises				X			X		
Ships of the former Haimark				X			X		
CroisiEurope				X					
Scenic Cruises				X					

Topics ebb and flow in popularity, but we have identified highlights of the themes on the calendars of the major river cruise lines and operators.

ART

AmaWaterways, Avalon Waterways and Crystal River Cruises all put the focus on art with cruises through landscapes that have inspired some of the world's best-known painters. Some itineraries feature a painting instructor on hand to give first-person advice on creating your own masterpiece.

AmaWaterways' Paris and Normandy itinerary journeys through regions captured on canvas by 19th-century masters Claude Monet, Pierre-Auguste Renoir and Paul Gauguin. Stroll through Monet's gardens then return to the ship to recreate the gorgeous setting with the guidance of an expert art instructor. All painting materials are supplied and you'll take home a one-of-a-kind memento.

Avalon Waterways invites guest to experience northern France with an art-focused itinerary that allows plenty of time to explore art museums in Paris, stroll through the gardens at Giverny, visit Château d'Auvers in Auvers-sur-Oise—the village where Vincent Van Gogh spent his final days—and take in Rouen Cathedral, the subject of Monet's well-known series of paintings.

Crystal's Crystal Mozart's "Paris and the Arts" itinerary offers an in-depth study of masterpieces housed in collections at Musée d'Orsay, d'Art Moderne de la Ville de Paris and the Louvre Museum. The ship sails to Rouen before returning to Paris.

FOOD & DRINK

Whether your personal tastes lean towards gourmet food, wine, beer or spirits, there's no shortage of **culinary theme cruises.**

Oenophiles may want to set their sights on AmaWaterways' roster of **wine-themed cruises** in destinations including Paris and the Seine, the Danube, the Rhine, Bordeaux, and Portugal's Douro River. Local wines are the focus.

Uniworld puts a special-interest twist on some of its most popular routes with date-specific Connoisseur Collection sailings focused on the **culinary** delights of France. Highlights of the culinary-themed "Paris & Normandy" sailings include a visit to La Couronne in Paris where renowned chef Julia Child first experienced French cuisine, an onboard Champagne tasting and a signature lecture: *From Vatel to Bocuse—Chef Dynasties in France.* Its 8-day "Burgundy & Provence" cruise includes an afternoon cocktail reception at Château de Seigneurs in Tournon, a visit to a truffle farm in the village of Grignan and a cooking demonstration and tea party at the Institut Paul Bocuse in Lyon. There's also a cruise in Bordeaux that includes a visit to Château Royal de Cazeneuve for a Sauternes wine-pairing lunch and a stop at the Rémy Martin estate in Cognac for a tasting.

Un-Cruise Adventures **wine-themed** sailings focus on Pacific Northwest vintners, bringing guests to the wineries and tasting rooms along the Columbia & Snake. A guest wine expert is onboard for the entire cruise. Highlights include a hosted lunch at Terra Blanca Winery & Estate Vineyard in Walla Walla, Wash.

Foodies flock to American Cruise Lines' *Food & Wine* itineraries. Lobster is a theme for cruises exploring the rocky coast and snug harbors of Maine. Head south to the Chesapeake Bay for a taste of Maryland's celebrated blue crabs (mallets and bibs, included). Hankering for a king-sized crab feast? Check out cruise itineraries for Washington's Puget Sound and San Juan Islands to indulge in Alaskan King Crab in all its glory.

Theme cruises aboard American Steamboat Company's *American Queen* include a **bourbon-themed** sailing that blends activities and excursions— music, food and workshops—with tours of some of the finest bourbon distilleries in the United States.

Avalon Waterways makes **beer** the focus on river cruises that include onboard tastings, visits to historic breweries and informative lectures about European brewing techniques. The 13-day Blue Danube Discovery River cruise begins with 2 nights in Budapest and includes port calls in Vienna, Passau and Regensburg (including a beer tasting).

You'll also learn about **craft beers** while exploring the Columbia & Snake on Un-Cruise Adventures' beer-themed sailings. Experts come onboard and there are beer pairings with regional cuisine, tours, tastings and informative presentations. Guest experts include Nate and Becca Schons, co-owners and brewers of Island Hoppin' Brewery in Washington's San Juan Islands, and Boe Trosset, co-owner of award-winning Aslan Brewing Company in Bellingham, Wash.

CULTURE

Uniworld's Monarch Collection is a series of **culture-themed** itineraries highlighting Europe's royal heritage. On a 15-day "European Jewels" cruise from Budapest to Amsterdam, highlights include a concert and dinner at Castle Weikersheim in Würzburg, Germany, a private cocktail reception hosted by Austrian Princess Anita von Hohenberg at her 13th-century castle home, and a private behind-the-scenes tour of Vienna's Spanish Riding School. There's also an 8-day cruise on the Danube that includes a private cocktail reception hosted by the princess, a private guided tour of Vienna's Spanish Riding School and an exclusive concert celebrating classical music by Mozart and Strauss at Vienna's imperial Hofburg Palace.

Or you might celebrate all things Americana aboard American Queen Steamboat Company's *American Queen*. Options include "The Mighty Mississippi," a 3-week journey along the Mississippi River and its tributaries, through landscapes that inspired American storyteller **Mark Twain.** American Cruise Line also does a Mark Twain Tribute Cruise itinerary from St. Paul to St. Louis on select dates.

CHRISTMAS MARKETS & HOLIDAY CELEBRATIONS

Festivals and holidays are a huge draw for river cruise aficionados, with itineraries focused on everything from local celebrations to major holidays. **Christmas Market** cruises, as operated by all the major lines in Europe, are extremely popular (whether designated specifically as "theme cruises" or not).

Oktoberfest on the American Queen brings a beer-fueled polka party. While the beer is domestic—a selection of German-style brews produced by homegrown breweries—a curator from the German American Heritage Center is onboard as a resource to share entertaining trivia and serve as a resource for information about culture, tradition and history of Oktoberfest. Polka lessons are provided; lederhosen optional.

Avalon's **Christmas Market** cruises through central Europe offer opportunity en route to indulge in sweet holiday treats while perusing handcrafted gifts at local Christmas markets. Local choral groups come aboard to sing Christmas carols; there are also on-board lectures about Christmas and New Year's traditions in Europe.

Uniworld celebrates the holiday season in a big way with an assortment of **Christmas-themed cruises** through European waterways. On "The Enchanting Christmas & New Year's" cruise guests listen to music played on the largest pipe organ in Europe on Christmas Eve in Passau and ring in the New Year with a gala dinner and ballroom dance in Budapest.

GOLF

Avalon Waterways invites golfers to make par on a **golf-themed cruise** on the Danube, with play at courses along the river. Experts are onboard to help you perfect your swing. Plan ahead for tee times at three select courses en route.

HISTORY

History buffs can learn about the **Civil War** while seeing the actual battle-fields on themed cruises operated by American Steamboat Company and American Cruise Line. Abercrombie & Kent brings a **World War II** specialist onboard select cruises on the Rhine, with excursions to battle sites in Arnhem and Remagen.

LIFESTYLE CRUISES

Couples Cruise (www.couplescruise.com) operates **adults-only** cruise itiner-aries created for people who enjoy an alternative lifestyle. For the second year in a row as we go to press, the line added a clothing-optional river cruise on an **Emerald Waterways** ship to its roster with Danube Delights. The 7-night cruise starts in Nuremburg and cruises through Germany, Slovakia and Hun-gary with stops including Budapest and Bratislava. On-board activities during the all-inclusive cruise—popular among swingers and nudists—include erotic theme parties and classes in BDSM and Tantra. While nudity and participating in erotic activities is optional, guests are encouraged to cruise with an open mind.

Several companies specializing in **gay cruises** charter river ships, including Brand g (www.brandgvacations.com) and RSVP Vacations (www.rsvp vacations.com). There are itineraries on rivers including Danube in Europe (including on ships operated by Emerald Waterways and Avalon Waterways) and in 2017, exotic itineraries in Myanmar and the Amazon. Olivia (Olivia. com), the leading company organizing **lesbian cruises,** was sponsoring one in China (on the Viking Emerald) as we went to press, in the Netherlands and Belgium (on Avalon Waterways) and on the Seine in France (on Avalon Waterways). Happy Gay Travel (happygaytravel.com) is a good resource for listings. Several companies also arrange **gay groups,** as opposed to full-ship charters, including Pied Piper Travel (www.piedpipertravel.com).

MUSIC

The rhythm is gonna get you when you board a **music-themed** river cruise. Groove to the beat of **Mississippi jazz and blues** aboard American Queen Steamboat Company's Mississippi "River Music Cruise" itineraries. Other options? Swing baby swing to the beat of Big Band sounds provided by the 13-piece Great American Swing Band playing original arrangements of tunes from America's **Big Band** Era. American Queen also has music cruises themed on **Country & Blues** (hosted by The Grand Old Opry's Dan Rogers), **Country Music** (with lectures including "The Country Side of Sun Records" and "Backstage at the Grand Old Opry) and **Elvis.**

Cruises for **classical music** lovers include Tauck's "Musical Magic" itinerary on the Danube, where you visit the haunts of Mozart, Beethoven, Bartók, Schubert, Liszt, Strauss and Haydn and listen to musical lectures and concerts along the way.

Avalon Waterways hits a high note with cruises along European waterways focused on **opera** and **jazz,** while UnCruise goes with smooth river sounds performed by **Pacific Northwest musicians.**

WELLNESS

Onboard spas may offer a respite from everyday stress, but a 13-day Avalon Waterways **wellness** itinerary sailing from Amsterdam to Vienna, is an immersive journey hosted by an onboard fitness trainer who runs stretching and yoga/Pilates classes while sharing her knowledge of fitness and a healthy lifestyle.

WINE EDUCATION

W ine lovers are attracted to river cruises, especially those that glide through such famous wine regions as France's Bordeaux, Burgundy, and Beaujolais, the Cote du Rhone and the Loire Valley; Germany's Mosel and Rhine Valley; and Austria's Wachau Valley.

These itineraries present rare opportunities to sip unique local varietals both on the ship and on shore; many itineraries include visits to vineyards and vistas of vines. If you don't find the wine cellar on your ship stocked with all the local varietals you want to try, pick up a bottle in the ports to bring aboard.

Here, Cleveland-based writer and wine lover Christine Jindra looks at wines you can sample along key rivers in Europe.

THE RHINE

A cruise on the **Rhine River** from Amsterdam to Basel takes you through The Netherlands, Germany, France and Switzerland; and to some of the world's northernmost vineyards.

The Rhine flows through nine of Germany's 13 wine districts, the Ahr, Baden, Hessische Bergstrasse, Mittelrhein, Mosel-Saar-Ruwer, Nahe, Pfalz, Rheingau, and Rheinhessen. Most of the country's best wines—which have a surprising elegance—are made from Riesling, the great white grape of Germany and king along the Rhine.

White grapes are treated with reverence in this part of the world, partly because Riesling once stood little chance of ripening so far north. After World War II, German vineyards reduced their risk and ensured a larger production by introducing the Muller-Thurgau grape, a crossing of Riesling and Madeleine Royale, developed in the late 19th century in a Swiss laboratory. The earlier-ripening grape allowed Germany to build a wine industry. It was also blamed for producing the bland, medium-sweet white wine that dominated Germany until the 1980s, such as Liebfraumilch and Piesporter. Remember the old Blue Nun label?

As tastes changed, German winemakers shifted to dry wines. Much of the Muller-Thurgau was replaced in the vineyards with higher-quality Riesling grapes, able to take more cold weather.

Germany also produces red wine—from Spätburgunder (Pinot Noir) and Dornfelder—two grapes used to create light-bodied

labels TO LOOK FOR

In Ahr: Jean Stodden Winery, H.J. Näkel Kreuzberg, Weingut Meyer-Näkel, Weingut Burggarten, Weingut Rudolf Fürst, and Weingut Sonneberg.

In Alsace: Jean-Baptiste Adam, Jean-Marc Bernhard, Meyer-Fonné, Bott-Geyl, Hugel et Fils, Zind-Humbrecht, Lucien Albrecht, Albert Boxler, Marcel Deiss, Rolly-Gassmann, and Cave de Ribeauvillé.

In Baden: Schloss Staufenberg, Schwarzer Adler, Schloss Neuweier, Danner, and Bercher.

In Hessische Bergstr: Der Stadt Bensheim, Simon-Bürkle, Brücke-Ohl, and Krupka.

In Mittelrhein: Toni Jost, J. Ratzenberger, Friedrich Bastian, Randolph Kauer, Lanius-Knab, Walter Perll, and August Perll.

In Mosul: J.J. Christoffel Erben, Donnhoff, Fritz Haag, Reinhold Haart, Heymann-Löwenstein, von Hövel, von Kesselstatt, Dr. Loosen, Joh. Jos. Prüm, Robert Weil, and Schloss Saarstein.

In Pfalz: Rebholz, Müller-Catoir, and Siegrist.

In Rheingau: Schloss Johannisberg (a winery that has been in production for 900 years), J.B. Becker, Georg Breuer, Domdechant Werner, Reiner, Joachim Flick, August Kesseler, Kloster Eberbach, Knyphausen, Peter Jakob Kühn, Franz Künstler, and Langwerth von Simmern and Leitz.

In Rheinhessen: Gunderloch, Balbach, Josef Drathen, Sankt Antony, and J. & H.A. Strub.

easy-to-drink wines. In Alsace, red wine is 100 percent Pinot Noir, resulting in a rose-colored light taste or a more intense red Burgundian style.

Ahr

Cruising down the Rhine from Amsterdam, the first wine region you'll encounter is the little-known German **Ahr,** west of the river and south of Bonn. Ahr's steep, sheltered slopes are the perfect environment for Spätburgunder (Pinot Noir) grapes and a varietal called Fruhburgunder. The warm, almost Mediterranean summer climate and the shelter from the Eifel Mountains allow Spätburgunder grapes to thrive. These reds (some vintners going light and others more full-bodied) are seldom, if ever, available in the United States because most wineries sell out of their bottled wines domestically.

Mittelrhein

On the east bank of the Rhine, the **Mittelrhein** wine region starts just below Bonn and follows the river 60 miles south to where the Rhine makes a one-quarter turn to the east. A long-growing season here is helped by the large volume of water flowing through the Rhine, which keeps temperatures warm in early spring and late fall. Mittelrhein's Riesling wines have a distinct acidity from the clayish/slate soil. The best wines are usually consumed locally.

Mosel

Back on the east bank, below the Ahr region, the **Mosel-Saar-Ruwer** river valleys empty into the Rhine at Koblenz. Mosel wines, most made from Riesling, excel in their mineral notes because of the microclimate—deep-angled slopes are south- and south-west facing and close enough to the river to catch the reflective warmth. The heavy amounts of slate in the soil store up and reflect the sun's heat and drain away the region's frequent surplus rainfall.

Mosel is Germany's third largest wine region in terms of area and the most internationally known; Riesling is the most prominent grape, other favorites are Kabinett and Spätlese wines.

Rheingau

After the Rhine makes its sharp bend near Wiesbaden, it flows west for 25 miles before flowing south, giving the vineyards on the right bank in the **Rheingau** wine district a southern exposure and more sun than most others. The steep slopes above the river are protected from northern storms by the Taunus Hills. The Rheingau produces most of Germany's highest-quality wine and the district has been key in the trend towards making drier German Rieslings.

Rheinhessen

The **Rheinhessen,** on the west bank of the Rhine, between Mainz and Worms, is Germany's largest wine region in area, and second to the Pfalz in the amount of wine produced. Much is for generic bulk wine and Rheinhessen is where the sweet Liebfrauenmilch, a big hit in Britain and America, was developed. But there is more than just mass-produced wines here. World-class Riesling is also produced in Rheinhessen from a stretch of vineyards on the river between Nackenheim and Nierstein, called the Roter Hang (Red Slope).

Pfalz

Germany's **Pfalz,** to the east of the Rhine, is a topographical extension of Alsace, which is to its south in France. It is an up-and-coming district with new, young producers of the dry style. It's one of the warmest German wine-growing regions; the climate is mild enough for almonds, figs and lemons to thrive. Pfalz's vineyards produce both white (60 percent) and red (40 percent) wines.

Alsace

South of Pfalz is **Alsace,** the Germanic region of France between the Rhine and the Vosges Mountains. To the north and east it shares a border with Germany; to the south with German-speaking Switzerland and to the west with the French provinces of Lorraine and Franche Comté.

Alsace wine is famous worldwide, and visiting wineries a favorite activity—the area is sometimes referred to as the Route du Vin.

Vineyards are along the eastern slopes of the Vosges foothills. The area is also famed for its pretty villages with brightly painted half-timbered houses.

Most Alsace wines are white, in the German tradition. Alsace vineyards are famous for their Silvaners, Rieslings and Gewurztraminers not produced anywhere else in France. The best wines are intense dry Rieslings, delicately dry Muscats and rich Pinot Gris and Gewurztraminers. There is also cultivation of Pinot Blanc (also known as Klevner), Chasselas Blanc and Tokaji (or Tokay) imported in the 16th century from Hungary.

The reds are from Pinot Noir. Most used to be almost rosé-colored and very light in taste, but recently a combination of climate change and improvements in winegrowing and winemaking has Alsace wineries turning out more intense red Burgundian styles of Pinot Noir. Try the wine with Alsace's wonderfully pungent Munster cheese and sweets.

Baden

Baden is the southernmost of Germany's wine regions, a long, slim strip that extends from near Heidelberg in the north to Lake Constance in the south along the Swiss border. Most cruise ships dock at Basel, the Swiss city where France, Germany and Switzerland converge.

Shielded by the Odenwald hills and the Black Forest on one side and the Vosges Mountains on the other, it enjoys the sunniest and warmest climate in Germany. Its grapes are varied and produce fresh white wines that are fragrant, spicy and aromatic and reds that are velvety to fiery.

Switzerland along the Rhine also produces some wines, mostly reds that cannot be compared to those of Germany. The primary types are Schaffhausen, Mariafeld, and Blauburgunder. Most Swiss wine is produced along the Rhone Valley between the Bernese and Valais Alps. It costs four times as much to produce wine in Switzerland than it does in France, so it is not commonly exported. The Rhine also flows through Austria but most Austrian wine is produced on the eastern side from north of the Danube to the southern border (see below).

THE UPPER DANUBE

As you cruise the Upper Danube River from Bavaria to Budapest, you pass impressive wine districts, including Germany's Franken region and the Wachau, Austria's historic wine region dating back to the 5th century.

Franken

Franken is **Bavaria**'s only wine district and most of its vineyards are on hilly slopes lining the Main River north of Nuremberg. But when cruising along the Upper Danube in Bavaria, particularly in Regensburg, you will find Franken wines—most of them dry white wines.

Franken's climate has cold winters, high annual rainfall and early frosts, making the area unsuitable for the late-ripening Riesling found throughout much of Germany. In Franken, the grapes are the Müller-Thurgau, Silvaner and new crossings, such as Bacchus and Kerner. The best Franken wines are traditionally bottled in the distinctive Bocksbeutel, a squat green or brown bottle with a round body.

The Wachau

As you travel into **Austria,** the Wachau, vineyards between Melk and Krems, with their silt sediments and rocky steep riverbanks, benefit from the daily

labels TO LOOK FOR

In Franken: Bürgerspital, Staatlicher Hofkeller, Hans Wirsching, Norbert Muth, Horst Sauer, and Stein.

In Wachau: Domäne Wachau, Emmerich Knoll, Franz-Xavier Pichler, Franz Hirtzberger, and Peter Veyder-Malberg.

In Austria's Other 15 Wine Regions: Forstreiter, Mantlerhof, Stadt Krems and Birgit Eichinger. For the Kamptal district, look for the Hirsch, Fred Loimer, Brundlmayer, and Schloss Gobelsburg labels.

mixture of cool, moist air from forests in the northwest and the warmer air coming from an eastern plain. A dramatic drop in nighttime temperatures, with the moderating influence of the Danube, creates fresh white wines. You can sample vibrant and spicy Grüner Veltliner and the dry, mineral-rich Riesling grapes. Among the most established and well-regarded in Austria, Wachau accounts for less than 5 percent of Austria's wine production.

Most of Austria follows a wine classification systems based on ripeness and harvest. However, Wachau wines have a unique system classifying them as Steinfeder, Federspiel, or Smaragd, all referring to the level of alcohol and the style of the wine: light, medium or full-bodied respectively.

Most of the Steinfeder wines, the lightest style, are consumed in Austria. Named after a grass grown near the vineyards, they are fresh, fruity wines with a maximum alcohol level of 11.5 percent. These wines are crafted from the earliest picked grapes in the Wachau and are the least expensive.

The second-tier Federspiel wines, named after a falcon hunted in the Wachau, are strong with a generous character. These wines have an alcohol level between 11.5 percent and 12.5 percent.

Smaragd wines, rich in weight and flavor, are the most coveted wines of the Wachau. They are made from the ripest grapes with the highest concentration of sugars. Alcohol level is a minimum of 12.5 percent and is suitable for aging. Smaragd wines are named after an emerald-lizard that lives in the vineyards.

More of Austria & Slovakia

As you travel the Upper Danube, you can sample Grüner Veltliner and Riesling grapes wines from many of Austria's other 15 wine regions, including Kremstal, Kamptal, Niederösterreich, Burgenland, Steiermark (also called Styria), and Wien (Vienna)—yes, even Vienna produces wine but its vineyards are no longer within the city's prestigious inner-walled First District but in other districts and city outskirts.

The DAC (Districtus Austriae Controllatus) label on the grapes of nine districts, including Kremstal and Kamptal, indicates the producer's name and location, the wine's region/village/vineyard of origin, its sweetness, the grape variety it's made from, and an indication of the grapes' ripeness level.

As you continue toward Budapest, the Grüner Veltliner white grape will be found in Slovakia, but you will also encounter grapes most likely new to you. The white Welschriesling grape is grown in Hungary, Croatia, Czech Republic, Romania and Slovakia, as well as in Austria. Despite its name, the Welschriesling is unrelated to the great German grape Riesling. The Welschriesling, also called Olaszrizling, is dry with a fruity aroma evoking green apples.

Slovakian wine comes mostly from vineyards clustered around Bratislava and scattered east toward the border with Hungary. The best-known Slovakian wines of the country's six wine regions are related to its ties with Hungary and its internationally known sweet Tokaji wine. At the end of World War I, the eastern fringe of the Tokaji region was annexed to Slovakia, giving the country a reliable consumer base. Sweet Tokaji wines from this corner of Slovakia have the right to be labeled as Tokajsky. (Also see Hungary below.)

THE LOWER DANUBE

A cruise on the **Lower Danube River,** with its beautiful and diverse terrain, is an adventure along a route less traveled by Westerners. The area, still struggling economically more than 20 years after the fall of Communism, is full of historical, architectural and cultural delights. Wine is one of them.

In the Lower Danube River region, the white Welschriesling (as mentioned above) produces a dry wine with a fruity aroma. Unlike on the Upper Rhine, you are unlikely to visit any vineyards, but you will have opportunity to taste local wines on your ship.

Hungary

But it's near Budapest that you will encounter Hungary's most famous red wine: Egri Bikavér, which translates to Bull's Blood because of its deep color, full body and robust flavors. Bull's Blood is often served with beef tenderloin.

Hungary is also known for **Tokay,** a dessert wine made from the Furmint grape and whose sweetness is measured in *puttonyos,* or baskets of sweet grapes used—the sweetest being six puttonyos.

Croatia

Croatia has produced wines since Roman times but has more recently come of age, with 300 wine regions and some of the best producers seemingly intent on celebrating native grapes over the more commercially expedient international varieties. Along the banks of the Danube, the country's easternmost sub-region, Podunavlje, has wine-growing areas including Srijem and Erdut and Baranja (where there's a European Union-designated wine road). As in the neighboring and better-known sub-region, Slavonia, the dominant grape is Graševina, which is used to create a dry, refreshing wine with floral and fruit aromas, but there's also Traminer and in the past few years Chardonnay, Sauvignon, Rhein Riesling, Cabernet Sauvignon and Merlot (a 2008 Merlot from Belje won a gold medal at the Decanter World Wine Awards).

labels TO LOOK FOR

In Croatia: Erdutski Vinogradi, Ilok Cellars (Iločki Podrumi), and Belje.

In Serbia: Čoka Cellar, Palić Cellar, WOW, Vinski Dvor, Braca Rajković, Aleksic, Temet, Maurer, Ivanović, Vino Budimir, and Spasić.

In Bulgaria: Bessa Valley, Todoroff, Edoardo Miroglio, Asenovgrad, Starata Izba, Parvenetz, and Borovitza.

In Romania: Avincis, Liliac, Prince Stirbey, Nachbil, Rotenberg, LacertA, Villa Vinea, Petro Vaselo, and Bendis Brut.

Serbia

Serbia's nine wine regions, not as clearly defined as those in countries with better developed wine industries, basically follow the path of the Velika Morava River as it approaches its confluence with the Danube.

A large number of small producers create quality wines. Eager to highlight its native grapes, Serbia is revitalizing the red Prokupac and white Tamjanika grapes. Prokupac goes well with roasted lamb, pork and a stuffed cabbage dish called *sarma*. Tamjanika is best with light white meat, vegetable and fruit salads and medium and light-bodied cheeses.

The most planted local grape is Smederevka, known for producing large quantities of unremarkable white wine. To increase the potential interest of the wine, Smederevka is blended with Welschriesling, often called Laski Riesling.

As the country modernizes its wine industry and makes wines for export, Riesling and Sauvignon Blanc have been imported into Serbia. Serbia's imported reds are based on the French varieties of Pinot Noir, Gamay, Cabernet Sauvignon and Merlot.

Bulgaria

Bulgaria is gradually finding its identity as a modern wine-producing nation, discovering new *terroirs*, grape varieties and styles. Most of the Bulgarian wine industry is in the Danube Plain and Black Sea regions. At the height of the Communist rule in the 1960s, Bulgaria imported French varieties such as Cabernet Sauvignon, Merlot, Chardonnay, Riesling and Muscat.

Today Bulgaria is trying to re-establish traditional Bulgarian grapes. Red wines include: Mavrud, a spice and fruity varietal with high tannins; Melnik, reputably the favorite wine of Winston Churchill, with a captivating taste much like that of Châteauneuf-du-Pape; Pamid, a pleasant light and fruity red wine that goes well with the country's heavy cuisine; and Gamza, also known as Kadarka, a fresh, harmonious and gently fruit wine.

Dimyat and Keratsuda are two white grapes being reestablished. Dimyat, sweet with a strong aroma, is Bulgaria's most widely grown indigenous white grape. Usually not aged but used to make high-quality Brandy and Rakia. Keratsuda is a simple table wine, with a strong aroma and a characteristic golden color that turns rose-amber once the wine is opened. Keratsuda is used to make fortified wines, which resemble Sherries.

Pelin is not a grape but a traditional Bulgarian style of wine flavored with wormwood—the same herb used as a chief ingredient in Absinthe. Pelin can be made from red or white wine, often with a lower alcoholic content, and can even be carbonated.

Romania

Romania, one of the oldest wine regions in Europe, dates back more than 6,000 years. Homer and Herodotus wrote of Thracian wines. The ancestors of the Romanian people, the Daci, were great agriculturists who cultivated the grape vine and also made wine, as noted by ancient Greek and Roman historians.

Today Romania cultivates two categories of grapes—traditional Romanian varieties and international varieties that were imported after the 1880's epidemic when North American phyloxera insects spread throughout Europe killing most of the vine strands in the region.

Romanian local varieties are **Black Maiden** (Feteasca Neagra), **White Maiden** (Feteasca Alba), **Romanian Incensed Maiden** (Tamaioasa Romaneasca), and the **Royal Maiden** (Feteasca Regala). The Black Maiden produces higher-end red wines that range from dry to sweet and are better when aged. White Maiden creates a dry or semi-dry white wine and is the most popular vine in Romania. Sweet wines are a Romanian specialty. Popular international varieties are Sauvignon Blanc and Cabernet Sauvignon.

BORDEAUX

A cruise around the **Bordeaux** region in southwestern France explores the Garonne and Dordogne rivers and Gironde estuary. Voyages begin and end in Bordeaux and visits to wine chateaus outside of towns including Margaux, Haut-Medoc, Lafite-Rothschild, Sauternes, Saint-Emilion, and Graves are part of the fun. Cruise lines stop at a few wineries, but do-it-yourself types must plan ahead as Bordeaux-area wine estates typically are open only by appointment. You'd also have to hire a car or taxi to get to the estates.

Bordeaux produces dry, medium-bodied red wines, the finest (and most expensive) of which come from the great chateaux of the Medoc, eight appellations or geographic designations, located on the Left Bank of the Bordeaux, particularly those in Pauillac and Margaux. Many complain about high prices for Bordeaux wines, but much of the attention is on the First Growths wines (high scoring classification), most in Medoc, and wine from the Right Bank districts of Saint-Emilion and Pomerol.

With nearly 10,000 wine producers, brand recommendations are impossible. Bottles of Bordeaux dry red wine are sold anywhere from a few dollars to those from the top chateaux priced at several thousand dollars.

Look for wines from up-and-coming appellations, which offer less expensive wines, such as Cotes de Castillon, Lalande de Pomerol, Fronsac, Canon Fronsac, Bordeaux Superieur, Entre Deux Mers, and Cotes de Bordeaux.

Merlot is the dominate grape used in most red, Bordeaux value wines, but Cabernet Sauvignon, Cabernet Franc, Malbec, Petit Verdot and Carmenere are also used.

Often inexpensive and refreshing white Bordeaux wines are produced from a combination of Sauvignon Blanc, Semillon, Muscadelle, Pinot Gris, Ugni Blanc (also called Trebbiano), and Colombard.

RHONE-SAONE

The 500-mile-long **Rhone-Saone River** wends its way through the heart of French wine country—the Burgundy, Beaujolais and Rhone Valley wine districts—before flowing into the Mediterranean. On the Saone, the town of Chalon-sur-Saone is the gateway to the Burgundy wine region; in the south, a river delta empties the Rhone into the Mediterranean near Marseilles. Here the Rhone is in Provence and the wines—and the people—are warm and welcoming, full of fruit and spice.

Burgundy

Burgundy's key grape varieties are Pinot Noir and Chardonnay; their lessor cousins are the Gamay and Aligote grapes. The district's better vineyards are classified as **Grand Cru,** the highest-quality; **Premier Cru,** very high quality but not on par with a Grand Cru; **Village,** wines of good quality but without the Grand and Premier status; and **Regional,** the lowest level of classification.

These wines, even at the lowest level, come from one of the best wine regions in the world, the region that made Pinot Noir and Chardonnay famous.

Beaujolais

The **Beaujolais** region starts 130 miles to the south near Lyon where the Rhone and Saone rivers meet. Its widespread plantings of vibrant and fruity red Gamay make Beaujolais one of the few regions of the world largely focused on a single grape. White Beaujolais Blanc, from Chardonnay and Aligote grapes, is also produced here.

Beaujolais wines are classified as standard **Beaujolais,** Beaujolais Villages, and the youthful **Beaujolais Nouveau.** The region's highest-quality wines are those of the Beaujolais Cru. They come from ten vineyards that present the best of the Beaujolais: serious, delicious, and often age-worthy, wines.

labels TO LOOK FOR

In Burgundy: Georges Duboeuf, Domaine Henri Perrot-Minot, and Joseph Drouhin Chorey-les-Beaune.

In Beaujolais: Richard Rottiers, Clos de la Roilette, Domaine de la Bonne Tonne, Julien Merle, and Jean-Paul Brun.

In Rhone Valley: Chapoutier, E. Guigal, Yves Cuilleron, Auguste Clapes, Jean-Michel Gérin, Château de Beaucaste, Andre Brunel, Le Clos Saint Jean, Mayard, Domaine de Marcoux, and Mas de Boislauzon.

Rhone Valley

From Lyon, where the Rhone and Saone rivers meet, the Rhone flows south through the important Rhone Valley wine region; its vineyards in the north are dramatically perched on steep slopes of granite and enjoy a continental climate of hot summers, moderate rainfall and cold winters. In the flatter south, the rocky, sandy soils enjoy the warmer winters of a Mediterranean climate. Rhone wines are crafted and inspired by a variety of grape and growing environments, giving pleasure to wine-lovers worldwide.

The smaller, more quality-driven northern Rhone uses Syrah to make prestigious red wines such as Côte Rôtie, Hermitage, and Condrieu. White grapes here make Viognier, Marsanne, and Roussanne. The larger and more prolific south has more grape varieties, including the red Grenache and Mourvedre, which are combined with Syrah to produce the GSM blend—Grenache-Syrah-Mourvedre.

The world-famous **Chateauneuf-du-Pape** area is in Avignon in the south of the Rhone wine region and produces powerful, full-bodied red wines made predominantly from Grenache, Syrah and Mourvedre.

Both the north and the south Rhone wine areas can claim the regional Cotes du Rhone appellation for their red, rosé and white wines. A higher status Cotes du Rhone Villages designation is restricted to about 20 villages clustered in the southern section of the Rhone near the town of Orange which produce slightly higher quality wines. These vineyards can add their village name to their wines, resulting in colorful but long-winded names such as Cotes du Rhone Villages Saint-Pantaléon-les-Vignes.

DOURO

Vineyards along the **Douro River** Valley, from Porto, Portugal's Atlantic costal city, to the Spanish border, are spectacular. The Portuguese stretch between the towns of Mesão Frio and Pinhão, where the vineyards cling to the steep terraces on either side is the most beautiful part of the Douro. Tastings at port lodges and wineries are very much part of the Douro cruise experience.

The **Douro** wine region produces Portugal's best quality Port, the fortified wine. The region near Pinhão, the center of Portugal's **Port** wine production, is a UNESCO World Heritage Site in honor of the economic impact of 2,000 years of winemaking. The Douro Valley was defined and established as a protected region in 1756, making it the oldest defined and protected wine region in the world. Italy's Chianti (1716) and Hungary's Tokaji (1730)

labels TO LOOK FOR ALONG THE DOURO

Graham's Quinta dos Malvedos, Taylor's Quinta de Vargellas, Symington Family Estates, Niepoortt Vinhos, Quinta Vale D. Maria, Quinta do Vallado, Quinta do

Crasto, Quinta do Vale Meão, Dow's Prats & Symington Chryseis, Casa Ferreirinha, and Quinta do Pôpa.

regions were defined earlier but without regulations. Port varieties range from inexpensive **Ruby Port** and 2-year-old **Tawny Port** to **Aged Tawny Port** (with is aged in casks 10, 20, 30, or 40 years) and **Vintage Port,** the best and most expensive—the full declarations of Vintage (agreed upon by the majority of shippers) so far this century have been 2000, 2003, 2007 and 2011. New on the market is a **Rose Port.**

The same red grapes that you see in Port are mostly used for the region's dry red wines, which tend to be robust and full-bodied and often are aged in oak.

Grape varieties, which are bottled alone or blended, include Touriga Nacional, considered to be the country's finest grape; Touriga Franca, which is lighter and more perfumed; Tinta Barroca, grown primarily in the Douro region; and Tinta Roriz, called Tempranillo in Spain.

White grapes make up only a small fraction of the wines you'll find, and include Rabigato, Gouveio, Viosinho, and Malvasia Fina and are similar to White Burgundy.

ELBE

Most Elbe River cruises begin with hotel nights in Berlin and end in or near Prague in the Czech Republic (or vice versa), providing a cultural tour of Germany and Eastern Europe. From Dresden to Hamburg, the river passes by the vineyards of **Sachsen** in the German state of Saxony and the beautiful Sandstone Mountains, known locally as the Saxon Alps.

Sachsen, the furthest north and east of Germany's wine district, is one of two former East Germany wine regions added to the western region with unification in 1990. The other is Saale-Unstrut. Dry wines are favored here—of the type drunk by the Saxon kings and Martin Luther.

Most Sachsen vineyards are sheltered in the Elbe valley where the river moderates the cold winters and late spring frosts and help make grape cultivation possible. Summers are hot and many vineyards are terraced to take advantage of every hour of sunlight.

More than 80 percent of production is white wine with Muller-Thurgau, Weissburgunder and Riesling grapes. Two unusual white grape varieties grown in Sachsen are Goldriesling, a cross of Alsatian Riesling and Courtillier, and Elbling, central Europe's oldest grape variety. Because of local popularity and small production, finding these wines outside of Germany—or even outside of Saxony—is difficult; drinking Sachen wine is a perk of your visit.

labels TO LOOK FOR ALONG THE ELBE

Schloss Proschwitz, Sachen's oldest winery; Schloss Wackerbarth, Sachsen's	oldest sparkling wine cellar; and Klaus Zimmerling.

Index

See also Accommodations and Restaurant indexes, below.

General Index

A

Abercrombie & Kent, 18, 212, 219–220
World War II cruises, 329
Abu Haggag Mosque (Egypt), 318
Abu Simbel (Egypt), 319, 321
Activities, onboard. *See* specific cruise lines and ships
Adventures by Disney, 10, 136, 137
Ahr wine region, 332
Airport arrival, 52–53
Air travel
add-ons, 35
canceled or delayed flights, 53
Allianz, 40
Alsace Lorraine, barge cruises, 217
Alsace wine region, 333–334
Alte Nikolaikirche (Frankfurt), 243
Alte Oper (Frankfurt), 243
Altes Rathaus
Bamberg, 245
Nuremberg, 244
AmaBella, 138–139
AmaCello, 140–141
AmaCerto, 138–139
AmaDagio, 140–141
AmaDante, 140–141
AmaDara, 142–143
Amadeus Cruises, 212
AmaDolce, 140–141
AmaLegro, 140–141
AmaLotus, 142–143
AmaLyra, 140–141
AmaPrima, 138–139
AmaPura, 143–144
Amarapura, Myanmar, 308–309
AmaReina, 138–139
AmaSerena, 138–139
AmaSonata, 138–139
AmaVerde, 138–139
AmaVida, 141–142
AmaViola, 4, 136, 137–138
AmaVista, 138–139
AmaWaterways, 4, 5, 11, 131–144. *See also* specific ships
activities, 134
art cruises, 326
brief description of, 17, 131
children's program, 134–135
dining options, 132–133
entertainment, 135
fleet, 132
Frommer's Ratings, 137
itineraries, 134–135
overall experience, 131–132
passenger profile, 132
postcards, 56
pre- & post-cruise stays, 136–137

Privilege Rewards Program, 34
pros and cons, 131
service, 135
tours, 136
wine-themed cruises, 327
Amazon Discovery, 190–191
Amazon Dream, 299
Amazon River, Brazilian, 299
Amazon River, Peruvian, 11, 20, 293–298
highlights, 297
optional add-ons, 298
recommended food and drink, 298
Amenities, best river cruises for, 5
America, 152–153
American Cruise Line
Civil War cruises, 329
culture-themed cruises, 328
American Cruise Lines, 10, 147–153, 292. *See also* specific ships
culinary theme cruises, 327
American Empress, 10, 160–161
American Pride, 150–151
American Queen, 158–160, 328
American Queen Steamboat Company, 5, 10, 153–161, 292. *See also* specific ships
activities, 156–157
bourbon-themed cruises, 327
brief description of, 153
children's program, 157
Civil War cruises, 329
culture-themed cruises, 328
dining options, 156
entertainment, 157
fleet, 155–156
Frommer's Ratings, 153
itineraries, 154–155
music-themed river cruises, 329–330
overall experience, 153–155
passenger profile, 156
pre- & post-cruise stays, 158
pros and cons, 153
service, 157
tours, 157–158
American Society of Travel Agents (ASTA), 30
Amsterdam, 235–236
Angkor Archeological Site, 314
Angkor Pandaw, 196–197
Angkor Wat (Cambodia), 310
Anne Frank House (Amsterdam), 235
Antoinette, 79, 82–85
Aqua Amazon, 164
Aqua Expeditions, 161–166. *See also* specific ships
Aqua Mekong, 165–166
Arbanassi, 232
Arc de Triomphe (Paris), 267
Aria Amazon, 164–165
Arles, 263–265
Arles Amphitheatre, 264
A-Rosa River Cruises, 18, 212
Arromanches, 269
Art Basel, 236

Art cruises, 326
Asia, seasons, 19
Astoria (Oregon), 279–280
Astronomical Clock (Prague), 256
Aswan, Egypt, 318–319
Aswan High Dam (Egypt), 318
ATMs/banks, 41
Avalon Affinity, 128–129
Avalon Creativity, 128–129
Avalon Felicity, 128–129
Avalon Luminary, 128–129
Avalon Myanmar, 129–130
Avalon Scenery, 128–129
Avalon Siem Reap, 129–130
Avalon Waterways, 4–6, 121–130. *See also specific ships*
activities, 123
art cruises, 326
beer-themed cruises, 327
brief description of, 17, 121
children's program, 123
Christmas Market cruises, 328
dining options, 123
entertainment, 123
fleet, 122
Frommer's Ratings, 122
golf-themed cruises, 329
itineraries, 124–125
overall experience, 122
passenger profile, 123
pre- & post-cruise stays, 126
pros and cons, 121
repeat-passenger discounts, 34
service, 124
Suite Ships class, 126–128
tours, 125–126
wellness cruises, 330
Avignon, 262–263
Ayeyarwady River (Irrawaddy River), 305–309

B

Baden wine region, 334
Bad Schandau, 259
Bagan, 307
Baggage limits, 45–46
Bakeshop (Prague), 257
Bamberg, 245
Bamberg Cathedral, 245
Bamboo Bridge across the Tonle Sap (Cambodia), 314
Banks, 41
Barca d'Alva, 253
Barge Connection, 219
Barge cruising, 216–220
The Barge Lady, 220
Basel, 236
Basel Münster, 236
Baselworld, 236
Bassac Pandaw, 197–198
Bastei Rock Formation, 259
Baton Rouge, 287
Bayeux Tapestry, 269
B.B. King Museum, 287
Beale Street (Memphis), 284
Beaujolais wine region, 339
Beaune, 263
Beer, 32

B

Beer tasting, Cologne, 237
Beer-themed cruises, 327–328
Beethoven Hall (Moscow), 273
Belgrade, 230–231
Belmond Afloat in France, 218
Berlin, 257–258
Best river cruises, 3–6
    for the best itineraries, 6
    best of the best, 3–4
    for cuisine, 4
    for families, 4
    for included shore excursions, 5
    for pre- & post-tours, 6
Beverages, 46–47
Biedenharn Museum of Coca-Cola Memorabilia, 286
Biking, Vienna, 227
Bishops' Residenz (Würzberg), 244
Bizet, 119
Blaye, 249
Blount Small Ship Adventures, 212
Boarding pass, 57
Bollywood Theater (Portland), 279
Bolshoi Theatre (Moscow), 273
Booking a cruise, 26–42
    air add-ons, 35
    choosing your cabin, 36–38
    costs, 30–32
    deposits and cancellation policies, 39
    on the Internet, 30
    Intra-vacation flights, 36
    money-saving strategies, 32–35
    pre- & post-cruise hotel deals, 36
    with travel agents, 26
    travel insurance, 39–41
Bordeaux, 246–250
Bordeaux wine region, 338–339
Bratislava, 227
Brauerei Fischerstube (Basel), 236
Brazilian Amazon, 299
Bucharest, 229
Budapest, 224–225
Budgeting, for shipboard expenses, 46–47
Bulgarian wine regions, 337–338
Burgundy barge cruises, 217
Burgundy wine region, 339
Burgundy wineries, 263
Busch Brewery stables (St. Louis), 289
Business hours, 41

C

Cabins, 14, 24. *See also specific cruise lines and ships*
    choosing, 36–38
    river cruising vs. ocean cruising, 13
    size of, 38
Café des Federations (Lyon), 262
Café du Monde (New Orleans), 285
Café Van Gogh (Arles), 265
Cambodia, 310–315
    recommended food and drink, 315
Canal cruises. *See also Barge cruises*
    captaining your own ship, 219
Canal du Midi, 217
Canals, Dutch and Belgian, 240
Cancel for any reason insurance, 40
Cancellations, 39
Carriage House Restaurant (Natchez), 286
Casa de Fierro (Iquitos), 296
Cash, 41, 47
Casual cruises, 23
Cathedral Basilica of St. Louis, 289
Cathédrale de Notre-Dame (Paris), 267
Cathedral of Vasily the Blessed (Moscow), 273
Catherine, 3–4, 79, 83–85
Caudebec-en-Caux, 269
Celebrating special occasions, 25
Cellphones, 41, 53–54
Century Cruises, 11, 166–171
Century Diamond, 170–171
Century Emerald, 170–171
Century Legend, 169–170
Century Paragon, 169–170
Century Sky, 170–171
Century Star, 170–171
Century Sun, 170–171
Cesky Krumlov, 226
Chalon-sur-Saone, 263
Champagne region, 217
Chardonnay, 117
Chateau de Bizy, 268
Check-in, 53
Children's programs, 24
China, 320–324
Chobe Princess houseboats, 300
Chobe River, 21, 300
Chongqing, China, 321–323
Christmas Market cruises, 328
"Christmas market" cruises, 62
Christmas-themed cruises, 328
Church of St. Dmitry on the Blood (Uglich), 275
Church of the Intercession (Kizhi), 275
Church of the Savior on Spilled Blood (St. Petersburg), 274
Church of the Transfiguration (Kizhi), 275
Ciqikou (China), 322–323
Civil War, 329
Clarkston, 279
Classical music cruises, 330
Clinton, Iowa, 288, 292
Clothes
    packing for your cruise, 43–44
    space for storing, 14
Club Ebony, 287
Coffee, 32
Cologne, 237–238
Columbia Gorge, 280–281
Columbia Gorge Interpretive Center Museum, 280–281
Columbia River, 21, 277–282
The Columbia River Maritime Museum (Astoria), 280

Copenhagen, 276
Cosmos, 6
Costs, cruise, 30–32
Côte de Beaune, 263
Côte de Nuits, 263
Côtes du Rhône, 263
Couples Cruise, 329
Credit cards, 29, 41
    lost or stolen, 42
Crew. *See Service*
Croatia, 336
CroisiEurope, 18, 171–177
    barge cruises, 219
Cruisecritic.com, 30
Cruise Lines International Association (CLIA), 30
Cruise resellers, 146
Crystal Cruises, 10
Crystal River Cruises, art cruises, 326
Cu Chi Tunnels (Vietnam), 313
Cuisine, best river cruises for, 4
Culinary theme cruises, 327–328
Culture-themed cruises, 328
Currency exchange, 56
Customs and Border Protection (CBP), U.S., 59
Customs regulations, 42, 59

D

Daily programs, 56
Daniel et Denise (Lyon), 262
Danube Delta, 233
Danube River, 6
    brief description of, 19
    locks, 55
    Lower Danube, 228–233
    Upper Danube, 221–228
    water levels, 48
Davenport, Iowa, 288
Deals, how to get, 22
Debarkation, 58
Delfin II, 213
Delta Interpretive Center, 287
Dendera, Egypt, 319–320
Departure time, 58
Deposits, 39
Deutsches Weihnachtsmuseum (Rothenburg), 245
Dining options. *See specific cruise lines and ships*
Disabilities, travelers with, 25
Discounts, 32–34
Dnieper River, 20, 259
Documents, 50–52
Douro River, 20, 250–255
    vineyards, 340–341
Dresden, 257, 258–259
Drinks packages, 46–47
Dubuque, Iowa, 288, 291
Dutch and Belgian rivers and canals, 240

E

East Side Gallery (Berlin), 260
Edfu (Egypt), 320
Egypt, 314–320
Egyptian Museum (Cairo), 318

Map List

Photo Credits

Published by

FROMMER MEDIA LLC

ISBN 978-1-62887-250-7 (paper), 978-1-62887-251-4 (e-book)
Editorial Director: Pauline Frommer
Editor: Pauline Frommer
Production Editor: Heather Wilcox
Cartographer: Roberta Stockwell
Cover Design: Dave Riedy

For information on our other products or services, see www.frommers.com.

Frommer Media LLC also publishes its books in a variety of electronic formats. Some content that
appears in print may not be available in electronic formats.

Manufactured in the United States of America

5 4 3 2 1

ABOUT THE AUTHORS

Fran Golden is a well-known travel writer and creator of USA Today's Experience Cruise website. She is also chief contributor for the cruise magazine *Porthole*. The former travel editor of the *Boston Herald*, she writes for numerous newspapers, magazines, and websites, including *Virtuoso Life* magazine and ShermansCruise.com, and she is the author or co-author of several travel books, including *Frommer's EasyGuide to Alaska Cruises and Ports of Call*. Fran is married to fellow cruise writer David Molyneaux, and when they are not at sea, they make their home in Cleveland.

Michelle Baran is a senior editor at *Travel Weekly*, where she has been reporting on the travel and river cruise industries since 2007. She has covered everything from Egypt's Arab Spring to Colombia's shedding its cocaine past, from traveling alone as a woman abroad to traveling on a cruise ship along many of the world's most well-known rivers. Baran has sailed the Danube, Rhone, Volga, Mekong, Yangtze, Nile, Amazon, and Irrawaddy rivers, among others, and she has also written about river cruising for *Travel + Leisure*, *Travel + Leisure Southeast Asia*, and *Budget Travel*. Her *Travel Weekly* cover story about women traveling the globe solo, "Courage and Caution," was a 2014 finalist for a *Folio* magazine Eddie Award. Prior to working at *Travel Weekly*, Baran covered the fashion industry at Conde Nast's *Footwear News*. She received her master's in journalism from Northwestern University and lives in Concord, California, with her husband, Jonathan.

CONTRIBUTING WRITERS

Sue Bryant
Anita Dunham-Potter
Chris Jindra
Peter Knego
Kim Foley MacKinnon
Theresa N. Masek
Lisa Matte
David G. Molyneaux
James Shillinglaw

ABOUT THE FROMMER'S TRAVEL GUIDES

For most of the past 50 years, Frommer's has been the leading series of travel guides in North America, accounting for as many as 24% of all guidebooks sold. I think I know why.

Although we hope our books are entertaining, we nevertheless deal with travel in a serious fashion. Our guidebooks have never looked on such journeys as a mere recreation, but as a far more important human function, a time of learning and introspection, an essential part of a civilized life. We stress the culture, lifestyle, history, and beliefs of the destinations we cover and urge our readers to seek out people and new ideas as the chief rewards of travel.

We have never shied from controversy. We have, from the beginning, encouraged our authors to be intensely judgmental, critical—both pro and con—in their comments, and wholly independent. Our only clients are our readers, and we have triggered the ire of countless prominent sorts, from a tourist newspaper we called "practically worthless" (it unsuccessfully sued us) to the many rip-offs we've condemned.

And because we believe that travel should be available to everyone regardless of their incomes, we have always been cost-conscious at every level of expenditure. Although we have broadened our recommendations beyond the budget category, we insist that every lodging we include be sensibly priced. We use every form of media to assist our readers and are particularly proud of our feisty daily website, the award-winning Frommers.com.

I have high hopes for the future of Frommer's. May these guidebooks, in all the years ahead, continue to reflect the joy of travel and the freedom that travel represents. May they always pursue a cost-conscious path, so that people of all incomes can enjoy the rewards of travel. And may they create, for both the traveler and the persons among whom we travel, a community of friends, where all human beings live in harmony and peace.

Arthur Frommer

Befor of an
Eas **sult**

FRE OM

FROMMERS.COM IS K

NI
The latest events (and deals

BL
Opinionated comment

FOR
Post your travel questions, g

SLIDE
On weekly-changing, practical but inspiring topics of travel

CONTESTS
Enabling you to win free trips

PODCASTS
Of our weekly, nationwide radio show

DESTINATIONS
Hundreds of cities, their hotels, restaurants and sights

TRIP IDEAS
Valuable, offbeat suggestions for your next vacation

*AND MUCH MORE!

Smart travelers consult **Frommers.com**